History in Stone

History in Stone

The Story of Red Rock Canyon

Ruth Obee

Enjoy this walk through time!
Ruth Obee

JOHNSON BOOKS
BOULDER

Copyright © 2012 by Ruth Obee

ISBN: 978-1-55566-448-0

Published by Johnson Books, a Big Earth Publishing company,
3360 Mitchell Lane, Suite E, Boulder, CO 80301
1-800-258-5830
E-mail: books@bigearthpublishing.com
bigearthpublishing.com

Cover and text design by Rebecca Finkel
Front cover photo: Upswept Fountain Fins in Autumn:
Red Rock Canyon, Colorado Springs, courtesy of Bill Koerner
Back cover photo: Winter Reflections, courtesy of Bill Koerner

Library of Congress Cataloging-in Publication Data on file

9   8   7   6   5   4   3   2   1

Printed in the United States of America

For all of those in the community
who helped make
Red Rock Canyon Open Space a reality

Contents

Acknowledgments

Just as it took a community to save Red Rock Canyon, it was the community that made possible the writing of this book. I am grateful for the help of many—first and foremost, Don Ellis, also known as "the Encyclopedia Britannica of Red Rock Canyon." Not only did Don share his extensive knowledge of Red Rock Canyon history, but he also lent enthusiastic support to the idea of a book that would serve to document the land's many stories. Don's voice provides a strong, illuminating counterpoint throughout the narrative.

Colorado College professor of biology Tass Kelso, who read the ecology chapter for accuracy and balance, was one of the first of my outside readers. Her encouragement and generosity of spirit helped propel me forward. Professor of geology Jeffrey Noblett at Colorado College devoted as much care and attention to the reading of my geology chapter as he would had I been one of his students. I benefited immeasurably from his close and highly expert reading and editing, and also from his geology guide that has become as well-thumbed as my aged *American Heritage Dictionary*. My thanks also go to Dr. Ken Carpenter, paleontologist at the Denver Museum of Nature and Science, and naturalist Melissa Walker, for time they devoted and expertise they brought to bear in the reading of the paleontology chapter concerned with the "new" Garden of the Gods dinosaur. And thanks to DMNS paleontologist Kirk Johnson for helping to rescue "Theio," the dinosaur, from dusty obscurity and wrongful identity.

I am grateful to geologist Jon Barker for his superb lecture at the Old Colorado City Historical Society, for taking my husband and me on a guided geology tour of the open space, and for answering a multitude of questions. Professor of geology Mark Izold at Pikes Peak Community College contributed to my understanding of geologic time, and his enthusiasm for this subject spurred me on. His lecture at the Colorado Springs Pioneers Museum and follow-up answers to my questions were tremendous aids in my efforts to come to grips with a complex subject. Thanks are due to geologist Ken Weissenburger and paleontology researcher Sharon Milito, who read early drafts of relevant chapters.

I am indebted to Len Froisland, resident historian of General Palmer's Glen Eyrie, who devoted an afternoon to driving my husband and me around the city founder's beautiful estate, while sharing his passion for the estate's history—deconstructing it stone by stone, while drawing on three decades of knowledge.

Thanks to Kenyon Jordan, editor of the *Westside Pioneer*, for excellent long-term coverage of Red Rock Canyon, and for use of photographs; and to reporter Bill Vogrin of *The Gazette* for his interesting and informative feature on the Bock property and for answering follow-up questions.

Botanist George Cameron both accompanied me on and conducted botanical walks and talks on the open space, which I attended. These formed the basis for the flower and plant list in the ecology chapter. The hours we spent working together to make certain that botanical descriptions of plants were accurate and correctly formatted proved both educational and enjoyable.

My deep appreciation goes to archeologists Steve Snyder (who answered repeated questions, in particular ones about the mysterious "D-figure") and Bill Arbogast, both of whom read the early human history chapter for accuracy, as did Ute historian and author Jan Pettit, whose classic work I return to time and again. Retired national park superintendent Jack Williams, author of two excellent monographs on Native Americans, likewise contributed his deep understanding and knowledge to the reading of the chapter on the early human history of the open space.

Colorado author and Chautauquan Richard Marold, whose knowledge of Colorado history runs wide and deep, kindly read the chapter on modern history, suggesting additional reading that led to new insights, while correcting a few ignominious errors. Founder-editor of the award-winning *Kiva* magazine, Richard first published my article on the Red Rock Canyon property and the effort to save it. This provided the heirloom seed out of which this book grew. I am grateful on all counts.

A variety of Bock associates, tenants, consultants, city leaders, Trust for Public Land officials, real estate brokers, activists, and developers agreed to interviews and patiently answered questions. I wish to extend my appreciation to the following for the willingness with which they shared information, anecdotes, and first-hand knowledge, as I attempted to patch together a better understanding of the property's history, not to mention that of the famously testy and gun-packing late owner, John Bock. These include: geologist emeritus of Colorado College, John Lewis; real estate brokers Tom Kay, Jeany Rush, and Zoltan Malocsay; developer Steve Schuck and architect and developer Bob Fairburn of Phoenix, Arizona; Tom Schmidt of the Broadmoor Development Company in Colorado Springs; local builder and civic leader Chuck Murphy, former city utilities director, the late Jim Phillips; former county planner and attorney P.J. Anderson; TPL negotiator Woody Beardsley; former city councilman Richard Skorman; architect Morey Bean; city official Chuck Miller; and friends and associates of Bock, including Dr. Erwin Cook, his personal physician, and Dick and Joan Lambert—all of whom were more than generous and engaged informants. Warm thanks also go to Chelley Gardner-Smith and Lou Colson who shared unforgettable stories of their years living in the beautiful Red Rock Canyon as Bock tenants.

A special thanks to the following Colorado Springs Parks, Recreation and Cultural Serivces officials: Chris Lieber, who always picked up his phone and never failed to know the answer to a question or how to find it, and who devoted so many of his personal leisure hours to negotiating purchases of parks and open spaces for the city; Terry Putman for his contribution in pulling off what amounted to a major coup, as only a low-keyed Texan with a faint drawl might do; and to Paul Butcher, who knows that an open space is "not somewhere you park your car," and who let Chris and Terry do their thing.

I wish to thank the excellent staff at the Colorado Springs Pioneers Museum, including Matt Mayberry, Leah Davis Witherow, Kelly Murphy, and Brooke Traylor, for assistance with archival material and research. My thanks also go to researchers at the Colorado College library for information about Richard Bock's attendance at the college, and those at Penrose Library for helping me to identify sources relevant to the historic quarries.

Scott Campbell and Josh Tenneson at the Palmer Land Trust deserve a tip of the hat for so clearly elucidating complex issues related to property easements and the nineteenth-century Land Act vis-à-vis Section 16s, essential to understanding our own recent acquisition of Manitou Springs Section 16 as public open space described in the Epilogue.

I wish to express appreciation to the consulting firm of Tweed Kezziah and Susan Watkins for answering questions about public process. The team skillfully facilitated public planning sessions and conducted polls, one of which indicated that a book on the open space bringing together its many stories would be of wide interest to the public, lending further encouragement to what, at times, seemed a daunting project. Kezziah and Watkins earned my further appreciation for demonstrating that public process as a function of grass roots democracy not only can, but does, work.

Numerous open space activists who worked to make Red Rock Canyon Open Space a reality also filled in some of the blanks on the, at times, byzantine politics and processes that helped ensure the success of the intensive, five-year campaign to save Red Rock Canyon. Many thanks to such key informants as Joe Fabeck, Lee Milner, Bill Koerner, Scott Flora, and the Friends of Red Rock Canyon, including past president Karlee Thompson, all of whom contributed so much and shared so many wonderful stories.

Railroad historians Art Crawford and Mel McFarland helped immeasurably in keeping me on the right tracks regarding complex railroading history that involved everything from switches in gauge and ownership to railroad names. Old Colorado City historian David R. Hughes provided first-hand information about John S. Bock's interest in building teleports and a world trade center in Red Rock Canyon.

A long-distance thank you is extended to retired diplomat and good friend John Dixon of Chevy Chase, Maryland, noted for his precision prose and silver pen, who bravely waded through early drafts of several chapters, including that on the Far West's "weirdsma" (to use John McPhee's term) geology, making needed corrections, and offering suggestions.

The celebration of Red Rock Canyon would be incomplete without the art that was inspired by the incomparable red rocks themselves. A picture is worth a thousand words and, in that sense, talented landscape photographer, Bill Koerner, and painter, Laura Reilly, contributed volumes with their timeless and beautiful work, for which I shall remain eternally grateful.

A special thanks goes to my editor at Big Earth Publishing in Boulder. Mira Perrizo brought a global and, indeed, a brilliant perspective to bear in the editing of my manuscript based not only on her understanding of the logic of grammar and mechanics, but equally on her insistence that content be accurate, complete, clearly expressed, and well-organized. Undaunted by the complexity of some of the topics addressed in this book, she was able to draw on impressively deep reserves of patience, thoroughness, and long experience. She was a joy to work with.

Last but not least, deepest appreciation goes to Kent Obee, my ever reliable "inside source," "outside reader," best friend, and intrepid life companion.

Every effort has been made to ensure historical and scientific accuracy of the text. Any mistakes are solely my own.

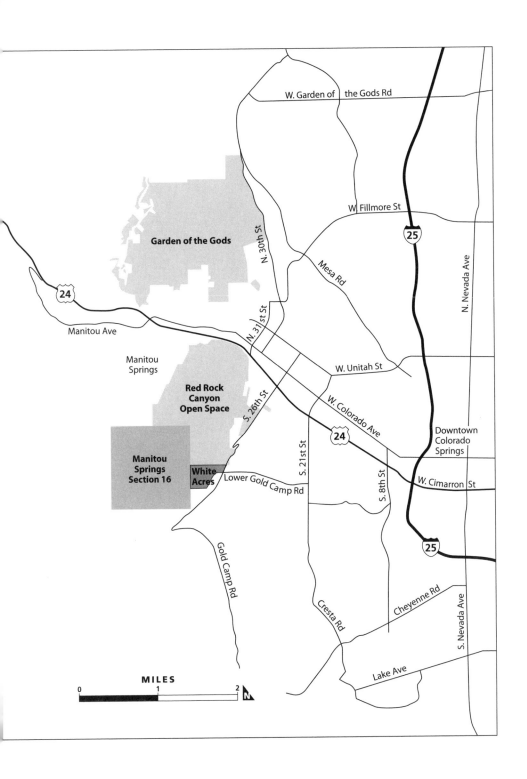

Introduction

"The far out stuff is in the Far West of the country—
wild, weirdsma, a leather-jacket geology in mirrored shades."
—John McPhee, *Annals of the Former World*

"To restore any place, we must also begin to re-story it."
—Gary Paul Nabhan, *Cultures of Habitat*

Why write an entire book about a relatively small parcel of open space—now comprising 1,474 acres, with the recent additions of historic White Acres and the widely popular Manitou Springs Section 16—which starts from the beginning of time, a la James Michener; and continues in the mode of Bill Bryson's *A Short History on Nearly Everything*? One simple, but very good reason is that the history of Red Rock Canyon Open Space is such a great story. And it is the story, first and foremost, of a truly heroic citizen effort against considerable odds to save the land as open space. Today, with the two additional adjoining parcels serving to complete the overall picture, it represents Colorado Springs' largest, most spectacular open space acquisition—surpassing in size its nationally acclaimed sister park, Garden of the Gods. Moreover, its grand narrative embraces many diverse "cultures of habitat," all reflective of the land's special heritage and identity. Like vanishing habitats, stories of the land themselves are worthy of preservation, of being gathered up and recorded as a matter of permanent record in order to produce a biography of place.

Chapter by chapter, Red Rock Canyon's epic and infinitely varied story recapitulates that of America's prehistory and, more regionally, the historic West. Indeed, in terms of both its rich and abundant natural and human history, few landscapes evoke the American past quite so vividly. Beneath our feet as we hike Red Rock Canyon Open Space are deeply layered and diverse narratives—colorful with the stories of ancestors and with the genesis-like stirrings of the earth's magnificent geologic creation. The possibilities for ranging wide within its perimeters are nearly limitless.

The present-day Red Rock Canyon Open Space is, indisputably, also one of the most beautiful sites in the Pikes Peak Region, drawing thousands of visitors annually, both locally and from afar. Its location alone is close to ideal—situated, as it is, at the gateway to the Rockies at the foot of Pikes Peak, on the west side of Colorado Springs (the state's second largest city), and in a place where time, space, and ecosystems come together at the juncture of the eastern plains, the great Southwest, the Front Range, and timeless Ute Pass—first used ten thousand years ago by the Clovis people.

Hardly anyone, except those who stand to profit from it, would question the merits of saving the Red Rock Canyon property, formerly described as "the last best place," from large-scale development. All it takes to convince most observers of the truth of this simple statement is a glance at its dramatically uplifted, fantastically shaped and tilted 323-million-year-old, rust-red sandstone spires and fins; its massive and extensively quarried red Lyons Sandstone; and its fossil-rich hogbacks, prominent visual backdrops to the city of Colorado Springs.

But for most, the property owned by the Bock family for eighty years was off limits. For the venturous few who chose to slip past the large "Keep Out" signs, there was the possibility of meeting the owner and his shotgun. Not surprisingly, the property came to be known among locals as the "Secret Garden of the Gods." Thus, as one of their first priorities, advocates for the open space were faced with the need to educate people about what was out there beyond the John S. Bock–owned stand of billboards and trailer camps, among his various enterprises for making money off the land.

While Red Rock Canyon or "the Bock property" had long been the target of both open space advocates and developers, Bock's non-negotiable price was deemed far too high by most to be affordable, and there was the additional liability of the roughly sixty-acre landfill that Bock leased out on the property—not only complicating the equation, but representing a potential liability of unknown proportions. These issues threatened at any moment to derail the entire process of negotiating an agreement on the sale of the Bock property, posing some difficult challenges for open space advocates.

Nonetheless, the goal of saving the property inspired a level of citizen engagement rarely seen, and one that offers lasting proof of the effectiveness of grass roots democracy in action. It was the community who, in 1999, put aside narrow party politics and ideologies to seize the initiative, setting its sights on the long-term goal of saving the Bock property as open space. With this objective in mind, and spear-headed by the citizen-based Red Rock Canyon Committee (organized by the Trails and Open Space Coalition), volunteers convened their first organizational meeting, then rolled up their collective sleeves and went to work, determined to make it happen.

Besides the many engaged and committed volunteers, several notable park officials and visionary civic leaders also played key roles in the five-year, hard-fought battle waged between 1999 and 2003, when a New Mexico developer rode into town with Red Rock Canyon in his sights and backed by big money and powerful interests. Given the imbalance in available dollars and the ability to afford legal council and other full-time resources, it appeared that open space advocates were up against impossible odds. In addition, there were the unpredictable twists and turns in negotiations with the famously difficult property owner himself.

Without the community-wide network of creative partnerships formed among neighborhood and conservation groups and public and private entities in support of the effort to save Red Rock Canyon, this beautiful site would doubtless look very different today. Had the developer succeeded in fulfilling his ambitious plans, it would more closely resemble a

Club Med–like mountain resort with exclusive clubhouse and luxury hotels, in addition to massive estate homes perched on the mesa, and a state-of-the-art golf course worthy of a glossy center spread in *Golf Digest* featuring dramatic red rocks and water-guzzling greens (in a drought-prone and arid high-desert region), and inaccessible to all but a few. Even earlier development plans drawn up in voluminous detail by the Bock family were, if anything, yet more grandiose—boggling the imagination in their sheer size and scope.

Several timely and positive developments, however, signaled early public support for the preservation of Red Rock Canyon as open space. In 1997, Colorado Springs presented citizens with an open space plan in which Red Rock Canyon was listed as a "candidate area." In the winter of 2001, Colorado Preservation nominated the Red Rock Canyon property for its list of "Most Endangered Places … because of its historic quarries, archeological sites, and imminent threat of development," demonstrating state-wide interest in saving the property. And in 1997, city voters approved (and then again in 2003 voted to extend through 2025) the .1 percent TOPS (Trails, Open Space, and Parks) tax. Red Rock Canyon served as the poster child for the critical extension.

The citizen-driven initiative, which involved one of the most intensive lobbying efforts in local history, and the passage of TOPS were, over the long term, two of the most critical factors in making it possible to save the Red Rock Canyon property as open space in perpetuity. Without either of these two key components, combined with generous and timely Great Outdoors Colorado funding (GOCO generates revenue through the lottery) and the strong, unflinching commitment made to the property by the Denver-based Trust for Public Land (TPL)—the open space as we know it today would not exist.

Thus, in the end, it was the many dedicated individuals, groups, and organizations contributing their dollars, time, and sweat equity, not to mention abundant skills and expertise, who helped make Red Rock Canyon Open Space a reality.

In preserving Red Rock Canyon land as open space to be enjoyed by all, including out-of-state visitors and tourists, the community made a difference. It also demonstrated a "conservation ethic" that can serve as a good starting point for the next generation. In *Hot, Flat and Crowded*, Thomas L. Friedman quotes Harvard political philosopher Michael J. Sandel who defines a "conservation ethic" as one which "begins with a sense of responsibility, a sense of stewardship, for the natural world [and] is an ethic of restraint that says we have a responsibility to preserve the earth's resources and natural wonders in and of themselves because they constitute the web of life on which all living creatures on this planet depend."

The effort to save the Rock Canyon property as open space was launched at a time when open space nearly everywhere in the country was under siege (as it continues to be to this day). Colorado and seven other western states are growing three times faster than the rest of the nation. The pressures of growth on wildlife habitats have resulted in numerous reports of species loss—from bighorn sheep in the West to little brown bats in the East.

• • •

My husband and I, both westerners by birth, have spent more than twenty years in the Foreign Service living abroad in countries in South Asia and Africa. We chose to return to our western American roots and were delighted to rediscover the beauty of the Colorado landscapes and the peacefulness of open spaces in our neighborhood—after having lived periodically (between overseas' postings) in our nation's capital, where the din of traffic noise and the roar of jet aircraft overhead were inescapable constants.

But before long, we began to see rampant development eating up those same beautiful open spaces that we associated with home and which had drawn us back. Scenic view corridors, foothill ridgelines, and popular outdoor recreational sites could no longer be regarded as sacrosanct or taken for granted, we now realized. We watched them disappear before our very eyes, virtually overnight. They were not, as we had once mistakenly assumed, an inviolable part of the landscape that we could count on always being there. We decided to get involved in the fight to save what was left before it was too late.

Life abroad had been more than illuminating, but never before had we been party to a citizen-driven effort comparable to the one that saved Red Rock Canyon as open space, and on a much smaller scale, the Stratton Open Space in 1998, with its five ecosystems and painterly view of the mountains, located in our own neighborhood. This much loved property, on the southwestern corner of the city, became the first open space parcel in recent history to be set aside for public use, thanks to the efforts of volunteers. It had been nearly a century since the Perkins family had presented the city with the splendid gift of Garden of the Gods for the express benefit and enjoyment of its citizens.

The Stratton Open Space success story, in turn, paved the way for more open space acquisitions that followed, including Blodgett Peak and Bluestem Prairie, as well as the New Cheyenne Mountain Park. In our past incarnations, my husband and I had made an effort to tell America's story abroad. But by coming home, we had a chance to witness some of the best of those stories being enacted.

Besides being drawn by and into the conservation community—I, for one, also wanted to get to better know McPhee's "leather-jacket geology in mirrored shades." After all, this Far West geology was a defining feature of the town in which I lived, even though, in the case of Red Rock Canyon, it wasn't my most immediate neighbor. I soon began to realize to what extent geology had called the shots on all the other history that had transpired over the millennia on today's open space—starting 1.75 billion years ago, if you count the Idaho Springs Gneiss found in Manitou Springs Section 16, and including paleontology, ecology, and human history. The geology is but the first chapter in a much larger narrative, each chapter of which involves masses of complex material.

As a layperson, in researching and writing this book, I began to think of myself as something of a translator. Aware of what I didn't know and understand, including some arcane, if picturesque, vocabulary, I thought that I could perhaps pinpoint the right questions and explain where needed in simple, understandable language and—

if the gods smiled on me favorably—I could accomplish this somewhat monumental task without too many egregious errors.

Above all else, I believed in the cause for which the community had so bravely stood up. Like so many others, I felt that it was vital to preserve Red Rock Canyon as open space and that the cause merited documentation, celebration, and testimony. Consider:

- Red Rock Canyon is not only one of the most beautiful sites in the Pikes Peak region, it's an important wildlife corridor and preserve for a variety of flora and fauna—from mountain lions to Great Blue Herons and such stellar wildflowers as the anemone, Indian paint brush, and mariposa lily.

- Red Rock Canyon is geologically continuous with Garden of the Gods, but less broken up. It boasts the most accessible and best geology found in any urban setting in the United States, according to Colorado College geologist Jeff Noblett.

- The story of how this "marvel of nature" was saved by the community can provide a useful, step-by-step template: a "how to" for other communities engaged in similar causes.

- New research has uncovered previously unknown marine fossils, including large predatory sharks that once dined on three-foot-wide giant clams, and dinosaur tracks from at least two species in the Cretaceous rocks of the open space.

- Since the land became public, archeologists have documented the long-ago presence of prehistoric humans on the open space, discovering embedded metates, arrowheads, and possible Ute defensive sites, overlooks and/or drift fences, helping to round out one of the earliest, most important chapters in the grand narrative.

- The Ute Pass Indian Trail, which borders Red Rock Canyon, is the oldest documented trail in the U.S.—first used ten thousand years ago by the Clovis people.

- The site's more modern human history embraces everything from trappers and miners to frontier cowboys and wranglers and the start of the Industrial Revolution, with its extensive rock-quarrying operations that provided building stones to other states and used in some of Denver's grandest mansions and most historic buildings.

- Western labor-mining history began, not with the mines in Cripple Creek as is widely believed, but with the gold refining mill owned and operated in what was once known as "Red Rock Canyon land," with its convenient rail connections built by wealthy copper baron Spencer Penrose.

- Red Rock Canyon was the target of grandiose development schemes of historic note including that of the Bocks, which envisioned a town of thousands complete with a world trade center, multiple lakes, a new-age teleport, dozens of high-rise buildings with the tallest scraping the clouds at thirty-six stories, and much more.

- The hematite red outcroppings that are the crown jewels of Red Rock Canyon, together with those in Garden of the Gods, gave the state of Colorado its singularly beautiful name.

- Red Rock Canyon Open Space is part of our natural heritage and identity, which—with its distinctive geographical profile and western frontier legacy—inspires creativity, history, and the arts.

- Red Rock Canyon Open Space promotes outdoor recreation and tourism, as well as education and our economy.

- Saving sites like Red Rock Canyon helps protect Rocky Mountain landscapes.

- Natural, historic, and cultural landscapes, in turn, connect people to place.

Red Rock Canyon Open Space represents a superb educational and recreational resource for all ages, and especially for young people. Recent research shows that children connected with the outdoors have improved learning skills and science scores, not to mention better health. Families and friends cement bonds by enjoying regular walks together in the great outdoors. We are talking here of "quality of life" indicators, which Professors Greenwood and Holt of the University of Colorado (Colorado Springs) argue in *Local Economic Development in the 21ˢᵗ Century* "encompass many non-market goods, such as health, education and culture, open space and parks, air and scenery …," and which, in the long run, represent a larger, more sustainable economic good. Richard Rogers, in *Cities for a Small Planet,* writes that, "The core of [the] concept of sustainability is the redefining of wealth to include natural capital [such as clean water], fertile land and the abundant diversity of species." Rogers further believes that "environmental sustainability should be at the core of subjects taught" in schools. Based on positive outdoor indicators and other criteria, *Outdoor Magazine,* in August 2009, declared Colorado Springs first in the top ten cities in which to live. To maintain such high quality-of-life ratings for clean air and access to open space requires constant vigilance and careful stewardship.

Red Rock Canyon Open Space is a geological archive and a natural history museum showcasing the best of Colorado's great outdoors. It took this book of considerable weight, written over a decade, to do full justice to the land's multitude of stories, recorded in the hope of raising new levels of awareness and appreciation for what's out there. At the end, it points the reader to a bibliography listing guides and texts by some of the most respected experts in their fields.

History in Stone: The Story of Red Rock Canyon endeavors to take the reader not only on a journey back in time, but also a journey forward, with stories written about the past for the future. This book is meant to inspire curious time-travelers, members of the general public, inquisitive students, educators, artists, and recreators alike to read and explore further—and thus to become more meaningfully connected to a very special, indeed, a magical place. If, as Walt Whitman once proclaimed, "These United States are essentially the poem," then Red Rock Canyon Open Space is surely among its most eloquent and enduring verses.

CHAPTER 1

Once Upon a Time Long, Long Ago ... The Epic Geology of Red Rock Canyon

"Mountains have the power to awaken an overwhelming sense of the sacred."
—Edwin Bernbaum

"Three granite mountain ranges wore away While I was coming here, ... A mountain range ago the sea was here, Now I am here, the falcons floating over. ..."
—Thomas Hornsby Ferril

"Once upon a time" is the way all good stories begin. And one of the best stories of all concerns the geology of Red Rock Canyon Open Space—an epic narrative that began about 1.75 billion years ago and spans hundreds of millions of years.

Chapter by chapter, the unfolding of the geological story on the open space (and of the Pikes Peak Region and beyond) reveals episodes of dramatic upheavals, tempestuous storms, rearranged landscapes, restless shifts of tectonic plates, and repeated transgressions of ancient seas. Five-hundred-million years ago, the land where the present-day city of Colorado Springs is located was submerged beneath a sea that stretched east to Kansas, in addition to covering much of the Southwest. There were at least four major periods of marine transgressions in which sea-level changes altered the shape of the "bathtub," but not the actual volume of water contained therein.

Shared Geology

Red Rock Canyon Open Space and Garden of the Gods are geologically joined at the hip. They are composed of the same types of rock and are graced by many of the same formations. As such, they share virtually identical geological histories—with their eye-catching and immemorial outcroppings of sedimentary red rock that at one time had been spread out in superpositioned (from the oldest on the bottom to youngest on top) and horizontal layers by ancient seas, later to be pushed up by the Laramide Orogeny, the great uplift that also gave us Pikes Peak and the modern Rockies.

Gene Smith, retired city parks department official, emphasizes this important point when he states that Red Rock Canyon and the Garden of the Gods should be viewed as historically and geologically a part of the whole. "They were all part of the same area," explains Smith. "It's just that there is a road separating them today and it's convenient to think of them as separate areas."

More Geologic Time than the Grand Canyon

Pike Peak Community College geology professor Mark Izold, whose enthusiasm for his subject bespeaks a geologist who has just found paradise, states that the rock in the open space—now including Manitou Springs Section 16—with its abundance of early Precambrian Idaho Springs Gneiss that is at least 1.75 billion years old—can claim more geologic time than the Grand Canyon. While the Grand Canyons' breathtaking bluffs, tiers, and monoliths contain more linear feet of rock, its strata stop at the Permian Period, 250–290 MYA (million years ago). In contrast, the massive sandstone formations which make up the crown jewels of Red Rock Canyon Open Space showcase five periods and two eras—from the earliest Pennsylvanian to the more recent Cretaceous.

> *"Kansas has a similar geological history, but you have to climb down an oil well to see it."*
>
> **—Jeffrey Noblett,**
> Colorado College professor of geology

It's important to note, in discussing the ages of rock, that geologic age is different from absolute age. Margins of error may consist of millions of years and timelines very from source to source.

"No city in the United states has more geological history located within the city limits than Colorado Springs. Every period is represented except the Silurian [417–443 MYA]," says Colorado College geology professor Jeffrey Noblett. Red Rock Canyon Open Space, together with Manitou Springs Section 16, is one of "the most geologically important parts of the natural history of the West. It's a wonderful place to teach beginning geologists in high school and college classes."

In short, while modern Colorado as we see it today—from the eastern plains to the central mountains and the western basins and plateaus—is still relatively young, the parent rock and overturned strata making up our most famous and breathtakingly beautiful mountain ranges and rock formations date much farther back into geological antiquity. Pikes Peak granite, for example, is more than one billion years old.

Colorado's mountain geology, with its superabundance of world-class rock, has influenced everything about us—from our earliest human history to our industrial and economic base, and the ways in which we recreate.

· · ·

A walk in Red Rock Canyon Open Space is a bit like stepping inside a vast time machine to be whisked, in the blink of an eye, back millions of years. If you take a close look around you, you will immediately notice that regardless of their size, texture, shape, color, or age, the type of rock making up all of the exposed outcroppings is sedimentary. This includes the limestone and shale that form the Dakota and Niobrara Hogbacks to the east that were deposited by an ancient sea; the fine-grained, windborne sandstone in the red Lyons Formation (named after Lyons, Colorado, the location where it was scientifically studied and recorded in a U.S. Geological Survey in 1905); and the rougher, more cobbled, river- and stream-borne gravel and conglomerate that compose the sunrise-red Pennsylvanian Fountain Formation (named in 1894 after Fountain Creek, near Manitou Springs).

Sedimentary rocks are themselves divided into two types: clastic, that is, made up of broken pieces of rock tumbled together by seas, glaciers, streams, and the like; and chemical precipitites. The evaporation of seawater is an example of a solution out of which rocks may be chemically precipitated.

In Red Rock Canyon Open Space, examples of formations made up of clastic rock include the Fountain Arkose, Lyons Sandstone, Lykins (shale), Morrison (shales and clays), the Dakota Group, most of the Benton Group, and the Pierre Shale. Among the chemical precipitites are the Lykins (limestone and dolostone), the gypsum member of the lower Morrison Formation, and the limestone in the Niobrara Formation.

"Most obvious layering of rocks is sedimentary," states geologist Halka Chronic. Because the sea floor was flat, the original sediments that composed these formations were laid down horizontally, too. These loose particles over the eons were changed into rocks by a process known as "lithification." Lithification can occur in one or two ways: the first is "compaction," in which sediment shrinks under pressure. The second is "cementation," in which the pores in the sediment are filled up with minerals deposited by water. Over time the minerals serve to bind the sediment into rock.

In the layers making up the sedimentary rocks, mud came from stream bottoms, sand dunes from the foot of mountains, chemical precipitites from salt in shallow seas, beaches from the edge of inland seas, and fossils from a variety of sources. Different and distinctive layers of sedimentary rock types are marked by sometimes small and gradual and sometimes abrupt changes in size and color of grains. Much can be determined about the rocks' origin by studying sedimentary "structures" such as ripple marks, cross bedding, and mud cracks, as well as animal tracks on the rocks' surfaces. After being formed, the rocks were shaped over the millennia by repeated cycles of uplift, caused by plate-shifting orogenies (mountain-building episodes), and the irresistible forces of erosion.

In learning more about the history of the dramatic rock outcroppings that distinguish the open space, it is helpful to be reminded of a geological principle formulated in the late eighteenth century—which is profound in its simplicity: "The present is key to the past." In addition, it is important to consider several key geological events that helped to shape the remarkable formations we see today. We shall thus follow the geologist's lead and begin with the theory of plate tectonics.

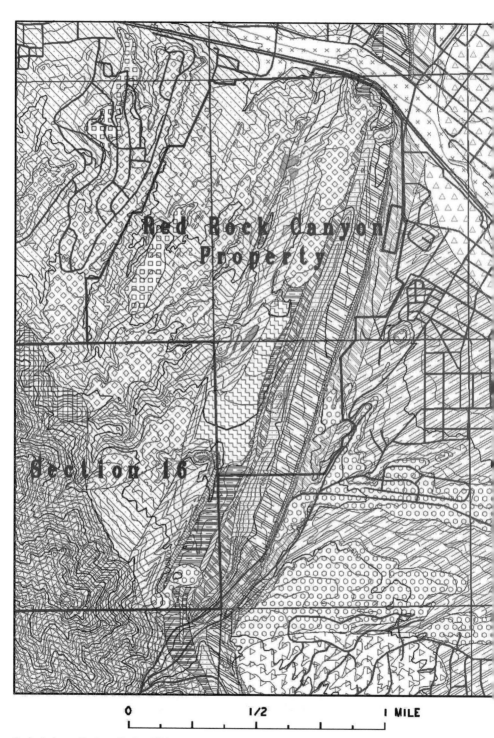

Red Rock Canyon Property

Section 16

0   1/2   1 MILE

Geological map. (Designed by Don Ellis)

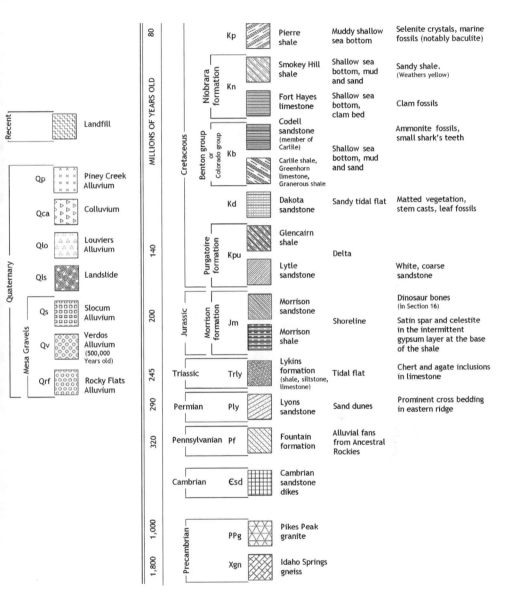

Geological timeline. (Designed by Don Ellis)

Wind-blown tidal pool ripples in the Dakota Sandstone. (Photo courtesy Don Ellis)

Cross-bedding in Lyons dunes. (Photo courtesy Bill Koerner)

Plate Tectonics

Plate tectonics is the theory that the earth is made up of large, jig-saw-like plates, which are in constant motion. Working like a conveyor belt, earth's plates move laterally and when they collide, they push, shove, and vibrate up and down. The plates, in turn, are driven by the magma-generated energy of convection currents. Their movement is both massive and slower than a tortoise's—indeed, averaging speeds of approximately 4 centimeters (two inches) per year, about the same as the rate at which a fingernail grows. Plate tectonics helped create the earth's crust and is associated with earthquakes, volcanic activity, mountain-building, and oceanic trench building—in which mid-ocean ridges rise and sink into subduction (where one tectonic plate slides beneath another).

Three Mountain Ranges in the Rockies' Genealogy

Early and nameless volcanoes emitting lava and poking their heads up in an arc above an ancient sea contributed to our oldest metamorphic rock. Next arose the ancestral Rockies, shedding huge volumes of sedimentary red rock as they wore down. Finally, the modern Rockies uplifted, and continue to the present day to fracture, break down, and disintegrate under the driving force of water, cold, heat, wind, and the impact of flora and fauna.

Rocky I: The Paleozoic Era Ancestral Rockies of the Pennsylvanian Period

Because much of the parent rock for the monumental outcroppings found in Red Rock Canyon Open Space was deposited by the long-since-vanished Ancestral Rocky Mountains, it is important not to overlook, in this geological, three-part sequel, the formative event popularly known as "Rocky I." Rocky I occurred during the late Pennsylvanian Period, between 290 and 323 million years ago.

During this event, two great Pennsylvanian islands, Uncompahgria and Frontrangia, were uplifted in approximately the same positions as the modern Rockies. These were, in turn, eroded with alluvial sand and cobble carried down by the lively streams flowing off them and by landslides. In the process, the mountains "shed" (meaning, they were carved down by streams, landslides, etc.) up to ten thousand feet of red, sandy sediment (or "redbed"), with the Ancestral Uncompahgria contributing its deposits, among others, to the Maroon Bells, near Aspen, and the top of Sangre de Cristo, southwest of Pueblo. The future location of Colorado Springs, however, received only about half of this amount, rising approximately four thousand to five thousand feet.

Frontrangia, to the east depositing its pink and red rock sediment in Garden of the Gods and Red Rock Canyon (as well as in the Boulder Flatirons and Red Rocks Amphitheater, west of Denver), together with the inland sea that once covered the area, are largely responsible for the magnificent red sandstone creations we see today. It took about 120 million years for the Ancestral Rocky Mountains to be worn down again roughly to sea level.

Rocky II: The Mountain-Building Laramide Orogeny

Most authorities agree that the raising up of the modern Rocky Mountains can be traced directly back to the major mountain building event that began about sixty-five million years ago, known as the Laramide Orogeny—also referred to as "Rocky II." This was an upheaval in the earth's crust that was first identified in the Laramie Range of Mountains in Wyoming and Colorado. With its pulsing crests and upthrusts, it moved in a slow and ponderous fashion. The rucked-up wrinkles in the earth's surface that it produced were not unlike those in a heavy carpet being pushed to the corner of a room.

The Laramide Orogeny was first set in motion off the West Coast of North America. Although its exact cause and age are open to debate, the most widely accepted explanation for the disturbance is that of the massive shifting of ancient tectonic plates hundreds of millions of years ago, with the Farallon Plate (named after the islands west of San Francisco) sliding under the North American Plate. This massive underthrusting (or subduction) set off a rolling wave that moved millimeter by millimeter, inch by inch, for millions of years. The ongoing tectonism from the Triassic, about 225 million years ago, is today largely experienced in the Sierra Nevada of California.

It was not until sometime in the Late Cretaceous Period, sixty-five to seventy million years ago, that this transformative, mountain-building event in a long, drawn-out process eventually reached the Pikes Peak region itself, having slowly penetrated into the interior of the continent to make its impact, at last, fully felt. As the powerful geological wave uplifted the modern Rockies and emptied out the seas, it also thrust up the mile-deep layers of old sediment, in effect deforming them, so that all the strata on the open space were pushed up to vertical (but with the layers still in order with respect to their geological periods and timelines). Fossil-bearing sediment has helped to establish the date of the onset of this mountain-building pulse that uplifted both the entire Front Range and the famous red sedimentary rocks found in the open space and Garden of the Gods.

Pikes Peak: From Fire to Ice, a Player in Rocky II

Over eons, Pikes Peak, a sky-scraping vision in our view corridor and a star player in the region's geology, has been shaped into a landform of breathtaking beauty by the forces of wind, rain, snowstorms, freezing, and the recent Ice Age. The top of Pikes Peak has a "scooped out" area, produced by the sculpting of a glacier, with everything not the peak having been cut away by forces of erosion. At one time the melt from the peak's receding glaciers may have provided watering holes for wooly mammoths.

In geological terms, Pikes Peaks is known as a batholith, which is a large mass of igneous rock formed by the melting and recrystalization of older rock that turns to molten magma deep within the earth. It takes thousands of years for the pooled magma beneath the earth's surface to cool. The Pike's Peak batholith covers some 1,300 square miles—roughly the size of Rhode Island.

Igneous (meaning "fire") rocks are the oldest rocks in the world. They are a product of magma formed and cooled underground. The magma (unlike lava from volcanoes) never reaches the surface. All granite is igneous. The pink color of the billion-plus-year-old Pikes Peak granite is due to various iron minerals, and represents a tie back to the Ancestral Rockies. Pikes Peak's coarse-grained texture, with its large crystals of feldspar, means it crumbles and weathers easily, explaining why every slope and hill in the region is covered with loose gravel as it continues to erode and wear down.

It was some fifty-five million years ago that the world-wide Laramide Orogeny uplifted Pikes Peak to a higher elevation. Many geologists believe that the energy generated from the peak's uplift, in turn, triggered a massive chain reaction as it slowly began to push up and overturn the Dakota and Niobrara Hogbacks and to tilt the unforgettable red Lyons and Fountain Sandstone Formations, setting them at jaunty angles. Without Pikes Peak there would, in short, have been no visible red rocks today. Additional small pulses led to further adjustments in some of the leaning red towers of stone, helping to explain why they don't all necessarily stand at the same angle.

The tectonism of the Laramide Orogeny was responsible for exposing 80 percent of the unprecedented bumper crop of rocks found in Colorado's geology. It overturned mile-deep layers of sediment that had been laid down in different and quite distinctive layers and compressed over thousands of years, displacing the rock on the open space (both vertically and laterally), and in the process folding, warping, bending, and upending previously buried strata. Nonetheless, the vertical rocks are lined up side by side in a somewhat predictable order. This means that as you move from east to west, they appear in roughly the right geological sequence in accordance with their ages and the principle of "superposition," with the oldest layer of rocks on the bottom. Due to the unevenness of the related warping and bending, the farther you move away from the mountains toward the east, the younger the rocks become; and the closer you are to the mountains in the west, the older the rocks are.

Faults in the Open Space and the Surrounding Areas

In addition to tilting the red rocks at unexpectedly jaunty angles, the Laramide Orogeny (Rocky II) was a major catalyst in the faulting that occurred in the open space and its bordering areas. Uplift, folding, tilting, and faulting results from the lateral movement between tectonic plates, causing stress to rock strata. Faults, in turn, are defined as breaks in the rock, along which relative movement has occurred, normally causing earthquakes. The amount of movement along the break determines the extent to which strata are displaced as they grind up against each other and are pulverized. In its handiwork of mountain building, the Laramide Orogeny—at its most intense— caused enormous chunks of rock to break off and rip apart. Comparatively speaking, Garden of the Gods has only minor faults, but they are numerous. Red Rock Canyon, on the other hand, is nearly fault-free. However, some small faults can be observed near the Ridge Road parking area and in Sand Canyon.

A good example of a more extensive fault in the area is the one that runs along Rampart Range, where it borders the open space to the north and extends all the way to Perry Park, north of Monument. This fault played a significant role in the casting and adjustment of the relative positions of the red rocks and helps explain their notably different attitudes, with some dramatically upturned at highly tilted angles and others lying flat as a billiard table.

There is yet another major fault running through Manitou Springs Section 16, south of Red Rock Canyon Open Space. This is the relatively well-known Ute Pass Fault. It was caused when an enormous block of the exposed Pikes Peak batholith was thrust upward and forced over the sedimentary strata to the east. Thanks to the road cut through Ute Pass, it is possible to get a close-up look at this remarkable example of upthrusted and overturned rock strata, demonstrating that "progress" not only has its unintended consequences, but some unexpected benefits as well.

Rocky III

Jeffrey Noblett writes in his *Guide to the Geological History of the Pikes Peak Region* that the current orogeny, or mountain-building event popularly known as "Rocky III," "began in the Pliocene (5 MYA) and continues today as the modern Rockies develop."

As a result of ongoing and mild tectonic activity generated in the region by Rocky III, it is possible, though not certain, that the new range of Rockies is continuing to rise. (Pike's Peak is thought to be higher than it once was, although this could be a mistake in its original measurement). The modern Rockies are also continuing to erode at a pace that may be equal to the possible uplift generated by Rocky III. The frequent earthquakes that continue in the region as a result of this orogeny are so mild we seldom feel them, but their constant movement is being monitored on a daily basis at the National Earthquake Information Center, located on the campus of the Colorado School of Mines in Golden.

Jeff Noblett sums up the Pikes Peak region's early geology this way: "Starting about 1.7 billion years ago … the volcanism and piling up of sediments where the tectonic plate was moving created a land mass in the Southwest, including Colorado." In this geological process "a large number of granites were formed and intruded in Colorado. The underthrusting of the earth's crust and the merging of plates through tectonic movements converted old ocean floor into new continents."

A Journey Back in Time through the Five Parallel Valleys and Past the Rock Ridges that Divide Them

Red Rock Canyon Open Space's remarkable topography is a product, as we have seen, of juggernaut-like forces of uplift and erosion. Unstoppable and relentless, these forces have worn down, buckled, coruscated, and shaped the open space's softer strata of crumbly shales and siltstone that originated as swamps and mudflats and which pave the valley floors, while the stronger sedimentary sandstone became the successive, parallel ridges. The result is a series of five, north-to-south-running, parallel valleys or canyons that are bracketed, in turn, by crested ridges and eye-catching red outcroppings, which span two hundred million years.

Going from east to west, the five parallel valleys, or canyons, are known respectively as: Hogback Valley (some early accounts call it Wild Horse Valley), Gypsum Canyon, Red Rock Canyon, Greenlee Canyon, and Sand Canyon. Each possesses its own distinctive character and unique charm. The crests and valleys tend to be higher toward the south as they approach Manitou Springs Section 16, sloping downward as they run north toward the drainage of Fountain Creek. Starting in the east, as previously noted, the rock formations are the youngest; while the farther west you go in Red Rock Canyon Open Space, the older they become. With the valleys thus properly named and identified, we can now begin to discuss the geology of the ridges among which they lie.

The Niobrara and Dakota Hogbacks

Geological names are often derived from the area where a given formation was first studied. The Niobrara Hogback, named in 1862 after the outcrops recorded near the Niobrara River in Nebraska; and the Dakota Hogback, named in the same year after the Dakota Territory and River, also in Nebraska, form the first in a succession of ridges on the open space. Younger than either the Lyons or Fountain Formation, and less visually arresting and colorful, the hogbacks, nonetheless, have equally, if not even more, fascinating stories to tell.

During the Cretaceous Period, the Dakota Formation resulted from the depositions of a sandy tidal flat, while the Niobrara, with its Smoky Hill Shale and Fort Hays Limestone members, as well as the Pierre Shale and the Benton Group, were products of a shallow sea bottom; and the even older Purgatoire Formation grew out of a tidal delta.

The up to six-hundred-foot-deep Western Interior Seaway, notable for its marine deposits, covered a vast area—from the Gulf of Mexico to Alaska and from western Utah to the Midwest. Over time, ripples and waves that formed peaks and troughs, and which were caused by the lapping of the tide on a sandy flat, were permanently recorded and preserved in the ancient rock—like artistically embossed prints. These watermarks can be easily discerned in the higher ridges of the Dakota Hogback.

During this period, there were also lakes and rivers; and if you look closely at the boulders that have rolled down from the hogbacks, it is possible to detect small grains of sand, indicating that some of the sediment in the rock formations had been carried for long distances—indeed, from rivers as far away as Utah.

Zeroing in on the Niobrara Hogback

The lower and eastern-most Niobrara Hogback is made up of a formation that is extensive throughout the West and is the focal point of big oil shale drilling interests. Beginning at the base of the lower hogback, you first encounter the approximately eighty-million-year-old Cretaceous Period Pierre Shale—not a member of the Niobrara itself, but a separate formation. The product, as suggested, of a muddy, shallow sea bottom, some layers of Pierre Shale contain expandable clays of coarse, thick, grey-brown sedimentary rock that breaks into slabs. These layers are composed of grains of silt and clay cemented together (dried, compressed muck). Much of Colorado Springs is built on Pierre Shale and it forms the under-story of all of eastern Colorado. In some places reaching a depth of a mile-and-a-half, this formation is the thickest of all local sedimentary strata.

As you walk up the slope, you come next to the slightly older Smoky Hill Shale (or Chalk), which is a yellow chalk-limestone type of rock. Near the top of the hogback, you arrive at the small white cliff of Fort Hays Limestone. Fort Hays Limestone and Smoky Hill Shale are members in good standing of the Cretaceous Niobrara Formation. ("Cretaceous" means "chalk" in Latin.) "Niobrara" refers to the prominent, white band easily seen from a distance. At roughly one hundred million years old, the limestone is the older of the two members. Limestone is a shallow warm-water sediment made up of precipitated material, indicating the presence of shallow seas of several hundred feet at the time it was formed. Usually white or grey in color, this sedimentary rock, deposited as a limey mud, is made up mostly of calcite (calcium carbonate, a mineral of many forms, often found in caves). Limestone is notable for its abundance of marine fossils. At the top of the Niobrara Hogback, the white cliff of Fort Hays Limestone meets the crest of the Codell Sandstone, which is part of the four-member Benton Group. Older and higher than and west of the Fort Hays Limestone, with its ironstone concretions, the Codell, like all the strata in the hogbacks, is a product of a marine environment. (With their wealth of marine fossils, these rocks represent a precious resource to be enjoyed by all. Please abide by park rules against collecting.)

Local historian Don Ellis reminisces about his "Hogback Memories" in an essay he wrote for the *Red Rock Rag* (Vol.4, No.12), the newspaper he founded to support the preservation of the Red Rock Canyon property as open space. In those days, Ellis lived on three acres of land, approximately two miles south of Colorado Avenue. "Once, hiking along the cliff of white Fort Hays Limestone on the lower hogback, we found a slot in the cliff just wide enough to slip through," he recalls. "Behind the slot softer stone had been eroded into a ramp which let me walk to the top of the ridge unseen. ... And, another Wild West fantasy unfolded in my mind."

In addressing the important geological refrain—the time/mind-bending question of "overturning strata" as observed in the hogbacks—Ellis describes it in closely observed detail in the *Red Rock Rag* (Vol.3, No.3). He notes, for example, that in some areas along the hogbacks:

> The rock strata separate and fan outward from one another like the pages of a book. This results in overturning of the strata so that older strata are found above younger strata [this phenomenon occurs locally, but not everywhere.] The Highway 24 road cut at the north end of the Red Rock Canyon property shows two prominent areas where the strata separate, fan out and bend over, forming eastward turning arcs. Pigeon caves in the northern part of the Dakota hogback were formed by spreading of Dakota sandstone.
>
> The hogback area formations in which overturning is most widespread are Fort Hays (Niobrara) limestone and Codell sandstone. Fanned out layers of Fort Hays limestone are evident in the limestone pit west of 31st and Robinson Streets; and fanning of the layers of Fort Hays limestone has created well-defined bands ... far below... the prominent ... band along "White Ridge" to the south of this excavation. However, the most prominent location where overturning of the Fort Hays limestone has occurred is west of the old gravel pit on 26th Street, in the vicinity of the landfill road. Here, there is a prominent exposed band of overturned Fort Hays limestone ...

But the overturning, when considered in the greater scheme of things, is "a small piece at the end of the story," observes geologist Jeff Noblett.

Hogback Valley

Between the Niobrara and Dakota Hogback ridges lies the Hogback Valley. On the lower, eastern side, like a sleeping basilisk, stretches the aforementioned Niobrara Hogback. The progressively older and higher ridge of the approximately 120-million-year-old tawny Dakota Sandstone rears up on the other side of and to the west of Hogback Valley. The sunny, broad, flat, virtually treeless Hogback Valley, with its spiny yucca plants, follows the incline up between the two.

Proceeding west across the Hogback Valley between the two hogback ridges, geology buffs and time travelers will hike over, if not actually encounter as a large outcropping, members of the aforementioned Benton (Colorado) Group that pave the Hogback Valley floor. The soft black shales and thin limestone of the Benton Group are easily eroded, lending themselves to the formation of draws and canyons. The group includes (from east to west) Carlile Shale, Greenhorn Limestone, and Graneros Shale—a black, marine sea-bottom deposit that, of the three, is the most evident and easy to spot.

The Benton Group also contains a yellow sticky clay (bentonite), which is expansive when it gets wet. Bentonite was originally deposited by volcanic ash carried on the wind from far away. When it swells and expands, it exerts tremendous pressure on its environment—up to thirty thousand pounds per square inch. Houses built on the clay have a noticeable tendency to develop enormous, destabilizing cracks in their foundations.

The Dakota Formation

Moving farther west and higher up, one arrives at the more prominent, and older of the two hogback ridges that bracket Hogback Valley. Handsome and suntanned, this buff-colored, marine sandstone—interbedded with gray shales—in its placement and location comes after (below stratigraphically) the younger Benton Group that lines the Hogback Valley floor. Highly visible on the open space, the Dakota Formation is among the oldest of Colorado's Cretaceous rocks, second only to the Purgatoire Formation.

Because of its economic importance and the fact that it is fossil-bearing, the Dakota Formation has always been of great interest to geologists and paleontologists. In addition to fossils, it contains rich reservoirs of oil, gas, coal, and water. Its location on the charts and maps is consistent with our journey back in time.

The product of beach sands of a sandy tidal flat at the edge of a large sea, the Dakota Formation is not only extensive in Colorado—stretching all the way from Loveland, north of Denver, to Walsenburg, south of Colorado Springs—but it also extends well beyond the state, from the Black Hills of South Dakota to Central Nebraska; from Santa Fe, New Mexico, to Moab, Utah. Much of the ground water for the state of Colorado is pumped from the Dakota Formation. Its shale has been mined for oil and gas and its clay used for pottery.

The Niobrara and Dakota Hogbacks, in short, not only form a prominent backdrop on the skylines of Colorado Springs and Old Colorado City, but are also of significant historic and geologic importance throughout Colorado and much of the West.

Heading West: The Progressively Older Formations

Located between the Dakota Hogback and the Lyons Formation are the Cretaceous Purgatoire, Jurassic Morrison, and the Triassic Lykins Formations. A mix of shale, silt-stone and limestone—the Lykins is the oldest of the three. The thin-bedded Purgatoire Formation is a product of river deposits. The sands of this later unit were probably deposited in a floodplain environment. Noblett, in his geological guide, reminds us that this formation appears not only in Red Rock Canyon Open Space, but also in "both the Garden of the Gods and Bear Creek. It includes a white conglomeratic sand-stone which is graded and cross-bedded suggesting fluvial deposition. Contrast these features with the Lyons Sandstone to get a feeling for recognizing river versus wind deposits. A thin black shale separates it from the Dakota."

The Purgatoire Formation, located along the Lion Trail and extending north all the way to Highway 24, is made up of two members: Glencairn Shale and Lytle Sandstone. A discontinuous ridge of Lytle Sandstone is the site of a possible Apishapa structure. (Apishapa were prehistoric hunter/gatherers and are discussed in the chapter on Early Human History.) Being spongy rock, the sandstone also serves as a reservoir for water to support the ponderosa which grow along that formation.

Gypsum Canyon

Proceeding west from the Dakota Hogback ridge and before reaching the first ridge of the Lyons Formation, you come to what Colorado College geologist John Lewis once called "the world's most beautiful dump," based on its world-class setting. Now off limits, the dump was once a true canyon. The appropriately named Gypsum Canyon was, once upon a time, the deepest of the five canyons located on the Red Rock Canyon Open Space, with its distinctive pink, cauliflower-shaped nodules, its swallowtailed crystals, and gypsum flowers found in the shale that lined the canyon bottom. Gypsum Canyon, before it was effectively filled, submerging its Jurassic-age Morrison Formation, might well have been a repository site for dinosaur bones.

The Morrison Formation—with its Baskin-Robbins colors—is made up of purple, red, and green shales, sandstones, limestone, conglomerates, and a thick base of gyp-sum. These rocks were a product of a warm, moist lowland climate, near sea level and shoreline, with sluggish rivers; and with depositions occurring in tropical lowlands. Because of its soft shales, the Morrison rock wore down more rapidly than the stronger, more resistant sandstone formations on the open space. For this reason, it does not form ridges that are easy to see.

Once abundant in its namesake canyon, gypsum is a rock that is a chemical pre-cipitite. It was precipitated from the evaporation of the warm shallow seawaters of the Jurassic Period to become in its densest form, alabaster, which is often carved into decorative ornaments. Chalk and plaster of Paris are also derived from gypsum.

Gypsum Canyon held many attractions for a youthful explorer growing up in the area. One of these was a cave. On the one hand, it was intriguing. On the other, for the likes of Don Ellis, it proved to be a tantalizing but unrealizable challenge. Ellis longed to descend into its unexplored depths—a would-be spelunker. However, he was unable to discover any footholds that would allow him to safely make the descent. Today the prospect of caving for young people on this site no longer exists.

Thanks to the accumulation of citizens' garbage over several decades, Gypsum Canyon has been filled to the brim like a giant bathtub, with the equivalent of a prohibition-era bootlegger's noxious swill percolating below its surface. In some places, the garbage is buried to a depth of more than one hundred feet, effectively entombing the bones of whatever large fauna fossils may have been present in this formation. And, as recently confirmed, dinosaurs did in fact once roam the open space, to be further described in the following chapter.

Because Morrison Formation shale is an expansive sort of clay, the landfill was reportedly lined with it—conveniently excavated from the site itself. After the landfill was closed in 1987 to meet State Health Department requirements, it was capped with clay and sod and re-seeded with grasses. The site covers approximately fifty-one acres, with another eight to ten acres located in Section 16 on the edge of Manitou Springs.

The Triassic Lykins Formation

Laid down before the Morrison, the older, approximately 245-million-year-old, limey mudstone of the reddish-brown and green-grey Triassic Lykins Formation contains few fossils, indicative of a salty and harsh environment of mixed shoreline and lagoonal conditions not conducive to life forms. The Lykins, however, does record impressions of communities of photosynthetic cyanobacteria (blue-green algae) found within its dolostone (rock with a high percentage of dolomite) and gnarly limestone deposits. Chert and agate can also be found embedded in its limestone. It was at the boundary of the Triassic Lykins and the even earlier Permian Lyons, some 280 million years ago, that the Great Permian Extinction occurred, ushering in the Age of Dinosaurs.

Continuing on west from Gypsum Canyon, one arrives at the edge of Red Rock Canyon, the heart and soul of the open space, with its unmistakable Lyons Sandstone Formations rearing up on either side. Then, just one valley (Greenlee Canyon) beyond it, rise the monolithic Pennsylvanian Fountain fins. These two formations are defined by their fancifully weathered and sculpted shapes, their warped, bent, and tilted angles, their distinguishing textures and, perhaps above all else, their trademark color, all of which offer valuable clues to "reading" their past history; and which, in turn, raise seminal questions. What, for example, explains those wonderful hues of red in the rocks that are so beloved of artists and poets?

The Quite Literally "Rusty Red Fins"

Geologically speaking, the Lyons Sandstone outcrop with its frozen dunes, and the Fountain fins with their cosmic eye holes, blades, pinnacles, and mushrooms, are not only breathtakingly beautiful, they are spectacularly unique. Sculpturally inimitable, these modeled and upswept red sandstone formations are rendered even more dramatic by their hematite red color, which can be attributed to the effect of iron in their mineral makeup. Eye catching as it is, it is simple oxidation that is responsible for the striking rust-red color in the rocks—in the same way that oxidation explains the rust

A fountain fin showing its tilted angle and distinguishing texture. (Photo courtesy Bill Koerner) that builds up on an improperly seasoned cast iron skillet. The description "rusty red fins" or "rusting outcrops" is, thus, far more than just a poetic turn of phrase. And while oxidation of iron fixes the color more or less permanently within the rock, leaching can and does occur under the right conditions.

The Permian Lyons Formation

To either side of Red Rock Canyon—with its gentle valley dotted with scrub oak communities, wildflowers, and native grasses—rise the substantial and handsome red Lyons Sandstone ridges. How did two such massive and extensive embankments of the Permian Period Lyons end up flanking the jewel in the crown of Red Rock Canyon? The answer is that there was a soft spot in the Lyons Formation that eroded over millennia, in turn creating a valley between the whaleback ridge on one side and the castellated embankment on the other.

The character of the 250–290-million-year-old Lyons Formation, in terms of its makeup, is somewhat mixed, although it is nonetheless quite easy to profile. On the one hand, its ridges, laid down in horizontal layers according to the principle of "superposition," are mostly composed of fine red sand. But it also has some conglomerate and arkose (coarse sandstone with significant feldspar and quartz) properties found to a far greater extent in the Fountain Formation and which, indeed, constitutes one of the latter's most distinctive features. Paradoxically, the Lyons Sandstone is often described as "a strongly cemented and resistant" rock—even though any rock with sand in it is, by definition, "weak rock." Thus there are some unpredictable variables in the characteristics of this famous rock band. But its incontrovertible history is one of changing climate and depositions that went from alluvial fan to dune and back again.

During the Permian Period, Red Rock Canyon Open Space was part of a coastal desert. The Ancestral Rockies had begun to erode and be buried under their own debris—first having been reduced to rocks, then to fine grains of reddish sand that ultimately piled up as Lyons dunes. Lime and shale were still being deposited in a shallow sea. The climate was thought to be analogous to modern Morocco, with Sahara-like dunes by the sea in close proximity to old mountains—a comparison further prompted and reinforced by the appearance of the extensive series of wind-swept, sandy dunes in the lee of the eroding Ancestral Rockies.

For the next one hundred million years, the future Red Rock Canyon was near the edge of the sea with a fluctuating shoreline and meandering streams. As the ancient winds blew, they gave rise to the rippling Lyons Sandstone dunes, shaping them into a series of progressively older waves, crests, and troughs, while moving them across the plains. The Lyons Formation, in general, recorded and preserved few fossils in the forms of prehistoric flora and fauna. The harsh conditions were clearly inhospitable to the preservation of all but a few life forms.

Near the site of what was once the Bock House and where now stands a pavilion built of the blocks of native Lyons Sandstone salvaged from the original structure, it is possible to get an initial close-up impression of one of the striking red Lyons fins *in situ*. By running your fingers over its surface, you immediately get a sense of its fine-grained composition. A magnifying glass further reveals that it is mostly composed of small grains of sand of uniform size, indicative of dunes deposited by wind. Piles of sand in riverbeds, by way of comparison, have many different sizes.

While the Permian Lyons Formation is typically hematite red, there are also some startling and unexpected examples of bleached-out white Lyons occurring as well. Even in the absence of its uniquely defining red color, the rock's minerals and texture offer irrefutable proof that it is, in fact, Lyons. According to Noblett, petroleum geologists speculate that the bleaching out may have been caused by petroleum oil passing through its strata. A very small outcropping of the sui generis—white Lyons—can be found near the "graffiti cave," also known as the "hippie cave," as you go up the Red Rock Canyon Trail to where there is a Bock road branching off to the east. This small rib is all the more unusual in that it displays the transition in its stripes between red and white Lyons. Nothing like it has been observed to date in either Manitou Springs Section 16 or Garden of the Gods.

Writing for the *Red Rock Rag* (Vol.4, No.12), local historian Don Ellis once again takes us back to his western-style, Huck Finn boyhood as he engages in explorations of Manitou Springs Section 16 at the south end of the open space. "I walked along the crest of the ridge of red [Lyons] sandstone. Found a little arch that I could reach through and shake hands with myself. Saw a twisted dead tree that had grown in a crack in the rock and been bent by the wind. Watched mosquito larvae in a bathtub-size rain water pool in the rock on top of the ridge. Experienced joy and wonder. Marveled at it all. I was no more than eight the first time we went there."

Cross-Bedding and other Archival Hieroglyphs

Taken as a whole, the monumental red Lyons outcroppings on the open space contain a variety of seemingly obscure, but nonetheless interesting, structural details from their past history—doing so in the hieroglyphs of their wind-swept ripple marks, in cross-bedding (where thin layers slant obliquely between the main horizontal layers), and in mud cracks. The irregular diagonal lines in the red Lyons that mimic the shapes of moguls on ski slopes are, as suggested, the tracks of ancient dunes driven by the wind. Each distinctive and successive fossilized imprint represents a still older, slumped down, eroded, scallop-domed sandy dune, with individual beds characterized by differences in grain-size and variations in color.

These ancient dunes, geologists believe, strongly resemble the modern dunes that can be seen today in the Great Sand Dunes National Park, west of the Blanca group of the Sangre de Cristo range. It is believed

> *"There's a spot in Red Rock Canyon Open Space where you can see the direction the wind was blowing 280 million years ago. It's a spot that makes my heart pound. You look east from the top of Quarry Pass and see petrified sand dunes."*
>
> —**Ken Weissenburger,** geologist

that these latter-day surviving relics can help us better understand the conditions that prevailed long ago when their ancient counterparts were laid down in the Permian Period.

In effect, the profiles of the ghosts of the Lyons past are indelibly recorded in the ancient rock, with prominent cross-bedding observable in the eastern ridge. Here is clear evidence that rather than being formed of water-born sediment, as were the older red Fountain fins, the Lyons Formation instead was shaped and formed by the shifting of sands blown by ancient winds. These early dunes, once they were formed out of red sandy beach and shore deposits, were subsequently buried, only to resurface again as today's familiar and architecturally muscular, relatively smooth-surfaced rocks.

If you make your way to the juncture of the Quarry Pass Trail, it is possible to view good examples of cross-bedding, first in the stair-stepping cut walls of the nineteenth-century sandstone quarry that once operated at this site, and then as you turn and face east to see prominent cross-bedding in the Lyons embankment rising up on the opposite side of the former quarry, close to the designated climbing wall that rock climbers, for good reason, refer to as "the ripple wall." The extensive cross-bedding apparent here helped to protect this landmark red sandstone wall from being sliced up into flagstones or cut into building blocks.

Red Rock Canyon's Sandstone Quarries

Because the red Lyons is both a handsome and easily carved sandstone (more resistant than Fountain, albeit less than Dakota), it was the object of one of the biggest and most productive quarry operations on the site of the present-day Red Rock Canyon Open Space. Indeed, by the late 1880s, several large quarries sited at the very heart of the future open space were operating on the west side of Red Rock Canyon (described later in greater detail). The most prominent were the Kenmuir (operated by the Greenlee family) and the Snider quarries located in the Lyons outcrop separating Greenlee and Red Rock Canyons. Of the various types of stone mined for industrial purposes from today's open space, it was unquestionably the red Lyons that underwent both the most extensive and conspicuous extraction, as evidenced by the monumental stair-stepping stone structure that remains—where six-foot-square blocks were once systematically drilled, cut, and blasted away.

In the nineteenth century, of course, the earth was beginning to be viewed more in terms of an industrial model (as it often continues to be to this day). It was possible then to view the American West, with its clear waters, abundant minerals, and virgin forests as representing limitless resources to be exploited for purely capital gain and material benefit, rewarding those with capital to invest and the will to work or, better yet, the ability to hire others.

Regardless of its historic use and abuse, the good news is that today the open space has been saved from future depredations. And in making a concentrated effort to see the glass as half full, it does become possible to re-imagine the quarried Lyons Sandstone with its giant pyramidal staircase as something approximating a sunlit Aztec temple or perhaps even an outsized modern work of cubist sculpture. In this way, the rock's disfigurement can be, to some degree, rationalized. Of less appeal, if of undoubted historic interest, is the evidence of some early graffiti scratched into a rock face.

Completing the Journey Back in Time to Rocky I and the Pennsylvanian Fountain Fins

The 323-million-year-old, hematite-red Pennsylvanian Fountain Formation, located at the far west of Red Rock Canyon Open Space, rises dramatically between the western-most two of the five, north-to-south-running parallel valleys—that is, Greenlee Canyon (under which lies some of the softer Lyons Formation) and Sand Canyon.

"In geology, there is nothing more permanent than change."

—**John Lewis,** geologist

To the east of Greenlee Canyon, running north and south, stretch the slightly younger and more solid-bodied rust-red Permian Lyons Formation. Then, to the west of Greenlee Canyon appear the unmistakable, vertically tilted, deep salmon-red outcrops of the Pennsylvanian Fountain Formation. This outcropping—with its jutting upswept fins and arched backs—leaps up like some great and mighty school of surfing, prehistoric leviathans. It brackets both sides of the last remaining of the five valleys, the appropriately named Sand Canyon.

By the Pennsylvanian Period (about 290–323 million years ago), the shallow sea covering the region had begun to recede and empty out. The Ancestral Rockies (Rocky I), as noted earlier, were on the rise—surfacing as a ring of islands with their heads breaking through the water at a rate of approximately a millimeter a year—rapid in geologic time. The deposition of more shales, sands, and mud that were laid down in successive layers continued. This process was accompanied by the erosion of great volumes of rock as the ancient mountain range was simultaneously wearing down.

The weathering and erosion of hematite-red rock and granite would continue into the more recent Permian Period when the Lyons Sandstone was formed. The material that would ultimately compose the even older Fountain Formation was initially deposited as alluvial fans along the flanks of the Ancestral Rockies.

Once the sea receded, the mud and sand sediments deposited at its bottom were carried down to the flatlands below by high-energy streams like today's Fountain Creek above Manitou Springs. In contrast to the Fountain Forma-

"Everything is Interrelated."

—**Alexander von Humboldt**

tion, in other depositions meandering streams from ancient seas and the force of blowing winds played a more formative role. As the range of Ancestral Rockies continued to "shed" tons of reddish sandy sediment off its east side, it was Frontrangia that was in the forefront, contributing its parent rock to the creation of the sublime Fountain fins (and later the Lyons) in Red Rock Canyon Open Space.

In the course of the Triassic Period (about 206–250 million years ago), the Ancestral Rockies were worn down to their roots. Despite the constant wearing down and erosion,

Ancient leaning towers. (Photo courtesy Bill Koerner)

with the eventual disappearance of entire mountains, noted Harvard biologist E.O. Wilson's principle of "consilience" was being adhered to. This theory posits that, based on cause, effect, and synthesis, everything from cultures to tangible phenomenon can be reduced to the laws of physics and an interconnectedness that "transverses the scales of space, time, and complexity."

The parent rock from the Ancestral Rockies found itself, thus, being recycled not only into the famous red sandstone formations in the open space, but also into such colorful and majestic ranges as the Maroon Bells, the Sangre de Cristo's, and the Flatirons. Different generations of mountains and rock formations, metaphorically, stood on the shoulders of older, earlier ranges made up of hematite red sandstone and granite.

In the Pennsylvanian Fountain Formation, the word "arkose" refers to the composition of its rock, with its sizeable amounts of quartz and feldspar (the earth's most abundant group of minerals) derived from granite. Geologist Halka Chronic in her book *Roadside Geology* defines "conglomerate," as "rock composed of rounded, waterworn fragments of older rock, usually in combination with sands." Some of the quartz grains may measure up to four inches or more in diameter. Conglomerate rock results from the deposits of high- to low-energy shallow streams flowing from steep to flatter areas, such as the base of mountains. More than ten thousand feet thick in nearby Manitou Springs, the Fountain Formation provides evidence of gravels that were carried directly down by streams from the eroding Ancestral Rockies. In some cases, the rocks in the conglomerate are large, indicating that their source was relatively close at hand, since even powerful streams would not have carried rocks of that size for great distances.

Small cobbled stones in the Fountain fins can be easily felt, rough to the touch, and seen enfolded within the compressed strata of the red-and-white striped rock. Upon close inspection, it becomes immediately apparent that the 323-million-year-old rocks—with their composition of dark red siltstone and red-and-white striped sandstone mixed with gravel, cobble, and boulder conglomerate—is of a much coarser material than its Lyons Sandstone counterpart. (The bleached-out white stripes are a result of "solution and chemical changes in the iron mineral hematite," states Halka Chronic.) The grand and monumental rougher-textured Fountain fins—soaring up from their broad pediments like sculptures in a museum—incorporate not only noticeably large pebbles, but also the small boulders once carried along by forceful alluvial streams.

By great good fortune, unlike the Lyons Sandstone, the incomparably beautiful Fountain fins in the open space, with their ferruginous blades and turned-up tails, have been spared industrial use by virtue of the fact they were never considered particularly "good rock" for quarrying. Hence, unlike the more desirable Lyons, these geological treasures were spared.

A Spectacular Walk Showcasing the Immemorial Fountain Fins

One of the most beautiful walks on the Red Rock Canyon Open Space, in order to enjoy a close-up view of the Fountain fins, begins with the Contemplative Trail. It starts from the Highway 24 main parking lot, goes west on the Sand Canyon Trail, then heads south and ultimately completes a circle on the bottom quarter of the open space. The walk takes about an hour at a brisk pace.

Large evergreens sprout from enormous rough-surfaced rust-red boulders, offering piney shade, while various viewpoints open up to vistas of the outrigger brown foothills and of Pikes Peak. In some places, the tumbled rocks contain narrow cleavages, in others, weathered and eroded mini-arches frame pieces of cobalt blue sky.

By viewing the Fountain fins up close, it is possible to recapture some of the same spirit of pure wonder and awe previously described by Ellis in his essay. The fins appear to be limitless in their protean shapes, sizes, and forms—their unending inventiveness. Their bulky, composite-filled bases are differently contoured from their angular and tilted tops, like sculptures on a stand. At their trunks they are often massively rounded or folded, with skin that is smooth and ruddy in some places; in others they are rough, erosion-pocked, and knobbed with large stones.

Some of these groupings evoke Homeric images of the sleeping, heavy-limbed bodies of Cyclops. On the barnacle-clad face of one of these giants, young junipers struggle to establish a foothold. If you look carefully, you will also spot the beginnings of a mini-arch, opening up like a Cyclops's singular and unblinking eye—through which shines the lapis lazuli blue of an Aegean Sea. But when you look again, you notice that indeed there is another eyehole, poorly aligned and farther off, in a manner suggestive of a drawing by Picasso.

In the timeless formations of the Fountain fins you are free to imagine any number of fanciful shapes, depending on the viewer, and whether they are seen through the

Garden of the Gods with lightning. (Lithograph by Archie Musick, circa 1938, courtesy Pat Musick)

eyes of a contemplative, a child, an artist, or anyone who pauses for a moment to suspend disbelief, engage in a bit of playfulness, and to dream. Hugely metaphoric and shaped by processes of weathering and erosion, nothing if not dramatic, these formations tease the imagination and boldly inspire.

On some of the higher points of the Contemplative Trail there are breathtaking views that show off the Fountain fins in all their grandeur as they march along together in lockstep. The manner in which they majestically progess across both our flagship parks—Red Rock Canyon Open Space and Garden of the Gods Park—then close up the space between them as they head east towards the plains, is proof positive of their age-old geological link and of their common history. Theirs, unquestionably, is a splendid processional.

Not far from the trailhead along the Contemplative Trail, in the narrowest passage between the high red walls of the Fountain Formation, a small fault line can be observed in the ancient rock. Not far from it, on the rock wall opposite and facing south, there appears a crudely lettered warning in fading black paint. Put there by the property's late owner, John Bock, this warning from the recent past reads: "Keep out. This means you." Happily, the warning no longer applies.

It is, nonetheless, sobering to realize that had the open space not been typical of arid, high desert country, and instead had been characterized by a moistly tropical one with constant high levels of precipitation, the red rocks may have been reduced by now to piles of red sand and a profusion of tropical growth, punctuated by tall trees. As it is, the incomparable leaning towers of red stone that we see and rejoice in today have been spared by both man and nature.

The Alluvial Gravels

There is a final feature on Red Rock Canyon Open Space's geological map to be noted. This is the generous deposits of alluvial sand and gravel, much of it disintegrated Pikes Peak granite that was washed down by precipitous streams from the new range of Rocky Mountains between ten thousand and two million years ago. They became something far more attractive than your standard roadside construction-area dumps. As if guided by a higher aesthetic, they instead formed the flat-topped hills and snub-nosed mesas. Several of the Fountain fins on the open space are capped by mesa gravels.

The three types of alluvial gravels are all quaternary-era rocks and a more modern phenomenon, dating back to as recently as between .01 and two million years ago.

The oldest of the three is the Rocky Flats Alluvium, which is found in Red Rock Canyon around the 26th Street Trailhead. The somewhat younger, six-hundred-thousand-year-old Verdos Alluvium of disintegrated Pikes Peak granite caps the main part of the mesa between Greenlee Canyon and Sand Canyon. It also gathered at the toe of Red Rock Canyon, where the Dakota Hogback may have acted as a barrier to eastward water flow. Youngest of the mesa gravels is the Slocum, which is found in Sand Canyon. These large dumps of mesa gravels and boulders, which would later supply the late owner of the Red Rock Canyon property with his highly lucrative gravel quarry, are spread throughout the open space. (The gravel quarry has subsequently been reclaimed and is now a revegetated, grassy area joining the Red Rock Rim and the lower Hogback Trails.) Indeed, the quaternary mesa gravels top nearly everything in the Pikes Peak region. We can only shake our head in wonder at the horrendous storms that must have taken place millennia ago to account for the magnitude of such huge slides of rock in the eternal, sometimes violent, play of the elements. (Or, alternatively, perhaps things just piled up, waiting for a good flood to come along and facilitate the disintegrated rock's transport and delivery.)

What We Can Learn from Red Rock Canyon's Geology

We have now, either with map in hand or in our mind's eye, completed a millennia-long journey back in time—during which three different sets of Rocky Mountains have been formed, several marine incursions have occurred, numerous layers of sedimentary rock have been laid down and overturned in mountain-building orogenies, and climates and landscapes have likewise undergone dramatic alteration. Among the constants in this dynamic, ongoing geologic process are time and, of course, change itself.

> "When it comes to geology, it's all about time."
>
> —**Judy Gerber,** geologist

Through a study of the geology of Red Rock Canyon Open Space we can gain a better understanding of other important features of the natural world as well. Such knowledge sheds light, in turn, on questions of how we fit into this amazing and interconnected world-old story, including the historic interplay of our unique environment and our long and diverse cultural history. Closely related to the story of the geology of the open space are its rich paleontology, ecology, and archeology—fields in which recent research has brought to light entire new chapters of documented finds and discoveries.

Geologist Jeff Noblett believes that the study of geology is a wonderful way to come to some sort of understanding of "the concept of time." He elaborates with an analogy helpful to the average layperson. "If we were to scale earth's history on a one-year calendar, with the earth forming on January 1 and today being midnight December 31, the oldest rocks we find in Colorado would not appear until the beginning of August. The detailed sedimentary record of the seas begins about Thanksgiving and humans reach Colorado only near the end of the final hour."

Our knowledge of plate tectonics and of continents that continue to drift and change, and of the ceaseless forces of erosion and weathering that over millennia have reduced mountains to rubble and sand, merely serves to underscore this useful analogy. In another hundred million years, Colorado and the continental United States as we know them today will no longer exist.

In the meantime, Red Rock Canyon represents a wonderful educational resource, as well as a spiritual and recreational one. The astonishing billion-year-old story to be read in stone (or painted, photographed, written about, and communed with) contains important lessons for the next generations of stewards to learn and pass on. Earth's long and eventful history, as represented by the open space, manifests shock and awe on a grand scale. It is calculated to induce both infinite respect and true humility as we struggle to better understand and more fully grasp both the timelessness and the temporality of the fragile, changing planet we all inhabit and call home.

CHAPTER 2

The Stories the Rocks Tell: Ancient Life Forms

"Let there be firmament in the midst of the waters,
and let it divide the waters from the waters ... and bring forth
abundantly the moving creatures that have life."
—Genesis, chapter 1

"To experience the world as an extended self and its story
as our own extended story involves no surrender or
eclipse of our individuality. ... Our recognition of this may be the
third part of an unfolding of consciousness that began a long time ago,
like the third movement of a symphony. In the first movement,
our infancy as a species, we felt no separation
from the world around us.
—Joanna Macy

George Finlay of Colorado College was a highly regarded geologist at the turn of the twentieth century. Among his many achievements was the survey he conducted for the *Colorado Springs Folio* (published in the 1916 *U.S. Geologic Atlas*), which included Red Rock Canyon and Garden of the Gods. In his erudite *Colorado Springs: A Guidebook* (1906) describing "the rock formations in the vicinity of Colorado Springs," Finlay wrote metaphorically that, "Rock strata are the pages in the book of the earth's geological history. They were deposited in order, one above another, like the leaves of a book lying flat. The succession of living forms on the earth has been, from first to last, in a definite progression." That iteration of a basic geologic truth remains as relevant today as it was more than a century ago. And within those stratified pages are to be found the fascinating stories of ancient life forms, studied and elucidated by paleontologists, while geologists work to de-codify the all-important context of time, place, and prevailing conditions in the grand narrative.

The Long Overdue Need for Scientific Study and Research

Since the Anglo-European settlement of Colorado, Rock Canyon Open Space has always been privately owned, and for the past eighty years by the same family. Until the site was purchased by the city in 2003, its potentially rich repositories of ancient fossils had never before been studied. No experts in the field until now had enjoyed the opportunity to document and assess the richness of the site's geology, paleontology, and archeology.

This absence of data was of concern to scientists, researchers, and citizens alike. Because experts had not conducted an inventory of the Red Rock Canyon property, "nothing had been recorded," says Meg Van Ness in the Office of Archeology and Historic Preservation at the Colorado State Historical Society. "This doesn't mean it didn't exist. It simply meant it hadn't been looked at." Registered sites on public land can be protected, but not on private land. And as Van Ness sums it up: "How do you know what you're losing [or gaining], if you don't know what you've got."

But all of that has changed, thanks to the successful grassroots effort made to save Red Rock Canyon, not only as an open space, but in perpetuity, with the benefit of an easement held by the Palmer Land Trust (details of this community-wide initiative are recounted in a later chapter). Now for the first time, two volunteers trained as paleontology researchers have combed the rocks hoping to unlock some of the secrets of the ancient past. Had Red Rock Canyon Open Space been subjected to development, the truth about these treasures might never have been known.

What Stories Do the Rocks Tell?

Most of the fossils buried in the 1,474 acres of Red Rock Canyon, like the red rocks themselves, are millions of years old and span a time when three mountain ranges had uplifted and two of which vanished again. At one time Red Rock Canyon was an inland sea that subsided and left behind its rich deposits in marine fossils, along with its soft mud shales and mudflats that gradually eroded into valleys and canyons.

In some cases it is possible to recapitulate the stories the rocks tell in relatively precise detail as a result of field study. In other cases we may only be able to make intelligent guesses about what fossils are most likely to be found in a particular formation based on what has been found to exist in the same formation elsewhere in the region. This is particularly true if the stratum is buried deeply or is otherwise inaccessible by earth-friendly methods. In such cases, the stories the rocks tell are predicated not so much on hard facts as on solidly reliable sources.

Paleontology Helps Us Understand the Earth's History

Paleontology, states Halka Chronic in *Roadside Geology of Colorado* is "the branch of geology devoted to the study of ancient life as shown in fossils, which are petrified remains or impressions of ancient animals or plants." If geology is a book made up of chapters, fossils are its index. But to get to them often requires some digging. Not surprisingly, the word "fossil" comes from the Latin word *fossilis,* literally meaning "dug up."

By studying the fossils of ancient plants, marine life, invertebrates, vertebrates, birds, dinosaurs, and the like, we can begin to answer any number of tantalizing questions about the earth's history—including its five major and various minor episodes of extinction. Paleontology can tell us about other conditions as well.

For example, according to Sharon Milito, an elementary school teacher and one of two researchers to engage in the first-ever paleontological survey of the original open space, the sooty-looking soil found on the site was probably deposited by volcanic eruptions on the West Coast millions of years ago. The ash first settled onto the water of the ancient sea that covered the area of the future Colorado Springs some seventy million years ago. Then it was submerged by water and later covered by a layer of shale, with more sedimentary layers to follow. The process repeated itself a surprising number of times. By sifting through and counting layers of soil, researchers can estimate how many eruptions may have occurred.

Facts, Clues and Detective Work

Mike Poltenovage, an engineer with a deep interest in large fauna of the past who wanted to model examples of volunteerism and outdoor activities for his kids, was the other half of the two-person team who participated in the two-year paleontological study of the open space. The "Paleotrails Project" was conducted under the supervision of experts at the Denver Museum of Nature and Science (DMNS) and in cooperation with the city of Colorado Springs Parks, Recreation, and Cultural Services department.

The Paleotrails Project focused on the stratigraphy of the open space, starting on the east side with the hogbacks. "Stratigraphy" refers to the study of rock strata. In order to secure approval for the project, Milito and Poltenovage were required to write a proposal, secure authorization, and, finally, to be issued a collection permit from the state archeologist at the Colorado Historical Society (CHS).

Among the team's stated goals was opening up potential educational and scientific opportunities for the community at large, which is also in keeping with one of the preeminent and core conservation values of the open space itself. Drawing on the team's scientific research and a careful analysis of their findings, the city would later incorporate results into the Interpretive Master Plan for the open space.

It was under this broad mandate that, starting in September 2006, the paleontology research team of Milito and Poltenovage began to clamber over rocks, sifting through light-colored soil and sooty volcanic ash and, in general, scouring the rough and rugged outcrops and the massive overturned formations that are the hallmark of the open space. One occupational hazard of the team's fieldwork was the unpredictable mountain weather. Among the benefits was the chance to enjoy Colorado's world-class wildlife.

Quoted in the May 2007 *Westside Pioneer,* researcher Milito remarked on two geological features that make Red Rock Canyon Open Space an ideal laboratory for study and, at the same time, distinguish it from its sister park, Garden of the Gods. First is the amount of time one can travel in so little space, with rock formations from different time periods easily accessible and relatively close together. And while the open space is stratigraphically continuous with Garden of the Gods Park, unlike the park itself, the open space is not as severely faulted and broken up, facilitating the study of various rock formations in their proper sequences. A small fault, as previously noted, can be observed in the Fountain Formation on the northwest end of the open space in Sand Canyon at the start of the Contemplative Trail, and another south of the main parking lot where the Fountain was cut away, exposing a fault.

Based on this relative absence of faulting and also the excellent exposure of what are typically considered fossil-rich strata in the state, paleontologists and geologists alike regard today's Red Rock Canyon Open Space as being something of a textbook model for geological points of interest. Furthermore, the heavy excavation for commercial use of sandstone for building blocks, gravel for road surfacing, and limestone for cement along the Dakota and Niobrara/Codell Hogbacks had at least one positive result—it exposed previously hidden fossils.

In the course of months of fieldwork, the team searched the open space several times a week for clues leading to evidence of ancient fossilized flora and fauna. When something identifiable, important, or of interest was found, it was subsequently measured and photographed. After completing days of fieldwork, the pair hunkered down to analyze, then described the results of their observations based on such characteristics as shape, color, patterns, markings, size, location of find, and geologic age. Highly selective in the rock samples they took, they left most of what they observed *in situ*.

Fossil Traces as Differentiated from Body Fossils

Paleontologists make a clear distinction, when describing ancient fauna, between "fossil traces," meaning tracks or footprints and "body fossils," which are skeletal body remains. By close examination of the tracks of dinosaurs, researchers can often determine what kinds of giant reptiles were resident in the area, when they were present, and how they behaved socially. Among other things, they calibrate the space between footprints of an individual and count toes. Fossil traces can reveal whether individuals were bipedal or quadrupedal, and also, but with somewhat less certainty, whether they were carnivorous or herbivorous.

What Life was Like for Ancient Fauna

Paleontological research can help us learn more about what life was like for various forms of terrestrial and marine fauna in their ancient environments and how they adapted and changed over time. It can also help us begin to address such existential and thought-provoking questions as: "Who are we and where did we come from?"

"For whatever we lose (like a you or a me)
it's always ourselves we find in the sea."
—e. e. cummings

On the basis of scientific study and research in paleontology and evolution we already know, for

"Ideal Landscape of the Age of Reptiles." (1874 sketch by Alexander Winchell)

example, that our ancestors, half a billion years ago, were jawless, fishlike creatures that had a rod of cartilage along their backs, giving rise to the signal and all-important evolution of vertebrates. A few million years earlier, between 525–565 MYA (million years ago), the Cambrian Explosion led to the development of all of the major body plans, or phyla.

By approximately 450 MYA, arthropods had evolved in the shallow seas, developing their armor of an external skeleton, or exoskeleton. At this point, a very odd-looking, four-foot-long shrimp, who was the first predator, developed eyesight. Another major breakthrough came when fish became migratory and developed a brain with memory. And so the story continues, as eventually the fins of fish begin to evolve into limbs and amphibians moved up on shore.

Among the first animals to invade the land were the *Myriapoda*, or millipedes and centipedes. They provided the early blueprints for modern spiders and insects. One of the largest of the arthropods was the three-foot-long giant scorpion that became a top predator. Even the millipedes in those days, observes geologist Kirk Johnson in *Ancient Denvers* were "as large as snowboards." The millipedes and scorpions we see in Red Rock Canyon Open Space today are the smart-car versions of these earlier models.

By 300 MYA, in the Pennsylvanian Period, giant insects took to the air in flight, while others scuttled along the ground, early forerunners of some of the scaled-down versions that can still be found on the open space today. By this time, *Meganeura monyi* had arrived on the scene. An ancient dragonfly the size of a giant kite, it could be found darting first among the Fountain fins and then, close to one hundred million years later, among the sandy undulation of the frozen dunes of Lyons Sandstone forming along the ancient shorelines. With its approximately two- to three-foot wingspan, it was the biggest insect that ever lived. The dragonfly you see flitting about Red Rock Canyon Open Space today is, in essence, a flying "fossil" that has been radically downsized over time.

In the Pennsylvanian Period, the revolutionary development of the amniotic egg made it possible for reptiles to reproduce on land. Vast forests of tall scaly club mosses (*Lycopsids*) grew along the mountain range to the west of the open space. Horsetails and tree fern covered the land, and cycads and plants resembling palms first appeared.

Besides being holdovers from the prehistoric past and, in effect, living museum specimens, many of the arthropods that skitter, fly, jump, and crawl about Red Rock Canyon Open Space today afford clear evidence that in nature—as it slowly adapts, refines, experiments, discards, but never wastes—"small is beautiful." Thus, during the Mesozoic Era when dinosaurs grew feathers, sprouted wings, learned to sing, and took to the skies, they were also scaled way back in their size.

The Dakota Formation: "Dinosaur Freeway"

In the second phase of their paleontological survey of the open space, Poltenovage and Milito investigated and analyzed the fossil-rich Dakota Formation, hoping to make some findings not previously described in scientific literature. Thousands of feet deep, this massive formation extends across several western states. Because it and the Purgatoire (as well as the Morrison) are notable for their abundance of dinosaur fossils and footprints, these formations are popularly known among paleontologists as "stomping grounds" or "dinosaur freeways."

According to University of Colorado professors Lockley and Hunt in their book *Dinosaur Tracks,* "Shorelines have an important bearing on the distribution of tracks

"Albertosaurus," a theropod weighing 3 tons and measuring 30 feet long and 11 feet tall, came equipped with knife-sharp, serrated teeth and powerful jaws made-to-order for a carnivore. This fierce predator lived in the Late Cretaceous Period. (Paleoart by Tracy L. Ford)

because shoreline environments provide an ideal setting for the accumulation of foot-prints." The shoreline of the Western Interior Seaway, with its "mosaic of wetland and waterways ... provided suitable substrates [underlying layers] for abundant tracks to be formed."

This is one reason why fossil traces of dinosaurs and other ancient species of fauna have a high probability of being found in the Dakota Formation on the open space. Indeed, the entire state of Colorado has the right geology for dinosaur hot spots and has proven itself to be fossil-rich. Moreover, several famous and well-documented ancient fossil finds had already been made locally in the surrounding foothills and mesas of the Pikes Peak Region and in nearby Garden of the Gods.

Furthermore, good preservations of fossils in the upland areas of the state was as-sured because in the ancient past there had been only one truly major flood that had penetrated that far inland. This flood of Noah-like proportions (the aforementioned Western Interior Seaway) was one of the largest of all times and occurred in the Late Cretaceous Age. Last but not least, the aridity of the landscape helps ensure that body fossils and traces or tracks are easy to spot in the already abundantly exposed rock, once you know what you are looking for.

Embedded in the Cretaceous formations of the hogbacks is the larger story of the struggle for dominance between marine and terrestrial life, in their different and con-textualizing depositions, as seas advanced and retreated. The stratified layers are laid out like display cases in an ancient museum, with their contents preserved according to a clearly demarcated (if geologically relative) timeline—suggesting when ancient fossilized flora and fauna first appeared, and then later—and sometimes quite myste-riously—vanished from the record altogether.

The Permian-Triassic Extinction

The earth in its long and eventful history has experienced five major extinctions and a number of minor ones. Of these, by far the most apocalyptic was the great Permian-Triassic Extinction, which occurred between the younger Triassic and the older Per-mian Periods, 251.4 MYA. One of the most massive and extensive extinction events of all time, it wiped out an estimated 96 percent of all marine species and 70 percent of terrestrial vertebrate species. It is the only extinction to have killed off insects on such a large and unprecedented scale, obliterating 57 percent of all families and 83 percent of all genera.

No one knows for certain what caused the Permian-Triassic Extinction, which fore-shadowed the long Age of Dinosaurs, and from which the earth was slow to recover. Some experts believe a series of catastrophic events may explain it, such as giant leaks of methane gas from the ocean floor, eruptions of huge volcanoes, the impact of an enormous meteor, and/or dramatic climate change, characterized by the earth's cooling or warming.

The Triassic, Jurassic, and the relatively more recent Cretaceous Period (in that order) are the three periods included under the category of the Mesozoic Era, while the preceding Paleozoic contains, among others, the early Devonian, Ordovician, and Cambrian Periods, respectively. The ancestors of all major marine animals had their origins in the Cambrian Period, at which time they took on the protective armor of shells, and continued to evolve and proliferate into the Ordovician. Land plants established themselves in a profusion of green in the subsequent Devonian Period. As for the first one-celled organism—the microbe—it has been detected in even earlier rocks. Indeed, it appears to possess the astonishing ability to survive in the obsidian-like, volcanic glass of three-billion-year-old igneous rock—which of all rock types is the world's oldest—in some cases getting its food energy from chemicals such as iron.

The Age of Dinosaurs

Dinosaurs were dominant in the Mesozoic Era, which began 251 million years ago— when the giant reptiles first appeared on earth—and ended 65.5 million years ago. The Latinized Greek *deinos* means "fearful," while *saris* equates with "lizard." Enormous, scaly-skinned, non-swimming reptiles, dinosaurs hatched their young from eggs. Most were herbivorous, at a ratio of thirty to one.

Because of the range and variety of their often bizarre and apparently impractical, Maurice Sendak-like design features—seemingly programmed for a kind of evolutionary obsolescence—cartoonist Gary Larson refers to this as the "Awkward Age … considered a hazardous time for most species." Darwin himself was inclined to refer to these big, bizarre beasts as "less improved" forms. But the question remains, as Denver Museum of Nature and Science (DMNS) paleontologist Dr. Kenneth Carpenter is quick to ask, "Why would evolution select for 'handicaps'?"

At the peak of the Jurassic Period, the single continent of Pangaea split into Laragia and Godwin. As in the stories of Genesis, the seas continued to rise up and retreat. Fluctuating shorelines, coastal dunes, and swampy conditions characterized the age when the great reptiles ambled through muddy swamps, leaving behind immense footprints frozen in mud over which late-arriving *Homo sapiens* would one day marvel.

By the late Cretaceous Period, the world's continents had begun roughly to resemble the shapes we are familiar with today. These major tectonic changes and the resultant geology affected both the adaptation and distribution of the proliferating species of dinosaurs that first appeared in the Triassic and reigned supreme in the Jurassic, continuing through the Cretaceous, until their ultimate extinction at the K-T Boundary (in "K-T" the Greek "K" stands for the Latinized "Cretaceous"; and the "T" for "Tertiary"). This boundary is a geological signature marking the end of the Mesozoic Era and the beginning of the Cenozoic Era.

Whenever one writes of dinosaurs, one is strongly inclined to set everything in uppercase boldface type. These behemoth and unlikely precursors of birds have always been a big source of fascination for amateurs and experts alike. How lucky we are, then, that this abiding interest can be easily satisfied at various sites and museums located around the state. Indeed, Colorado, with its fossil-rich geology, has provided museums the world over with some of the best proof found anywhere of the life and times of these outlandish reptiles that once walked the earth.

Often in connection with building construction or new roads, exciting new discoveries in the state continue to be made, just as they have been recently by the less-invasive methods of scientific study in Red Rock Canyon Open Space. The state has more than a dozen major dinosaur sites, including North America's busiest, longest dinosaur trackway—a late Jurassic site with thirteen hundred prints located near the Purgatoire River in southwestern Colorado. The first dinosaur fossils in western North America and the first of *Tyrannosaurus rex* in the world (the infamous *T. rex*) were found in Colorado.

Old Bones on Nearby Mesas

Geologist and Colorado College professor George Finlay reported in his nineteenth-century guide that "recently" a mastodon tooth was discovered in the mesa gravels north of Colorado City. A Jurassic reptile was also found close to Garden of the Gods, while a skeleton of a *Mosasaurus manitouensis* was discovered "in the Jurassic shale east of the band of white gypsum." The *Mosasaurus* was a carnivorous marine lizard (not a dinosaur) that lived in the Late Cretaceous Period, and had the immense linear body of a serpent on steroids. Its fossil skeleton was subsequently housed in the Philadelphia Academy of Natural Sciences, founded in 1812. More recently, the growing list of fossil finds (in this case, of a mammal) was added to when, in 1950, a Colorado College geology class found a six-foot-long Columbian mammoth tusk on a Pikes Peak–area mesa. DMNS paleontologist Dr. Kenneth Carpenter discovered a fossil of a prehistoric ground sloth near Widefield in the southern part of Colorado Springs in 1965. The right conditions need to exist for bones of dinosaurs and prehistoric mammals to survive. Their bones must be buried quickly after they die. It usually requires millions of years for them to fossilize.

An Enormous Case of Mistaken Identity

In nearby Garden of the Gods Park in the spring of 2008, paleontologists from the Denver Museum of Nature and Science announced at a special event held for the news media and public at the park's Visitor and Nature Center that the replica of a much-prized dinosaur skull, which had long been featured in its exhibits, was of a species and genus never before seen in the world. For more than a century it had suffered from an enormous case of mistaken identity based on incorrect profiling.

The error first came to the attention of Colorado Springs–born, DMNS paleontologist Dr. Kenneth Carpenter. Carpenter's interest in dinosaurs can be traced back to his boyhood when he was enthralled by the Japanese series of sci-fi thrillers that featured the *über* mutant dinosaur, Godzilla. Not coincidentally, perhaps, Carpenter is today well known in the scientific community "for his work in re-examining dinosaur fossils using the latest forensic technology to correctly identify the fossils by period and species."

Because of his close work and familiarity with the partially crushed remains of the original fossilized skull and his expertise as curator of lower vertebrate paleontology at DMNS, Carpenter had long suspected that the dinosaur's original identity might be mistaken.

Carpenter decided to follow up on his hunch and conduct further study in collaboration with DMNS Research Associate Kathleen Brill. On the basis of lab tests and evidence made available in archival material, the researchers were able to trace soil samples that still adhered to the dinosaur's skull to a specific site in Garden of the Gods Park, lending credibility to Carpenter's hunch.

The Long Journey Home

Carpenter himself had manufactured the cast of the so-called and previously long-lost *Camptosaurus* skull, after Dr. Kirk J. Johnson, Vice President of Research and Collections and Chief Curator at DMNS, had gamely undertaken the task of hand-carrying the precious, semi-crushed fossil (half the skull is missing) on a flight

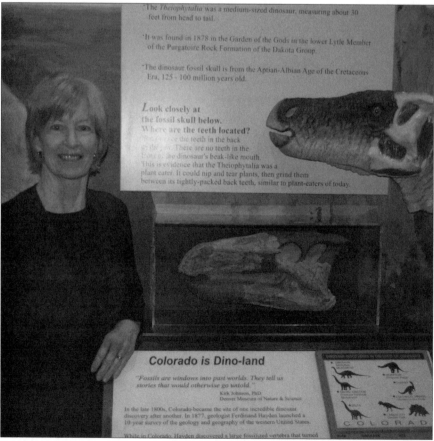

Naturalist Melissa Walker, with the newly identified and recovered Garden of the Gods dinosaur, "Theiophytalia kerri." It was Walker who first unearthed "Theio's" story, a news-making event celebrated at Garden of the Gods Visitor and Nature Center in the spring of 2008. (Photo by Les Goss, courtesy Melissa Walker)

back from the Yale Peabody Museum in Connecticut—from which it was taken out on loan—to Denver. (Dr. Johnson, a famously intrepid chaser of dinosaur fossils, is sometimes described as the museum's "very own Indiana Jones.")

In the unfolding of this amazing saga, Melissa Walker, past Program Coordinator at Garden of the Gods, played a key role by first raising the question of the possible existence of a Garden of the Gods dinosaur with experts at DMNS. Walker hoped to be able to set up a dinosaur exhibit for the new Garden of the Gods Visitor and Nature Center that was scheduled to open in 1995. In addition, her archival research, with the assistance of co-worker Lenore Fleck, brought to light an entire new body of information about the missing dinosaur's original discoverer, James Kerr. The researchers unearthed Kerr's scrapbooks and handwritten letters, which had long gathered dust in the Colorado College and Pioneers Museum archives. Kerr's papers offered proof positive of Walker's original guess that the geologist had been a Colorado College professor. In addition, his papers contained a number of important facts about his nineteenth-century discoveries, serving to nail down the 1878 date of the dinosaur find itself. One of the more useful clues to surface from Kerr's letters was that the dinosaur had been dis-

Colorado College Professor James Kerr, who discovered the Garden of the Gods dinosaur in 1878. (Image courtesy *Kiva* magazine)

covered at a site located "in one of the ridges in Garden of the Gods." It was then that Dr. Carpenter recalled having seen relevant information about such a dinosaur in his own files at DMNS.

In 1997, well over a century later, the freshly made cast of the rediscovered (if badly misidentified) Garden of the Gods' fossil, known then as *Camptosaurus,* was officially presented to Colorado Springs in a symbolic welcome-home ceremony—a most generous gift to the city from the DMNS and one that has been vastly enjoyed and appreciated by citizens and experts alike.

James Kerr Discovers "Portions of 21 Different Sea Monsters"

In 1878, Yale-trained Colorado College Geology Professor James Kerr, a sufferer from T.B. like many in the nineteenth century, had come to Colorado Springs to recover his health. He found the climate to be salubrious and, no doubt, the geology, too, so much to his liking that he stayed on. In that same year, Kerr reported in his letters and scrapbooks that he had discovered the bones of a large herbivorous dinosaur on a ridge of rocks in Garden of the Gods. In addition, he reported finding at the same site what he described, somewhat fancifully, as "portions of 21 different sea monsters." He subsequently wrote of his discovery to his Yale colleague, the fiercely competitive O.C. Marsh, whose bitter rivalry with his fellow paleontologist Edward Drinker Cope is so well known in paleontological circles that it is popularly referred to as "the bone wars."

O.C. Marsh, characteristically enough, wasted no time in responding to Kerr's report. He arrived on the scene in Colorado Springs, hastily identified what he thought was a *Camptosaurus* and shipped it, prepaid at a cost of $4.25, to Yale University where it was received on October 29, 1886. There it remained, far removed from its place of origin and all but forgotten, for the next nearly century and a quarter, albeit, it was studied and described by Charles Gilmore in 1909, and according to Dr. Carpenter, "sporadically referred to in the intervening years by other paleontologists." Additional bones from the same site were also collected by Professor Kerr. These were boxed and stored in people's basements and garages around town for lack of adequate storage space at Colorado College. The fossils have never turned up.

A Dinosaur with a Brand-New Identity

And now the 125-million-year-old, formerly lost and misidentified dinosaur has a brand-new identity and a new first name based on a combination of the Greek words for "belonging to the gods" and "garden." The dinosaur's second name comes from her original discoverer—hence *Theiophytalia kerri*, or "Theio" for short. And, while Theio is an iguanodontid, which are known globally, what sets her apart is the fact that she is a brand-new species and genus. Thus she can famously lay claim to being "one-of-a-kind," says Carpenter. In short, Theio is a new and previously unknown type of ornithopod dinosaur (meaning "bird footed") from the Lytle Member of the Purgatoire Formation.

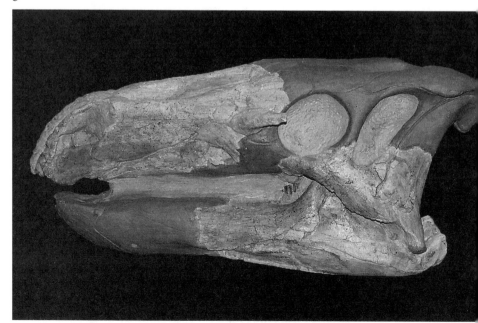

Reconstructed skull of "T. kerri" on display at the Garden of the Gods Visitor and Nature Center. (Image courtesy *Kiva* magazine)

Theio: A Probable Visitor and Intriguing Link

Theio, as it turns out, is *not* a Jurassic-age dinosaur as was originally thought. She lived during the Early Cretaceous Period, twenty-five million years later than the Jurassic Age when *Camptosaurus* held sway. During this period shorelines were lush, the landscape was flat, the Ancestral Rockies had worn down and the modern Rockies had not yet arisen. It is possible that Theio's fossil remains were preserved because her bones found their way into a grave of non-marine river sediment.

"Theio." (Computer-generated profile courtesy Dr. Kenneth Carpenter, Denver Museum of Nature and Science)

When she walked the earth, Theio was no dainty specimen. She weighed roughly three tons, measured at least thirty feet in length, and had a tail that stuck straight out. She stood up on her hind legs to browse, tearing leaves from the trees with her beak-like mouth. Her profile was both distinctive and different from *Camptosaurus'* in that her skull was larger and her snout longer; the shape and position of nasal and eye-socket openings were also different. Furthermore, and as is common in ornithopod dinosaurs, she had a "palepebral," or bone protrusion, in front of her eyes.

If you take a close look at Theio's profile, you will first note the beak-like mouth, in addition to the long, equine-like snout, resembling some slightly dim and haughty in-bred member of royalty. Based on any family portrait that included Theio and other members of the *Iguanodon* group, you might immediately jump to the conclusion that they were somehow related. And you would be right. While Theio is new to science, she is also, as Dr. Carpenter put it, "... just another piece to the puzzle of understanding the evolution of *Iguanodon*. What's surprising," says Carpenter, "is that *Iguanodons* are proving to be far more diverse in variety than ever thought."

The fact that Theio had a beaked mouth, lived in the immediate neighborhood, and enjoyed a close family connection (one is tempted to say "kinship") with *Iguanodon* hints at a vital and important linkage with another new find—the *Iguanodon* tracks that paleontological researchers have recently discovered in the Dakota Sandstone Formation in Red Rock Canyon Open Space.

Ken Carpenter, at Denver Museum of Nature and Science, with one of his authentically reconstructed dinosaur skeletons mounted with real, old bones. (Reproduced with permission of the publisher from Kirk Johnson and Ray Troll, *Cruisin' the Fossil Freeway* [Golden, CO: Fulcrum Publishing, 2007], 163)

Dinosaur Bones Identified in Jurassic/ Morrison Formation

In Red Rock Canyon Open Space, most of the approximately two-hundred-million-year-old Morrison Formation, with its easily eroded mudstones of maroon, green, and white, interbedded with sandstone and some limestones and conglomerate, is located in the deep valley beneath the city dump that was opened on the property by the late John Bock. Not only was the garbage-filled Gypsum Canyon the deepest valley in the open space, but it also encompasses a stratum of rock where dinosaur fossils are most likely to be found. It is impossible to know what fossils may have existed there and that now lie buried beneath two decades of accumulated refuse from the residents of

Colorado Springs. This is one reason why the possibility of finding fully intact body fossils in the open space remains remote. Today this potential graveyard of dinosaur bones appears pristine, and with its hummocky slope, more like a grassy cemetery plot. Thus, we can only speculate about whether this might at one time have been a hotspot for dinosaurs, based on other fossils discovered in this same formation elsewhere in the Pikes Peak region and the state.

We do know that dinosaur bones have been identified in the Morrison Formation on a proximate local site by local hikers. Because the bones, in this case, are disarticulated, it is difficult to say whether they belong to one dinosaur or represent an entire group caught in an ancient flash flood. There is good evidence from the Morrison Formation that dinosaurs were sometimes surprisingly social in their behavior and may even have lived in family units.

Among the dinosaur bones preserved in the Morrison Formation on this nearby site that were identified by Colorado Springs science teacher John Spengler were a dinosaur clavicle, an assortment of rib bones, a probable hip bone and periosteum, which is the fibrous outer covering of bone, as well as Haversian canals. Haversian canals are tubular channels in the bones with cavity-like openings of varied sizes and complex patterns that resemble a Martian landscape. Haversian canals conduct nutrients to the body. The diameters of the cavities that mark the openings to the Haversian canals may bear a direct relationship to the size of the dinosaur whose bones they represent.

Theropods, Sauropods, and Pterosaurs

There are more than three-dozen major fossil footprint sites that have been found in the Morrison Formation across the American West. These sites typically record the activities of theropods (carnivorous dinosaurs, characterized by small forelimbs) and sauropods (the largest of the dinosaurs, noted for their long necks). There is also some evidence in this formation of pterosaurs (extinct flying reptiles, such as pterodactyls). All were found in the Cretaceous and Jurassic Periods. The Morrison is famous for yielding the skeletal remains of well-known dinosaurs from the past such as *Apatosaurus* (a.k.a. *Brontosaurus*), *Allosaurus,* and Colorado's state dinosaur, the *Stegosaurus.*

Where would We Be without the Cyanobacteria?

While the fossil records for the Permian Triassic Lykins Formation that preceded the Jurassic Morrison are relatively sparse, this formation does contain impressions within its dolostone and limestone layers of once viscous, crinkly communities of photosynthetic bacteria or "cyanobacteria" (commonly known as blue-green algae), which obtain energy through photosynthesis and produce oxygen as waste, a new development in metabolic processing.

As the climate in what is present-day Colorado Springs changed and the sea subsided about 245 million years ago, the land was covered in extremely saline, shallow pools of water. This solution worked to preserve innumerable mounds of carbonate mud known as "stromatolites," which are considered the world's most ancient fossils. Dating back as much as three-and-a-half billion years ago, the stromatolites, an organic museum of microorganisms, are visible in layers of dolomitic limestone. They have a coarse, mud-speckled appearance like a bad job of spackling, where sediment was trapped, cemented, and laminated in the crinkly mats of cyanobacteria. *Homo sapiens* can today rejoice in an oxygen-rich atmosphere, as could the air-breathing dinosaurs long before us, thanks to these ancient life forms.

Dinosaurs Once Roamed the Open Space

While fossilized marine life is of deep and abiding interest, the confirmed reports of dinosaur tracks identified in Red Rock Canyon Open Space raised public interest to new levels. Several tracks made by at least two types of these over-sized, mostly benign, dragon-like beasts have now been scientifically identified and documented on the open space, thanks to the research of Milito and Poltenovage, with some results reviewed and/or confirmed by Dr. Kenneth Carpenter from Denver's Museum of Nature and Science.

We know that dinosaurs were gigantic, mostly herbivorous, spectacularly varied and diverse land-loving reptiles that lived for over 160 million years during the Mesozoic Era before becoming extinct. Despite their panoply of uniquely individualized and sometimes truly strange appendages, they did not live in the sea or fly, but were capable of walking well, and even running—working up to respectable rates of speed when the occasion required. Some dinosaurs walked on all fours, while others were bipedal. The smallest was the size of a dog, and one of the largest, the sauropod *Barosaurus,* weighed more than the equivalent of eight elephants.

As diapsid (a subclass of reptile, having two temporal arches) reptiles and descendants of thecodonts (the ancestral group of archosauromorphs)—dinosaurs are, perhaps not so surprisingly, related to modern crocodiles. The difference, however—and it's an important one—lies in the manner in which their knee joints and feet were designed. While the crocodile sways from side to side when it moves, dinosaurs were able to stand and walk upright, at least some of the time, while supporting huge weight. Their new, improved hinged (as apposed to swivel) knees were designed to be a more efficient form of locomotion. This new design feature also enabled bipedal browsing. At the same time, the feet of these gigantic and imposing creatures were newly adapted to propel them forward at higher speeds. This meant they were capable of moving even faster than their next-of-kin—that fearsome and once dominant "worm of the pebbles," *krokodilos*—no sluggard himself when it comes to quick and lethal snapping up of prey.

When it comes to hips, knees, and feet, in short, dinosaurs had more in common with their more modern, winged, avian descendants than with their ancient, terrestrial, sun-bathing, distant cousins, the reptilian crocodile. All dinosaurs, including *Iguanodon,* walked on their toes (just as modern horses do), which were typically long and slender—the better for grip. Nearly all dinosaurs, thus, have a three-toed footprint that resembles those of birds, but on a much larger scale.

Based on fossilized evidence, we know that some of these whimsical-looking creatures roamed widely to the far corners of the planet, skirting large seas by crossing land bridges when continents were still loosely joined. The state of Colorado, as previously noted, has an unusual preponderance of dinosaur fossils and stomping grounds—in part due to the geological conditions that made possible their excellent state of preservation.

Words Fail to Describe the Thrill ...

... Milito felt the day she looked up from a lunch break and happened to spot a huge dinosaur footprint just above her head in the sandstone she was surveying in Red Rock Canyon Open Space as a part of the Paleotrails Project. This serendipitous find proved to be one of her most exciting discoveries. "I think, if there is one footprint, there should be more," she stated. And she would soon be proved right as, adding to the general excitement, Milito and her partner Poltenovage further identified on at least one rocky ridge in the eastern part of the open space the existence of tracks of three or four dinosaurs from more than one species. These tracks appeared to mark the progression of several enormous plant-eating dinosaurs (as well as one possible carnivore) as, long ago, the Mesozoic giants sloshed through the mud of a coastal forest.

Iguanodon Discovery Confirmed

On the basis of distinctive tracks made by the giant plant-eating dinosaur *Iguanodon*, paleontology researcher Sharon Milito reported in a City Parks and DMNS-sponsored study called "Fossils and Geologic Points of Interest in Red Rock Canyon Open Space," issued March 2008, that this close relative of Theio was a presence on the open space well over one hundred million years ago. This exciting new track discovered in the Dakota Sandstone, documented by the team of Milito and Poltenovage, was initially described as having been made by a large ornithopod—possibly a hadrosaur, but more likely an *Iguanodon* (Theio's close relation). Upon further examination, the track was unmistakably identified as belonging to the genus *Iguanodon*.

The *Iguanodon* was a slender-toed, bird-like type of reptile. Huge, and mostly bipedal, it could also walk on all fours. Weighing a substantial three tons, as noted earlier, it measured at least thirty feet in length. The *Iguandon* group—as typified by *Theophytalia kerri*, the Garden of the God's dinosaur—had a toothless beak and closely crowded teeth similar to a modern-day iguana's. It claimed as its close relation the duck-billed dinosaur tribe. Its large conical thumb spikes were its most distinctive feature and were thought to have been used for defense against predators. Among other well-known members of this "clade" (a group of organisms that have evolved from a common organism) is *Camptosaurus*. *Camptosaurus*, however, may be better represented in terms of geographic distribution and documented numbers of fossil finds than *Iguanodon* is to date.

The body fossils of an *Iguanodon* were the first dinosaur bones to be discovered in the world, having been identified in Europe in the early nineteenth century. It was not until the mid-1980s, however—when the jaws and teeth of an early *Iguanodon* came to light near Grand Junction, Colorado—that the *Iguanodon* was even known to exist in North America. This important discovery of the oldest known specimen in the world—found in sediments approximately 135 million years old—further extended the range of *Iguanodons* to North America and even suggested the *Iguanodon* may have originated here.

The *Iguanodon's* bipedal shoreline tracks are known today to be fairly common in the Dakota Group of Colorado and in other states across the American West. Even so, *Iguanodon's* officially confirmed and documented presence in Red Rock Canyon Open Space represents a major and an exciting find.

Ankylosaurus also Makes a Big Impression

Another dinosaur that is famously reported to have put in its heavyweight appearance in Red Rock Canyon Open Space—having left his signature fossil traces impressed in the rocks—is *Ankylosaurus,* who lived between sixty-five and seventy million years ago. This dinosaur track was first reported several years ago by geologist Hal Proska. Preserved on the western face of one of the hogbacks, it is unusual in that it is the "cast" of a track seen from the underside. This means that the muddy indentation of the footprint dried, filled with sand, hardened to sandstone; then, the softer mudstone of its outer layers eroded and were undercut, resulting in a cast. (Kirk Johnson, in *Cruisin' the Fossil Freeway,* has a fascinating description of how to spot casts of dinosaur footsteps while breezing along the freeway at sixty-five mph by "reading road cuts the way you read billboards.")

Ankylosaurus was a huge and ponderous Cretaceous reptile. In any ring-size wrestling match, it is said the *Ankylosaurus* would have given the mighty *Tyranosaurus*

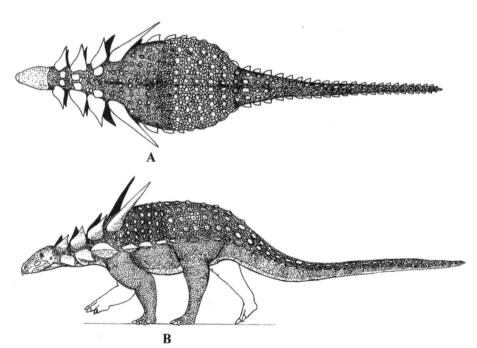

A

B

"Sauropelta," meaning "lizard with shield," is an ankylosaur type. Well-armored, it measured about 16.5 feet in length and weighed about 1.5 tons. It roamed the earth in the Early Cretaceous Period. (Paleoart by Tracy L. Ford)

rex a run for his money. Low-slung like a lizard, *Ankylosaurus* was seemingly at a bit of a disadvantage, however, given his comparative shortness of stature. Measuring about four feet tall at the hips, he compensated for lack of height with impressive bulk and length. In terms of body armor, *Ankylosaurus* was unusually well equipped to hold his own against potential predators. Not only was he built like a tank, he was armored with thick protective plates and boney spikes. But when it came to defending himself against such potential meat-eating predators as the deadly *Tyrannosaurus,* one of his most effective pieces of hardware was his heavy, well-armored club of a tail, which he could swing like a boom at competitors. With his formidable switching tail stretching to between twenty-five and thirty feet in length, *Ankylosaurus,* the largest known member of his family weighed in at an estimated three to four tons.

As a large herbivore, *Ankylosaurus's* intestine was undoubtedly cavernous and presumably came equipped with a large fermentation chamber in order to process the huge volumes of tough plant material he would have required to sustain himself.

"Beast-Footed" Theropod Footprints

Milito and Poltenovage, in the course of their investigation, discovered what appeared to be another species of tridactyl (three-toed) dinosaur track in the Cretaceous Period Dakota Sandstone. The apparent theropod trace, preserved in the form of a cast, was difficult to study at close range because of its condition and location. Despite its name of "beast-footed," this group of mostly carnivorous dinosaurs had bird-like feet. They used their sharp-clawed hands, attached to short forearms, to attack and seize prey.

The theropods, sometimes described as the ferocious killers of the dinosaur world, lived from between 220 to 65 million years ago. A diverse group of bipedal reptiles, including *T. rex,* the largest carnivore ever to have struck fear into the heart of its prey, theropods are thought to have been the fastest moving dinosaur. Surprisingly, birds are considered to be the direct, lineal descendants of the smaller theropods, some of which evolved prototypical feathers. A giant, but "very bird-like theropod," was found recently in the Mongolian Desert. Comparatively speaking, the fossil records of the theropod are fragmentary, and its remains are considered rare.

Perhaps future studies will reveal the truth about this and other tantalizing clues to earth's early fossil history yet to be explored in the open space.

Dinosaur Diners

A majority of dinosaurs were herbivores and, based on analysis of their tramping grounds, some were thought to have been gregarious, forming social units and moving in herds. To satisfy their abundant appetites must have required enormous amounts of forage, just as is it does for today's modern elephants. Conifers may have been the preferred choice of the tall, long-necked tribe of bipedal dinosaurs. Similarly, the giant, fast-growing, scaly club mosses (Lycopsids) that grew near water and that evolved 375 MYA in the Devonian Period, were a likely food source for the sauropods. While these giant club mosses were destined to become a casualty of the Permian-Triassic Extinction, small varieties did adapt and evolve into the Jurassic. Club mosses and such familiar and primitive yet modern plants as the horse tale (*Equisetum*), which grows along waterways today, were also probable forage for herbivorous dinosaurs.

Based on empirical evidence, it is thought that the more gregarious of the dinosaurs who were governed by herd instinct were probably to some extent migratory, moving from place to place in order to avoid the dinosaur equivalent of overuse of local resources and environmental degradation, brought about by over-consumption and trampling.

The Famous K-T Boundary near Denver

The mystery of the sudden demise of these large and ungainly reptiles and its probable cause continues to excite debate and speculation among the experts today. In the course of this massive extinction, known as the K-T extinction event, roughly 50 percent of the world's animals disappeared, as well as some plants and marine species. The most widely credited theory today is that the massive extinction was caused by an asteroid impact that occurred about sixty-five million years ago at the boundary of the Tertiary and the Cretaceous Periods. The supporters of the bombardment hypothesis tend to cite in its defense the unusually high amounts of iridium found in soil at K-T boundary sites, of which there are at least a dozen in southern Colorado. Iridium is a common element in meteorites, but is rare in terrestrial rocks. Other researchers, however, believe that the extinction, sometimes called "the great dying," resulted from sea and climate changes that came about more slowly over a period of two million years, somewhere between 64 and 66 million years ago.

The K-T boundary was first famously identified and described in the 1940s, west of Denver on South Table Mountain. Because of the importance of the K-T boundary layer, the Smithsonian Museum collected a two-and-a-half-ton sample of the strata from south of Trinidad in southwestern Colorado for its exhibits in Washington, D.C.

Whatever the probable cause for the world-wide extinction of dinosaurs, there are some scientists who suggest that these dumb-as-dirt and mostly gentle Mesozoic giants exhibited several rather serious design flaws from the start, perhaps rendering them less than adaptable over the long term. According to this argument, dinosaurs, despite their 180-million-year period of dominance, from the Triassic to the K-T boundary, were ultimately programmed for a kind of evolutionary obsolescence. Nonetheless, compared to humans, the dinosaur had a good long run of it. After all, *Homo sapiens* (Latin for "wise," or "knowing human") only originated in Africa about two-hundred-thousand years ago.

The world-wide event that so dramatically ended the Age of Dinosaurs doubtless did serve its purpose, however, when viewed from a purely human perspective. It arguably helped to pave the way for the later Age of Mammals. Early man, for example, was able to deal effectively enough in hunting or defending against the towering and super-sized, long-tusked, wooly mammoth. In fact, so effective was he in hunting these enormous shaggy pachyderms that he may have contributed to their ultimate extinction. But taking on *T. rex* with primitive stone tools and atlatls (throwing spear used by Paleo-Indians) would have posed another magnitude of challenge altogether.

All of us in the Pikes Peak region and beyond can rejoice in the fact that some of the remarkable links in the evolutionary stories that distinguish earth's early history are waiting to be discovered—playing themselves out over the millennia—right here in our own backyard.

Ancient Ecosystems

It was during the Cretaceous Period that insects, including pollinators such as bees, wasps, and butterflies appeared, and flowering plants bloomed. The leaves preserved in our Dakota Hogback, as if pressed in an album, record some of these revolutionary and evolutionary developments.

Colorado, in the long-ago days when dinosaurs reigned supreme, basked in a climate that was subtropical, having been shoved within approximately five degrees north of the equator by a massive tectonic shift. Palm trees and other tropical plants were common. But the ancient ecosystems underwent a change and according to Schuchert and Dunbar in *Outlines of Historical Geology,* "by the middle of the Cretaceous Period the forests were essentially modern."

Alexander Winchell wrote the book *Sketches of Creation* in the 1870s, and he affirmed that "the existence of a succession of [prehistoric] forests of different prevailing species has been satisfactorily established" by researchers world-wide. He further speculated that some of the seeds from these ancient forests may have survived for thousands of years and successfully reseeded themselves. The fossilized trees, leaves, and plants preserved in the rocks can tell us a great deal about the changing ecosystems that existed millennia ago.

The Dakota Hogback in the open space itself has maintained a good, if semi-permanent record of ancient trees ("semi-permanent" because the rock is constantly weathering and fossils are fragile). Impressions have been documented in this location of large fossilized tree trunks, branches, bark, vegetable litter, ferns, conifer cones and needles, and imprints of leaves from deciduous trees. One root system identified from the early Cretaceous may be that of a tropical mangrove tree.

In diversity and type, ancient tropical forests resembled the still-extant equatorial rainforests found in southern zones today. Proof of Colorado's once-tropical climate is found at Castle Rock, south of Denver, which is the site of what is "now recognized as the oldest and best-preserved fossil rain forest in the world," as DMNS paleontologist Kirk Johnson points out.

By the time modern trees appeared in the middle Cretaceous, they began to bear a strong resemblance to the varieties—such as willows, cottonwoods, and poplars—that we see throughout the Southwest and on the open space today. Here is yet another example of the geological principle formulated in the eighteenth century that, "The present is key to the past."

An eternal autumn of fossil leaves preserved from ancient forests in the Dakota Formation of the open space. (Photo from a private collection)

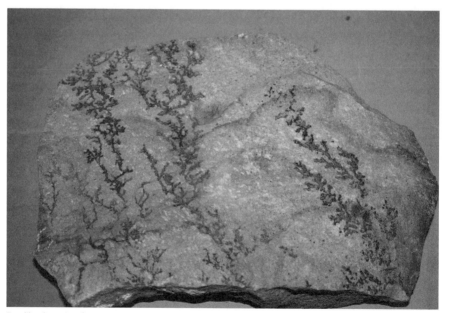

Fernlike deposits of manganese dendrites. (Photo from Colorado Springs Pioneers Museum)

The fossilized leaves identified in the Dakota Hogback suggest some of the same vivid colors and artistry as seen in a richly embroidered Kashmiri shawl. Most are appropriately colored in autumnal hues of faded orange, beige-gold, and lavender, with numerous leaves randomly positioned at different angles. Based on the handsome illustrations found in *Outlines of Historical Geology*, it is safe to assume that some of these fossilized leaves are narrow and curved in shape, while others are fan-shaped with veined webbing. The visual effect, roughly surfaced though it is, with its stamped, overlaying patterns, evokes autumn in the modern Rockies—but in this case the season remains virtually unchanging and eternal.

Ancient Tracks, Trails, and Homes of Crustaceans

Fossilized animal burrows and trails, as well as the tracks of crustaceans, have been identified in the Dakota Sandstone as well as in the Fort Hays Limestone and Benton Shale. The worm-like creatures that created the many burrows in this formation chewed up the sediment so thoroughly that its surface today appears to be rippled and incised. The technical term for this process is "bioturbation." Among the many burrows dug out of the sediment, at least one of them was called home by a ghost shrimp. Many other varieties of invertebrates are represented by small creatures that blazed the numerous burrows and narrow meandering trails in the rocks in quest of prey, and who in turn, were threatened by their larger and equally hungry predators.

Ancient Marine Life Dependent on Tooth-and-Jaw Survival Strategies

If you look closely at the rock faces of the Dakota Sandstone, you will notice clear evidence of ripple marks caused by the ebb and flow of ancient wind-blown tidal pools—

"There's a lot of neat stuff in the hogbacks!"
—Don Ellis

rhythmic, timeless, and unmoving. Indeed, both the Cretaceous Niobrara and the Dakota Hogbacks, dating back from between approximately 65 and 150 MYA, are a treasure trove of ancient marine life forms, in addition to terrestrial ones. The eastern side of the open space—with its exposed Niobrara and Codell Sandstone Formations and its chalky layers and ridges of shale—has yielded rich and abundant finds. Successive layers in the sedimentary rocks, laid down over millions of years like chapters in a book, document the existence of many different species of marine animals such as giant clams and shell-crushing predatory sharks, each in their respective periods of dominance.

Baculites, Ammonites, Predatory Sharks, and Giant Clams

At the base of the lower and eastern-most Niobrara Hogback is found the grey-brown Pierre Shale. It underlies much of Colorado Springs, but is not a member of the Dakota or Niobrara Formations. Pierre Shale is typically rich in fossils such as baculites (a rod-shaped mollusk with a number of chambers, rather like a straight nautilus). While this formation did not figure significantly into the Paleotrails study, it is worth noting that baculites had previously been reported in the nearby Pierre Shale by a few sharp-eyed and observant hikers familiar with the geology of the open space.

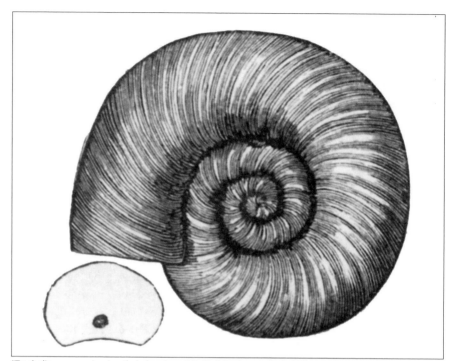

"Trocholites ammonius. A coiled-chambered shell of the Trenton Period." Ammonites or cephalopods are a good fossil index to rock layers and are found throughout the world. A large body print of an ammonite, measuring 1.5-feet wide, has been identified in the Codell Sandstone in the open space. (Sketch by Alexander Winchell, 1874)

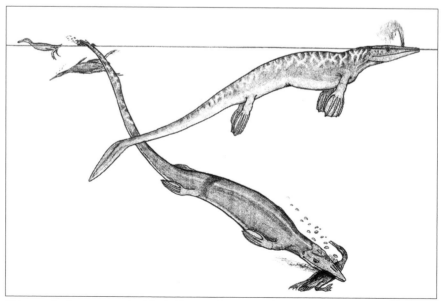

"Tylosaurus," a giant mosasaur that blended features of the monitor lizard and snake, reaching lengths up to 49 feet. It was a dominant predator of the Western Interior Sea that once covered the open space. A mosasaur tooth was reportedly found in the open space. (Paleoart by Tracy L. Ford)

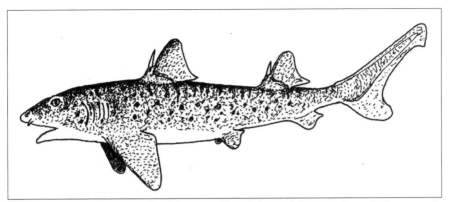

"Ptychodus," a genus of extinct shark, with batteries of flat grinding teeth for consuming mollusks, measured about 32 feet in length and weighed in at about 1 to 2 tons. This giant predator cruised local waters that, in the Cretaceous Period, covered the open space. (Paleoart by Tracy L. Ford)

Older and higher up than the Fort Hays Limestone, the Codell Sandstone rises to a point where it first meets the Fort Hays Limestone, then crests the ridge of the Niobrara Hogback. Forming most of the ridge and west face of the lower eastern hogback, these two members of the Benton Group preserve an abundance of marine life in the sediments laid down by ancient seas.

Among the ancient marine fossils preserved in the Codell Sandstone are the whorled ammonites, related to modern squid and octopus and the favored food of mosasaurs. Named after the Egyptian god, Ammon, like Ammon's headdress, the ram-horn-shaped shells of ammonites are spiraled and striated. Their body prints, preserved in stone, resemble gigantic lobster tails. An ammonite body print the size of a large platter has been identified on the present-day open space. One of the largest specimens ever found measured more than six feet. Ammonites are geographically ubiquitous and are reasonably common on our own site.

Other exciting finds from the Codell Formation include numerous small, rounded sharks' teeth, measuring about an eighth of an inch in length. The teeth originated from several different varieties of shell-crushing sharks. Among these was the formidable *Ptychodus whipplei* that was present in the shallows of the Western Interior Sea that penetrated inland covering the land of today's Colorado Springs. The *Ptychodus whipplei* (one species of Ptychodus) ranged in size from 1.5 to 9 meters (about 5 to 29 feet) in length. They were generously endowed with a redundancy of teeth, arranged in parallel rows of graduated sizes, with no less than 600 teeth per jaw in some species.

Once a living clam bed, the white cliff of Fort Hays Limestone, a member of the Niobrara Formation, was deposited in the Western Interior Sea when the waters were deep. It formed the conspicuous white band near the top of the Niobrara and has long been known as an abundant warehouse for clam fossils. *Ptychodus whipplei,* armed with their multiple rows of teeth and powerful jaws, preyed upon the clam-like Cretaceous bivalve known as "*Inoceramus,*" which are well preserved in this stratum and were abundant ninety million years ago. One sub-genus of *Inoceramus* is known as "*Platyceramus.*" Of the Cretaceous bivalves, this enormous flat-shelled species of clam

Fossil clam shell specimen, 2.75 inches high x 3.5 inches wide x 6 inches in length, collected from Red Rock Canyon. (Photo from Colorado Springs Pioneers Museum)

was known to have reached unprecedented sizes, setting records with its potential for achieving a diameter spanning up to ten feet. The largest *Platyceramus* found on the open space measured a respectable three-and-a-half feet in width (sufficient for a very large pot of New England clam chowder). *Platyceramus* occur in both Smoky Hill Shale and Fort Hays Limestone. Another large and common species of inoceramid clam identified in the open space from the Cretaceous Smoky Hill Shale is the *Volviceramus*.

Easily visible in the Fort Hays Limestone and Smoky Hill Shale, the giant *Inoceramus* clams that were dinner to predatory shell-crushing sharks also supplied homes and nutrients for the organisms, or Epizoa, growing on them, which included oysters. Serving well in their specialized ecological niche, the giant clams provided large, umbrella-like shelter and shade for a variety of other fish as well. Guests may have risked being, quite literally, eaten out of house and home. Members of the bivalve, "level-bottom community," oysters and clams evolved in the Permian and were found globally by the Jurassic and Cretaceous Periods.

The *Inoceramus* were a popular *a la carte* choice, not only for *Ptychodus whipplei*, but also for *pycnodont* fish. *Pycnodonts* were a medium-sized fish with batteries of peg-like, round, flattened teeth, well adapted for feeding on their hard-shelled prey. In turn, *pycnodonts* were preyed upon by the long-nosed goblin shark (*Mitsukurina owstoni*). Yet another formidable variety of large shark that boasted impressive, chainsaw-like jaws, with smooth-edged teeth in the front and shorter grinding teeth in the back, goblin sharks were admirably equipped both to dine on fish or crush the giant *Inoceramus* clams—just one more example of nature's tooth and jaw at work in the ancient sea world. While the molar of a *pyncodont* was identified in the cretaceous rocks by the researchers, none has to date been found for the ancient, evolutionary goblin shark, which is today still extant.

Teeth that Last for 90 Million Years: The Dental Bill of Good Health

One of the most common of the five species of predatory sharks identified by the researchers, which swam in our own local waters, was *Squalicorax falcatus,* or the crow shark. The crow shark's teeth are an ideal fossil index for the late Cretaceous, both because they are abundant and because they are easy to spot. Often found in Codell Sandstone or Fort Hays Limestone, they are triangular in shape with serrated edges. The crow shark,

typically two to three meters (six to ten feet) in length and a fast swimmer, resembled the modern tiger shark, but boasted an even more powerful bite. A tooth was found on the open space of this extinct shark that once swam in the Western Interior Sea.

The fact that shark skeletons are made up of soft cartilage, whereas teeth are composed of hard enamel, may help to explain why more fossilized shark teeth are found in the rocks than are shark skeletons. Also, since shark teeth were embedded in flesh rather than in the jawbone, they were frequently

Fossilized shark's tooth, measuring .25 inches x 1.5 inches, collected from the Codell Formation in the open space. (Photo from Colorado Springs Pioneers Museum)

shed. Fossilized bones and scales do, however, occur in the shales of the open space.

Thanks to dental proof of their long-ago existence, we know that most sharks that cruised the Western Interior Sea—with their enormous, razor-sharp and toothy grins designed to strike terror into the hearts of prey—could have served as cinematographic prototypes for *Jaws.* In terms of their size and lethalness as predators, some of these species were more than a match for today's Great White Shark. They had superstar-quality and would have made formidable leads in any chilling sci-fi film that focused on marine life in the ancient deeps.

Mosasaur: A Dominant Predator in its Time and Element

Also collected from the Codell Sandstone was a "probable" tooth that may have belonged to a mosasaur. As measured by relative degrees of ferocity and the number of intimidatingly sharp teeth, the mosasaur was clearly one of the fiercest of the denizens of the ancient sea world.

In a reversal of more standard evolutionary patterns in which, for example, fish moved up on land and exchanged their fins for legs and feet, the mosasaur evolved from land reptiles and returned to the sea. On a vastly enlarged scale, the mosasaur was a composite of blended parts. The shape of the mosasaur's head, mouth, and body resembled those of today's monitor lizard, to which it was closely related. But its long, lean frame and serpentine tail emulated that of its closest kin, the snake. Unlike the monitor, however, this scaly marine reptile had teeth. Yet like the snake, it possessed a double-hinged jaw, enabling it to swallow its prey nearly whole. In place of legs and feet, the mosasaur—which at its largest could measure as much as fifty-two feet in length—came equipped with paddles.

The mosasaur was not only notoriously ferocious, but it was also a powerful swimmer, making it the dominant predator and carnivore of the warm, shallow seas of the Late Cretaceous. So at home was the female mosasaur in its natural watery element that it gave live birth there, finding no need to return to shore in order to lay eggs in imitation of the turtle. The mosasaur, in short, was a multitude of things. But the one thing it was not—and never could be—was a dinosaur.

The earth, on land and in sea, was literally teeming with newly evolving life forms in an astonishing range and variety. The narrative being told was often one of not-so-big about to be eaten by bigger and on up the food chain—with the pyramidal hierarchy of needs being played out at the most basic level in a Darwinian struggle of the fittest for survival. If the ancient sea world and its coastal environment were often beautiful and mysterious, they were also equally fraught with the unexpected, with lurking perils and ever-present dangers as life unfolded.

These, then, are among the fascinating stories the rocks tell about the long history of the open space, recorded and preserved for the edification of inquisitive and interested *Homo sapiens*—who happened along much later in the greater scheme of things; were conveniently bipedal; endowed with an opposable thumb; and possessed of the gift of language, not to mention with an uncanny ability to observe, scribble down notes, use a laptop, and operate a digital camera.

Fossils in the Pennsylvania Fountain Formation

Despite the fact that the stunning, hematite-red Fountain Formation is a visually prepossessing and extended presence on the open space, the number of fossils found in this more than three-hundred-million-year-old structure proved negligible. Expectations for fossil finds in this stratum on the open space were never high. Fossils would not have fared well in the rough and tumble of buffeting and fast-paced ancient streams cascading off the Ancestral Rockies, which were close by and which contributed to the formation of the nearly vertical Fountain spires uplifted by the Laramide Orogeny. The proof of this is in the size and angularity of the rocks transported and embedded in the Fountain fins, which indicate the presence both of strong waters and short distances. By contrast, smaller rocks carried longer distances, over time, wear down to well-polished, rounded shapes.

A Scattering of Ancient Animal Tracks and Paleo-Mud Cracks

Similarly, during the Permian Period when the hallmark, hematite red Lyons dunes were created, the fossil record suddenly becomes as scarce as it was abundant in the more recent Cretaceous. Like the Fountain Formation, the Lyons yielded little in the way of fossil remains, despite the close scrutiny of the Paleotrails researchers. This is due largely to the harsh conditions that prevailed in its desert environment roughly between 250 and 290 MYA.

Of greater interest (at least to geologists) than the few fossil traces identified in the Lyons are the fossilized dunes themselves, with their distinctive pattern of crossbedding (with thin layers slanting obliquely against horizontal ones) caused by ancient winds blowing in a southerly direction. Also of particular geologic interest are the fossilized paleo-mud cracks that can be observed in this formation at the south end of the open space and on into Manitou Springs Section 16. This unusual effect is the product of the evaporation of water from ancient mud puddles of fine clay in an arid climate. Eventually the original mud eroded away, leaving the sand outlines of the cracks. Where the polygonal shapes of the cracks are numerous, the rocks' raised rough surfaces have a lumpy scalloped and mottled appearance.

What Does It All Mean?

A primary goal of the Paleotrails Project was to contribute scientific information on open space fossils and geology to the Interpretive Master Plan of the City's Parks, Recreation and Cultural Services department. This information would, in turn, be made available free to the public in a variety of formats ranging from signage to an interpretive exhibit housed in the new open-air pavilion, a generous gift of the Friends of Red Rock Canyon Open Space. Besides contributing to two time-loop interpretive trails on the open space with a focus on geology and paleontology, the project would also help establish guidelines in striking a balance between the sometimes conflicting goals of preservation and interpretation.

Several of the long-term objectives of the Paleotrails Project continue to be realized: to build on efforts to educate the public, to help preserve our precious geological treasures, and finally, to further document the marvelous stories that—chapter by chapter, over millennia—the rocks tell.

Help Us Preserve Our Open-Air Museum

Decades ago, when there weren't quite so many of us living in the Pikes Peak Region, individuals randomly and perhaps unthinkingly collected fossils. This practice, however, denies the next generation and other members of the public an equal opportunity to learn about and observe relics from our prehistoric past *in situ*. Our unique geological and paleontological legacies require and deserve respect, careful stewardship, and a long-term commitment to preservation.

Natural history museums and public libraries alike function well solely because of public trust and support. Red Rock Canyon Open Space might appropriately be thought of as earth's ancient open-air library, permanent archive, and natural history museum, all in one, that belongs to each one of us and of which we are all custodians.

If you have found yourself picking one up, please drop the rock. As for dinosaur tracks, once exposed, they are very fragile and easily eroded. Even the millennia-old fossils come with an expiration date. Please keep to the trails and tread gently on this old earth, with its ancient fossil imprints and enormously fragile, easily eroded fossil traces; its bristling humped and gnarly boned ridges; its dramatically overturned and exposed rock outcroppings, filled with amazing stories from the past.

"Probably all the organic beings which have ever lived on this earth have descended from some one primordial form, into which life was first breathed. ... There is grandeur in this view of life ... that, whilst this planet has gone cycling on according to the fixed law of gravity, from so simple a beginning, endless forms most beautiful and most wonderful have been, and are being evolved.

—**Charles Darwin,** *The Origin of Species,* 1859

CHAPTER 3

The Diverse Ecology of Red Rock Canyon

*"Dead leaves when they lose themselves in soil
take part in the life of the forest."*
—Rabindranath Tagore

"Cultural Diversity is itself dependent on biological diversity."
—Evan Eisenburg

The indigenous plants and animals found in a region or ecosystem help in important ways to define its character and to inspire nature study, storytelling, folk beliefs and myths, as well as the arts and sciences. By becoming more aware of and better
informed about our region's ecology, we can arrive at a deeper, truer sense of the place
we call home. We can also become more effective mentors to the next generation of
land stewards and conservationists.

Ecology is defined as the study of the relationship of plants and animals and their
environment; and within this framework, the interrelationship of the vast and varied
communities that make up all living organisms. The word "ecology" itself derives from
the Greek word for "house." Planet earth, by logical extension, is "home" to all the vast
and varied communities that inhabit it. As interdependent parts of a greater whole,
these complex communities, in turn, are strongly influenced by their underlying geology. Life and habitat, in short, are inseparable.

Among the ecological features that distinguish Red Rock Canyon Open Space and
set it apart is the fact that it is a point of convergence where several distinctive ecosystems meet. Its juniper and piñon pine woodlands alone clearly mark it as a transitional
zone between the grasslands of the eastern plains and prairies, the arid high desert of
the Southwest, and the Gambel's oak–clad foothills of the Pikes Peak region. Piñon
pines do not occur, for example, on another of the city's well-loved public properties—
the Stratton Open Space—and the existence of the single-seed juniper on that site is
a rarity. Because of its ecological diversity as well as its location, Red Rock Canyon

Open Space thus plays host to an interesting and rich blend of plants, mammals, birds, reptiles, and insects.

In a 2003 study initiated by the city parks department, Colorado College biology professor Tass Kelso, together with Scott Reis and Phillip Halteman, noted that the "ecological contiguity of the Red Rock Canyon property with Section 16 and Pike National Forest provides a corridor for both wildlife and plants [that] showcases regionally significant flora and fauna." At the same time, the additional space required by "wide-ranging megafauna" also helps to minimize "potential for human-wildlife conflicts at the urban edge." "Wide-ranging megafauna," in this case, is an unmistakable reference to black bear and mountain lions, as well as mule deer. At an earlier time in our history, the reference might also have included the grizzly bear and gray wolf.

But regardless of whether we are speaking of flora, "wide-ranging megafauna," or, more specifically, *Homo sapiens*, the interactions of these broad communities will inevitably prove to be one of two kinds—either competitive or cooperative, and often both at once. The aim, ultimately, is to achieve dominance or balance within the greater ecosystem.

Even a brief glance at the deeply complex and multifaceted human and natural history that distinguishes Red Rock Canyon Open Space brings to mind a number of examples. Take the case of noxious weeds—whether they are invited guests or not, they inevitably move in to stay. The more disturbed the ground, the more the noxious weeds take over, with less and less diversity assured in the process.

Noxious, non-native weeds can out-compete native plants in any number of ways. They can make it impossible for seedlings to become established by overshading local plants or grabbing nutrition and water from them. Because, as Kelso points out, they are Eurasian imports that have escaped the biological controls of their home territories, "They run amok in the New World." In pursuit of their destinies as colonists, they end up wiping out established local cultures. Furthermore, they can be harmful to wildlife, not to mention livestock. (Indeed, noxious weeds with economic impact have attained not only a botanical, but also a legal definition along with mandates for their control.)

The critical problem of weed eradication and containment, what Tass Kelso refers to as the "botanical dark side," poses an age-old dilemma. On the one hand, there is the all-too-human propensity to over-manage things. On the other lies the necessity to avoid creating monocultures by eliminating invasive and aggressive non-native species that kill and crowd out local communities. But in general, states Kelso in *Botany of the Pikes Peak Region*, "Most biologists see weeds as one of the most severe threats to native ecosystems at the current time."

By contrast, one of the best examples of a mutually beneficial, cooperative relationship established among communities is that of the plant and its pollinator. And of these, one of the most fascinating is between Yucca (*Yucca glauca)* and the night-flying pronuba moth. Yucca is also known as "soapweed" or "Spanish bayonette," and grows abundantly in dry sunny places in Red Rock Canyon. According to Dodd and Linhart in a study reported in 1994 in the *American Journal of Botany* (81:815–825), the pronuba night-flying moth is the primary pollinator of the yucca (flies may also serve

Chickadee on yucca. (Courtesy *Kiva* magazine)

as secondary pollinators). Apparently the relationship is not considered to be as mutually "obligate" as once thought. Nonetheless, the moth does rejoice in having a specially designed proboscis, unusually well suited to accomplish the task at hand, in what amounts to an elegant nighttime dance on the order of a pollen-naise.

Boring a hole into the ovary of the plant, the pronuba moth lays an egg inside. Then it collects a wad of pollen from the anther, which it proceeds to stuff deep into the funnel-shaped style. Pollination eventually produces hundreds of seeds—enough to feed the hungry young larva that hatch within the host plant, while not denying extra seeds to feed the birds and start new plants as well. It is a win/win situation for all participants, with symbiosis brought to new and harmonious heights. Adding yet another layer of complexity, the yucca can apparently abort seeds with larvae inside.

Ladybugs are often found in abundance on yucca plants. Botanist George Cameron aptly describes this relationship: "The ants are the shepherds, herding the aphids [which they milk for honeydew], while the ladybugs are really the wolves dressed up like Little Red Riding Hood. They eat the aphids. For this reason ants try to keep the ladybugs away."

Yucca, a member of the Agave family, is one of the southwestern plants that was most useful to Native Americans. Its fiber was utilized by Ancestral Puebloans to weave sandals and baskets, while its roots provided soap for bathing and for washing the handsome hand-loomed blankets and carpets woven by Navajos.

Lichen upholsters some of the open space's outcroppings and rocks in rough, gray-green and russet patches. Here, too, is another fine example of two very different but cooperative species interacting to the mutual benefit of each other. Lichen are made up of algae and fungi. Fungi provide water absorption and nutrients, while algae bring in the food through photosynthesis. Lichen enjoy a multitude of uses, from reindeer food to dye. Lichen can even be used to monitor the levels of pollution in the atmosphere.

Recycling is another important theme that manifests itself in the ecological functioning of the wild flora and fauna found in the open space. There is very little waste in nature—even in waste itself. Indeed, everything in the biosphere is recycled in one way or another. The large mammals, for example, play a role in the redistribution of seeds for future growth—whether it's by the browsing mule deer or the chokecherry-dining black bear, the seeds consumed find their way back into the soil via animal droppings, along with additional recycled nutrients.

One of the most critical elements in nature's overall scheme that's essential to the open space and the world at large is the process of photosynthesis by plants and the exchange of carbon dioxide for oxygen, the very air we breathe, which did not even exist in earth's early history and took hundreds of millions of years to evolve. We can thank the plants and the trees for the part they, and even the lowly lichen, play in this life-enhancing process.

Flora Found in Red Rock Canyon Open Space

Alexander von Humboldt, the brilliant late eighteenth to early nineteenth century German naturalist and explorer, after whom one of Colorado's fourteen-thousand-foot peaks was named, once said: "We respond to trees because their life cycle is something like ours. They have this magical quality of the forest. How can you avoid being moved."

One hundred and forty years ago, as is dramatically illustrated in old photographs of Colorado City, there were very few trees growing in the region. Fires set by lightning or, in some cases, the Utes in order to stop the pursuit of plains Indians or facilitate hunting, periodically swept through the area (frequently to the benefit of forest ecology, as accumulating biofuels and undergrowth were significantly reduced and overall vigor and health promoted). At lower elevations, however, the high desert climate with its aridity was perhaps most favorable of all to the growth, not of slow-growing conifers and water-loving deciduous trees, but instead to yucca and native weeds.

Nonetheless, Red Rock Canyon Open Space is home to an interesting variety of native trees and shrubs that are characteristic of the West. Indeed, each of the ridges, outcroppings, and valleys harbor different types of flora based on its geology. Geology holds the key to biodiversity, and while the deciduous trees continue to express themselves in life cycles related to the seasons, the ancient communities of conifers, which evolved about three hundred million years ago, have the "magical quality of the forest."

Aspen Groves

A few isolated aspen *(Populus tremuloides)* groves, known as "clones," occur in the open space. The aspen is the most widely distributed tree in North America, with its largest populations occurring in Colorado and Utah. As a vital keystone species, it supports diverse forms of wildlife—from mammals to insects to birds. In addition to the tree's leaf-trembling beauty, it is of particular interest because of the way in which it reproduces. These landmark Rocky Mountain trees that put on such a spectacular show in autumn—equaling the richest, most glittering of boom-town gold strikes— generally prefer higher elevations. But they do grow at lower elevations and can be started from seeds. Most, however, replicate themselves through a system of shoots that eventually grow up into trees that are genetically identical to and a part of the root system of the mother plant. Aspen clones exhibit synchronous behavior, meaning that all trees leaf at the same time.

Clones of aspen have achieved world-class records both for size and longevity. One famous aspen grove in Utah, nicknamed "Pando" (from the Latin for "I spread"), is considered by some experts to be the world's largest living organisms. Aspen clones may also rank among the world's oldest living organisms. There are clones in the U.S. that are estimated to be eight thousand years old. While the trunks of old trees die off, roots can continue to survive underground almost indefinitely, achieving a certain kind of immortality. Because modern aspen leaves so closely resemble fossilized ones, some researchers even assert that there are living aspen clones that may be as much as a million years old.

Aspen trunks with their papery white bark produce a white powder that rubs off easily on the hands. This white powder is said to have been used by Indians as a kind of sunscreen. When food was in short supply, Indians relied on dried strips of the aspen's inner bark, which was ground into meal and mixed with other starches to make bread or mush. Aspen bark strips were also fed to horses. The trunks of older aspen are frequently scarred by elk teeth and the incisive hieroglyphs of bear claws.

On the east side of the Red Rock Canyon Trail there are two aspen groves that are fairly prominent. The Utes, however, would not have encountered these particular groves, since they are reasonably young. But there may have been older groves here that were cleared away or died off. The young trees may even have regenerated from the offshoots of an older, established "mother tree."

The Dominant Mountain Shrub Community

While there is a coming together of several distinctive ecosystems and communities in Red Rock Canyon Open Space, there is also a clearly recognizable and defining uniformity. As the Kelso report unequivocally states: "The dominant community type found throughout the Red Rock property is the mountain shrub community." This community includes three major types: Gambel's oak *(Quercus gambelii)*, also known as "scrub oak," mountain mahogany *(Cercocarpus montana)*, and three-leaf sumac *(Rhus trilobata)*.

The three-leaf sumac, according to botanist William A. Weber, is related to both poison ivy and the mango tree. Three-leaf sumac produces dense clusters of berries that black bears relish. Indians gathered and dried the berries, relying on them as a food source. (In their dried state, these small red berries are mouth-puckeringly tart.) In addition, the bush produces blazing displays of color in autumn, specializing in burnt oranges and deep reds, a visual feast to human eyes. Another shrub common in thickets is the honeysuckle. There are twenty native species in North America. Hummingbirds are attracted to this plant, and it is used in herbal cough medicines.

The understory of native grasses in this mountain shrub community includes bromes, muhly, needlegrasses, and native species of grama grasses. Blue grama (*Chondrosum gracile*), of which Weber lists three species, is one of the dominant grasses of the short-grass prairie. It thrives in sunny areas. As described by botanist George Cameron, "Its flag-like inflorescences bounce on wiry stems in late summer." These inflorescences, according to one young observer, strongly resemble helicopters. The presence of grama grasses, Colorado's state grass, is a clear indicator of the ecological good health of areas where it is found.

Some yucca and prickly pear cactus (*Opuntia macrorhiza*), or "Bigfoot," with its spectacular yellow blooms, also appear in the stands of shrubs facing south. There is also a strong possibility of the existence of a related species of prickly pear that produces pink blooms, which has been spotted on a nearby property.

The west slope of the Dakota Hogback, to the east of the landfill site and the gravel quarry, is populated by the densest of the shrub communities on the property.

Piñon-Juniper Community

Another common community type in Red Rock Canyon Open Space is that of the piñon pine (*Pinus edulis*) and the one-seeded juniper (*Juniperus monosperma*), conveniently shortened to the "PJ."

The transitional and desert-loving PJ community is associated regionally with sedimentary rocks, mixed with mountain shrubs. Thus this community is found solely on the western edge of the property on exposed slopes in rocky soil. Ponderosa pine is also occasionally found amid the PJ woodlands. Its preference, however, is generally for cooler valleys with south-facing rocky slopes or on ridges where the porous rocky sandstone soil may contain more water.

Bears and Mountain Utes alike have long depended on nutritious and high-fat piñon pine nuts, as well as high-carbohydrate acorns to supplement their diets. (In a good season, acorns falling off the Gambel's scrub oak sound like popping corn as they hit a hard surface. Even mule deer have been observed munching on nature's popcorn.) Early on, the Utes recognized that, while cedars need more water than piñons, the two often grow together. According to linguist and anthropologist James A. Goss, when seen growing together, the trees are thought of by the Utes as enjoying the kinship of sisters. The paired trees are thus known to the Utes as "pa" (meaning "water") and waap (the word for "piñon pine") or "pa-waap."

Cool Conifer Community

While piñon pines are generally found in the drier, more desert-like areas, where grasses tend to grow in isolated clumps, the "cool conifer community" prefers lower montane settings, deep canyons, or ridges with north-facing slopes. Members of the cool conifer community include Douglas fir *(Pseudotsuga menziesii),* Colorado blue spruce *(Picea pungens),* and ponderosa pine *(Pinus ponderosa),* as well as white fir *(Abies concolor).*

It is of interest to note that spruce and other trees occasionally develop growths known as galls, which are like benign tumors. In the case of the spruce, the galls are sticky and resemble pinecones. Galls are usually caused by a small insect or a fungus, and do not kill the tree. Spruce galls are useful in cancer research.

The tall, steepling, puzzle-barked ponderosa, with its straight red trunk and sun-struck halos of needles, like the Colorado blue spruce, is among the world's most beautiful trees. In this case, "cool" is the operative word applied by the younger set of aspiring naturalists. They are quick to discover that the ponderosa's sun-warmed bark smells deliciously of butterscotch or vanilla. Indeed, its sap is used in the manufacture of artificial vanilla.

With regard to the ponderosa, there are numerous interesting points to ponder and reflect upon concerning the tree's natural history and the traditional Ute and Jicarilla Apache cultural uses. Don Ellis offers this interesting fact: "The bark of the young ponderosa is dark gray, almost black. As the tree becomes large and mature, the bark lightens to a ruddy yellow, just as we get lighter hair at a certain stage in life. Some older books mistakenly distinguish the black-barked ponderosa from the yellow-barked ponderosa as though they were different species, calling them, respectively, 'blackjack pine' and 'western yellow pine.'"

Coloradan Jack R. Williams worked for thirty years for the National Park Service, first as a ranger and then as a superintendent. He is a life-long, self-described student of American Indian cultural arts. He notes in his book *Ute Culture Trees: Living History* that first Americans have been using pines, such as the ponderosa, in a multitude of ingenious and practical ways for thousands of years. Some of these uses resulted in scarring or deforming. All relate back, in a broad sense, to their daily lives and culture.

Supple young conifers, for example, were sometimes bent by the Mountain Utes in order to mark a trail, especially in dense forest. This practice, however, probably did not affect the tree's growth much. On the other hand, blaze-faced ponderosas, if they are well over a century old, may have been used by Utes and their allies, the Jicarilla Apaches, as a food or pitch source, in which case the scar on the tree will be elliptic and shows signs of having been cut by a sharp-edged tool.

The Utes and Jicarilla Apaches used pine bark and resin in similar ways. The cambium was eaten, the pitch was used as medicine, and the women used it to seal the baskets they wove. Pine pitch was also chewed to refresh the mouth and clean the teeth, giving birth to today's chewing gum. The flavor of the cambium of the ponderosa pine is described by one source as having a sweet, acidic taste not unlike lemon syrup.

Despite these historic cultural practices on the part of the Utes, the majority of deformities we see in ponderosas today are most likely to be nature-caused. This can happen in any number of ways. For example, young trees growing on north-facing ridges are sometimes beaten down by winter storms. The tree then lies recumbent, while a few upright branches continue to grow vertically. Because of the tree's location in shade, snow melts slowly. The tree subsequently becomes bent and warped, in some cases, developing an extreme, swan neck–like crook or curvature.

Tree scarring may also result from the girdling of hungry porcupines or bark-eating Abert's squirrels. The incisions made in the thick ponderosa bark simply continue to enlarge as the tree grows, creating an even bigger, more disfiguring scar. Additional nature-induced growth problems may be caused by wind, lightning strikes, and freezes that cause a tree to burst.

Recently, the use of the term "prayer tree" has gained a certain popular and wide-spread currency in local reporting. However, Williams and others would argue that this term is misleading since it does not fully begin to embrace the rich and complex history of the multiple ways in which the Utes used pines, such as the ponderosa and piñon. (For the most part, such uses did not end up actually killing the tree itself or involve cutting it down. One is reminded, instead, of the way in which Vermonters annually tap maple trees for syrup.)

In short, not every bent or blazed ponderosa we see today was Indian-caused. Most are too young for that to be the case. Nor is every Indian-bent or blazed tree, *ipso facto*, of spiritual importance. As Williams points out, a few Ute trees were, in fact, venerated, while others were considered to be curative. In addition to "medicine trees," the Indians had "ceremonial trees" and some rather famous, shade-giving "council trees." (In Delta, Colorado, a magnificent two-hundred-year-old plains cottonwood (*Populus deltoides* ssp. monilifera) with a girth of seven feet was designated a Colorado Historical Landmark to commemorate the memory of Chief Ouray and his wife Chipita. Under this tree—a species also found in Red Rock Canyon Open Space—numerous meetings took place between tribal members and settlers.)

The Niobrara Community—from Rabbitbrush to Fremont Man

The Niobrara community occurs only in the alkaline, salt-rich layers of the Niobrara Formation on the eastern edge of the property. Here the soils lend themselves to the growth of an entirely different set of species. These include four-winged saltbrush (*Atriplex canescens*), winterfat (*Kraschennikovia lanata*), and mountain mahogany (*Cercocarpus montanus*). Where the Niobrara limestone and sandstone soils intermix, members of the mountain shrub community are also found, along with rabbitbrush (*Chrysothamnus*) or "chamisa."

Rabbitbrush turns a beautiful yellow in fall and often figures, with its bright splashes of color, into stunning landscape paintings by well-known artists of the Southwest. Early Fremont pictograph painters also recognized its value as a color and a dye. These pre-historic rock artists manufactured a black powder using a mixture of piñon gum, sumac, and yellow ochre obtained from rabbitbrush. Reds were produced from red ochre and the roots of mountain mahogany. These resourceful early artists (some of whom may have been shamans) also fashioned fiber brushes from the chewed ends of yucca. In the right place and season, supplies were readily at hand at no extra cost except for the labor involved.

Sand Bench

This is the mesa top between Greenlee Canyon and Sand Canyon, and is mostly covered by thick mountain shrub communities. Several natural grassy meadows occur here with diverse native grasses and very few invasive species. The grasses include dropseed, wheatgrass, and ricegrass. The meadows, together with the oak and mahogany thickets, provide excellent bird and butterfly habitat.

Sand Canyon: Home to the Rare Narrowleaf Cottonwood and Common Chokecherry Communities

In Sand Canyon, which is steep, narrow, and wet, there is a small pond where willows and cattails grow. Here chokecherries also flourish along the stream corridors. This, as might be expected, is classic black bear country. It is also the home of the narrowleaf cottonwood community. This increasingly fragmented and rare community of trees gets a "number one heritage rating" as being of preeminent conservation concern and value by the Colorado National Heritage Program (CNHP). The deeper, cooler canyons, by contrast, not only play host to cool conifer forests, which include the previously noted Douglas fir, Colorado blue spruce, ponderosa pine, white fir, and piñon pine, but also shrubs such as willow, wild rose, box elder, snowberry, and ninebark.

The artificial lakes or wetland areas on the open space fill another ecological niche, offering refuge to great blue herons and Canada geese. Other species that are listed as probable denizens of this area include: the tiger salamander, woodhouse toad, western chorus frog, northern leopard frog, painted turtle, bullsnake, western terrestrial garter snake, mallard, green-winged teal, killdeer, spotted sandpiper, and the red-winged blackbird.

Colorado's Mixed Grass and Native Tree Communities Are Being Lost

Mixed native grass and tree communities, states the Kelso report, "are becoming increasingly rare in Colorado and constitute important foraging ground for many animal species." Arguably a preserve such as Red Rock Canyon Open Space can play a critical role in helping to protect rare communities of native grasses and trees. It is important to note, however, that the species themselves are not so rare, as they do occur individually. Rather, it is the native plant and tree communities themselves, such as the heritage-rated narrowleaf cottonwood, with all their ecological interactions, which are becoming increasingly fragmented as a result of development.

The Colorful Parade of Colorado Wildflowers in the Open Space

Certain flowers and plants are so unmistakably associated with the southwestern landscape in their vivid splashes of color, unique and varied functions, and in their eye-catching displays that they might well be regarded as iconic. Red Rock Canyon Open Space is fortunate to play host to them all. I have chosen to begin by highlighting these particular plants because they tend to announce themselves so plainly and are among the first any new arrival or visitor to the region is apt to notice. My admittedly biased list of thirteen iconic flowers includes the previously described yucca, prickly pear, and rabbitbrush. Prickly pear here merits an additional note because of its historically important relationship with the scale insect called cochineal. Also in the running are the anemone or pasque flower, the sand lily, Indian paintbrush, mariposa lily, bee balm, green gentian, spiderwort, ball cactus, penstemon, and the Kansas gayfeather.

The well-known naturalist Aldo Leopold once said: "The chance to discover a pasque flower is a right as inalienable as free speech." Sometime in early spring—mid- to late March through April—this inalienable right can be enjoyed to its fullest in Red Rock Canyon. Pasque means "Easter" in French, and the crocus-like bloom that is of such great and delicate beauty, with its pale purple and white sepals, can usually be counted on to make an appearance just in time for the holiday.

As house-bound winter days draw to a close, the pasque flower inspires neighbors and naturalists alike to begin looking for the first bloom in some warm and protected spot. The quest for spring's first anemone has become, for many enthusiasts, an annual rite to mark the changing seasons that is as much anticipated as the traditional egg hunt.

If you've lived in the area for a while, perhaps you have by now been able to take full advantage of the opportunity to hike some of the many fine trails that have recently been added to the city's open spaces. If so, the search for the first anemone may have already become as much a harbinger of spring for you as the appearance of the first robin or the sound of the courtship song of the chickadee.

With the chickadee's tuneful and unmistakable song of "spring's here, spring's here," its presence soon becomes as easy to recognize as it is to spot the anemone's first bloom. Indeed, there may be more than one anemone in bloom. A sociable flower, anemones tend to grow in small clumps or mini-communities—the floral equivalent of baskets full of Easter eggs dyed in pale purples.

Recalling elegiac memories of growing up in close proximity to a "natural Red Rock Canyon," Don Ellis, like many in the area, recalls "the floral face of spring in the larger, hairy, almost disheveled, yet delicately beautiful pasque flower," as opposed to the garden-grown, domesticated crocus. Such a harbinger appealed to his youthful sensibility, as it still does today, not only as being different but in the most desirable sense, both "wilder," and "more robust."

In the spring of 2005, open space advocate Martha Rosenau enthused that "spring has sprung in a big way in Red Rock Canyon. There are at least a hundred pasque flowers in bloom along the quarry trail, with the greatest volume in White Acres. I'm not exaggerating on numbers at all!" As botanist George Cameron observes, one good rule of thumb is: "Every dry year is the same; every wet one is different."

In the annual spring and summer parade of wildflowers, some of the showiest begin to appear after Memorial Day in May or in early June, which is also a good time to start looking for vetch, penstemon, and paintbrush. Each flower has its season.

Sand Lily *(Leucocrinum montanum)*: A beautiful bridal-white lily, with its miniature bouquet of star-rayed tepals. It grows in April and May in sand and clay on slopes, hills, and abraded open paths. One of the loveliest and most delicate of the wildflowers to bloom in a bad neighborhood.

Indian Paintbrush (*Castilleja integra*): This flower's name is self-descriptive. It produces a striking, fiery orange, brush-like flower. It splashes its color across the hillsides in June, July, and early August. Partly parasitic, it taps into roots of sage and grasses and steals water, engaging in water wars at a floral level.

Mariposa (Sego) Lily (*Calachortus gunnisonii*): This beauty can be found growing in the open space from late June to early July. "Mariposa" means butterfly in Spanish and the mariposa does indeed resemble an earth-bound butterfly. Moreover, function follows beauty. Its bulb was milled into flour both by Native Americans and Mormon settlers, who may have learned about this resource from the Indians themselves. On the Mormon

Indian paintbrush. (Photo courtesy Bill Koerner)

trek to Utah, its bulb is credited with having helped to stave off starvation. Not surprisingly, the mariposa lily is Utah's state flower.

Prickly Pear Cactus (*Opuntia polyacantha*): With its waxy yellow blooms that turn into red-purple fruits, the prickly pear is the most abundant cactus to be found on the open space. Blooming in May and June, it plays host to the female scale insect called cochineal from which the crimson-colored dye carmine is derived—which is also called cochineal. These insects are about the size of a pinhead and produce a dye that was highly coveted by Indians for dying rugs and blankets. Originally used by the Incas and Aztecs and cultivated in Oaxaca, Mexico, during the Spanish Colonial era, cochineal was more valuable than gold. For this reason, it was illegal to carry it out of Spain or share the secret of its production on penalty of death.

Bee Balm (*Monarda fistulosa menthifolia*): In the intriguing world of wildflowers this also deserves special mention. It is a member of the mint family, and is also known as "wild oregano," which makes an acceptable substitute for that herb. The

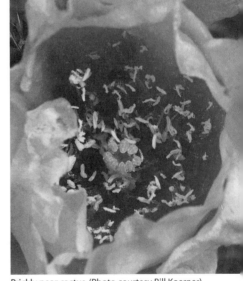

Prickly pear cactus. (Photo courtesy Bill Koerner)

flowers of bee balm are usually pale purple to lavender. Bee balm was used as a dye by the internationally known New Mexico potter Maria Martinez in her distinctive black-glazed, pueblo-style pottery.

Green Gentian or Monument Plant (*Frasera speciosa*): This striking plant, with its typically three to six foot tall flowering stalk and large basal rosette of leaves, takes between twenty to eighty years to produce flowers, after sufficient nutrients have been stored in its roots. Then one year it produces its summer blooms, makes seeds, and dies. It favors open sunny spots in foothills and meadows. The monument plant is sometimes mistaken for mullein. However, its leaves are shiny instead of downy. Its flowers are green and white and star-like. A constellation of some six hundred blooms can appear on a single plant and sometimes a patch of green gentian will bloom together simultaneously.

We've only recently learned these interesting facts about this plant's unique life history as a result of the long years of research by Dr. David Inouye at the Rocky Mountain Biological Laboratory in Gothic, Colorado.

Spiderwort *(Tradescantia occidentalis)*: With its three spreading petals of blue, it is one of the loveliest of wildflowers to bloom in the foothills from mid-May through June and into July. The petals, taken together with its slender, spider leg–like, curved and elongated leaves, may vaguely resemble a spider in its configuration. As Don Ellis writes in the *Red Rock Rag* (Vol. 4, no.5), "wort" comes from the Old English "wyrt," meaning plant.

> One species of spiderwort has found a very unusual scientific application … as a radiation monitor. The stamen hairs of this spiderwort are each a chain of single cells, like beads on a string. The stamen hairs grow by the successive addition of cells to the chain. In this particular species, the cells of the stamen hairs are usually pink. But, there is an occasional blue cell. The blue color is the result of a single point mutation in the cell's genetic material. The likelihood of this mutation occurring is proportional to the radiation to which the cell is exposed. So, counting the number of blue cells in the stamen hairs give an estimate of the radiation to which the flowers were exposed. Since the cells in each hair grow sequentially, the location along the stamen hairs of the blue cells tells when the radiation exposure occurred. This species of spiderwort was once planted around a nuclear power plant in Japan to monitor the release of radioactive material. Not only did the spiderworts tell how much radioactive material was released and when, they also told how the wind dispersed the radioactive material.

The spiderwort was named in 1753 for John Tradescant, who served as gardener to Charles I of England. While the delicate three-petaled flowers are typically blue to purple, we once spotted a white one. Each flower lasts but a single day. The spiderwort grows in gravelly areas and on rocky slopes.

Ball Cactus or Pincushion Cactus *(Pediocactus simpsonii)*: Radiant is the perfect word for the spectacular, sunset-colored, bright magenta blooms that grace this ball-shaped spiny plant. An early bloomer, its flowering time is from May to July. Visitors, including one Siberian botanist the author was privileged to meet, often express surprise to see cactus growing among conifers in a mountain setting, especially after the first snowfall. Colorado's highest growing cactus, however, is hardy and cold resistant. It reaches to altitudes of ten thousand feet. There are two other species on the open space.

The ball or pincushion cactus germinates both from seeds and from tiny new balls resembling miniature pincushions. Clusters can expand to several inches across. Smaller versions are sometimes nestled beneath forest litter, making them hard to spot. In winter, the cactus retreats, shrinking into the ground, then, in spring, it inflates again like a ball, up to six inches in diameter.

Kansas Gayfeather *(Liatris unctata)*: The flowers of this pert purple plant are arranged on a long narrow stock, with distinctive featherlike styles, reflective of the plant's common name. It puts on an unmistakable and showy display of blooms in vibrant patches, blooming from July to October.

Penstemon (Species include *P. secundiflorus, P. virens, P. virgatas,* and *P. angustifolius)*: Penstemon in their many varieties are a study in shades of blue—from pale blue to cobalt to sky blue to orchid and purple. Another striking bloom and easy to identify, it clusters in sandy patches from May to July. Growing from eight to fourteen inches tall, its tubular, five-lobed flowers cover much of the upper part of the stalk of each plant. Its name refers to its five stamens, one of which is sterile. Its purpose is unknown. Perhaps it's a landing strip for pollinators.

Blue penstemon. (Photo courtesy Bill Koerner)

Other Wildflowers to Look for

In nearly all cases, the wildflowers described previously and compiled in the list that follows were observed growing in the open space by Colorado College biology professor Tass Kelso, or while on a walk in the company of botanist George Cameron, and/or they figured into the Greystone Environmental Consultants' habitat study requested by the city parks and recreation department. The initial lists were added to and expanded over a three-year period. The result is not intended to be encyclopedic. The hope is that it might provide a useful framework on which to build, while referring to some of the classic field guides listed in the bibliography.

There is a high probability that many of the same plants found in Garden of the Gods will also be found in Red Rock Canyon Open Space—given similar soil types, slope aspect (generally north-facing at an angle of 40 degrees), and elevation. Based on an inventory of plant species identified in Garden of the Gods and conducted as part of its master plan, we might expect to find more than one hundred and fifty species in the open space, surpassing the probable count in Garden of the Gods. Indeed, Red Rock Canyon Open Space is more biologically diverse than Garden of the Gods because it includes cool conifer forests, which Garden of the Gods does not have.

The Private Lives of Wildflowers and Some Other Interesting Facts

Botanist George Cameron, author of *Vascular Plants of the Stratton Open Space* and an instructor at Pikes Peak Community College, observes that the unity among all plants is manifested, among other things, in their reproductive structures. For example, in flowering plants, the carpel (the female structure of the plant) is related to the spiraling scales on a gymnosperm cone (pine cone). The ponderosa pine has separate male and female cones. The male cone of the ponderosa pine is tassel-like in appearance.

These male cones dispense pollen in copious and even wasteful amounts, like the residue of yellow chalk on a blackboard, while the female structure swells up to its decorative, Christmas cone–shape after being fertilized.

Orchids, says Cameron, with approximately twenty thousand species world-wide, are the biggest flower family in the world. About twenty species are found in Colorado. The second largest, with fifteen thousand–plus species globally, is the composite family, with at least four hundred represented in Colorado. Included in this extended aster family *(Asteraceae)* are sunflowers, daisies, fleabane, bachelor buttons, and thistles—all of which are found in Red Rock Canyon Open Space. The composite's flower, in its Zen-like composition is, in reality, the head of many flowers contained within a central disk. Yet, we see what we think of as a single flower.

Herbal Knowledge of the Cheyennes and other Tribes

In addition to the Mountain Utes and other tribes, the Cheyennes made good use of local plants, both for food and medicine. Several plants found in Red Rock Canyon Open Space are among the varieties that were eaten, including lambs quarters *(Chenopodium berlandieri)* and the roots of American licorice *(Glycyrrhiza lepidota)*. Another species is the source for the popular confection, as historian Elliott West writes in *Contested Plains*: "The groundplum milkvetch *(Astragalus crassicarpus)* [in season] also put out its succulent, sweet fruits that staved off thirst." As medicine, Indians applied puccoon *(Lithospermum incisum)* to paralyzed limbs, while aromatic sumac *(Rhus aromatica)* was mixed with tobacco and enjoyed as a smoke. And the list goes on.

Additional Common Wildflowers Identified in Red Rock Canyon

In the following list of common wildflowers identified on the open space, a genus may be represented by one or more species whose identity is uncertain or unknown. This is designated by the standard botanical abbreviations: "sp." for the singular, and "spp." indicating the plural.

Alumroot *(Heuchera parvifolia)*: This plant prefers rocky canyons and cliffs. The flowers of this species are yellow; its roots produce an astringent used to treat superficial sores, including on the mouth and gums.

Mountain Bladderpod *(Lesquerella montana)*: Clusters of yellow, four-petaled flowers bloom on hairy curved stems about eight inches in height. Its hairy fruits are bladder-shaped. Seen along roadsides and sandy slopes in late spring and early summer.

Mountain Candytuft *(Noccaea montana)*: An early blooming wildflower that grows in three-inch tall patches. In this member of the mustard family, clusters of white flowers with pointed sepals and four white petals top stems with alternate leaves. Commonly found on canyon slopes and in valleys.

Senecio *(Senecio spp.)*: means "gray-head," related to "senile." Multiple yellow flowers with narrow, ray-shaped petals. Most species grow on low stems with long, thin, blade-shaped leaves often in meadows and ponderosa woods. Plants are covered with balls of grey seed after flowering, hence the name.

Meadowrue *(T. fendleri)*: An herbaceous plant, about two feet tall, related to the mountain columbine, its leaves resemble those of its relative.

Lambert's Loco *(Oxytropis lambertii)*: Too much selenium in this plant makes cows crazy, causing spasms. Loco has a beak on its keel, distinguishing it from vetch, which it strongly resembles. Both plants are members of the sweet-pea family.

Common Skullcap *(Scutellaria brittonii)*: This eight-inch tall member of the mint family blooms in summer and has an elongated two-lipped flower, ranging in color from blue to pink to white. The helmet-shaped lower lip of its bloom accounts for its name.

Evening Primrose *(Oenothera coronopifolia)*: A native species. White blooms open in evening and close in the morning.

Prairie Goldenrod *(Unamia alba)*: A small population exists on the eastern edge of the gravel quarry. It is a state-ranked conservation species by the Heritage Program. A member of the aster family, it flowers from July to September.

American Milk Vetch *(Astragalus spp.)*: Vetches are members of the pea family. Their colors run from purple to violet to white, with flowers resembling the domestic sweet pea. Growing from four to six inches high, they flower in April and May. Easy to confuse with Loco.

Kittentail *(Besseya plantaginea)*: Purplish corolla on six-inch tall plant, with leafy bracts. Prefers grassy slopes and parks. Its common name refers to the fuzzy alpine species.

Wild Tarragon *(Artemisia dracunculus)*: A plant associated with desert steppes. Frequent in the region and sometimes considered "weedy," it is easy to identify with its long, narrow leaves resembling domestic varieties (and perhaps the tongue of a dragon?) and its profuse beading made up of small flower and seed heads. Flowers are bunched and yellow. Some wild varieties bear the unmistakable scent of tarragon and are used in parts of Europe as flavoring. "Dracunculus" means "little dragon."

Fendler Sandwort *(Arenaria fendleri)*: Related to chickweed, partial to open dry areas, grows up to ten inches tall with clusters of white star-like flowers, each with five elongated petals.

Wooly Plantain *(Plantago patagonica)*: An eight-inch plant with hairy stem, topped by a spike of fuzzy green bracts that conceal small white flowers. Blooms in April to June.

Gumweed *(Grindelia squarrosa)*: A one to two foot tall member of the aster family, abundant on packed, worn soil along trails and roads. Flower heads are covered with a sticky gum.

Yellow Stonecrop *(Sedum roseum)*: Distinguished by fleshy leaves and small, bright, star-like yellow flowers, low-lying, a good survivor in rocky dry areas from early to late summer.

Copper or Globe Mallow *(Sphaeralcea coccinea)*: Blooms from June to September. Grows to eight inches in height. Has bright, sorbet-colored, red-orange petals in a round corolla of five petals. Three- to five-part leaves are grey green. Grows in dry areas along roads and on slopes.

Puccoon *(Lithospermum multiflorum* and *L. incisum)*: Grows in leafy clumps with fringed, small yellow, trumpet-shaped flowers. *L. multiflorum* grows in shrubland and blooms in July. *L. incisum* grows in open grassland and blooms in spring meadows.

Mullein *(Verbascum thapsus)*: According to *Peterson's Field Guide to Rocky Mountain Wildflowers,* thapsus comes from the name of an ancient town in North Africa. The leaves of mullein are gathered for medicinal purposes. Its seeds supply small birds with food when other sources are snow-covered.

False Dandelion *(Agoseris glauca)*: A member of the aster family, it resembles the common dandelion. It is one of our earliest blooms. Yellow heads and wavy strap-like leaves hug the ground. Common in meadows, on slopes, in fields, and open glades.

Perky Sue *(Tetraneuris acaulis)*: A member of the aster family with cheerful yellow ray flowers on eight to twelve inch stalks.

Lanceleaf Chiming Bells *(Mertensia lanceolata)*: Flowers are small, blue, bell-shaped, drooping clusters. Blooms in April, May, and June. Provides food for early arriving hummingbirds.

Whiplash Daisy *(Erigeron flagellaris)*: Red Rock Canyon Open Space supports several species of this huge genus, including *E. vetensis.* In spring, the whiplash daisy flowers in an upright cluster. Long, whip-like stems form after flowering.

Sunflowers *(Helianthus* spp.*)*: Helianthus, true sunflowers, grow on the open space, with *H. annuus* most common, growing in disturbed ground. Two other species grow here as well.

Prickly Poppy *(Argemone polyanthemos)*: Sometimes called the "cowboy's fried egg," it flowers from April to August, producing a spectacular, white papery five-inch bloom, with a yellow eye of clustered yellow anthers. Its spines and poisonous alkaloid act as a defense against predators. Pharmaceutical labs are researching its possible use for medicinal purposes.

Dogbane *(Apocynum androsaemifolium)*: In Vol. 3, No.5 of the *Red Rock Rag* in his column "Tidbits," Ellis reports that on the first quarter mile of the Manitou Springs Section 16 trail, dogbane is abundant. Its genus name is *Apocynum,* he writes, meaning "noxious to dogs." The plant, with its poisonous milky sap is not only harmful to animals, including cattle, but also distasteful and they usually avoid it. In our area, dogbane produces a bush-like plant about three feet high, with a multitude of small pink to white, bell-shaped flowers. It also produces fibrous stems. Several Indian tribes used the fibers from dogbane to make cords, nets, and cloth. In the Southwest, the fibers were used for basket weaving—several old and beautiful examples of which are preserved in museums. In the past, dogbane was sometimes referred to as "Indian hemp." South Asian Indian hemp (that is, from India) is better known as "marijuana."

Western Wallflower *(Erysimum capitatum)*: In the mustard family, stands up to twenty inches tall, and has four mustard-colored petals and an abundance of narrow leaves.

Easter Daisy *(Townsendia* sp.*)*: Produces large striking, stemless blooms in white or pale pink, growing from March to June in sandy or gravelly soil, often in or at the edge of trails, close to the ground.

Wild Geranium *(Geranium caespitosum)*: Has five pink petals and palmate leaves. Blooms from May to August.

Nodding Onion *(Allium cernuum)*: Grows from six to eighteen inches tall and has a nodding umbel with a pink flower. A smaller wild onion *(Allium textile)* has white flowers. Both are abundant but have different blooming times. Wild onions were used by Indians. Lewis and Clark reportedly used them to season meat dishes.

Fringed Sage *(Artemisia frigida)*: Small and feathery with finely divided leaves, this sage is a composite in the mint family and related to wormwood. Named after Artemis, goddess of healing, it is thought to have curative powers. Ellis in the *Red Rock Rag,* Vol. 8, No.1, writes that it was used "by some Native Americans as a dressing for wounds, after the leaves were first chewed. Because of its bitterness, it must be used sparingly, but it has been used as a spice for corn dishes and to help 'mask the greasy rancid odor of dried meats.'"

Prairie Sage *(Artemisia ludoviciana)*: Writing in the same edition of the *Rag*, Ellis states the following: "Prairie sage or white sagebrush grows one to two feet high in Red Rock Canyon. It has simple linear or elliptic leaves, sometimes toothed at the tips, and tiny … flowers that bloom in late summer. Prairie sage is used in sweat lodges and for smudging by the Lakota and other tribes. Evil spirits are dispelled by smudging with the smoke from prairie sage, while good and beneficial spirits are attracted by smudging with sweetgrass. Sacred objects are often wrapped with sage in medicine bundles. Some Native American traditions associate four sacred fragrant plants, sage, sweetgrass, tobacco, and cedar, with the cardinal directions."

Western Figwort *(Scrophularia lanceolata)*: Also known as "Bunny-in-the-grass," it grows in moist soil. Interesting, but often overlooked, it has a five foot tall square stem and reddish-brown flowers made up of a two-lobed upper lip and three-lobed lower lip, it was once used as a folk remedy for scrofula and "fig warts."

Aster or Michaelmas Daisy *(Aster laevis)*: Tall with many lavender ray flowers at the top of a thick green branching stalk with alternate leaves; tiny shingled bracts. It blooms in late August, early September.

Broomrape *(Aphyllon fasciculatum)*: This mole-like plant is an oddity. With no leaves, it makes no chlorophyll. Instead, it lives underground and is parasitic, tapping into the roots of the fringed sage. It pokes its head above ground only to reproduce.

Yellow Sweet Clover *(Melilotus officinalis)*: Also known as "Honey Clover." Member of the pea family.

Prairie Violet *(Viola pedatifida)*: A classic violet that flowers in early spring, this is another sensitive species that may occur in the open space. Also known as birdfoot violet, its rich purple-blue flowers can seem nearly hidden in the dry tan grasses of early spring.

Dayflower *(Commelina dianthifolia)*: This is a rare species known from a few locations in our region (such as Aiken Canyon). It also occurs in the open space. Its spathe, or large shielding bract, is drawn out to a point and holds three blue petals. Its leaves resemble those of dianthus. A member of the spiderwort family, it favors talus slopes in canyons.

Poison Hemlock *(Conium maculata)*: Non-native member of the same family as parsley, which it resembles. Its deadly poison killed Socrates.

Blue Flax *(Linum lewisii)*: Blooming from May to August, the saucer-shaped, sky-blue flax flower with its five petals measuring one-half to one inch, borne on long, slender stems, enhances open and cleared areas and roadsides. The plant was named for Captain Meriwether Lewis, hence *"lewisii."* Its stem, covered with alternate leaves, is fibrous, as is also the case with cultivated flax. The latter has a multitude of uses—from linseed oil to Egyptian mummy wrappings. Flax growing on re-vegetated land also include *L. perenne.*

Those who give wildflowers their common names are themselves anonymous. But it's safe to say that the names bestowed are inspired by one of three elements: the plant's appearance, its location, or its blooming season. Some plants, such as the ball cactus, go by a number of aliases—in which case the Latin or scientific name may prove helpful with its identification. Yet occasionally, scientific names also undergo change. Still, this nomenclature tends to work just about everywhere. Scientific names may, in fact, represent one of the world's few, truly functional, universal tongues. In our own family, a much-esteemed elder, Dorothy Shaw, introduced us to the common name of a species of purple aster. Because it blooms around the time of the saint's day in September, it is called "Michaelmas daisy." Dorothy was partial to the name for a good reason. Her husband, educator Lloyd Shaw, celebrated his birthday on the same day as the dragon-slaying saint. The name, however, simply added to our confusion. If it were an aster, why was it called a daisy? The argument, in the first instance, was settled by a close-up look at the flower's tiny shingled bracts on its underside. Clearly, an aster by any other name is still an aster. (But now I'm informed that the nomenclature of "aster" is under debate.)

Arrowgrass *(Triglochin maritima)*: A plant that likes moist conditions, found growing in the shallows ponds that are present in the Lyons stone quarry when it rains. This plant with its spiky raceme of small green flowers has long, narrow leaves that resemble grass. Not a true grass, however, it can, under some conditions, be toxic to animals feeding on it.

Wild Asparagus *(asparagus officinalis)*: Escapees from gardens, wild asparagus grows up to six feet tall and strongly resembles the domestic variety. Young stalks are edible.

In addition to the trees and grasses previously described, sedges, rushes, wax currants, and gooseberries also grow on the open space.

Noxious Weeds

Some noxious weeds are as beautiful as Cleopatra and as subversive as Tokyo Rose, while others are merely obnoxious. The latter may be very little trouble, just so long as they are not in the wrong place at the wrong time, or to put it another way—just so long as they are not being "inappropriate," or "politically incorrect." But, in general, noxious weeds may not be nearly so innocent as they look and should, in fact, be taken quite seriously.

The experts in the field consider noxious weeds to be a very serious matter, indeed—so much so that the weeds have attained a legal classification all their own, beyond their botanical definitions. It's little wonder why. Of the three thousand native species of plants in Colorado, five hundred, or 17 percent, have already been displaced by noxious weeds, reports the Colorado Weed Management Association in *Troublesome Weeds of the Rocky Mountain West* (Eighth ed.). "Noxious weeds" are those designated by federal, state, or county governments to be injurious to public health, agriculture, recreation, wildlife, and any public or private property.

In 2003, the Colorado Noxious Weed Act was amended to assign noxious weeds to one of three categories labeled A, B, and C. Species in the "A" category are mandated by state law to be eradicated wherever they are found. The "B" list includes well-established species that need to be stopped. Many of the weeds listed in the statewide "B" category also appear on county lists. As such, their control is a requirement.

The harm associated with species on the "C" list needs to be reduced. Government entities at the local, state, and federal levels are prepared to provide a variety of support services for locally initiated plans to control weeds in the "C" group. For species found on the "C" list, the hope is to provide additional educational, research, and biological controls where needed and/or requested.

In the management of some weed types, the U.S. Department of Agriculture has successfully implemented the use of "biocontrol insects." Under the supervision of entomologists and other experts, biocontrol insects have been used, for example, to control leafy spurge in the northern plains and elsewhere—along with several species of knapweed. Such controls as these, when carefully done, can be a powerful and effective tool in the effort to stem the relentless tide of proliferating and invasive weeds.

A Brief History of the Origin of Noxious Weeds

Native plants have been evolving for millions of years to fill specific ecological niches. In the so-called "primal" wilderness, as it once was, non-native, ecologically damaging weeds as we know them today did not exist. (In fact, the land in the American Northeast and South was already being cultivated by Indians when the early seventeenth-century colonists first set foot on shore, arriving aboard vessels from "old Europe." Not surprisingly, the Indians, with their long experience, had a far better knowledge and understanding of crop rotation and the use of native seeds appropriate to the local soil and growing conditions than did the new arrivals. At any rate, non-native invasive plants were first introduced principally from Eurasia by colonists. Seeds were most probably carried via clothing, animal feed, and other goods, as well as in the dirt used as ballast in ships.

In the case of plants used for dyes, reseeding, or decorative purposes in home gardens, the plants or seeds were purposely transported and later replanted. However, these attractive and more visually pleasing ornamental plants proved to be every bit as invasive as their weedy-looking counterparts. While in their native habitats, insects, diseases, and competitive species had served to keep them in check. However, these same biological controls did not exist in their new-world environment.

In short, invasive weeds are not only hardy master survivors, but they can reproduce rapidly, thereby effectively reducing the diversity and quantity of native plant communities. The Bureau of Land Management (BLM) estimates that each day on public lands, weeds spread to approximately four thousand additional acres. Many weeds produce a virtual explosion of seeds. Knapweed, for example, produces up to a thousand per plant. While a certain percentage germinate, the rest remain, often for years at a time, in a seed bank in the soil, waiting for the right conditions to sprout. Furthermore, once a weed infestation has been identified on a site, it is often so large that containment becomes not only difficult, but also costly.

Some Noxious Weed Facts

- Noxious weeds not only contribute to erosion, but they are significantly less fire-resistant. According to the Colorado Weed Management Association, cheatgrass can accelerate the frequency of fire in sagebrush communities from approximately fifty to seventy-five years to three to five years.
- Noxious weeds take over important wildlife habitat areas, depriving animals of essential forage.
- Noxious weeds are often thorny, scratchy, and grow in dense patches, making hiking and other recreational activities difficult to impossible.
- Noxious weeds increase the cost of maintaining recreational facilities. The Bureau of Land Management states that leafy spurge alone costs North Dakota an estimated $87 million a year.
- Wildflowers such as Colorado's state flower, the Colorado blue columbine, cannot compete with invasive ornamental plants for soil nutrients, water, and sunlight.
- Noxious trees, such as the Russian olive, deprive birds of valuable nesting sites.
- Noxious weeds have the capability of taking over and totally destroying native communities of plants.

There is an important distinction to be made between non-native, ecologically damaging weeds and "early succession" plants that are sometimes called "weeds." Plant succession, as defined by one plant biologist, is "an ecological process in which one plant community replaces another over time." Sometimes early succession plants are described as "weeds" simply because they appear in a site intended for some other purpose, such as an agricultural crop. However, early succession plants often supply vital needs of wildlife, including ground-nesting birds, because of their high production of nutritious seeds. To further complicate matters, the pioneering early succession plants, like noxious weeds, can benefit from disturbances in the land.

That is the bad news on noxious weeds. The good news is that there is a growing awareness and appreciation of the problem among the public, starting with school children, thanks to some creative educational programs implemented by science teachers and encouraged by such entities as the BLM. In 1996, the state of Colorado passed the Noxious Weed Act, which enables county and city governments to implement and support a wide range of management programs.

Some Noxious and Troublesome Weeds and Trees Found in Red Rock Canyon

Just as it takes a village to raise a child, it may take a community to eliminate a well-established weed. Since weeds are a threat to our fragile ecosystems and because of their ubiquitous and destructive natures, we all, in a sense, have a role to play in their control and elimination. Volunteer groups, for example, can work together to help eradicate Siberian elms (as they have and continue to do on the Stratton Open Space); others can contribute through educational programs. Taking the time to learn to identify some of the primary offenders may also help to stem their destructive and rampaging march into uncolonized territory.

One writer on the subject of noxious weeds and their control reported that her grandmother from Nebraska was all too eager to dig up some toadflax to replant in her garden at home. This response to the ornamental toadflax is by no means uncommon. Returning more than a decade ago to my own western American roots, I found myself visited by a similar impulse. After all, the toadflax were not only aesthetically pleasing—they were clearly thriving, far more than anything in my own small and struggling garden. Soon, however, I learned about the botanical dark side ...

Dalmatian Toadflax *(Linaria dalmatica)*: Dalmatian toadflax is unfortunately spreading rapidly, especially along the foothills in places like Manitou Springs Section 16 and Red Rock Canyon Open Space. Dalmatian toadflax is on the list of "Teller County's Top 10 Noxious Weeds." An ornamental plant that closely resembles yellow toadflax, it was introduced from Europe. It has attractive yellow snapdragon-shaped blooms with orange centers. A creeping perennial that is rapidly invading dry rangeland as well as the foothills, it reproduces both by its abundant seeds and its underground rootstalks. It is very aggressive and difficult to manage, crowding out vegetation that is desirable forage for wildlife and domestic stock.

Yellow Toadflax *(Linaria vulgaris)*: "Butter and eggs," another deceptive beauty, is massively present throughout southwestern Colorado. It strongly resembles Dalmatian toadflax with its yellow and orange snapdragon-like blooms, except for its leaves which are narrow and linear as opposed to the broader leaves of Dalmatian toadflax. This invasive species is also present on Red Rock Canyon Open Space.

Cheatgrass ranks as another major noxious weed of the West. Less fire-resistant than native vegetation, it overruns native plants and is troublesome to livestock. Cheatgrass is ubiquitous throughout the West. It occurs in Red Rock Canyon Open Space, where it represents a small to medium problem.

"Unfortunately," says Colorado College professor of biology Tass Kelso, "one side effect of the history of the Red Rock Canyon property is that it is extremely weedy, with many of at least the B and C list species occurring in abundance on the open space. This will be a long-term management issue," she states.

Additional Noxious Weeds Identified or Probable on Red Rock Canyon Open Space

Russian Thistle or **Tumbleweed** and **Sweet Clover:** Neither of these plants is on the official Colorado noxious weed list, but deserve to be.

Bindweed *(Convolvulus arvensis)*: A member of the Morning Glory family, this creeping perennial arrived from Europe. It is one of the most competitive of the perennial weeds and is a problem throughout the state. It can store a two- to three-year food supply in its extensive root system, while its seeds may remain viable in soil for up to forty years.

Knapweed, Diffuse Knapweed (*Centaurea diffusa*), **Spotted Knapweed** (*Centaurea maculosa*).

Soapwort, Bouncing Bet (*Saponaria officinalis*): This alien escaped from old gardens during mining days. Its crushed leaves make a soapy lather.

Leafy Spurge (*Euphorbia esula*): An African plant. This weed is listed among El Paso County's top 10 most noxious weeds. This common plant occurs mostly in grasslands.

Myrtle Spurge (*Euphorbia myrsinites*): This spurge appears on the state's A list. This spurge is common in the foothills, such as those above Garden of the Gods. Many people still plant it and it escapes easily.

Thistle: There are several species of thistle in the open space. All are common in the region. These include **Canadian Thistle** (*Cirsium arvense*), **Bull Thistle** (*Cirsium vulgare*) and **Musk Thistle** (*Carduus nutans*).

Chinese Climatis (*Clemantis orientalis*): In El Paso County, this handsome but noxious weed is abundant. A perennial vine that grows to twelve feet, it covers rocks, young trees, and shrubs. It is also called "old-man's beard" because of its long, feathery styles that give the plant a silvery appearance. Its inflorescences consist of striking pale yellow sepals three-quarter inch wide. It blooms from August through October and is allelopathic, meaning it secretes a fluid that is toxic to other plants, in this case, especially legumes.

Tamarisk or **Salt Cedar:** No more than three plants have been spotted growing on the open space. While tamarisk is found along Monument Creek, there are insufficient watercourses in RRCOS for Tamarisk to flourish. Hence it is a non-problem.

Russian Olive: Of minimal concern in RRCOS.

Siberian (Chinese) Elm (*Ulmus pumila*): Like all noxious weeds and weed trees, the Siberian elm is aggressive and competitive—unlike "friendly" native elms of North America. And like the equally pesky locust, it is an introduced tree and fast growing in dry regions. To successfully eradicate a Siberian elm, listed as a Class C weed, requires nothing if not great persistence. There are thousands of these weed trees in the open space. Their growth was promoted by the contouring of the land done by the former owner. The contours served as ready-made water catchments where young saplings could all the more readily take hold. The larger, regenerative elms are as efficient as an assembly line in their production of millions of seeds that are widely dispersed by wind.

Siberian elms are true pests and the only way to get rid of them is to employ the cut-stump method on large trees. This requires the use of loppers or a saw and the application of herbicide. Only a small amount is required—not enough to be transported beyond the cut stump.

In the aftermath of the Dustbowl, great numbers of *U. pumila* were planted as shelter belts across the prairies due to its tolerance for draught and cold. Among horticulturalists, the Siberian elm is known as "the world's worst tree."

In summary, there is an overwhelming consensus among the experts in the field—whether Colorado botanists such as Guennel and Weber, or the specialists at such entities as the Colorado Weed Management Association, BLM, and the U.S. Department of Agriculture—that noxious weeds know no boundaries and should not be welcomed. Indeed, they should be carefully managed through an integrated program involving plant removal, digging out of roots, the introduction of natural predators (goats may eat knapweed and thistles, for example), education programs, and prevention—and, in some cases, the application of safe and effective chemicals where necessary (as in the elimination of Siberian elms).

Given the fact that noxious weeds do occur in great numbers on the Red Rock Canyon Open Space, in turn posing a threat to the biodiversity and ecosystem stability of its native plant communities, it is important to consider a few simple preventive measures.

While there are already any number of good reasons for not straying off trail—whether hiking, riding horses, or biking—among them is surely the presence of noxious weeds on the open space. Seeds can inadvertently be picked up and transported on clothing, the soles of shoes, the wheels of vehicles, or the fur of animals—thus to be sown even farther afield, thereby contributing to an already troublesome (or perhaps nettle-some) problem. By adhering to trails, we as land users can all do our part to help prevent the additional spread of these unwanted, ecologically damaging invaders.

Poison Ivy Alert

According to recent studies, poison ivy, which is neither poisonous nor ivy—but which does emit a toxic, itch-and-red-rash-inducing resin called "urshiol"—has been growing faster, bigger, and more toxic as the climate warms. In the open space, poison ivy has been identified growing where the Red Rock Canyon Trail meets the Round-up Trail. The plant has three leaves, just like its close relative, the sumac. Alternate, ovate, and shiny, the leaves have a few coarsely rounded "teeth" near the top. In some places, poison ivy grows several feet tall, but in Red Rock Canyon it is usually only about a foot in height. It favors the edges of trails and banks of streams.

Wide-ranging Megafauna

Underlying geology strongly influences plant communities and their growth, which in turn either positively or negatively impact the numbers, as well as the health and diversity of fauna found in the region and on the open space itself. As humans have continued to populate the region, wildlife has either vanished altogether or opportunistically moved into urban areas.

Indeed, habitat loss has become the single biggest threat to local wildlife as, increasingly, there has been no place left for the indigenous wildlife to retreat to. There has also been a proportionate rise in the numbers of interactions reported between humans and the "megafauna [meaning black bear, mountain lion, and mule deer] at our urban edges." At the same time, as the numbers of large predators have either been dramatically reduced or extirpated, as in the case of the gray wolf, so have the numbers of lesser fauna, such as mule deer, undergone a commensurate population explosion resulting in significant and noticeable imbalances.

In order to avoid contributing to such imbalances, while steering clear of episodes of "conflict," some citizens have made a deliberate and conscious decision to move over, pay closer attention, and learn more. They hope to learn to adopt some realistic and creative measures that will enable them to co-habit, peaceably and safely, in shared habitats with the larger mammals whose numbers are rapidly diminishing.

Black Bear

Bears, according to *Mammals of Colorado* (Fitzgerald et al.), are "closely allied to canids." Black bears are described as Colorado's "largest surviving carnivore," having replaced the grizzly, which is now extinct in Colorado. In the state of Colorado today it is estimated that there are between eight thousand and twelve thousand bears. Loss of habitat, illegal killing, and destruction of bears that pose a threat are the main cause of mortality. Indeed 85 percent of adult mortality is human-caused and in Colorado, if a bear becomes troublesome, in the best case scenario it's "two strikes and you're out"; often enough it may be just one.

While the black bear's diet is omnivorous, its teeth are adapted to the consumption of meat. The pelage or fur of so-called "black" bears can bleach out to a punk-like blond or change color with maturation and/or the seasons. Some black bears, manifesting the second of its two phases, sport an unusually handsome and striking coat of cinnamon-bark red fur.

Black bears are common in montane shrublands and subalpine forests. Being omnivorous (as well as opportunistic) feeders, they eat berries, fruit, plant material (including dandelion leaves, grasses, and forbs), acorns in fall, insects, and a selection of small mammals, including rodents. They feed mostly during the day or at dusk, bulking up in round-the-clock foraging just before the winter period of dormancy. Fresh black bear scat on trails is recognizable as shiny onyx to dark brown mounds filled with seeds, while pawprints are five-toed and clawed. The claws of a bear are non-retractable, unlike those of a cat.

Mother bears typically give birth to a litter of two or three cubs during hibernation in their dens—established in a rocky cavity or in excavations under brush and trees. As Dr. D.J. Obee writes in his book *Mammals of Rocky Mountain National Park and the Colorado Rockies*: "A female of one color may have cubs of the other color, or one of each color in the case of a litter of two, which is the most common number. ... The cubs are born in the middle of winter [around January or February] and, considering the size of the parents, they are extremely small, weighing less than a pound at birth. This is truly a remarkable adaptation because, her young being born when they are, the female would not have an adequate supply of food for larger offspring, not to mention the fact that in some cases the den itself might become crowded."

Besides being tiny, cubs at birth are covered with fine hairs and are blind. However, they do put on weight rapidly. Cubs typically stay with their mothers for the first year of life. (In Colorado, cub survival rates are a little over 50 percent. Comparatively speaking, Colorado has a very low population density of black bears.) During the approximately two hundred–day period of hibernation, bears may develop new footpads. Dens are returned to, in some cases, year after year.

Black bears are good climbers (no pitons required), hence the climbing scars observed on trees in groves of aspen. Cubs can, with enviable ease, shimmy up a towering ponderosa in split seconds, to peer down with their curious button eyes and furry rounded ears, while looking for all the world like a carved totem pole. Adults, despite their lumbering gait, are good runners, achieving bursts of speed up to thirty-five mph. Bears have excellent hearing and a keen sense of smell.

Bears are easily habituated to humans. Moreover, they've developed an unhealthy preference for the fast food on tap from garbage cans and bird feeders. At least one observer is convinced that some members of the local bear population are beginning to show signs of obesity. The garbage habit is, in any case, not a healthy one. A bungicord attached to a garbage can, despite the best intentions, will prove insufficient to foil a hungry bear. They are much too smart, resourceful, and strong. Bird feeders must be ingeniously rigged far from a climbable tree or a long reach, possibly on pulleys. House doors with lever-style handles are easily opened by bears. Keeping such doors securely locked—not to mention keeping easily entered, low-lying windows closed—is a good way to prevent bears from becoming house burglars. Mother bears and cubs that break and enter are most often exterminated. Garbage should ideally be stored in strong bear-proof garbage sheds or some kind of 100 percent guaranteed bear-proof receptacle. Even with these precautions, the best strategy is to wait until the last possible minute for trash day pick-ups.

The city parks and recreation department has designed, among other wonderful resources, an attractive user-friendly picnic area for visitors to Red Rock Canyon Open Space. Users are advised not only to exercise extreme care in disposing of their garbage, but to "pack it out!" in order to avoid setting up a fast-food joint for the enterprising bruins. Troublesome bears (which face the maximum sentence for violations) are all too often created by human carelessness.

If a park visitor should happen to surprise a bear or to be equally surprised by one, the advice generally given is to raise your arms high up over your head, making yourself appear as large as possible. Speak audibly and calmly and back away as you face the bear. Bears are generally not dangerous. However, one should take pains to avoid encounters while they are eating or when they are, one is tempted to say, "hungry as a bear," in the late spring or early summer, after emerging from winter dormancy and the end of the spring period of "walking hibernation."

A sow with cubs is to be strictly avoided. She will be more than protective, particularly if a "two-legged" gets between her and her cubs. A foot stamp or a snorting— almost pig-like—"huff" constitutes a warning, and to stand frozen like a statue might be interpreted as a challenge. Follow the instructions and concede to the sow or, as the case may be, the boar's desire for more flight space.

Droppings and tree claw marks along trails are proof that bears appreciate the ease of traversing the hills on a path, just as much as humans do, not to mention hoofed mammals, such as deer and elk. Indeed, it was the trails made by animals throughout the West that were first used by Indians. These trails, in turn, were later followed by explorers, trappers, militia, missionaries, and early settlers.

The Mountain Ute enjoy a special relationship with bears, which will be further explored in the chapter on early human history.

Mountain Lion

One day, quite early, not so many moons ago, a well-known jogger in these parts was taking his morning run. Perhaps it was a premonition or a sense of being watched. Whatever it was, his focus suddenly shifted to a rock ledge above the trail where he was running. There in early morning light, lazily sunning itself like a magnificent sculpture was a large and handsome solidly muscled feline sporting a handsome tan coat. He stretched to six feet in length, and weighed in at about one hundred and thirty pounds. His heavy, graceful black-tipped tail that seemed to have a life of its own was a point of pride, like an elder's walking stick used for purposes of balancing. His topaz-gold eyes were fixed on the runner's every move.

Can you spot the mountain lion? Scott Flora had this to say about the photograph he took of the large feline: "This is the original photograph. … I was a little intimidated to get any closer without a camouflage blind, a baseball bat, or a large SUV. I did feel brave at the time!"

Mountain lions are known to purr or to utter a coughing snarl or a high-pitched screech—like a tomcat with a megaphone, if it happens to be an amorous male. But this big cat, with its many names—from cougar and puma to panther and catamount—remained silent. Despite its vaunted ability to purr, in no sense could it be regarded as simply a very large kitty cat with enormous paws. Wild it was and potentially dangerous. The runner, with a sudden spurt of adrenaline, got back to his car in record-breaking time. When he reached his vehicle, a small eternity later, he discovered that his neck ached from all the swiveling action. But his attempt to locate the big cat had been in vain. Ghost-like and secretive, it had vanished with the morning mist. It's unlikely, however, that the lion perceived the runner to be a delectable breakfast morsel. Mule deer on the hoof would be its strong preference.

On another occasion, a group of Japanese tourists bristling with Nikon cameras was led on a guided tour of Red Rock Canyon Open Space. Suddenly they spotted a mountain lion flashing through the brush. They were thrilled. But unlike our early morning jogger, they wanted to turn back for an even closer look, in the hope of getting some National Geographic quality shots. The sighting of the mountain lion in its natural habitat not only made their day—it was a highlight of their Colorado visit.

Mountain lions are counted as a keystone species, defined as a "species critical to [the] natural function and maintenance of [a] particular biotic community" (Fitzgerald, et al.). They help keep deer herds healthy by weeding out the sick and weak, sustaining themselves on approximately one deer a week. It is interesting to consider that while the tooth-and-claw relationship between predator and prey, in this instance, is a competitive one, it also has an overall positive and beneficial effect for both communities.

Mountain lions are active throughout the year. These powerful animals can leap forty feet and jump eighteen feet straight up in the air (see *Pikes Peak Region Traveler* by Melissa Walker). Covering large distances, their daily range can be as much as seventy miles. Mostly nocturnal, their favorite habitat is the foothills of the Front Range. Geographically, they are the most widely distributed of any native mammal—yet, today, on the East Coast, native populations are either endangered or extinct. In the state of Colorado, among adult populations, human-caused mortality can be as high as 50 percent. Cubs are sometimes killed by porcupine quills and occasionally by adult males.

The bleached bone–littered lair of a mountain lion was first discovered a few years back in a brushy, overgrown area on a rocky slope in Red Rock Canyon Open Space. The tales of the early morning jogger and the Japanese tourists, not to mention the detail about the lion's lair, may serve to raise alarm. Yet the fact remains that statistically the risks of hiking in the open space are far less than those of crossing a busy street in New York City.

The main thing to keep in mind, as wildlife officials and field biologists are quick to point out, is that when we move into a wildlife area (or when we walk in an open space where such wildlife ranges), we become responsible. That responsibility begins with the need to inform ourselves and become aware of and respectful towards wild animals and their behavior. These experts advise keeping kids close at hand and avoiding solo hikes—as well as dawn or dusk activities—in true wilderness areas. They also stress the importance of keeping pets on leash or safely secured in kennels with a top and sides.

Mountain lions rarely attack humans. In the unlikely event of a mountain lion encounter, the advice given is similar to that when meeting a bear. Raise your arms and your walking stick. If you have a coat, use that, too. Make yourself big. Back away. Speak calmly. Raise kids up high. If you are attacked, do not crouch. Fight back with sticks and stones, aiming for nose and eyes.

It helps to keep in mind that more people are killed in the U.S. each year by dogs, as well as by deer (and this statistic does not include car accidents), than by larger mammals or carnivores. It also pays to be informed and alert. For more information on wildlife and safety, visit the Colorado Division of Wildlife's website at http://wildlife.state.co.us.

In a 2004 Colorado Springs *Independent* story, UC (Davis) field biologist Kent Logan was asked whether or not he thought humans and mountain lions could successfully coexist over the long term. He answered "yes," but said he would call it "a managed coexistence," adding that he personally "wouldn't want to live anywhere where there aren't big, hairy animals."

Mule Deer

Mule deer are the most ubiquitous of our larger mammals. Periodically their numbers have undergone significant declines due to habitat loss and over-hunting. Most recently, such a decline occurred from the 1950s through the mid-1970s. Currently, however, Colorado has the largest population of mule deer in the country.

Mule deer are easily distinguished from their eastern plains cousins, the white-tailed deer. The former have large, mule-like ears. Their satellite dish–like ears that constantly twitch make for acute hearing. They also have big feet, the better to dig for water in arid climes. The mule deer's tail, instead of being white, bushy, and held erect, is thin, drooped, and black-striped. The rump, however, has a large white patch.

Instead of running in graceful leaps like the white-tailed deer, the mule deer bounces like a pogo stick when alarmed. This gait is referred to as a "pronk" or a "stot." When alarmed, a mule deer goes pronking or stotting off at a goodly pace, stopping to take a last look around. The pronking gives him both speed and visibility. Mule deer can also walk, trot, and gallop.

The antlers of mule deer are branched equally (dichotomously) into four main tines, although old bucks may have six or more tines, called "points." Mule deer antlers are not only configured differently, but are generally smaller than the white-tailed deer. The growth of antlers is both initiated and controlled by the length of the day.

Mule deer are adapted to a wide range of habitats. We love seeing them in Red Rock Canyon Open Space and in the surrounding foothills, but are somewhat less enthusiastic about their presence as living yard art in our gardens.

Mule deer are most active in morning, evening, and on moonlit nights. They like to take siestas in a cool spot mid-day. As the Wild Forever Foundation points out, a spotted fawn on its own may appear to be abandoned, but probably isn't. It's just as likely that the mother went off to browse and will be back shortly to collect her young one—or at the very least before nightfall.

During the mating season, the neck of the bucks swell, making them appear bigger than their average weight of 155 pounds, and the height of five feet measured at the shoulder. Being in rut also makes them cranky and potentially dangerous to confront. After mating, young females typically give birth to one offspring; while older, healthy females may produce twins, either in May or June. Fawns lose their light dorsal spots after the fall molt in August.

Lesser Fauna

There are any number of smaller mammals that call Red Rock Canyon Open Space and the nearby foothills home. Several, if not all of the following, have been observed in their natural habitats or passing through. These include, among others, the bobcat, coyote, rabbit, skunk, red fox, raccoon, vole, bat, Abert's squirrel, and rock squirrel.

Interesting Facts about the Smaller Mammals in the Area

Abert's Squirrel: Abert's is one of the most beautiful of the squirrels and is easily recognized by its tufted ears and handsome black glossy coat and bushy tail. The Abert's squirrel makes its home in ponderosa pines, where it builds the squirrel equivalent of a starter castle. Its large spherical nest of twigs and leaves may measure as much as three feet in diameter. Like all squirrels, Abert's sometimes forget where they've hidden a cache of seeds. Thus, they become by default cooperative gardeners as the seeds they so industriously buried germinate into new trees. The piles of shredded pinecones stripped down to seeds, which squirrels eat, are called "kitchen middens."

Skunks: There are four species of skunks in Colorado, the striped skunk being most widespread. The skunk boasts a powerful "scent" that won't let you forget, which it can spray to a maximum distance of twenty feet, with a range of accuracy of half that distance, thus effectively establishing its claim to its designated territory and beyond. The unmistakable and long-lasting spray is made of a sulfur-containing compound.

Both spotted and striped skunks are reported to be able to break open bird eggs by throwing them backward between their legs up against a hard surface. Skunks have also evolved a high resistance to snake venom, possibly because their usual defenses don't work with snakes. This is surprising since snakes are able to pick up odors with their chemically sensitive receptors, including paired pouches that open in the roof of the mouth cavity. But the skunk's built-in immunity has turned the snake into prey. Skunks are mostly nocturnal.

Raccoon: Until recently, raccoons were uncommon in Colorado. Changing habitats, however, have resulted in their increasing numbers. The raccoon's bandit-like mask, ringed tail, and shadowy black and gray markings provide an effective camouflage, making it difficult for nighttime predators to see them. Raccoon paws, with their long slender "fingers," five in number, resemble small human hands, except for the claws. Raccoons can open, unlock, and unscrew just about anything.

Bobcat: Larger than the domestic cat, the bobcat, with its short, black-tipped bobbed tail can move easily through dense brush. Tawny with a reddish hue in summer and grayish buff in winter, it has dorsal spots, stripes on its legs, bars on its tail, tufted ears, striped cheeks and a ruff about its face. Its habitat is piñon-juniper woodlands and montane forests in rocky hills and canyons. Mostly a nocturnal hunter, the bobcat ambushes its prey of rabbits and rodents. The occasional chicken or turkey is also sometimes taken, explaining why in some states this distinctive feline is still regarded as a "varmint." According to Fitzgerald et al in *Mammals of Colorado,* "bobcats scent-mark with feces, urine, and anal gland secretions, rubbed on objects or discharged on the ground."

Coyote. A well-established pack of coyotes serenades the western skies in Red Rock Canyon. (Photo courtesy Bill Koerner)

The Porcupine

Recently, the family dog had an unexpected encounter with a very large porcupine busily stripping the bark from a ponderosa. Little Bear, pushing his luck with total disregard for the consequences, ended up with a nose full of quills. The effect was all three: alarming, funny, and pathetic. The porcupine's quills are not, as commonly supposed, shot from his well-stocked quiver of some thirty thousand quills. Instead they are administered with a well-aimed slap of the tail, as the porcupine turns in a defensive circle. The quills (which are actually rough, hardened hairs) are sharp and barbed at the end. They swell with blood, increasing the difficulty of extraction. According to *Mammals of the Rockies* (Fisher *et al.*), porcupine quills may cause infection, "blind an animal, prevent it from eating, or even puncture a vital organ."

It takes a skilled and steady hand and a large pair of pliers with a wide flat grip to remove them. In this case, we counted some thirty quills extracted, while making certain none was left to fester. The dog moaned pitifully throughout the procedure and even bled, but did not attempt to bite the family member holding him or the one performing surgery. Twenty minutes later, he was none the worse for wear, but his people were still a bit shaken. Did he learn his lesson?

Coyote: The coyote, like the fox, is viewed as being clever, wily, and imbued with special powers, particularly in Ute creation myths. The elimination of its main predator, the gray wolf, among other causes has resulted in increased population densities throughout the West. According to information from the Colorado Springs Wild Forever Foundation, it is only the alpha male and female of a pack that mate. Thus, when one member of the alpha pair dies, the pack is no longer regulated, since new pairings and/or random mating may result in more than the average number of litters. This may help explain why their numbers have increased despite the human attempts to regulate them.

Dr. D.J. Obee observes in his book on Colorado mammals that while the red fox enjoys a reputation for cleverness, the coyote surpasses him in this attribute. He states that "… the extreme craftiness of this species, along with the fact that he is able to make himself at home" just about anywhere, may also help explain why its numbers have increased despite being hunted and trapped. Coyotes or "song dogs," as they are sometimes known, are famous for their yip-yipping vocalizations. Obee describes the unforgettable effect of moon-lit coyote choruses: "Where present, his typical howling, heard usually at night, is just as much a part of a mountain evening as the sunset itself."

Red Fox: The red fox sports a red coat, black stockings, and a black-tipped tail and rejoices in a reputation for being cunning and clever, hence the name "Reynard" in French (from *renard,* referring to someone who is too clever to be vanquished). The body of the red fox is dapper and lithe, particularly after shedding its warm and luxuriant winter coat. With its light frame and long legs, it is able to leap gracefully from ground level up to a flat surface six feet above.

After mating in the winter months, females give birth to a litter of between one to ten kits in spring. One mother, however, was observed feeding thirteen small, furry gray kits who were as playful and rambunctious as kittens. Since Ma Fox comes equipped with only eight mammary glands, the pups took turns and she stood up to accommodate the maximum number at a feeding, which included all thirteen, both queue-jumpers and late comers. The most eager of the eaters would jockey for position, attempting to nudge others out of the way.

Two adults, presumably the parents, worked together to supervise the nursery where day-long games of tag, pouncing and wrestling in a safe, sun-warmed spot provided invaluable training for later hunts. The adults job-shared. While one adult vigilantly guarded the nursery, the other hunted for food, often in early morning and late evening. Prey, including rodents, was carried back to the den. By late summer the kits were dispersed—except for a quartet who apparently decided to adopt as their personal territory their natal birthplace. Red foxes have a high, raspy bronchial bark. If a prey is out of reach, they may stand and bark out of simple frustration and pique.

Bats: Bats have been evolving since the Eocene Epoch, fifty to sixty million years ago. They are the only mammals capable of flight. Because of their thick skin, they, like elephants, are sometimes referred to as "pachyderms."

The Microchiropters found in Colorado are the small echolocating bats (as opposed to the Old World fruit bats). The Microchiropters emit ultrasonic sounds that produce echoes, by which they navigate. Of the eighteen species of bats in Colorado, the Western Pipistrelle is the smallest. This two-and-a-half inch long bat weighs slightly more than a penny and has a slow, erratic butterfly-like flight. It is common in canyonlands.

Another common bat is the Little Brown Bat. It migrates to areas in the foothills in the fall where there are caves, which do exist in Red Rock Canyon Open Space. Before hibernating, the bats mate. After winter hibernation, sometime in late June and early July, females give birth to one or two offspring.

The Townsend's Big-eared Bat is listed as a "species of special concern" in Colorado by the Colorado Department of Wildlife (CDOW). These insect-gleaning bats, with their dumbo-sized ears, typically roost in rock outcroppings, caves, and tree cavities. Like other bats, Townsend's can catch insects with the membranes of their wings and tails and shovel them up to their mouth. The manmade lakes in the open space offer ideal foraging habitat for the bats. Red Rock Canyon property was described by Greystone Environmental Consultants in their 2004 report as affording "medium to high quality habitat for the bat," whose numbers are diminishing.

Because Microchiropters are insectivores, they are good citizens, providing a useful service by consuming large numbers of night-flying insects. While rabies in bats is extremely rare, caution is advised in handling them, as they do bite. A bat that is active during the day is not behaving normally and should not be handled.

Other small mammals and rodents that are probable residents of Red Rock Canyon Open Space include the pocket golfer, deer mouse, prairie dog (in small numbers), and the gold-mantled ground squirrel.

Reptiles: Snakes and Lizards

While snakes often figure in mythology as symbols of fertility (among Hindus, snakes such as the cobra are considered sacred and are fed bowls of milk), they also provide an important service. Bullsnakes, rattlesnakes, and other predators help control rodent-born diseases as well as the vectors that carry them. Snakes, in turn, are preyed upon by foxes, coyotes, badgers, hawks, as well as eagles, among others.

Red Rock Canyon Open Space, with its arid, high-desert scrubland and rocky outcroppings, provides good habitat for the bullsnake (also known as the Great Basin gopher snake), as well as for rattlers. Most experts appear to agree that bullsnakes do not, as is sometimes reported in popular literature, eat rattlers. But they do compete for habitat—with the result that where there are bullsnakes, there may be fewer rattlers.

Bullsnakes are sometimes mistaken for rattlers because they have a diamond-shaped head and, when alarmed, will coil and brush their tail against dry brush to make a rattling sound. However, the bullsnake is much more striking in its appearance, with its large, brown-black blotches on a soft yellow background. Long and heavy bodied, measuring between thirty-six to one-hundred inches, the bullsnake tends to be more docile than the rattler, but it can hiss impressively when disturbed. A powerful constrictor, this legless reptile rejoices in an interesting love life. It finds its mate by following a scent trail she lays down like a scented lace handkerchief in a Victorian romance. A bullsnake has been observed in the open space undulating through the grass.

Like bats, the bullsnake, as noted, provides an important service. Harmless, if imposing, he is an effective eradicator of unwonted rodents, helping to maintain balance. The bullsnake thus occupies an important ecological niche. Ranchers, for example, have come around to a genuine appreciation of the bullsnake, welcoming him as a friend and valued ally, whether in field or barn.

The Rap on Rattlesnakes: Some Cold-blooded Facts

There are an estimated thirty to fifty species of rattlesnakes in the New World, depending on the source, with the greatest concentration being found in the Southwest and Mexico.

Of the twenty-five species of snakes in Colorado, the western or prairie rattlesnake and the massasauga are the only venomous species. The western rattlesnake appears in most habitats throughout the state. The massasauga, however, is limited to the southeastern grasslands. There are four subspecies of the western rattlesnake and one is very commonly found in Garden of the Gods and in Ute Valley Park. Since these parks have the same plant communities and rock types as Red Rock Canyon Open Space, it is a good bet that it will be present here as well.

The rattlesnake is a member of the pit viper family (Crotalidae), well represented by 182 species world-wide. The pit viper not only has rows of teeth, it possesses fangs. In addition, it sports a pair of telltale pits on either side of its head. These infrared sensing devices are located between each slanted eye (with its vertical as opposed to rounded pupils) and each nostril on either side of the head. Able to detect variations in temperature, the heat-sensitive pits help the snake to locate its warm-blooded prey.

The rattler also employs its flickering forked tongue—in addition to its heat-sensitive head pits—to hunt. Its tongue is said to act as a chemical receptor, picking up chemicals emitted by its prey. With this combined and sophisticated apparatus, it experiences no problem in hunting at night. Although the rattler's vision is not acute, it can see movement. Unresponsive to airborne sound, it is alert to vibrations from the ground.

Measuring on the average of 33.5 inches in length, the western rattlesnake (a.k.a. Prairie rattler) has a thick body with a dull skin as opposed to glossy. Its dorsal scales are keeled. The rattler's broad, triangular head (unlike that of the bullsnake) is noticeably larger than its body. The head is set on a narrow neck above a splotchy skin that is tannish in the background, with a tapestry of dark blotches, the numbers of which depend on the snake's length. These desert fatigues of tan, stamped with dark, Rorschach-like graphics that flatten out to rings on the tail affords the western rattler an effective camouflage.

The rattler carries his rattle at the tip of his tail, which vaguely resembles a bony, finger-like extension, with its segmented, bead-like rattles terminating in a blunt edge. The rattlesnake reportedly likes to travel with his tail pointed up. Perhaps he is displaying a certain pride of ownership in his fine instrument—to which no other snake can lay claim.

Composed of the horny material keratin, a new segment of the rattle is produced each time skin is molted, which may be a few times a year for a healthy snake. It is these bead-like tail segments knocking together that produce the rattling sound. Occasionally, rattles may be broken off or lost, but molting snakes will get a new one. If a rattlesnake gets his tail soaking wet, his rattle will not rattle. Crossing a creek thus may reduce him to silence. Newborns do not have rattles. Adult rattlesnakes, it should be noted, do not always necessarily rattle before they strike, and sometimes they administer what is known as a "dry bite," meaning they have already used up their venom or they are not unduly disturbed or, more accurately, not too badly rattled.

It's the Pits: Some Strange and Counterintuitive Facts about Snakes

- Snakes are ectothermic. They avoid temperature extremes, preferring to hunt in mild conditions during the day in good weather, possibly at night in the heat of summer.
- Rattlers can bite even after they have been injured or killed until rigor mortis sets in.
- While most snakes lay eggs like reptiles, the female rattler, who typically mates in spring, gives live birth to a brood, averaging about twelve babies. Moreover, the babies are as potent as their elders, but their size limits the amounts of venom they are capable of delivering.
- Some ground squirrels show an interesting and unusual resistance to snake venom and are even known to kick up dirt at the snakes.
- In winter, rattlesnakes crawl into rocky crevices and caves and lie dormant. Sometimes up to a hundred snakes or more use the same crevice as a communal den. (One den in a basement in Kiowa County was cited as having contained three hundred snakes, 50 percent of which were rattlers.) Rattlesnakes will sometimes occupy the burrows of small mammals such as prairie dogs.

To prevent unwanted rattler encounters, be observant. Sweep the trail with your eyes, look before you sit down, watch your step among boulders, rock outcroppings, on ledges, and when stepping over log—and don't poke your hand into crevices without looking first. If you should meet a rattler, stop, remain still for a moment, until the *snake* calms down, then back away and give it a good flight distance. Rattlers can strike faster than the eye can see and at distances of up to two-thirds of their body length. If the snake is upset, it may not assume the S-coiled position.

In the highly unlikely event of a bite, it is no longer advised to suck out the venom or incise the puncture. Instead the best procedure is to immobilize the affected area, keeping it lower than the heart. Remove anything that constricts circulation in the region of the bite. Remain calm and seek medical attention immediately. It is reassuring to know that no one has ever actually reported having seen a rattler in Red Rock Canyon Open Space. Furthermore, bites from rattlers these days are rarely fatal.

Hammerson in his classic text, *Amphibians and Reptiles in Colorado*, states that the number of western rattlesnakes is on the decline due to persecution by their foremost predator, humans. He reminds us that rattlesnakes are "an interesting and significant component of Colorado's natural habitat, and they warrant the protection and careful management afforded other wildlife. They pose very little risk to humans (much less than riding in an automobile, playing most sports, or smoking)."

Lizards

At least two, and probably more, varieties of lizards may occur in Red Rock Canyon Open Space. These include the boulder sun-basking and scurrying western fence lizard, with its ridged brown scales and blue belly; and far less likely, but possible, the horny toad or horned lizard. The western fence lizard has a most unusual feature. If a lyme-carrying tick feeds on it, the lyme bacteria will be neutralized by a protein that occurs in the blood of the lizard. The result is that the tick's bite will no longer prove harmful to humans.

As for the horned lizard or horny toad, it sports a double ridge of spines running from front to back leg on a brown to gray body (protective camouflage that does not change like the chameleon's, but does blend color-wise into its environment). Wide and pancake-flat with distinctive horns that seem to bristle like an arsenal, together with its spine, it resembles nothing so much as a small dinosaur. On earth long before humans were, horned lizards are a member of the iguana family. They have been evolving for millions of years. Widely distributed and with many species, they are native only to western North America, where their numbers are dwindling due to habitat pressures.

The favorite food of horny toads is harvester ants. During rainfall, the horny toad has been observed to lower its head and hunch its back in such a fashion that the rain is able to funnel conveniently off it into its mouth. Hammerson cites credible studies that support the idea that horny toads do on rare occasion squirt blood from their lower eyelid as a defense mechanism, employed strictly against foxes and coyotes, but not other potential predators. The blood is evidently distasteful to these carnivores.

> Don Ellis writes about horned lizards/horny toads in an informative and charming *Red Rock Rag* piece that can be viewed on the Friends of Red Rock Canyon website (RedRockCanyon Openspace.org). Ellis describes finding horny toads and carrying them in "a boy's pocket" to Midland School, a half mile east of the Red Rock Canyon Open Space, when he was growing up. He also notes that the horny toad seemed to occupy its own unique ecological niche determined by, among other things, the protective camouflage of its color. Never could this observant young naturalist find a horny toad outside the parameters of a certain well-defined area. It was as if a line had been clearly drawn. Where there was gray-brown Pierre Shale, there were also horny toads. While the probability of its presence in the open space is not high, the horny toad may occur in a few spots where Pierre Shale in the habitat matches its coloring.

Ancient peoples were both inspired and intrigued by these miniature rhino-like reptiles, and they found their way as models, along with other lizards, into artistic southwestern pottery designs as well as the rock art of pre-historic peoples.

Because of their partiality for ants, horned lizards have been used in the past for ant control, sometimes having been shipped to states and countries where the environment was unsuitable. For this and other reasons, several states have placed the horned lizard in a protected status.

Birds in Red Rock Canyon Open Space
Hummingbirds

One of the most celebrated long-distance migrants, despite its diminutive size and four-inch wingspan, is the broad-tailed hummingbird and—slightly later in summer

(July and August)—the feisty and territorial rufous, whose name describes his color. If the rufous weighed ten pounds, he'd rule the world.

The male broadtails, with their twittery calls and the hum and whistle of their wings, arrive in Colorado Springs about mid-April, before the females, in order to establish their territory. The Starsmore Discovery Center advises hummer aficionados to put out feeders by tax day and leave them up until October. Departure is in mid- to late September, but there may be a few stragglers. The last to leave are the females and juveniles.

O birds, your perfect
virtues bring
Your song, your forms
your rhythmic flights ...
—Ralph Waldo Emerson

There is no need to worry about tempting hummingbirds to overstay their visits, say the experts, even by the long-term availability of food in feeders. You will not be setting up an unhealthy dependency, since hummingbird migration patterns are purely a matter of instinct. (Feeders should, however, be cleaned regularly and filled with a mixture of one cup sugar to four cups water, brought to a boil, then with heat reduced, simmered just a short time until sugar is thoroughly dissolved. Cool before filling.)

The male broadtail is an iridescent green and sports a chic, rose-red gorget that is absent in the female. Brilliant as a Spanish matador, his spring courtship displays feature spectacular aerial sky dives and acrobatics. He performs these displays while facing the sun in order to show off his resplendent plumage to the admiring female. After mating, the female lays two, coffee bean–sized eggs. The nest is built of soft materials, such as moss and leaves, with lichen providing the camouflage. The tiny nest is then held together by the structural steel of spider webs.

Man, he sure is showin' proud
Lookin like tiger yiye in na sun
Wid his sword held high
He goona take y'all on.
—Clinton Boy Jackson

Hummingbirds are called "flower kissers" by the Portuguese. According to *National Geographic* (Jan. 2007), hummingbirds visit up to one thousand flowers daily to lick up the nectar with their long tongues (thirteen licks per second state Miller and Nelson in *Hummingbirds of North America*). They are partial to tubular flowers and the color red. By transporting pollen that falls on their heads and beaks, they help pollinate other plants.

Broadtails are long-distance migrants, capable of traveling non-stop in their five hundred mile, twenty-hour-long crossing of the Gulf of Mexico. The rufous's journey is even more impressive, covering twenty-five hundred miles—all the way from Mexico to Alaska. Not only do hummers travel great distances, unlike any other bird they can hover and fly backwards. Their wings sometimes get dirty and sticky from all that darting about and whirli-giging. To clean them, they fly through sprays of water.

Great Blue Heron

From petite to big—in both size and appearance, the great blue heron contrasts dramatically with the hummer. It measures approximately forty-six inches in length and boasts a seventy-two inch wingspan. As a waterbird, with its long, stilt-like legs ideal for wading, it is a surprising and unexpected presence in high desert country. Large, elegant, and immovably statuesque, with its beautiful gray-blue wings folded when at rest or hunting, herons have been observed on ledges and trees near the manmade lake at the entrance of Red Rock Canyon Open Space.

Like hummingbirds, great blue herons are seasonal migrants from the south, arriving in March. Males compete for the best locations in their large, slightly untidy looking condo-style rookeries, with the dominant older males getting the choicest sites. By March 22, the females have begun to arrive from their holiday resorts. The preening males greet their arrival by extending their necks and fanning their handsome slate blue plumage, while squawking invitingly in their best baritone buffo style. The females then commence to look things over. For them, everything is about "location, location, location." A female indicates her interest by accepting a ritual offering of a twig.

At the end of courtship between the 10th and 15th of April, the female lays between three and seven eggs. Pairs job-share in incubating the eggs, which, to say the very least, is a labor-intensive process. The parent who is in residence (while the other is away gathering food) stands up every twenty to thirty minutes and gently turns each egg with its beak, so that it warms evenly. This pattern continues for close to a month, when in Mid-May, the eggs in the clutch begin to hatch in the same order they were laid. If seven eggs were laid, that adds up to an astonishing, Guinness Book world record of (if my math is correct) approximately 10,080 egg rolls per clutch during the month-long period of incubation.

Raptors

The raptors in the open space and surrounding hills and plains are both strong and endowed with incredible sight. They can spot their prey from miles off. They are also the chief predators of snakes, as well as rodents, since snakes cannot sense their aerial approach through vibrations transmitted on the ground.

Golden Eagle: The third-largest raptor in western North America and has been sighted in Red Rock Canyon Open Space. It has mottled brown feathers covering its entire body. Even its legs and toes are feathered. Its prey includes rabbits, ground squirrels, prairie dogs, snakes, and carrion.

Red-tailed Hawk: The most common and widespread hawk in North America. It is a large bird that holds its wings in a shallow "V" during flight, with a wingspan of fifty inches. The red-tailed hawk displays breathtaking aeronautical skill as it circles, glides, soars, and dives. Such displays are at their peak at mid-morning, when the thermals it rides are at their best. The red-orange of the wedge-like uppertail and the paler color of the undertail are beautifully illuminated by bright sunlight during the red-tail's flight in the vast blue dome of a Colorado sky. The scream of red-tailed hawks, while they are courting, hunting, or warning others away, is both dramatic and unmistakable—indeed, blood-curdling enough for an Alfred Hitchcock thriller.

Peregrine Falcon and Prairie Falcon: Two other beautiful and sensitive species among raptors that may be sighted sailing in the lake-blue sky or arrowing swiftly down for a sudden strike as they scope out some scurrying rodent in the fields below are the peregrine falcon and the prairie falcon. When bounty-hunting was at its peak in the 1920s and 1930s, the ranks of the prairie falcon were decimated. But its numbers today, while significantly reduced, are beginning to stabilize. It is listed as "threatened" by CITES (the Convention on the International Trade in Endangered Species of wild fauna and flora).

The bald eagle, our national symbol, and the Mexican spotted owl, are two other raptors singled out in the Greystone report as being among either listed or sensitive species that have the potential to occur on the Red Rock Canyon Open Space. Because the bald eagle builds its nest in large living trees, typically near water, and hunts for fish and prairie dogs, "which constitute a large prey base," the probability of occurrence of bald eagles on the property is not high. However, it may visit the site on a temporary basis while foraging—especially near the manmade pond.

Red-tailed hawks generally prefer rural settings for their nest building, but have been known to make national news by setting up housekeeping (a bit too messy for some, with their dropped bits of raw meat and tendency to white-wash façades of elegant buildings) in a swank, high-end condo apartment building in upper Fifth Avenue in New York City. This pair, famously known as Pale Male and First Mate, inspired both heated controversy and a loyal and devoted following. Pairs are known to stay together for extended periods and may be monogamous for life, returning to the same nest season after season. During incubation of eggs, the attentive male appears regularly with life support.

Another popular pair of red-tailed hawks has built a nest at the Franklin Institute in Pennsylvania, where the twosome and family are being constantly monitored by camera and enthralled fans.

Bald Eagle: The bald eagle has a wingspan of six and a half feet and mates for life. Although a sensitive species, it is no longer considered endangered and was removed from the endangered species list in 2007. The bald eagle represents a good news story when it comes to preservation, testifying to the success of laws that in 1972 banned the use of DDT, as well as to the effective implementation of the Endangered Species Act. Across the U.S. the numbers of bald eagles have surged from five hundred to ten thousand nesting pairs. The female is bigger than the male, weighing up to fourteen pounds. Bald eagles can live in the wild for up to thirty years. Because of Colorado's relatively mild winter, some twelve hundred bald eagles winter over in the state. Bald eagles can often be seen near reservoirs.

Mexican Spotted Owl: These owls roost in old growth and mixed coniferous forests. Greystone rated the Red Rock Canyon wildlands as being "critical habitat for the Mexican spotted owl." The report is also quick to point out that this does not necessarily mean the Mexican spotted owl is present throughout the area. The field survey suggests instead that it would most likely be present along the sides of the canyons, primarily to the south and west, where there are denser ponderosa pine and Douglas fir stands.

Additional raptors that are considered likely candidates to use the area include: Swainson's hawks, sharp-shinned hawks, American kestrels, merlins, Cooper's hawks, northern goshawks, northern harriers, and ferruginous hawks.

Other Common Avian Visitors and/or Year-round Residents

All birds have both a call and a song. The chickadee's call (which is issued as a warning and a declaration of territory) repeats its name with a hoarse, scolding "dee, dee, dee." Its lyric, flute-like song of romance sounds more like "spring's here, spring's here," sung in clear and perfect thirds with repeated refrains. The nuthatch runs up trees and then precipitously down them again, headfirst, as it forages in the bark for insects. Look for nuthatches in conifer forests.

The bold and noisy family of jays, who are related to crows, are easy to spot, whether it's the crestless scrub jay (a year-round nesting species) with its blue head and wings and long blue tail (juveniles are grayish above), or the darker, uniformly blue Steller's jay (a year-round visitor) with its black head and long black crest. The Steller's is providential enough to bury acorns for the winter, in imitation of the squirrel. The blue jay (a spring, summer, fall visitor), with its black-barred wings, white patches, and blue crest is the most showy and sartorially splendid of the three.

Not related to jays, but equally striking in its appearance is the western rufous-sided towhee, (a resident nesting species), which is a bit smaller than the robin—with its white spots and stripes on an orange-brown background and its habit of rustling around in leaves at ground level, where it builds its nest.

Various types of sparrows and the cosmopolitan American robin (who doesn't sing to attract mates or advertise territory, but rather to announce the fact that a new clutch of eggs is about to hatch), along with the thieving, black-billed magpie (a resident nesting species) and the scolding American crow (a year-round visitor) will doubtless make their presence seen and heard. Not to be ignored is the wood-tapping and attractive northern flicker (a resident nesting species), with its red shafts.

Both in its call and plumage, another attention-getter is the liquid burbling red-winged blackbird. A lovely, fluted warbling is the specialty of the house finch (a resident nesting species). With any luck, in summer one may also be privileged to hear the melodic, heart-lifting song of the meadowlark. This may be punctuated by the hoarse honking of Canada geese, their flight-forming "V" flung out like a fishing net. A summer-nesting resident to look for is the blue-gray gnatcatcher. The sad cooing of the mourning dove offers a nostalgia trip that is always pleasurable.

Canada geese in snow. (Photo courtesy Bill Koerner)

Don Ellis grew up not far from Red Rock Canyon Open Space. He records his memories in a lyrical account appearing in the *Red Rock Rag* (Vol. 3, No. 4). Spring, he recalls, was heralded, not by the robin, "businesslike in his red vest, industriously extracting earthworms from the front lawn, but by the meadowlark standing erect on a fence post, yellow bib bared to the world, trilling" its song, which is unmistakable in its variable series of bubbling, flute-like notes. This experience, he believes, is one reason why he is "so passionate about preserving a natural Red Rock Canyon, preserving a wild place where our increasingly urbanized and regulated community can readily reconnect with the meadowlark and the pasque flower, the dynamic order of nature in contrast to the designed and manicured order of the city." Ellis concludes his reminiscences with the affecting observation that, "If I could choose to live again the springtime of my life, I would again choose to live it where the meadowlark announces the season of reawakening."

The western meadowlark sports a black "V" on its bright yellow breast. It favors grassland and open fields, weaving its nest out of dry grass into a hair-lined bowl. The young leave the nest before they can fly. This renders the unfledged hunter-gatherers vulnerable to predators as they search for food. Thus, to preserve the western meadowlark, grasslands must also be preserved.

Not to be forgotten in any preliminary list of birds found in Red Rock Canyon Open Space is the raven. Because of its size, its big bill, its all-black glossy plumage, and its deep throaty croaks and hoarse vocalizations—as well as its aerial stunt-like rolls, tumbles, and dives—the raven has inspired a large body of lore and literature. From the myths of the Athapascan-speaking coastal Indians of the Northwest to Edgar Allen Poe's well-known poem "The Raven," this bird gets central billing. In Poe's poem, the raven is described as "this ebony bird beguiling my sad fancy into smiling." Throughout the poem, the bird repeats again and again, like a Greek chorus, that saddest of all words in the English language—"nevermore."

Ravens are considered to be among the smartest of birds. They are also some of the most fearless and expert at aerial maneuvers. Larger than crows, their tail feathers in flight are rounded to a wedge, unlike the crow's, which are squared off. Epic in fields of battle, ravens will challenge hawks twice their size in flight and consistently win— often causing the hawk to drop its food, which the raven then makes off with.

Ravens engage in a variety of complex courtship displays and are thought to pair not only for the year, but for life. According to Donald & Lillian Stokes in their book *Guide to Bird Behavior* (Vol. 3), when nest building, ravens do not pick up twigs from the ground. Instead, they will break off large sticks from trees. These can measure up to three feet in length and be close to one inch in diameter. Nesting sites may be used for up to one hundred years.

From Crickets to Butterflies to Wolf Spiders

Crickets, grasshoppers, bees, beetles, ants, butterflies, including the monarch, and other arthropods such as the black widow spider, the wolf spider, scorpion, millipede, and centipede are among the animals that occupy the open space. Of all the phyla, arthropods are the largest in number of species. By the 1980s, according to Smallwood and Anderson in their text *Biology*, "one million different species [had] been named and described." The list continues to get longer, with countless millions more remaining unknown in tropical rain forests. One defining characteristic of the vast phylum, which includes insects, arachnids, and myriapods, is their segmented body—in addition to the presence of an exoskeleton and the absence of a backbone. Among these invertebrates, the highly diverse order of beetles has the largest number of described species. While no official census has been taken, there are doubtless vast numbers of insects that hop, buzz, scurry, skitter, crawl, scuttle, sting, jump, burrow, spin, and flutter as they pursue their various arthropod lives in the Red Rock Canyon Open Space. Often they play beneficial roles as nature's sanitation engineers and pollinators, with each fulfilling a clearly defined need in its own highly specialized ecological niche.

Insects

The field cricket is a wonderful homebuilder as well as a singer. But in late summer, usually around August, it is the male tree cricket that tunes up so audibly for its nightly serenades. (A different species of cricket altogether sings in spring. But it fails to achieve the same dramatic effect or fortissimo as its late summer counterpart, that is the true Pavarotti of the cricket world.) The female cricket does not stridulate or rub her wings together to produce a song. Instead, she plays the role of music critic, deciding which vocalist stands out as the best performer and holds the greatest appeal.

The cricket's instrument is its specialized and enlarged veins on its wings. The scraper on the left wing is rubbed against the file on the right wing to produce sound. The performers themselves "hear" the sounds of other crickets through the tympanum located on their front legs—in effect, hearing with their elbows. Their vocalizations, which can be affected by the temperatures and even the amount of moisture in the soil, include chirps and trills, and a repertoire of several types of songs. These include the "calling," "mating," and "staying together" song, as well as a "rivalry" song (to warn off competitors vying for the attention of their lady love). While the chorus may sound as if it's singing and pulsating in unison, some individuals deliberately sing in a contrapuntal, offbeat cadence, so as to stand out better from all the competition. These annual and highly vocal cricket concerts, commencing at dusk in late summer, serve as a prelude to coming fall.

The dragonfly is an ancient species. This flying fossil favors riparian settings where things are moist and they can prey upon abundant mosquitoes. As a sensitive species, its presence is considered an indicator of the health of wetland environments. Dragonflies come in a range of luminescent colors. The fatter, shorter varieties are called "darters," as they dart about, stitching up the sun-spun invisible fabric of the atmosphere. The longer, thinner species that fly up and down and swoop for their prey are called "hawkers."

The adult monarch butterfly and its larva eat milkweed. Milkweed contains a potent poison, which the butterflies store, rendering them poisonous to their predators.

Besides nectar, monarchs need minerals and salts, which they get by gathering in moist places. These congregations are called "puddling clubs."

The monarch chrysalis is jade green and pointillated in gold dots. The caterpillar is colorfully striped in orange and black. The male monarch has a scent gland, which he uses like cologne to attract females.

In terms of its sheer fragile beauty and its record-making flight distances in its annual migration, the monarch is a match for the hummingbird. Monarchs east of the Rocky Mountains overwinter in forest habits in central Mexico. Those living west of the Rockies head to California and areas along the Pacific Coast. However, unlike the hummers, and depending on the latitude, it is the second or third generation who makes the return flight, guided by an internal compass and a hereditary map developed over ten million years, and stored perhaps in their DNA.

It is an impressive pilgrimage, considering how small and fragile is the bark and how great the metaphoric sea. And there are fewer places these days to stop to refuel than there once were—as open fields with milkweed growing in them become increasingly rare commodities. However, some people are beginning to help by planting special gardens at which the wayfarers can stop as they make their way on their long and difficult journey.

Beginning in September, monarchs cover an average of one hundred miles a day, avoiding mountains en route and taking shelter from storms. Some butterflies cover as much as four thousand miles in their migration. By the time the migrants arrive at their destinations, they are doubtless a bit battered and travel-weary. Their arrival in Mexico coincides with *El Dia de los Muertos* or "The Day of the Dead," celebrated by Mexicans and other Hispanics. According to local folk beliefs, the monarchs are the returning souls of dead relatives. One of the monarch's favored destinations in Mexico is a town with the eponymous name of El Rosario. There the monarchs cover the trees in clusters, like thousands of delicate fluttering petals, a virtual forest of butterflies, or perhaps the many strings of a rosary.

Myriapods

Their numbers include the many-legged, light-sensitive centipedes and millipedes, which are often found under rotting logs. They do occur in Red Rock Canyon Open Space as does a harmless western species of scorpion. The only North American species of scorpion harmful to humans is the Arizona bark scorpion, and it is not found in Colorado.

The scorpion, with its long tail and stinger, is active at night. It uses its stinger to paralyze its prey, usually insects and spiders. After sundown, the scorpion goes about busily hunting its prey, which it ambushes. It is, in turn, hunted by centipedes, tarantulas, lizards, birds (especially owls), small rodents, and bats.

Arachnids

The black widow spider is easy to recognize. It is described by Smallwood and Alexander as having "a black body and a large round abdomen with a red or orange hourglass figure on the ventral surface." Its bite causes acute distress, but almost never is fatal. Medical treatment can relieve symptoms. If you do trail work, keep an eye out for the black widow. Lift a rock and you may find a black widow at home.

The wolf spider is one of Colorado's largest arthropods and because of its size (as much as two inches in length) and its hairy appearance, it is frequently mistaken for a tarantula. Wolf spiders do not spin webs, but instead forage for their food. These beneficial, non-poisonous spiders dine out on insects, helping to keep numbers in balance. The conscientious and hard-working females carry their egg sacks around with them in order to protect them from predators. Newly hatched spiderlings climb up on their mother's back, where they travel like babies in carriers. The life span of most spiders is a year. Wolf spiders, however, may live for two or three years.

• • •

From the cricket to the mountain lion to the green gentian or monument plant, the story of the life of any one of the myriad insects, plants, animals, reptiles, or birds that pass through or inhabit Red Rock Canyon Open Space could become the subject of a lifetime's study. The more you look, the more you see how multi-layered, how rich and complex, how limitless is the ecology of this beautiful piece of open space.

Restoration and Planning: A Cooperative Undertaking

A new chapter of this ultimately successful story continues to be written as engaged citizens, city park officials, and volunteer groups, such as the Friends of Red Rock Canyon, work cooperatively on a wide variety of plans and projects to help restore the open space and preserve it over the long run. To this end, citizens of all ages have turned out in sizeable numbers to contribute sweat equity to the building and clearing of trails and to assist in city park department–organized tree plantings, such as ones held on past Arbor Days when hundreds of native trees were planted.

In the years ahead, the problem of noxious weeds and trees growing in Red Rock Canyon Open Space will need continued remediation. John G. Bock, after he began assembling the property parcel by parcel in 1924, undertook to implement a self-directed program of conservation on the land. This included the construction of earthen dams to re-direct water run-off and the planting of trees, shrubs, grasses, and clovers. Some of these measures were ill advised based on our current understanding of the role played by invasive species introduced into native communities. Unlike early succession native plants that colonize an area after fire or floods and prior to the development of mature ecosystems, noxious weeds are pushy and ruthlessly competitive. They immediately set about establishing their dominance and, in no time at all, can wipe out the natives.

For example the Siberian elms, Russian olive trees, and the type of clover John G. Bock may have inadvertently introduced as a part of his conservation plan fall into the invasive, difficult to eradicate category. These dominant and aggressive competitors introduced into the otherwise mutually cooperative communities of native trees and grasses not only obliterate the natives, but often deprive wildlife of important nutrients and protective cover.

The Gravel Quarry

Prior to Red Rock Canyon's acquisition as city open space, the Trust for Public Land (TPL) and the Bocks, working together, had begun to re-seed and restore the gravel quarry, located west of the Dakota Hogback and originally owned and operated by John S. Bock, son of John G. The restoration work was undertaken in order to meet conditions originally outlined in the quarry's licensing contract. After the land was purchased, the city parks department continued in the restoration work already begun on the site. Tons of topsoil were hauled in by truck to replace those previously stripped away by bulldozers. The area was completely re-seeded and planted with native grasses, and a culvert was installed to improve drainage.

The Bock gravel quarry supplied gravel for road resurfacing, including the Pikes Peak Highway. (This same gravel would eventually wash down from the road into fragile mountain tundra, in the process destroying wide swathes of alpine plants and silting up the pristine mountain streams below.) The gravel quarry would prove to be one of John S. Bock's most successful money making enterprises, among several others including the garbage dump, several small trailer camps, and some large and unsightly billboards that operated off of, and capitalized on, the land itself.

The World's Most Beautiful Garbage Dump

As recorded on a Certificate of Designation issued in June 1970 by El Paso County, John S. Bock was granted the right to operate a "sanitary landfill for disposal of solid waste," in return for a fee of $25.00. Bock's fifty-one-acre garbage dump (there's another eight to ten acres in Manitou Springs Section 16) is where western Colorado Springs disposed of most of its garbage until 1987, when it was closed.

Citizens who grew up in the area nostalgically recall looking forward to Sunday drives to the dump for the simple reason that it was located in such a breathtakingly beautiful setting. The city's accumulated waste, however, would eventually fill up Gypsum Canyon—at one time both the deepest and most geologically (as well as paleontologically) interesting of all the canyons on the property. It is one of the supreme ironies in the history of the Red Rock Canyon Open Space that the landfill also was destined both to scare off developers and prove a major stumbling block in its preservation.

It was reportedly John S. Bock's intent to fill Gypsum Canyon in order to create a site for a golf course. This idea was taken up again, some thirty years later, by the Santa Fe developer who hoped to acquire the property and develop it as a world-class golf course, complete with majestic red rocks as a backdrop, worthy of a glossy centerfold in *Golf Digest*. The site, with its flattened and re-seeded grass surface, continues to this day to ferment and settle like a witch's brew, emitting methane gas. The fumes are being siphoned off by a number of chimney-like vents originally installed by Bock at the behest of the State Health Department and is regularly monitored by the city parks and recreation department. (See Chapters 5 and 7 for more details.)

A Brief Note on Wildfire History and Ecology

In the past, fires have occurred in the dump, which, in turn, have been duly managed and repressed. Wildfires, however, were once a common occurrence throughout the grassland and forests of Colorado. Whether lightning-caused or started by native peoples, forest fires have helped shape the ecological adaptations of the ponderosa pine forests, which have evolved over thousands of years. Frequent fires serve to maintain the diversity of forested areas and reduce accumulated bio-fuel, while contributing to park-like open meadows and grasslands, essential to native species of flora and fauna.

Many trees have adapted in highly specialized ways to ancient fire regimes. Some, for example, depend on fires to activate their seeds. Others, such as the aspen, may be charred to sticks by a high-intensity blaze. Yet their growth is actually promoted since their roots underground are adapted not only to survive, but also to regenerate.

Scrub oaks are another fire-adapted species and are meant to burn every fifty years or so. Likewise do the piñon-juniper woodland communities benefit from a regime of frequent fires of moderate scope and intensity. Too many young trees in an area, moreover, can seriously disrupt the benefits of fire ecology, serving instead as a fire ladder carrying fire to the upper canopies of old, established stands. This is especially true of the ponderosa.

Combining Long-term Conservation Goals with Public Use and Information

Starting in mid-September of 2007, at the conclusion of an informative series of educational lectures on Red Rock Canyon Open Space, a related series of public-process meetings was held. Sponsored by the city parks and recreation department, the Pioneers Museum, and Friends of Red Rock Canyon, the goal of the public process was to formulate, with citizen input, an interpretive master plan. The meetings were a classic example of how well and effectively grass-roots democracy in action can work. Skillfully facilitated by Tweed Kezziah and Susan Watkins of Kezziah Watkins consulting firm, the public process offered proof of the power and dynamism of citizen input.

From the start there was wide-spread agreement by citizens that the open space should be kept as much as possible in its undeveloped natural state—allowing, of course, for some judicious landscaping, essential trail and facility building, long-neglected restoration, and the removal, over time, of noxious weeds and trees.

Participants also suggested that, while signage should be informative, educational, and strategically placed to cover topics of interest concerned with geology, human history, ecology, and the like, it should also ideally be kept "minimally invasive." There was a consensus that archeological and paleological sites should be well-protected, but that relevant information could be placed in exhibits in the covered pavilion.

Karlee Thompson, president of the Friends of the Red Rock Canyon, defines "preservation" as including the long-term goal of educating the land stewards of tomorrow through outreach programs aimed specifically at schools. She believes that a critical value to be learned by the next generation of land stewards is "respect for the land itself."

The original concept of setting aside a park that is preserved for future generations to enjoy is generally attributed to the self-trained, western American painter George Catlin in the mid-nineteenth century. One of the first American artists to travel extensively among the Indians of the West, Catlin was both sensitive to and concerned about the potentially negative impact westward expansion might have on these first Americans. He recorded and paid tribute to their lives, not only in his famous and historically detailed series of sketches, portraits, and landscape paintings, but also in his diaries. Catlin's diaries, according to Ute historian Charles S. March, are generally regarded as some of the best of the period.

It was Catlin's deep and fervent hope that Indian civilization would be protected and that the awe-inspiring wildlands through which he traveled could be preserved. These ideas were given clear expression when he memorably wrote that he hoped such preservation could be achieved "by some great protecting policy of government ... in a magnificent park. ... A nation's park, containing man and beast, in all the wild and freshness of their nature's beauty!"

The idea of preservation is more than relevant when considering the abundant and extensive wildlife legacy represented by Red Rock Canyon Open Space, which includes several rare species of plants and animals, as well as endangered communities of trees and plants. To quote some of the conclusions reached by Greystone Environmental Consultants in its 2004 habitat study, the original 789-acre property contains:

> medium- to high-quality habitat for upland generalist species such as coyote, mule deer, raccoon, squirrel, rabbit, magpie, crow, blue jay, robin, and raptors. The man-made pond area provides medium- to high-quality habitat for riparian generalist species ... raptors, and the Townsend's big-eared bat. Medium- to high-quality peregrine falcon and Townsend's big-eared bat nesting habit is also located in several areas on the property. Mexican spotted owl critical habitat likewise does occur over a considerable portion of the property.

Furthermore, the peregrine falcon, a state-sensitive species, has been identified within the range of the property—with three additional areas having been confirmed within El Paso County where peregrines breed. The Arkansas Valley evening primrose and the prairie violet are also prime examples of sensitive plants that occur in the open space—the former in silty clays or looser rocky and sandy soils; the latter in open woodlands, forest openings, and rocky sites.

In addition, there are the communities of narrow-leafed cottonwoods, recognized by the Colorado National Heritage Program as "types of conservation concern." Also in this category, due to "increased fragmentation in the Front Range corridor" are the ponderosa pine and Gambel's oak community and the oak and mountain mahogany grassland. The report further states that the "wetlands area on the property ... although artificially created, could contain rare habitat types and plant species."

Moreover, not just regionally, but nationally, the open space claims unique significance not only for its rich and diverse ecology, serving as critical refuge and wildlife corridor for literally dozens of plant and animal species, but it is also celebrated for its stunning geology. Because the exposed rock in the open space is less broken up than that of its sister park, Garden of the Gods, it offers classic textbook examples dramatically illustrating such geological principles as superposition and overturning. Indeed, the geology of the open space causes geologists and their students alike to swoon— while captivating awe-struck visitors.

Thus, Red Rock Canyon Open Space affords a wonderful outdoor laboratory for future study and field trips that can and will, over the years, help sustain and contribute to the long-term preservation goals of the people who continue to love and support it.

CHAPTER 4

The Early Human History
of Red Rock Canyon

"Everything the Power of the World does is in a circle.
The sky is round, and I have heard that the earth is round like a ball. …
The wind in its greatest power whirls. Birds make their nests in circles,
for theirs is the same religion as ours. The sun comes forth and
goes down again in a circle. The moon does the same, and both
are round. Even the seasons form a great circle in their changing,
and always come back again to where they were.
The life of a man is in a circle and so it is in everything
where power moves."
—Black Elk (Lakota), 1931

"I believe in the infinite variety of human expression."
—Yo-Yo Ma

Everything in Red Rock Canyon Open Space is interrelated—from its ancient geology and ecology, with its abundant native flora and fauna, to its prehistoric and more modern human history. In one sense, Red Rock Canyon is a microcosm of the history of the American Southwest and specifically of Colorado, where human occupation dates back at least twelve thousand years to the end of the Pleistocene (Ice Age).

In another sense, Red Rock Canyon Open Space might be said to represent the reverse side of a telescopic lens. By examining some of the early human history of the greater Southwest—with its richly diverse confluence of three broad streams (Indian, Spanish, and Anglo)—we can learn more about what may have transpired over the centuries on the 1,474-acre open space here in the Pikes Peak region along the Front Range of the Rockies.

Landscapes in the Pikes Peak region are a painter's dream, with their cobalt blue skies, majestic mountains, chaparral and montane forests, and rufous red rocks, interspersed with rapidly shrinking parcels of open space—while in the distance stretch the eastern plains. Prior to its burgeoning population growth and development, the American West was easy to imagine as a vast, empty, un-peopled wilderness— until it was first "discovered" by the Spanish and later "developed" by Anglo settlers. But, on the basis of new evidence and study, we have begun to see the need to dust off some of these old myths and start to re-imagine a very different kind of reality—one which includes bands of hardy and resourceful prehistoric peoples roaming the Pikes Peak region thousands and thousands of years ago, in relatively sizeable numbers.

The Need for an Archeological Survey

Before the Red Rock Canyon property became open space in 2003, no archeological survey had been made of it. But everyone agreed such a survey was of critical importance. As Gene Smith of the Colorado Springs Parks, Recreation, and Cultural Services put it at the time: "We know the area is rich in archeology, in human history, as well as in natural history. The red rocks in Red Rock Canyon Open Space, Garden of the Gods, and Glen Eyrie were part of the same greater ecosystem. The rocks held the heat and the canyons offered shelter. American Indians sheltered and camped here in winter." Moreover, there were snow-fed streams along which to camp, with plentiful game available.

The importance of an archeological survey was further borne out when one was finally done in nearby Garden of the Gods Park in 1993, at which time several important finds were documented. Among these were hearths or fire rings (blackened stones from ancient campfires, often buried three or four feet deep), together with bones of buffalo and other animals that dated back more than three thousand years based on carbon dating. Petroglyphs (that are pecked out of the rock surface, as opposed to "pictographs," which are painted, using pigments from minerals or plants) have also been discovered in Garden of the Gods.

In 1994, a Master Plan was drawn up for the Garden of the Gods Park. Its chief priority was to address some major conservation concerns resulting from the park's high-density use, with an estimated 1.7 million visitors annually. As a part of the process, a workshop was held to which tribal leaders representing several Indian tribes were invited—including the Southern and Northern Ute, Kiowa, Apache, Cheyenne, Arapaho, and Lakota. This gave the tribal elders, as well as the general public, an opportunity to come together, share knowledge, and most importantly, have a say in the plan itself. The Master Plan resulted in trail development and restoration, signage and educational exhibits, and the somewhat controversial removal of several old buildings. It also led to the decision to build the Garden of the Gods Visitor and Nature Center, which was "crucial to the interpretation and stewardship of the park," according to Melissa Walker, a member of the original planning team and former park program coordinator. In the future, Red Rock Canyon would undergo a similar process.

Colorado's Three Prehistoric Hunting-Gathering Culture Stages

The dates for the earliest humans in North America keep getting pushed further and further back into the past as new evidence emerges. It is now thought possible that the earliest Americans may have crossed the Bering land bridge from East Asia sixteen thousand years ago, based on recent studies and DNA evidence, such as that derived from a study of a human coprolite found in the Paisley Caves in south-central Oregon and reported in 2011. Nonetheless, precise dates are subject to ongoing debates.

There are three prehistoric culture stages in Colorado that archeologists have identified and classified. These date back at least fourteen thousand years and include the Paleo-Indian, Archaic, and Late Prehistoric stages. The Paleo-Indian, in turn, consists of the Clovis—currently considered to be the oldest of the prehistoric groups, together with the Folsom and Plano peoples, respectively.

Significantly, we are located squarely in the middle of some of the oldest sites showing human occupation found anywhere in North America. In the state of Colorado alone, there are at least twenty-six thousand known or recorded prehistoric sites, with a total of approximately six thousand combined sites at Fort Carson, a dozen miles south of Colorado Springs, and in Piñon Canyon farther to the southeast beyond Fort Carson.

The Paleo-Indian Stage

The Clovis and Folsom were named after towns in New Mexico, where abundant tools and projectile points were found representative of these two groups. But it was in Dent,

"Pre-historic Man." (From *Sketches of Creation*, 1874, by Alexander Winchell)

"The Hairy Mammoth, ('Elephas primigenius') restored." Hairy mammoths no doubt found viable water holes formed by the glacial runoff from Pikes Peak. (From *Sketches of Creation*,1874, by Alexander Winchell)

Colorado, in the 1920s that the first evidence of Folsom people was discovered. According to E. Steve Cassells in *The Archaeology of Colorado*: "This was the first good association in America of man with mammoth." Clovis points and bones from extinct bison were also found on this site.

All of the early Paleo-Indian groups were remarkably skilled game hunters who crafted ingenious hunting weapons, such as hurtling spears and finely knapped (or flaked) projectile points. The fluting in the skillfully made early North American projectile points represented an innovation that was seen only in the New World. So fine, in fact, were the projectile points produced by the Folsom people that modern flint knappers fail in their efforts to duplicate them. The spear throwing atlatl (an Aztec word), with its reliance on a fulcrum-based design and the laws of physics, was a remarkable hunting weapon for the times.

Courage was also not in short supply as the Paleo-Indians hunted woolly mammoths, which had eight-foot-long tusks, weighed up to ten tons, and towered over their human pursuers. Giant, extinct species of bison, given their enormous size and the nature of the hunting tools employed, further helped ensure that the hunt was a distinctly sportsman-like activity.

More than ten thousand years ago, when the woolly mammoths and giant bison still roamed the earth, glaciers from the last ice age were beginning to recede. Bones from these giant mammals have been found in Colorado near ancient springs once fed by the glaciers, which served as gathering points. Previously, most of the mammal fossils found in the state dated back from between 10,000 to 20,000 BP—including the Columbian mammoth tusk discovered by a Colorado College geology class on a nearby mesa in Colorado Springs in 1950. However, in the fall of 2010, a large and exciting cache of nearly two dozen different Ice Age mammals, including a young female mammoth (appropriately named "Snowy"), several mastodons, a bison skull, a camel, giant sloth, and a Pleistocene horse, all dating back from 75,000 to 125,000 years ago, were unearthed during construction at Snowmass Village, Colorado. Continental mammoths died out about ten thousand years ago. The cause of the animals' extinction may have been overhunting by humans or possibly climate change. Yet another theory postulates that a comet or meteor, sometimes referred to as the "Clovis comet," fell through the atmosphere and struck the glacial ice sheet, killing off all North American megafauna and ending the Clovis culture. Such a meteor hit would have been considerably less cataclysmic, however, than the event that is theorized to have caused the extinction of dinosaurs. Researchers are still puzzling over the mystery of the demise of these ancient relatives of the modern-day elephant.

The Archaic Stage

The history of Archaic peoples ("Archaic" means "ancient" in Greek) is divided into three time-periods that include Early Archaic, Middle Archaic, and Late Archaic (from ten thousand to four thousand years ago). These descendants of the earlier mammoth

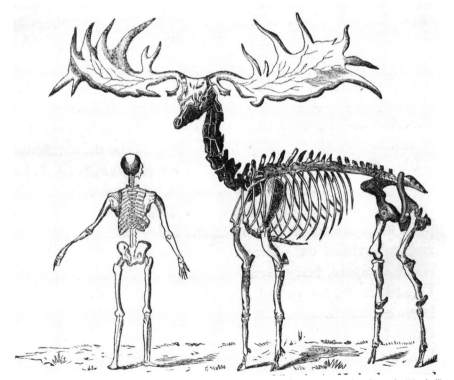

"Skeleton of Extinct Elk … in Comparison with Man." (From *Sketches of Creation*, 1874, by Alexander Winchell)

hunters, who migrated from plains to foothills to mountains in search of food, were all broader-spectrum hunter-gatherers, with ample evidence of the use of metates (large flat or trough-shaped stone mortars) to process foods.

By the time of the Archaic peoples, giant mammals had become extinct. But there was still plentiful game, and the small nomadic bands would follow the herds of elk, deer, antelope, bison, and big horn sheep in their seasonal movements. The Archaic peoples also became adept at the use of snares and traps to capture smaller mammals. In addition, they gathered edible plants such as Indian ricegrass, an attractive grass with a rice-shaped seed, which was used extensively as food by American Indians. (Indian ricegrass is typically found growing along trails and roadsides in Red Rock Canyon Open Space.)

Middle Archaic people not only followed the herds in their seasonal migrations, they probably used bison jumps or herded animals into blind canyons in order to maximize their take. While the Middle Archaic, plains-dwelling people were still using atlatls, by the end of the Late Archaic Period, the bow and arrow may have been introduced. The healthy diet of the Archaic people, which (thanks to improved technology) combined high-protein intake with varieties of roots, tubers, nuts, berries, seeds, and edible plants, resulted in a significant increase in their numbers.

The Archaic peoples, as they traveled from place to place in small bands made up of extended families, probably did not exceed in numbers many more than fifty to a group. They built pit houses as their summer and winter homes. The bark of juniper trees was peeled off in strips to braid sandals, sleeping mats, and ropes, and to make clothing. It is thought that these early people were the first to invent the high-energy power bar known as "pemmican," that consists of dried meat and berries. These ingredients were finely powdered on metate stones, then mixed with hot marrow fat to bind them.

The Late Prehistoric Stage

The Late Prehistoric stage is a broadly conceived term, the use of which was first proposed by William T. Mulloy, an archeologist working in Wyoming and Montana during the 1940s. It embraces all "post-Archaic peoples prior to historic contact," according to Cassells, and it includes a timeline that extends back to 1000 BCE, depending on the source, and ends around 500 CE.

This period includes the further development of new technologies and significantly improved domestic articles, such as pottery with cord marks that began to appear in the archeological record of eastern Colorado, as well as a continued growth of populations, with bands of hunter-gatherers making limited use of corn, and in some cases, game drives, not to mention their newly improved tools used both for hunting and food processing and storage.

• • •

Like later protohistoric and historic tribes of the Pikes Peak region, the Paleo-Indians, Archaic, and Late Prehistoric people were essentially egalitarian in their social structures, with emphasis placed on sharing and inclusiveness, rather than on hoarding and the exclusive accumulation of goods. Each individual was responsible for all other members of the band as well as the tribe as a whole.

When later historic American Indian tribes became more sedentary and did begin to accumulate some trade items and material goods, it was still not practical to accrue too much. It was implicitly understood that labor was teamwork, with goods and produce fairly divided. Hunters should share with all. Women worked together to tan hides and make tepees; older people were provided and cared for. Even gifts were meant to be shared with others and enjoyed. Moreover, it was simply not practical for semi-nomadic people to transport a large number of material possessions.

Historic Tribes

Tribes either occupying or visiting the Pikes Peak region included the Ute, their allies the Jicarilla Apache, the Comanche, Arapaho, Sioux, Kiowa, and Cheyenne. Pawnees and Shoshones also visited the region. The Ute and the Jicarilla Apache may have been in the region as early as the 1300s or 1400s (though many experts consider the 1500s a more likely date). However, in all probability—based on evidence provided by rock art, linguistics, and oral histories—the ancestors of the Utes, or "Nuche," meaning "people," were present in the region thousands of years ago.

Many of these historic American Indian tribes, like their antecedents, were nomadic or became nomadic as they acquired horses and moved farther west. Exceptions were the Pawnee who practiced agriculture, and the Jicarilla Apache who cultivated corn on small parcels of land. All except for the Ute and the Apache (including the Jicarilla) were pushed farther west and south by Anglos or hostile Indians who themselves had been displaced by the successive waves of settlers—as expansion in the 1800s continued from the East Coast, causing unrest and upheaval along the way.

The Mountain Utes: Why They Are Important

Why are the Mountain Utes important? Among other reasons, they have historically lived in Colorado longer than any other American Indian tribe, with probable antecedents dating far back into the prehistoric past. In addition, the Utes have historic links to southwestern culture extending all the way to Mexico. The Utes were known to be "friendly" by trappers, traders, and the early Spanish explorers. The Spanish traded guns, beads, and metal knives in return for such items as their much coveted and widely admired, softly tanned white hides and finely beaded moccasins.

Two of the earliest "probable" references to the Utes were made by the Spanish in 1626 and again in a treaty in 1680. In 1776, further references occur in the records of two Spanish priests from the Franciscan order, Fathers Francisco Atanasio Domínguez and Silvestre Vélez de Escalante, who according to Ubbelohde et al. in *A Colorado History,* "led the first white expedition through some of the most treacherous terrain in all North America." Not only did the Utes befriend the Spanish priests, they also acted as their guides.

Ute History

Shorter in stature than the Plains Indians, dusky-skinned and powerfully built, the Utes speak a Uto-Aztecan language, related to the Aztec spoken in Mexico and shared, among others, by the Hopi and Comanche, as well as the Shoshones—who are distant relatives.

Anthropologist and linguist (specializing in the Ute language) James A. Goss states in *Ute Indian Arts and Culture* that the Intermountain West is the probable "ancestral landscape" of the Uto-Aztecan language family, dating back ten thousand years, with populations gradually pushing out from this center as conditions changed. The Utes in Colorado and the Aztecs in Mexico are, in short, both Uto-Aztecan people. The linguistic evidence, alone, would suggest a very early date of origin for the Ute people in the Intermountain West.

Originally hunter-gatherers, the Mountain Utes believe that the Fremont people are their ancestors. Primarily Archaic hunter-gatherers, the Fremont people, named after the Utah River by the same name where their sites were found, also practiced limited agriculture. They occupied northwestern Colorado as well as southeastern and eastern Utah.

The lifestyle and economy of the Utes were dramatically transformed by their acquisition of horses from the Spanish. Thanks to this new form of speed and mobility, they became prosperous owners of many horses and hunters of bison, moving down to lower and warmer elevations in the fall, where women could harvest piñon nuts, acorns, grains, and berries. When it came to the hunt on the eastern plains, the women rode along with the men. It was easier to carry back the remains of a bison that had already been properly skinned and processed on the spot by the women—"so it was done right," according to one female elder.

The Ute people are currently made up of six bands: the Uncompaghre (Tabeguache), the White River, the Uintah, the Mouache, the Capote, and the Weemnuche. The Mouache and Capote are called the Southern Utes;

The Buffalo

For American Indians, including the Utes, the buffalo was more than meat on the hoof to be converted into stew or cut into strips and dried as jerky. It was also shelter (it required twenty stretched bison skins sewn together to make a tepee), clothing (a chief in his buffalo robe was both warm and elegant), and a source of tools (tendons were used for bows, the bison's stomach lining carried food and water). Cups and spoons were fashioned from the horns. According to historian Jack Williams, the Indians are some of the best users of natural resources in the world. There were literally dozens of different ways in which bison parts were used—everything, in short, except for the grunt. But the bison, by the late 1800s, was being rapidly exterminated—bison were being hunted for sport. Tom Nixon, a professional buffalo hunter, boasted of killing 120 bison in 40 minutes. Bison hides were being stockpiled by traders to feed a growing demand back East, where buffalo tongue had become a luxury item. Between 1872–1873, an estimated twenty-five million bison were slaughtered. Yet the buffalo was far better adapted to extremes of cold and heat and to the native grasses on which they grazed than the cattle that replaced them.

the Weemnuche are the Ute Mountain Utes. The Uncompaghre (Tabeguache), White River, and Uintah bands, collectively, are known as the Northern Utes. At one time the Utes called most of Colorado and the eastern part of Utah, in addition to New Mexico and Arizona, home.

In defense of their "shining mountains" home, the Utes managed to resist the white settlers the longest of any tribe. According to writer and historian Jan Pettit, "The Utes were the last tribe to fight a major battle with the Army, and the last to be forced onto a reservation."

Ute Pass, the Oldest Documented Trail in the Country

When it comes to Colorado history, all of civilization, it appeared, once passed over the old Ute Pass Trail. Indeed, it stands as a vivid and robust metaphor for sizeable portions of Colorado's past.

Astonishing as it may seem, the Ute Pass was first used in prehistoric times by the Clovis people. Proof of this exists in the form of a ten-thousand-year-old Clovis projectile point found buried eight feet deep near Fountain Creek (where a hole was being excavated for a septic tank) in the small town of Cascade on the old Ute Pass Trail. Clovis points have also been found in South Park, the beautiful, high green mountain valley that lies farther to the west and which would later become a major destination and campsite for the Utes when they traveled the Ute Pass Trail during seasonal migrations. In addition to its use by Paleo-Indians, Ute Pass in prehistoric times "afforded passage for great migratory herds of buffalo," states Pettit.

Robert Ormes and Robert Houdek observe in the *Pikes Peak Atlas* that the Ute Pass Trail "gives a greater appreciation for the breadth of Ute Pass. Not possessing dynamite, the Utes used this route to skirt Fountain Creek Gorge and Rainbow Falls. It starts just to the right of the old incline depot and stays above Ruston, then turns up Rattlesnake Gulch," eventually linking up with the Waldo trailhead.

White men would later follow the same approximate route. Passing today's Red Rock Canyon Open Space, Highway 24 parallels the historic Ute Pass Trail, as it winds up the mountain on a road flanked by sheer, rugged walls blasted out of solid granite. The highway is "one of the only roads leading west out of Colorado Springs into the mountains," observe past Colorado Springs Fine Arts Center Director David Turner and Curator Cathy Wright in the scholarly book that grew out of the first-ever Ute symposium on arts and culture to be held in the city, which they organized in 2000.

In her book *Ute Pass: A Quick History,* Jan Pettit writes, "Ute Pass has long been an important route through the Front Range of the Rocky Mountains of Colorado." Not only was the Ute Pass Trail known to the early Spanish, it is the oldest historically documented trail in the U.S. Later it became a major artery in the gold rush days, and after that a popular destination for settlers and tourists alike. In 1873, the intrepid Victorian adventurer, writer, and traveler Isabella Bird traveled Ute Pass. By 1887, the first standard-gauge railroad, the Colorado Midland Railway, had pushed through and up the pass to Divide, Colorado. In 1912, the Southern Ute chief Buckskin Charlie (who like Chief Ouray was half Jicarilla Apache) led a mounted procession of tribal members from Cascade to Manitou Springs as part of a dedication ceremony to commemorate the pass. He declared, "I [am] seventy years old and never been so happy" as when returning to the sacred ground of Manitou Springs.

The Utes as Mounted Warriors and a Changing Lifestyle

The Utes were reputed to be exceptional horsemen, both in the care and breeding of their horses and in their equestrian skill, having been the first to secure horses from the Spanish in the early 1600s. It was either Coronado in 1540 or DeSoto in 1541 who first brought horses to the Southwest. Later, some horses escaped or were abandoned,

Southern Utes on mounts, 1910. (Photo from Colorado Springs Pioneers Museum)

providing ready stock for the Plains Indian. For the Utes, horses symbolized wealth and prestige, while enabling them to be more successful hunters with a healthier diet.

Fierce and brave as warriors, "courage" was the watchword for the Utes. They were not by practice or temperament, however, inclined toward mindless bloodshed. It was considered a far braver feat for a Ute warrior to steal into a camp and make off with a fine horse than to kill a man. Such tribal raids have characterized nomadic cultures the world over—from Mongolia to Yemen to Timbuktu—since the days of horses and the bow and arrow.

From Wickiups to Tepees

Early Utes built wickiups, a shelter of brush and animal hides supported by poles of piñon or juniper wood and used as a temporary shelter when traveling. Later on they used tepees of brain-tanned animal hides like the Plains Indians. Unlike the Plains Indians, however, who relied exclusively on buffalo, the Utes often made use of elk hides for their tepees, which were lighter. Women were the homeowners, responsible for erecting and dismantling the tepees, while men were their honored guests. Women also owned the horses that were used to transport goods or pull a *travois*—a platform, netting, or folded tepee laid over two long supporting poles attached to and pulled by a dog or horse.

Northern Ute Leader Ouray

While there are many contradictory "facts" cited concerning his life, most experts agree that the great northern Ute leader Ouray was born in New Mexico in about 1833, of a Tabeguache (meaning "people who live on the warm side of the mountain") Ute mother and a Jicarilla Apache father. Both Ouray's father and Ouray joined his mother's tribe as would be expected in a matrilineal society. By the 1860s, the U.S. government had come to regard Ouray as Chief of the Confederated Bands of Utes because of his strong leadership abilities, but in actuality he represented only the Uncompahgre (Tabeguache) Utes. This was during a period when gold had been discovered and occupation by prospectors and settlers had moved the Utes out of their traditional hunting and foraging areas, creating discord and starvation.

Both Ouray and his wife, Chipeta, were respected leaders and influential advocates for peace between the increasing numbers of Europeans placing claims on the lands, and the tribes who had inhabited it for centuries. While visiting Washington, D.C., in 1880, Ouray was described by President Hayes as "the most intellectual man I have ever conversed with." In *Indians of the Pike's Peak Region*, Irving Howbert described Ouray as "cultivated and courtly" and of "noble demeanor and bearing."

> "We do not want to sell a foot of our land—and that is the opinion of all. The government is obliged by its treaty to take care of our people, and that is all that we want."
> —**Ouray (1873)**

Diplomatically skilled and multilingual, with a command of English, Spanish, Apache, and Ute at his disposal, Ouray worked hard to mediate peace and treaty agreements with both the U.S. government and the white settlers. It was Ouray's fervent hope that his people would be able to retain at least a small share of their natal lands as the settlers and gold prospectors continued to move in.

Ouray clearly knew how to get along and negotiate with Anglos. He counted among his personal friends Kit Carson, and the two men and their wives often enjoyed each other's hospitality. However, despite his impressive and well-honed diplomatic and negotiating skills, Ouray was not able to fix what amounted to permanently broken and deliberately ignored or forgotten treaties. Sometimes viewed as a traitor by his own people, Ouray was nonetheless among the first to recognize that the Utes could never realistically expect to overpower the white man, with his industrial-age weapons and surging numbers.

Ouray's Intervention in the "Meeker Massacre"

With the benefit of historic hindsight, a direct line can be drawn between the infamous Sand Creek Massacre on November 29, 1864, the "Meeker Massacre" on September 29, 1879, and the Uncompaghre Utes' long march to Utah. In the historically well-documented Sand Creek Massacre, John Chivington along with seven hundred troops, including his 3rd Colorado Volunteers, attacked a peaceful and sleeping encampment of mostly Cheyenne and Arapaho women and children—when most of the young men were away on a buffalo hunt. Not only did the troops slaughter about 150 in all, but they brutally mutilated their victims—despite the white flag of peace and the U.S. flag that the wise and peaceful Cheyenne Chief, Black Kettle, had flown in hopes of forestalling the attack.

The catalyst for the so-called "Meeker Massacre" in 1879 was the White River Indian Agent Nathan Meeker, who, most historians agree, was a notoriously inept manager with little knowledge of Indians. Added to this was a rigid and self-righteous determination to force the Utes to take up farming against their will. To this end,

Meeker plowed up a Ute horse racing track and subsequently was roughed up by the enraged Indian whose track it was, a Ute named Johnson. A panicked Meeker called for troops. His call was answered by Major T.T. Thornburgh, accompanied by nearly two hundred soldiers. A group of Utes subsequently headed off the major and requested that all but Thornburgh and five soldiers should remain, with the rest removing themselves to a point fifty miles distant from the White River Agency while issues were discussed. This request had been prompted by memories of the bloody and extensive Sand Creek Massacre that had occurred just sixteen years earlier, and the fact that it was illegal for troops to enter reservation lands.

Accounts vary as to what happened next, but apparently Thornburgh ignored the demand by the Utes. Thornburgh's refusal to comply spurred a Ute attack on the Indian agency in which Agent Meeker and ten male employees were killed. Taken captive were Meeker's wife and daughter, as well as a young mother with two children. The Utes then fought a pitched battle with Thornburgh and his forces at Milk Creek on the northern edge of the reservation, killing the major, thirteen of his officers, as well as horses and mules, and wounding an additional twenty-seven troops. The two Ute attacks in Colorado generated news headlines across the nation.

Meanwhile, Ouray had sent word to the Utes to stop fighting. Because of Ouray's intervention, the captive women and children were released unharmed twenty-three days later. Ironically, the Indian perpetrator of the Meeker conflict was a member of another band, not Ouray's. But because of the White River battle, the Uncompaghre Utes were forcibly relocated to the Utah Territory on August 28, 1881. "If one had stood on Piñon Mesa [near the junction of the Colorado and Gunnison Rivers], what a march of a retreating civilization he could have seen! Here was the last defeat of the red man" one commentator is reported to have said.

Due to Ouray's willingness to negotiate with white settlers and the U.S. government, he would later be stigmatized by some tribal members who believed Ouray had sold them out. Suffering from rheumatism and nephritis in his later years, Ouray sought relief in the warm mineral springs near his home on the western slope, as did his soul mate and wife, the legendary Chipeta. One of Colorado's 13,000-foot peaks was named after the famous leader, as is the old mining town of Ouray, and the county by the same name.

Ouray visited the Colorado Springs area often. We know that he and Chipeta camped in what is now Chipita Park (the spelling was changed to avoid confusion with a railroad siding called "Chipeta," where mail was sometimes mistakenly delivered), west of Red Rock Canyon Open Space, up Ute Pass. Ouray died on August 24, 1880, the last of the Utes to live on tribal land as opposed to a reservation.

Chipeta, A Leader in Her Own Right

Chipeta ("Chipit," means "water springing up,") was the trusted confidant and faithful wife and companion of the Northern Ute leader Ouray. Born in 1843, Chipeta was raised as a Ute, but may have been kidnapped as a child from the Kiowa Apache. Her legendary poise and intelligence, not to mention her kindness and compassion, along with her beauty as a young woman, are matters of historic record. These assets included a deep love of children (when she herself was childless) and a wisdom that was often sought after by Anglos, members of her tribe, and Ouray himself.

When Chipeta traveled with her husband, Ouray, to Washington, D.C., in 1880, she broke with accepted conventions for Indian women at the time by allowing herself to be photographed. She also participated in meetings and discussions with high U.S. officials as an equal member of the Ute delegation, establishing yet another new precedent.

In the course of her long life, Chipeta experienced heartbreak, displacement, disappointment, and bitter loss. She was a part of the forced dispersal of her people, the Uncompaghre (Tabeguache) Ute in 1881. From the "blue sky country" of Colorado, they were forced to march their livestock and families over rough and difficult terrain on a long hard trek to the desolate lands of northeastern Utah. The land they were given to farm once they arrived proved barren, waterless, and unfit for cultivation. Mormon leader Brigham Young had previously rejected the site for use by his own people—but in describing it to President Abraham Lincoln, he endorsed it highly for the displaced Utes.

The Utes' forced removal from their shining mountains occurred after the death of Ouray, whom Chipeta outlived by close to half a century. Despite her tragic life, and the squalid conditions and poverty she endured after being forced out of Colorado, Chipeta retained, to her dying day, her unusual gifts of great wisdom and unfailing kindness—according to two of her biographers Cynthia Becker and David Smith. She died on August 16, 1924, and by the end of her life, she was considered as the equal to Ouray and was widely celebrated. The little mountain town of Chipita Park, named after her, lies not far, as the crow flies (or any other way), from the open space up Ute Pass, heading west out of Colorado Springs. There is also a Chipeta Lake and a Mount Chipeta in Colorado.

Chipeta and Ouray, leaders of the Uncompahgre band of Utes (Ouray considered Chipeta an equal partner and often sought her advice) traveled to the nation's capital in the hope of securing a formal agreement that would allow their people to remain in the "shining mountains" of Colorado. Here they sit for a formal portrait during their visit to Washington, D.C., in 1880. (Photo by Walker Studio, from Denver Public Library, Western History Collection, X-30600)

Ute Cultural Traditions and Practices

Ute society was matriarchal. Young men married into the women's family. Women named children and passed their family names on to the next generation. Work was cooperative, as was true with all American Indian tribes. In the official guide to *Garden of the Gods and Rock Ledge Ranch Historic Site*, Gene Smith, formerly of the city parks and recreation department, observes that the Utes "worked together and formed groups or bands in order to help each other hunt, cook, and make camp. Camps were alive with laughter, music, ceremony, games, art, and education. The Ute people are known for their laughter and sense of humor," he writes.

The Utes, along with other American Indian tribes, share a long tradition of storytelling and legends. Typically animals—such as the frog, toad, crow, coyote, bear, porcupine, skunk, owl, tortoise, mountain lion, mosquito, and even water babies—figure as central characters in this rich folkloric body of tales. These tales, composing an extensive collection of oral literature or "orature," passed down from generation to generation, depend on superb and well-trained memories and draw strongly on creative and imaginative gifts for storytelling. It is of historical significance, however, that there are no Ute origin stories that feature migration—unlike those, for example, of the Hopi. In other words, the Ute oral tradition is consistent with increasingly well-substantiated historic fact—that is, that the Ute are truly an "aboriginal" people—meaning, "native from the beginning."

> **Ute Creation Myth**
>
> One of the best-known Ute creation myths draws on a familiar creature in the West, and one you may chance to observe in the open space as well. (Former RRCOS park ranger and current parks' official Scott Abbott reports that there are "lots of coyotes" in Red Rock Canyon, with at least one "very successful pack.") One day—the story goes—trickster Coyote, disobeying instructions from the Great Spirit, Sinawaf, opened a bag out of which jumped a multitude of people speaking many different tongues. This led to a fight over land. The Utes, however, were left behind in the bag until the very last. When he discovered the mischief that the wily Coyote had caused, the Great Spirit Sinawaf was mightily displeased, for Coyote's interference had caused much dissension among the tribes. Sinawaf, however, decided to reward the Utes by making them brave so they could defeat others. In this way, the Utes become a powerful and respected people, and among the most feared of all the tribes.

The Bear Dance

The Utes are famous for their Bear Dance, a ceremonial dance with feasting and socializing that occurs over a period of three or four days in the spring of each year after the first growl of thunder. The Bear Dance is unique to the Utes and is one of the oldest of their ceremonies. Of all the animals, the Utes consider the bear to be one of the wisest,

Mapescass. Described as a Ute medicine man, few details about this photograph are known except that the subject, although posed, is not in the least bit objectified and is fully engaged as a participant in the interaction with camera and photographer. (Photo from Colorado Springs Pioneers Museum)

surpassed in courage only by the mountain lion. *Mama-kwa-nhkap* celebrates the renewal of life, symbolized by the bear's coming out of hibernation and the return of spring. It is also a time of self-renewal and healing, of letting go of problems or feelings of anger and sadness that might cause disharmony.

In the Bear Dance, men and women stand facing each other in parallel lines. The men face east; the women face west. Next the women choose their partners, perhaps by tapping them lightly on a shoulder with the corner of their shawls. Then begins the slow and rhythmic shuffling movements of the dance: three steps forward and three steps backward (as a bear might move). The dancers move to the musical, rhythmic chants of singers, the hypnotic beat of a drum, and the loud rasping sounds of a notched stick (called a bear growler) being pulled over a large, long metal resonator (in the old days this was a hollowed-out log). These traditional instruments, still in use today, produce a sound suggestive of a bear's growl or thunder in spring. The vibrations are reportedly strong enough to be felt for miles. On the last day of the celebration, dancers break into couples or just a single pair, still facing each other while moving back and forth in the same established pattern.

Besides feasting, trade, and the exchange of news, courtships sometimes took place at this festive celebration that drew together many bands. New clothing was worn—with the Ute women no doubt showing off their handsome, soft white buckskin dresses to good effect. The ceremony, with its underlying themes and rituals centered on self-renewal and new life, was held not only to celebrate spring, but to honor women. The men did all the preparation and serving of the food, which often in the old days featured a delicious, thick, buffalo meat stew with vegetables cooked in a "big, big pot" and stirred with a new shovel (according to Jan Pettit, who attended many Bear Dances over the years). This was served with corn on the cob, rolls, and slices of watermelon. On the last day of the gathering, when the feast was held, families often filled large kettles brought from home with food to carry back with them for the return trip. The Bear Dance continues to this day to be an important annual celebration for the Mountain Utes. It is a time for fun and fellowship, in which women occupy a special place; and for new beginnings—represented by the spiritually potent resurrection symbol of the bear coming out of hibernation in the spring.

The Utes as Early Ecologists

The Mountain Utes, like most American Indians, knew the local landscapes like the back of their hands and had an enormous understanding of and appreciation for the plant and animal kingdoms. Indeed, the Utes have been described by some scholars as being our first ecologists. They were careful not to heedlessly waste or overuse resources, but perhaps more importantly, they held a deeply respectful attitude toward nature and found ways to express their profound gratitude for its many gifts.

James A. Goss points out that the Utes had a very precise lexicon to describe the flora, based on type and elevation. For example, they had words for high alpine areas, others "for the forested mountain slopes between the alpine areas and the more arid basins and plains. They had a term for the basins and plains." They had, in short, "an ecological model" that resembles any scientific diagram you might find in a contemporary scientific text, said Goss, in an interview conducted with former Colorado Springs Fine Arts Center curator Cathy Wright, and published in *Ute Indian Arts and Culture*. "If you stop and think about it, they [the Ute] were excellent ecologists because it wasn't just academic to them, it was important to their survival to know the environment," he said.

Ute Camps and Fortifications

In autumn, when the meadows up higher were covered with frost, the Utes came down to the area now known as Garden of the Gods Park, where they camped. And now, as a result of the recent archeological survey, a number of scientifically described and documented artifacts, along with other signs—principally centered in the Dakota Hogback—confirm the historic presence of the Utes in Red Rock Canyon Open Space as well. Doubtless, too, there were other American Indian tribes of the Pikes Peak region that wandered through the area or visited the site.

Why were the Utes in the Dakota Hogback? There are a number of plausible explanations. The hogback may have offered a desirable lookout point with commanding views of the eastern plains. Here the Utes could watch for the telltale cloud of dust indicating the approach of horse-mounted enemies. Perhaps they wanted to protect access to the sacred mineral springs in nearby Manitou Springs or to the buffalo trail up Ute Pass, or to guard the camp while the young men were off hunting. To pass the time, they may have carved arrowheads, placing all but the rejects into a leather pouch for later use. Pettit states that "the Comanche, Arapaho, and other tribes venturing into the mountain parks ... usually met well-armed Ute warriors. Most stayed out of the way."

If Only the Stones Could Speak: Drift Fences versus Ute Defensive Walls

Irving Howbert in *Indians of the Pikes Peak Region* describes the hogback area as containing "numerous circular places of defense built of loose stone, to a height of four or five feet, and large enough to hold three or four men comfortably. These miniature fortifications were placed at intervals along the ridge all the way from Fountain Creek to Bear Creek and doubtless were built and used by the Utes."

And, indeed, running along the Dakota Hogback are the remains of stone structures that some argue could have historically been Ute fortifications, reinforced by the natural ruggedness of the hogbacks themselves. On the recently preserved White Acres, to the south of Red Rock Canyon, the remnants of a stone wall appear as a continuation of the ridge-crest stone wall found in Red Rock Canyon. Its location on a high point overlooking the eastern plains may argue in favor of the theory that the structures were, indeed, intended as fortification walls. Unfortunately, "the part of the wall running south from the saddle [in Red Rock Canyon] has been largely destroyed," observes local historian Don Ellis. We will never know the full history of the purported circular Ute fortification wall, given that a significant portion of it was obliterated by the road John Bock built to the city dump that he opened near the site.

Jan Pettit, in discussing the "fortifications" with a group of Ute elders, was told the stone structures could have served an altogether different purpose. They may have been used for catching eagles in order to secure the feathers necessary for use in ceremonies. (After the removal of several feathers, the eagles were most often released unharmed.) Or the site may have been used as lookout points.

Yet another theory to explain the stone structures has been proposed. According to this hypothesis, which is favored by some experts, the stone wall was built as a traditional drift fence to funnel grazing animals, such as elk and deer, and also used as a hunting blind. While the animals grazed or drifted along the line of the fence, which typically was four to five feet high, the hunter, who was hunkered down out-of-sight behind the stone wall, waited for the right opportunity to pick off an animal. Moreover, similar drift fences have been identified throughout the region. According to the Old Colorado City Historical Society, "Arrowheads found in the area are most often small 'bird point' made of petrified wood from the Black Forest area, perhaps suggesting that the hunt was more common than the battle along the hogbacks."

Snyder et al. found that a "discontinuous, deteriorated rock wall stands on the hogback (unlike the circular, four- to five-foot high ones described by Howbert , although a circular wall *was* found on the southern end of the hogback.) While most of the stone structure is less than four or five feet in height, the wall has no doubt been degraded and reduced in size over time by people scrambling over it.

Snyder further observes that the wall in question "has lichen attached to the stone, but the lichen has not grown in between the rocks. Had the lichen grown in between the rock, a very early date could have been supported" for the construction of the wall. Nonetheless, both the recently documented "lithic scatter" in the Dakota Hogback and "previously collected projectile points suggest Native American activity on the ridge."

Sacred Landscapes

In the Pikes Peak region, both the Utes and Arapaho considered Manitou Springs, due west and adjacent to the open space, as a sacred site and, despite their enmity, declared it neutral territory. To honor this peacekeeping agreement, the Utes traditionally would store their weapons in a safe cache as they rode down the old Ute Pass trail, prior to their arrival in Manitou Springs. In addition to holding Manitou Springs sacred, the Utes and other tribes greatly appreciated the healing properties afforded by these naturally heated mineral pools. It was said that the Great Spirit, by breathing into their clear watery depths, had caused their effervescent bubbles and rippling surfaces. However, the name "Manitou" itself, which refers to an eastern Algonquin deity, is somewhat fanciful. It was thought up by the English financier William Blackmore in the 1870s. A better-than-average developer name, it is nonetheless totally out of context, inspired as it was by Longfellow's romantic poem "Hiawatha." Dubious spiritualism, in this case, went hand-in-hand with early commercial enticement.

The Garden of the Gods was also regarded as sacred by the Utes. Nonetheless the Utes did camp and hold dances and ceremonials in the park. But they treated the land with respect and showed equal veneration for the wonderfully shaped red sandstone rocks. Consistent with their beliefs, the Utes, in the Master Plan planning process, were strongly outspoken in their opposition to the idea of drilling holes into the rocks for anchor bolts in order to secure ropes, and to having rock climbers scramble all over these ancient formations.

How the Storied Red Rocks Got Their Shapes

As for the storied and sacred rocks in Garden of the Gods, with their haunting and fanciful shapes, the Utes recount a story about how once upon a time, long ago, these anthropomorphically shaped rocks had once been their living enemies. But the Great Spirit in his desire to help the *nuche* had turned their enemies into stone.

In *Man in the Garden of the Gods,* Richard and Mary Ann Gehling document another (presumably Ute, though they do not identify it as such) legend concerning the origin of the wondrous and amazing shapes found in the red sandstone formations. According to this story, which is not far removed from geologic fact, once a great flood covered nearly everything except for the top of [the Great Spirit's] mountain. When the waters at last subsided, the floating animal carcasses "turned to sandstone and rolled down the peak into a garden valley below."

Thus did the Indians paint the landscape with their stories and myths—in which if you scratch a myth, you find a fact. Tales of all Indian tribes typically contained some moral or practical lesson, intended to be passed on to youth in the retelling around the campfire. Such stories, along with dance, song, and instrumental music— for example, the courtship flute Ute men played when courting (referred to as "love magic," according to Pettit)—contribute immeasurably to the richness of the cultural landscape and to what western American writer Wallace Stegner suggests is a vital part of our "knowing" of a place.

Other Historic Indian Tribes in the Pikes Peak Region

In addition to the Mountain Utes and the tribes covered in the following section, several other historic tribes lived near, visited, or hunted in the Pikes Peak region. These include the Shoshone, Comanche, Sioux, and Pawnee. Most of these tribes were nomadic and originated in the north or the east, except for the Pawnee who came from the south (Howbert). However, I have limited myself in this chapter to ones known to have visited the immediate area for extended periods or who have figured prominently into local place names. It is not within the scope of this book to give an extended history of all of the tribes who figured into the history of the Pikes Peak region, but rather to sketch out some interesting historic facts associated with those tribes who in all likelihood were in the neighborhood and either geographically or contextually figure importantly into the early human history of the open space itself.

The Sioux, for example, probably did not occupy or claim any of the eastern plains or southern Colorado as a part of their domain. The chances of finding identifiable

Sioux cultural material in this area are likewise close to nil. For this reason, I have chosen in this chapter not to profile the Sioux, although they do figure onto historic lists of Indians known to have visited or traveled through the Pikes Peak region on hunting or scouting expeditions.

The Apishipa: Who Were They? Why Are They Important?

Roughly a thousand years ago, a nomadic people known as the Apishipa lived in the area. They were named by an archeologist in the 1930s after a tributary of the Arkansas River that runs southeast of Pueblo, where some of this early group's distinctive artifacts were first discovered. In *People of the Red Earth*, archeologist Sally Crum describes the Apishipa as the "part-time gardeners and house builders of the Plains."

The Apishipa carried tools and hunting spears with them as they walked about and hunted animals. They also used bows and distinctive, side-notched arrowheads, as well as stone knives; and for domestic chores, rounded pots. They built freestanding stone houses using massive slabs and pillars of stone, with a brush roof supported by rods of juniper wood. Their preferred building sites were on the rims of low cliffs. Besides their small stone dwellings, they also constructed larger brush-covered, arbor-like structures, akin to rustic *ramadas*, whose purpose may have been communal—as large numbers of buffalo bones, broken to extract fat and marrow, have been found in these areas.

The Apishipa were primarily nomadic hunter-gatherers who migrated with the changing seasons and hunted buffalo (tools for scraping buffalo hides have been found at Apishipa sites). Instead of carrying their homes with them, they built summer and winter shelters. While they did consume some agricultural produce (corncobs have been found at Apishipa sites), they were not thought to be intensive agriculturists, except in the cultivation of a few small plots.

While the Apishipa did not take to agriculture and settled village life in the same fashion as the pueblo-dwellers in the somewhat more temperate climes of present-day New Mexico, they did master the science of constructing rodent-proof, weather-safe storage areas for the wild food they gathered. These cists consisted of holes dug in the ground, lined with rocks and then sealed tight with a slab of stone.

Apishipa sites have typically been found in sandstone canyon environments, most notably at Fort Carson to the south of Colorado Springs and in the army's Piñon Canyon maneuver area covering thousands of acres in southeastern Colorado, where hundreds of archeological sites have been identified. These sites, however, are government-restricted in terms of public access. Apishipa sites have also been identified along the Purgatoire River in Picket Wire Canyon in southeastern Colorado.

Possible Apishipa Site in the Open Space

Of more immediate interest and much closer to home, however, are the remains of a possible Apishipa site identified in Red Rock Canyon Open Space itself. Situated between the Dakota Hogback and the Lyons Sandstone, the site consists of the rough, crude outline of building stones suggestive of Apishipa structures. The rocky outline, in its current state of deterioration, requires the trained eye of an archeologist first to spot it and then to recognize it for what it might be—in this case, the dimly scattered ruins of what could potentially be the oldest human structure ever to be identified on the open space. It was first spotted by Stephen Snyder, after he had written his initial assessment report.

Who would have dreamed that somewhere between six hundred to more than one thousand years ago, long before the original property owner John Bock had arrived on the scene, the Apishipa may have occupied Red Rock Canyon Open Space. However, they left no deed behind of their *de facto* right to ownership. Furthermore, archeological evidence of the Apishipa disappearing some six hundred years ago—possibly due to a drought in the Pikes Peak region—suggests there were no descendents left to press their claim. And having, in any case, left behind no written records, these early peoples have remained silent on the subject. Nonetheless, they were clearly in the area, probably as family groups, and if not in the actual millions, at least in the thousands, as they hunted and gathered throughout the Pikes Peak region and eastern Colorado.

The Jicarilla Apache

The Jicarilla Apache are closely allied to the Utes, although they speak a different language. Early hunter-gatherers, they originated in Canada and were among the numerous Apache bands who moved south along the Rocky Mountains into Colorado and New Mexico, probably sometime between the 1300s and the 1400s. They, along with the Navajo, were early arrivers in Colorado and both are members of the Athabascan/Apachean linguistic group. Indeed, the Jicarilla Apache and the Utes are regarded historically as the two earliest Indian groups to inhabit Colorado.

The Jicarilla Apache, who call themselves *Tinde,* "The First People," were originally ancient foes of the Utes, fighting with them over buffalo hunting ground. However, they eventually struck up an alliance, and in general, were regarded as being among the most peaceful of the tribes.

The Utes and Jicarilla Apache over time began to share many customs in common and they intermarried extensively. Like the Utes, the Jicarilla Apache are among the mountain tribes who acquired horses early—historians are not in agreement about the actual date, but sometime in the seventeenth century. They also earned a reputation for being highly skilled horse traders.

Jack Williams, in his monograph *Jicarilla Apaches: The Forgotten People of Pikes Peak and Southern Colorado,* writes that, "An 1846 map shows the Jicarillas had one permanent and two temporary campsites near Manitou Springs." Like other American Indian tribes in the Pikes Peak region, the Jicarilla considered the area sacred.

As was the case with most American Indians, the "mountain" or Jicarilla Apache struggled over the centuries to survive as "displaced persons." Yet they were able to keep their "core culture" intact, according to scholar Dolores Gunnerson, who has made an in-depth study of their origins and history. The survival of the Jicarilla Apache was based on their ability to adapt in the face of constantly changing political and social situations, without losing sight of their fundamental values.

The Jicarilla Apache were one of the last tribes to be permanently settled on a reservation. This occurred in 1887 in north-central New Mexico, where at the time, they died in huge numbers as a result of such rampaging diseases as tuberculosis, along with what has been described as "the untreatable illness of despair." At one point, their numbers were down to a few hundred, and it was feared that the tribe was on the verge of extinction. But their numbers eventually rebounded. Today the Jicarilla Apache are considered to be one of the most prosperous of the tribes in the region.

Each year, representatives of the Jicarilla Apache travel from Dulce, New Mexico, up to Colorado Springs to participate in the city park and recreation department's sponsored "First Nations Day," held at Rock Ledge Ranch in the fall—with its stunning view of the sandstone formations in Garden of the Gods. The Mountain Utes and Navajos, along with other tribes, are also well represented at this annual gathering.

Why the Jicarilla Apache Became the "Forgotten People"

Because the Jicarilla Apache did not have reason to attack the Spanish, they did not attract much attention from the conquistadores, who were hard put, in any case, to distinguish them from other tribes in the region. As a result, the Jicarilla Apache were largely ignored in the accounts of the day, and this scarcity of data from Colorado's early history continued on up into the present. Moreover, in the late 1800s and early 1900s, when the Jicarilla Apache visited Manitou Springs, they were frequently mistaken as Utes in what Williams refers to as a not uncommon form of profiling, based on the syndrome of "they all look alike." These are some of the reasons why the Jicarilla Apache became "the forgotten people of the Pikes Peak region and southern Colorado."

Weavers of Museum-quality Baskets

The Jicarilla are noted for their skilled basketry, hence the Spanish name "Jicarilla," meaning "little basket." To this day, Jicarilla women continue to weave beautiful baskets that combine the functional with the purely artistic, and which the Spanish were the first to acknowledge (even if they may have been short-sighted in some other respects). Using the "coiled" technique of basketry, Jicarilla artisans weave their baskets from strips and rods of willow and sumac, sealed with pitch. Several beautiful, museum-quality baskets woven by Jicarilla Apache women were on exhibit at the Symposium on Ute Arts and Culture held in 2000, under the auspices of the Taylor Museum, at the Colorado Springs Fine Arts Center.

The Cheyenne

Around 1825, the Cheyenne moved to Colorado from the Missouri River region. The catalyst for the move was pressure from the Sioux. Originating in Minnesota, the Cheyenne are members of the Algonquin language group. Moving on to Missouri, they lived in earth lodges and farmed patches of corn. Once they had acquired horses, however, they moved out to the plains where they became renowned as buffalo hunters and warriors, living in hide tepees and eventually trading with the French. In the mid-to late 1800s, in the absence of buffalo and good arable land to farm, the Cheyenne began to suffer from starvation, like so many of the tribes.

The Colorado gold rush further compounded the negative impact on the Indians of their displacement by the white man's arrival—this time by miners hoping to strike it rich. The lands that the Indians were being given were increasingly unfit for farming and often lacked a water source. The often-promised rations never seemed to arrive and the great herds of buffalo, as well as bear and antelope, had been decimated, in some cases deliberately by white settlers and militias. These negative effects were likewise suffered by the Cheyenne's close allies, the Arapaho, with whom they frequently intermarried.

The Arapaho

Described by Alfred Kroeber in his classic work, *The Arapaho*, as being "sensuous and imaginative" and by Crum as "outgoing and gregarious," the Arapaho were known for their skill as traders. Like the Cheyenne, they belong to the Algonquin language group, but in all other respects are quite distinctive. By the mid-1600s, the Arapaho had begun to hunt buffalo on the plains, becoming more nomadic in lifestyle. Like many American Indians, they held a cosmic belief in the central, life-sustaining importance of the sun.

> *"People seeing the beauty of this valley will want to stay, and their staying will be the undoing of the beauty."*
> —**Chief Niwot**

Sometime in the late eighteenth century, the Arapaho arrived in Colorado—by which time the Kiowas and their allies, the Comanches, were established in southeastern Colorado. Having originated in present-day Minnesota near Lake Superior, the Arapaho had once been farmers in the Red River Valley, dwelling in domed lodges of bark and cultivating corn, beans, and squash. The Arapaho regarded the Utes as their enemy, and also considered them to be the bravest of all the Indian warriors—except for themselves. After arriving in Colorado, the Arapaho and the Cheyenne shared the territory that more or less covered the eastern half of Colorado and the southeastern quarter of Wyoming. The Arapaho today live in the Wind River Reservation in Wyoming.

The Kiowa

Like the Arapaho and Cheyenne, the Kiowa figure prominently into local place names. Before settling in the Black Hills of present-day South Dakota, the Kiowa lived in the mountains of western Montana along the Yellowstone River. Eventually they became a buffalo-hunting plains people who owned more horses than any other tribe, and were closely allied with the Kiowa Apache and then the Comanche. They enjoyed a reputation for being the best sign-talkers of the plains. Sign language was necessary to make oneself understood from a distance, especially when the wind was blowing hard. It also helped overcome the language barrier, given that the American Indians spoke a multitude of tongues (exactly as in the Ute creation myth).

While the Sun Dance became an important ritual to both the Kiowa and Utes—unlike the northern plains tribes, they did not practice skin piercing and women were allowed to participate. Later, the Kiowa got caught up in what Williams describes as "the Ghost Dance craze" in an effort to ward off the white man's diseases, such as measles, that killed at least three hundred members of the tribe in 1891. By the end of the nineteenth century, the Kiowa had lost their reservation lands. Today roughly ten thousand Kiowa are scattered throughout the West—some living on "allotted tribal land" in Oklahoma; others in major cities, such as Denver.

With the opening of the Santa Fe Trail and the appearance of merchants carrying trade goods, diseases such as smallpox became another scourge of the tribe, wiping out more than half their numbers. Treaties were negotiated and broken, raids continued, supplies failed to arrive, and so the story continued. After the Sand Creek Massacre in 1864, in an unintended but not surprising consequence, the Kiowa, Comanche, and other plains tribes became both fierce and unrelenting in their attacks on white settlers.

Treaties and Lost Lands

When it came to the treaties that were constantly being renegotiated, the American Indians were woefully unprepared—not only in terms of their legal knowledge and inability to read the fine print, but in their fundamental belief system. It was antithetical to them to think that land could be bought and sold, anymore than one could buy and sell the sunshine or the fresh air or the rain. Nonetheless, they did understand what they stood to lose over the long term, and it included not only their land, but an entire way of life.

The Buffalo is Exterminated and the Kiowa Lose Their Horses

In the 1870s, the establishment of the transcontinental railroad brought buffalo hunters who helped ensure, in their heedless killing of the wild beasts sometimes just for sport, the extermination of the great, native grass-grazing herds on which the plains tribes depended for survival. This was aided and abetted by an apparently deliberate government policy, at the time, to rid the plains of the buffalo and thus of the American Indians. Lone Wolf and Satanta were two great and brave Kiowa chiefs who attempted to negotiate peace with the white settlers, but were instead held hostage by General Custer. By 1874, the buffalo had been exterminated; after which the Kiowas' horses were killed or auctioned off.

> *"We know that our lands have become more valuable. The white people think that we do not know their value; but we know that the land is everlasting, and the few goods we receive for it are soon worn out and gone."*
>
> —**Canassatego,** an Onondaga, in negotiation with Six Nations in the mid-1800s

Archeological Finds in Red Rock Canyon Open Space

In the investigation conducted by archeologist Stephen Snyder, with Michael Flowers and Rayond L. Morad, for the Parks, Recreation, and Cultural Services in February 2004, several fascinating discoveries in the open space from the Archaic Period were made and scientifically documented. These included a number of previously collected, but undocumented, projectile points that exhibited "characteristics found in all Archaic-stage points."

According to the Snyder report: "A core reduction flake found on the southeastern side of the Hogback has considerable patination, suggesting a very old manufacturing date." Cassells defines a flake as "a thin piece of stone detached from a core or partially finished artifact." The report further points to the fact that there is collaborating evidence of early human occupation in nearby Garden of the Gods, dating back thousand of years—as well as farther south at Fort Carson, which has abundant ancient sites.

Recent Finds and Artifacts from the Late Prehistoric Stage to Protohistoric and Historic Tribes

According to Snyder and his team, this evolving culture stage is generally characterized by the introduction of the bow and arrow for hunting and by the manufacture of ceramics.

Not surprisingly, artifacts from this extended period, principally arrowheads and flakes, as well as domestic tools such as drills and scrapers, had already been collected from Red Rock Canyon at the southern end of the hogbacks prior to the commencement of the Snyder study. More surprising, in view of the land's heavy modern occupation and use, is that in addition to these artifacts, a number of intriguing and identifiably prehistoric isolated finds

Embedded metate identified in the Dakota Formation on the open space may have served the Mountain Utes as a vertical grinding tool to process acorns or dried fruit, or, alternatively, as a whetstone. (Photo courtesy Don Ellis)

were also documented by the survey team. These included half-a-dozen gray and tan chert and brown quartzite flakes.

Several other exciting archeological finds were discovered and described in the course of the team's survey. They include one fine-grained "mano" (one-handed pestle) of brown sandstone that exhibited light to moderate use, and three brown sandstone metates (mortars). Such implements were of the type used for hundreds of years by both prehistoric and historic tribes to pulverize seeds, meat, berries, acorns, and piñon nuts, or to manufacture powders to be used as paint for ceremonial use or in dyes. Plant and mineral-based medicines were also ground with the use of similar grinding tools, manufactured from locally available stone of a suitable durability and texture.

One of the brown sandstone metates was broken and, on close examination, indicated light use. Later, after the completion of his survey, Snyder discovered another "trough-shaped" metate that had been removed from its original site (meaning it had been robbed of its archeological context) and set up on top of a pile of stones. Some angular white chert debris was also identified—the remains of the industry from some unknown ancient's long-since-vacant workshop.

The dates of metates are somewhat problematic because the rock of which they are made is, in itself, of ancient provenance. Therefore, to correctly assess their actual age, it is helpful to find residual foodstuffs—grains or pollens and the like—caught on their surfaces or in the general vicinity. Even when difficult to date, however, metates can show stylistic differences that offer clues to their origins. For example, in the case of Ute metates, the edges are typically rounded and the shape is oval or trough-like.

Nevertheless, at a bare minimum, the metates are estimated to be at least two centuries old and constitute solid archeological evidence of historic Indian tribes having spent time on the open space, principally in the area of the hogbacks. These and other recent discoveries in the Dakota Hogback indicate an entire complex of long-term use by the Utes—from campsite to possibly (although less likely) battleground. Further evidence of the use of the area as a campground is indicated by the discovery in the early 1950s of a stone circle and fire pit site ("tepee circle") south of Red Rock Canyon Open Space.

A Prehistoric Open Camp: Isolated Finds

Not far from the possible Apishipa structure on a ridge that makes up the southern boundary of the closed landfill overlooking Red Rock Canyon, a small "lithic scatter" was located. The term "lithic scatter" or assemblage refers to the number and variety of materials (stone flakes and tools) found on an archeological site, showing evidence of long-term human habitation. The evidence in this case suggests the long-ago presence of an open prehistoric camp. The site in question is located on a Dakota Sandstone ridge, with ponderosa pine, juniper, and Gamble's oak. It overlooks the Red Rock Canyon drainage "that was probably a grass and riparian area before the landfill was established," according to Snyder's survey. The scatter, as detailed in the survey, includes a tan ortho-quartzite core with one piece of angular debris and one flake. The site also revealed one broken, salmon-colored chert biface (which is defined by Snyder as being "a flaked stone artifact exhibiting evidence of facial thinning on both dorsal and ventral faces"), one chert-tested cobble (a rounded rock with percussive marks testing it for chert), and one Black Forest petrified wood flake. "The landfill cuts away at the northwestern boundary of the site, probably resulting in the loss of some material," the report concludes.

American Indian Artifacts in the Region

Although most of the recently documented and described archeological finds are associated with the Utes, the fact that the Jicarilla Apache, Cheyenne, Arapaho, and other tribes in the region once camped in and visited Garden of the Gods and Manitou Springs suggests their historical presence in Red Rock Canyon as well.

In addition, artifacts from most of the historic tribes of the Pikes Peak Region have been identified on the top of nearby Cheyenne Mountain. According to life-long, self-described student of Indian culture and former National Park Superintendent Jack Williams, it is possible to find evidence on Cheyenne Mountain of nearly all of the American Indians just named. The abundant archeological proof of camps and hunts consists of, among other artifacts, "… fire hearths, ossified bones, stone implements, burials, hunting blinds and/or shelters, glass beads, and metal objects such as projectile points, knives [and] lancepoints." Williams asserts that there's every reason to believe similar artifacts should be found in Red Rock Canyon Open Space.

In several cases this supposition has been borne out. Where archeological finds have been slight or non-existent, the reason can be readily traced to the recent human occupation of the open space, during which time some artifacts were collected and removed, while others were lost irretrievably as roads were bulldozed, dumps filled, houses built, and three trailer camps opened up as one of John S. Bock's private ventures.

Rock Art

In northwestern Colorado and Utah, the Fremont rock artists, whose sites date back more than 1,500 years, were some of the most prolific. Their subjects were trapezoidal human figures, some wearing horns, helmets, or kilts, others carrying shields or shown with a weeping eye, as well as plants and animals that included deer, antelope, birds, lizards, and mountain sheep. In Hidden Valley Cave in Durango, Colorado, there are pictographs of the popular flute player, Kokopelli, which may have originated in Basketmaker times. The Basketmaker people, so named because of their handsome, tightly woven baskets, were the first *Anasazi,* an Archaic group of farmers who cultivated corn and lived in pithouses about 2,500 years ago. In the Navajo language "Anasazi" means "Ancient Ones" or "Ancient Enemies." Today the preferred usage is "Ancestral Pueblo." Fremont petroglyphs were better represented and longer lasting than pictographs. The Fremont artists were highly skilled in the use of their medium, and the rock art of other groups lacks the innate artistry the Fremont demonstrated as they covered the rocks in tapestries of their figurative art.

Early rock art also exists in Ute country and is stylistically consistent with later examples of Ute rock art, even where content differs, offering "the strongest evidence [yet] supporting prehistoric occupation by the Ute people," states Pettit in *Utes: The Mountain People.* Despite stylistic similarities in the rock art of different prehistoric groups, it is perhaps not surprising that the content itself may change to reflect local geology, ecology, and changing histories. Some post-Spanish Ute art, for example, depicts horses. And, according to Polly Schaafsma in *The Rock Art of Utah,* in addition to wavy lines, snakes, circles, and spirals, the bear paw is "a prevalent element in Colorado [rock art] sites."

There is a Ute rock art panel in Garden of the Gods and a rock art district with prehistoric art at Fort Carson. Archeologist Terry Moody at Fort Carson cites the 1976 National Register of Historic Preservation (NRHP) nomination when referencing some of the many rock art panels found on the extensive, 137,000-acre base, located south of Colorado Springs. The nomination states that, "The art here is believed to be the work of Utes and were [thought to be] a form of communication."

A Crow's Nest and a Mysterious Petroglyph or "Engraving"

Other intriguing artifacts in the Dakota Sandstone, not far from the bedrock metate, include steps to a crow's nest (perhaps an eagle trap) and a D-shaped petroglyph or "engraving" suggestive of a bow, with a crosspiece and "a pecked trail at the bottom," pointing north, "that exhibits possible prehistoric characteristics or may be a brand," according to Snyder. But a review of Native American rock art and Colorado brands turned up no identification that would explain its origins, says Snyder, who refers to the figure as an "engraving." Snyder defines a petroglyph as "native American pecked rock art." Not all engravings are petroglyphs. In describing the faint engraving—which has faded significantly since first spotted fifty years ago by Don Ellis—Snyder further notes that it does not resemble the D-shaped engravings found in South Dakota late prehistoric rock art sites. Linea Sundstrom, a rock art specialist consulted by Snyder, did not "think it possible to identify the design with any confidence."

Ute Bedrock Metate Sites

While some metate sites in Colorado are from the Archaic Period, dating back at least eight thousand years, it is more likely that the sites found in Red Rock Canyon Open Space are comparatively recent and are Ute in origin. Among the more intriguing and unusual of the grinding stones identified in the area are funnel-shaped bedrock metates found in the Dakota Sandstone (see photo pg. 134). The metates in question are worn into the face of the rock at such an angle that gravity could have facilitated the flow of materials worked there downward towards the earth. At the top of each is a small rounded hollow. The troughs are narrow, not more than a few inches across at their widest. They measure about three feet in length and are situated fairly close together, with one in the group less distinct than the others. The metates are carved out of rock faces located on a site commanding a good view out over the eastern plains. However, the Snyder report states: "The metates on the hogback are problematic in that most metates have hard surfaces and exhibit a gloss from food preparation. The metate[s] on the hogback do not currently exhibit either of these characteristics but may have at an earlier time. A one-hand mano [hand-held pounding or processing tool] was collected 10 meters northwest of the metate."

But there may be another explanation for at least one of the more unusual bedrock artifacts. According to former national park superintendent, author, and self-described

Indian cultural enthusiast Jack Williams, it could be a lapidary stone. The Dakota Sandstone in which the deep grooves and shallow hollows are found is measured at #7 on the hardness scale for rocks (diamonds are at #10). Made up of grit and quartz, this formation offers ideal materials for sharpening tools. There is a strong possibility, Williams suggests, that the rock was used to sharpen and shape tools, such as stone axes and manos—a process which took a great deal of time and hard work and likely was done by a specialist. There appears to be a significant amount of patination on the top ("patination" refers to such undisturbed vegetation as lichen or desert varnish), indicating that the artifact may be very old.

One way or another, probable Ute metates were indeed found in Red Rock Canyon Open Space. Were they used to pound acorns into flour, or piñon nuts, process corn into meal, or to grind pigments for use for ceremonial purposes? The Ute women, for example, processed red pigment from the earth, which they removed only after addressing a prayer of thankfulness to the earth. They would then grind it to a fine powder and use it as a kind of rouge on sacred occasions.

While the portable metates used by the Utes were usually oval in shape, those used in pueblos for grinding corn were trough-shaped. Often the metates were too heavy to be conveniently transported. When it was time to pack up and move, the women would carefully turn the metate upside down and leave it in a safe place under a bush, to be returned to later.

When Jack Williams was a boy growing up in his native Colorado in the late 1930s, he discovered in southwestern Colorado near the Great Sand Dunes one of the largest metates ever found in the state. Currently on display at Great Sand Dunes National Park, the metate is bowl-shaped (typical of ones used by hunter/gatherers) and weighs an impressive seventy-four pounds.

Indian Burial Canyon

Indian Burial Canyon is a side canyon feeding into Greenlee Canyon. The name Indian Burial Canyon was featured on planning maps for the grandiose development scheme dreamed up by the late owners of the Red Rock Canyon property, John Bock and his brother, Richard (see Chapter 6). Local historian Don Ellis speculates that, "the name could derive from [the brothers'] boyhood fantasies." Nonetheless, the area was surveyed by archeologists for evidence of burials.

According to archeologists and historians, the Utes buried their dead in rock crevices, shallow graves, or placed the body in a cedar tree and cremated it. Personal belongings, along with favorite dogs and horses, were sometimes added to accompany the dead to the other world. A close survey of the site, with special attention given to rock outcroppings, revealed no evidence of such burials. However, Snyder and his archeological team did report having identified "a stone anomaly ... at the base of one of the red rock formations. "It is not clear," the report continues, "if the feature was prehistoric or historic."

There is yet another archeological find in Red Rock Canyon Open Space that can only be described as "puzzling," and even somewhat mysterious. It consists of a cairn of limestone in which were secreted crystals and steel bracelets. While in certain respects it sounds "new age," it may, in fact, be much older. The secrets of the limestone cairn, with its puzzling artifacts, are yet to be unlocked.

Colorado's Remarkable Prehistoric and Early Human History: A Vital Chapter in the Story of Red Rock Canyon

The recent archeological study conducted for the Colorado Springs Parks, Recreation, and Cultural Services by archeologist Stephan Snyder and his team has added an entirely new and exciting dimension to our understanding of the prehistoric and early historic human history of Red Rock Canyon Open Space and, by extension, that of the Pikes Peak region and beyond. In terms of past and present discoveries that for the first time have been scientifically described and documented, the study demonstrates anew the incredible richness and complexity of Colorado's human legacy as reflected in Red Rock Canyon and in the Pikes Peak region. It is a legacy that extends back thousands of years and embraces many diverse cultures—with its three broad streams (Indian, Spanish and Anglo), and many smaller tributaries—coming together at a rich confluence in the Four Corners region of the American Southwest.

A Storehouse for Ancient Artifacts

Understanding the human history of the past can help us to better understand the present. Unfortunately, much of Colorado's ancient human history has been lost due to systematic pillaging and looting of archeological sites throughout the state. When archeological remains are removed from a site, as the experts tell us, they lose their identifying historical and cultural context, which is essential to understanding their origins. The best storehouse for ancient artifacts and fossils, besides museums, is their natural setting in public parks and open spaces. Here they can continue to educate and illuminate while being left undisturbed *in situ*. In order to preserve and protect this non-renewable resource for future generations, we must all act as responsible stewards, showing artifacts the same respect we would if they were on display in a locked Plexiglas showcase.

CHAPTER 5

Modern Human History: The White Man Comes

*"Since the first pioneers laid claim to it in 1866,
Red Rock Canyon has been viewed as a cash cow—
valued more for the financial wealth it represented
than for its wealth of wildlife and natural beauty."*
—Bill Vogrin, *The Gazette*

The Utes, when first seeing a white man, may have thought they were seeing a "man without a skin," a fitting metaphor, perhaps, for the impact of the white man's arrival in the Pikes Peak region and on today's Red Rock Canyon Open Space. Indeed, in the one hundred and eighty years since their arrival, the Anglo settlers have had a greater impact on the region and the open space than all of the human history that preceded it. And for half of this time, one family dominated—the Bocks.

Just as time has inscribed its signature in the weathered forms in Red Rock Canyon Open Space, so has modern human history left its indelible mark—driven by the forces of the Industrial Revolution—frequently in the form of highly visible extractions and permanent disfiguring scars. Once again, time and change are the key players. But in contrast to geology's deep timelines—human history is brief, passing, and ephemeral, yet fascinating in the stories that make up its many individual and often colorful chapters.

From Explorers and Trappers to Squatters, Prospectors, and Settlers

In 1820, the first recorded Euro-American explorers reached the Pikes Peak region. The party of sixteen, led by Stephen H. Long, an eastern-born military man who taught mathematics at West Point, included cartographers, a naturalist and zoologist, a landscape artist, and, most importantly, a medical doctor, who was also a geologist and a botanist. This latter-day Renaissance man, Edwin James, became the first white man

"Pikes Peak and Colorado City," lithograph by J. Bien, New York, 1866. (From Old Colorado City Historical Society)

on record to climb to the summit of Pikes Peak and the first botanist on the North American continent to collect alpine flora above timberline. The first Colorado columbine was discovered on the Long Expedition. Many of the specimens of flora and fauna collected by James ended up at the Philadelphia Academy of Natural Sciences. Founded in 1812, it is the oldest natural science museum in the western hemisphere. It was here that the famous Long Expedition to explore the West had been organized.

For a short period the iconic Pikes Peak was even known as "James Peak," after Dr. James. But the Long party did little more than scratch the surface when it came to the riches the area contained—at a time when the buffalo still reigned supreme, once choking the creeks with dung, and rendering the water unfit to drink (see Noblett, *Guide to the Geological History of the Pikes Peak Region*).

In addition to early explorers and adventurers in the first half of the nineteenth century, Red Rock Canyon saw the arrival of mountain men and trappers, who, following the beaver trails, according to Ubbelohde et al. in *A History of Colorado*, became "the true explorers of the Rocky Mountain frontier."

According to John G. Bock in his short history, *In Red Rock Canyon Land*, as the fur trappers, or mountain men, followed Fountain Creek up to Ute Pass and the high mountain parks that lay beyond, they camped in the canyons of what is today's open space. To corral their horses and mules, they would simply fashion a brush fence to close off a convenient canyon. It may have been fear of trouble from Plains Indians that drove them to construct a stone and log fort at the mouth of Red Rock Canyon, which they called "Red Rock Fort." But with the decline in the fur trade, the trappers soon left and Red Rock Fort disintegrated into rubble, leaving behind it no trace.

With the onset of Colorado's gold rush in 1859, goldseekers flooded in, along with deer hunters, who supplied prospectors and squatters with food. These new arrivals began to stake out camps in what is today's open space. By the late 1860s, several had filed patents on all of the canyons making up the seven hundred–plus acres of the then–Red Rock Canyon land, which included Red Rock Canyon, Gypsum Canyon, Wild Horse Canyon (now Greenlee Canyon) and Sand Canyon.

Holders of Homestead Patents on the Future Open Space

Among the early petitioners for land in the open space, after the Homestead Act passed in 1862, was local entrepreneur and developer Anthony Bott. For the next two decades investors continued to record Declarations of Occupancy or Homestead Patents in the present-day open space.

In 1872, one of the most interesting and colorful of the Homestead Patent holders to make a cameo appearance on the open space was the noted English lawyer, writer, adventurer, and land speculator, William Henry Blackmore. Inspired by Longfellow's poem "Hiawatha"—Blackmore famously named Manitou Springs after the displaced Algonquin deity. Blakemore was a friend of Colorado Springs founder General William Jackson Palmer and a backer of the historic 1872 Hayden Expedition to Yellowstone. He and his wife Mary (nee Sidford) were socially well-connected, entertaining such prominent figures in their London home as Oliver Wendell Homes, Mark Twain, and Charlotte Brontë.

Demonstrating a deep interest in Native American culture and history unusual for the times, Blackmore established a museum in England to accommodate the famous Squier-Davis collection of early American artifacts, excavated from mounds in Mississippi and Ohio, which he had acquired in the course of his extensive travels. He also assembled one of the finest photographic collections of Native Americans in existence, including images taken by William Henry Jackson, whose work Blackmore helped to underwrite and support.

Not only did Blackmore partially subsidize the historic Hayden Expedition to Yellowstone, he himself accompanied it—as did his adventurous and intrepid wife, Mary. Tragically, she did not survive the expedition, succumbing to pneumonia while in Montana. Today her greatest and most enduring memorial is Mount Blackmore in Montana—named in her honor by the Hayden Expedition. A newly discovered mineral in the same location was named "Blackmorite," after her husband in appreciation for his support of the Hayden Expedition.

Blackmore was involved in numerous land deals, not only in the partnership he formed with William Jackson Palmer, but also in a promotional effort aimed at Robert Todd Lincoln, surviving son of the U.S. president. In the first instance, William Blackmore owned Spanish land grant property in the Southwest where Palmer wanted to run his Denver and Rio Grande Railroad. This led to both a business deal and a friendship.

In addition to his other investments, William Blackmore held claim to a sizeable and magnificent parcel of land at the very heart of Red Rock Canyon, with its massive and distinctive red walls of Lyons Sandstone. It was the same site where the Kenmuir Quarry would later set up its successful enterprise. John George Bock, in his canyon land history, documents the sale, in the autumn of 1872, of eighty-four acres made to William Blackmore by Frederick B. Hertel for the sum of $500. Hertel appears to have engaged in what may have been a shady, if not downright illegal, land speculation deal. It was not until a year after this sale, in 1873, that Hertel actually received the U.S. homestead patent on the land he sold Blackmore. In 1874, the deal-making Hertel then sold Charles M. Leibold both his own homestead and the parcel previously sold to Blackmore.

In short, William H. Blackmore deserves more than a passing mention in any history concerning the region, given his important role both in the exploration and development of the American West and in the preservation of Native American artifacts.

When it came to prospecting for gold on today's open space, Anthony Bott and other homesteaders and squatters on the land were quick to realize that the geology simply wasn't right for it. What little prospecting was done took place largely on adjacent Manitou Springs Section 16, where a few small gold mines were dug. The remains of these mining tunnels can still be seen today. As late as the 1920s and '30s, a miner's cabin stood near an old shaft on Section 16. One tunnel had even been converted by a squatter into a homey dwelling—complete with stone fireplace and stovepipe chimney.

Many of the squatters in Red Rock Canyon land began to look into more practical means of employment, rather than basing their hopes on the risky proposition of striking it rich by traveling to the high Rockies as lone prospectors. And before long, Red Rock Canyon land was dotted with rustic cabins, crude shacks, and bustling makeshift camps, peopled with immigrants to the frontier, hoping, if not to strike a bonanza, at least to discover new opportunities for securing a livelihood.

The Founding of Colorado City

The story turns once again to the entrepreneurial Anthony Bott, who—always quick to capitalize on any development opportunity—helped found Colorado City in 1859, together with several Denver investors. The new town was built on the site of a former ghost town known as "Eldorado" ("the gilded land," in Spanish). At the height of the gold rush, Colorado City was established to serve as a major supply hub and watering hole for miners headed for the gold camps. (Known today as *Old* Colorado City, this quaint, Victorian-era neighborhood on the west side of Colorado Springs has been designated a National Historic District.) Bott's timing was fortuitous. A year later, a major gold strike was made in South Park, up Ute Pass.

The Famous Red Rocks Inspire Nomenclature

As for the naming of Colorado City, Anthony Bott, in his *Life and Reminisces*, reports that it was inspired by none other than the nearby, immemorial, landmark red rocks. Colorado (or "red-colored," in Spanish) was the name given to the territory in 1861 and, in 1876, to the state itself—chosen from a baker's dozen of less appealing options, such as "Idahoe," "Nemera" and "Lula." The Colorado River did *not* inspire either territorial or state name, or that of the earlier Colorado City, as is sometimes erroneously assumed. At the time of Colorado City's baptism, that great river and virtual lifeline flowing through five western states was known as the Grand River—a name first used in print by William Jackson Palmer. Rather, it was the dramatic outcroppings of fountain fins and red Lyons Sandstone, first observed in Garden of the Gods and Red Rock Canyon, which gave the state its lyric and evocative name.

By 1860, some three hundred log houses had been built in Colorado City. Main Street was already known as "Colorado Avenue" and featured businesses with "attractive … square fronts." In the same year, Colorado City experienced something of a building boom, during which some additional "two hundred houses were built," as documented by Irving Howbert in *Memories of a Lifetime in the Pikes Peak Region*. As time went on, the quarries, which continued to be developed in Red Rock Canyon, would provide both building materials and employment opportunities for citizens in the growing town.

Sin City Gains Notoriety

Along with its growth, Colorado City began to gain a certain amount of notoriety, along with the label "Sin City." Its main street soon became better known for its saloons—where at one time Bob Ford, Jesse James' killer, liked to hang out, and for its brothels, including the famous Laura Bell's—than for its shops. Dorothy Aldridge quotes local historian David Hughes in her *Historic Colorado City* as remarking that in those days it was possible to order twenty-two drinks—and enjoy each one of them in a different saloon.

Close on the heels of the gold seekers and squatters, and the earliest patrons of "Sin City," came the settlers, entrepreneurs, and investors, in successive waves, together with the cowboys and wranglers, not to mention those unfortunates afflicted by chronic respiratory ailments for which they hoped to find a cure in the clean, dry, high-desert air and abundant sunshine for which Colorado is justly famous. Soon the Rocky Mountain West was also discovered by another hardy breed, the adventure tourist, who made the requisite stops to gaze at the monumental spectacle of Garden of the Gods, followed by a visit to the nearby famous mineral springs in Manitou Springs, and on up Ute Pass.

The arrival of a sizeable number of settlers in the Pikes Peak region caused additional demand in such communities as Colorado City—for a period of four days the territorial capital—and in Manitou Springs, Fountain, and elsewhere for building materials for houses and public buildings. Catering to this growing demand were the several quarries that began to operate on prominent sites located in the present Red Rock Canyon Open Space. In addition to tons of handsome building stones extracted from the massive outcroppings of Dakota and Lyons Sandstone, these quarries also yielded an abundance of building sand (from decomposed Lyons) and paving gravel (eroded Pikes Peak Mesa gravels), besides lesser amounts of gypsum, which had been discovered in the Lykins Formation, east of the red sandstone outcroppings, in addition to limestone. Some quarry operations left permanent and conspicuous scars in the rock faces, while traces of other rock mining operations have all but vanished.

Anthony Bott Establishes Early Quarries

By the 1860s, Anthony Bott—vividly described by John George Bock in his short, privately published, 41-page history *In Red Rock Canyon Land* as "a plainsman, Indian fighter and promoter of Old Colorado City"—had joined in partnership with a few other settlers in Colorado City to begin mining in Gypsum Canyon. Gypsum is used in the manufacture of cement and plaster of Paris. The Bott gypsum quarry, however, eventually closed—possibly because gypsum, with its seams and nodules, is not easily mined, and demand for some of its byproducts was diminishing. Below the Dakota Hogback, it is still possible to see the fading, overgrown tracks of the old wagon road where gypsum, as well as large logs of pine, were hauled out.

In the Niobrara Hogback of what is today's open space, Bott also started a limestone quarry. Lime is used to produce cement, mortar, paint, and other materials. However, when his cement plant burned down in 1894, Bott decided to stop mining limestone. The site of a small limestone quarry on the east side of the Niobrara is still visible where the eggshell-white sedimentary rock was mined. This sizeable, moon-shaped hollow in the hogback serves as a permanent reminder of the often irremediable and long-term effects of the human impact on the open space.

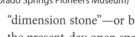

French-born Anthony Bott is described by John George Bock in his history booklet as "a plainsman, Indian fighter, and promoter of Old Colorado City." (1859 photo from Colorado Springs Pioneers Museum)

The indefatigable Bott was also owner of several large "dimension stone"—or building stone (as opposed to "crushed rock")—quarries on the present-day open space. These were located on the east face of the Dakota Hogback, the property's highest ridge, with several smaller quarries sited farther south.

The Bott and Langmeyer Building Stone Quarry

Bott was joined by his brother-in-law and business partner, John Langmeyer, in the operation of Bott and Langmeyer Building Stone. In 1875, John Langmeyer secured title for a piece of land that included today's White Acres in the Dakota Hogback. One of the company's more successful enterprises was in the mining of Dakota building stone from the hogback. As local historian Don Ellis explains the process, "the stone was cleaved from the quarry face along bedding planes." A simple pry bar was all that was required for this relatively low-tech and simple operation of cutting free the large handsome blocks of Dakota Sandstone, with their gradation of colors from tawny to beige to brown, and with their distinguishing hallmarks of red ironstone concretions (in the vernacular known as "rust balls").

A historic Dakota Sandstone quarry on the open space. Quarried Dakota Sandstone from the open space was used in several of the buildings and walls in Colorado Springs and may also have figured into the construction of walls and outbuildings on General Palmer's grand estate, Glen Eyrie. (Photo courtesy Bill Koerner)

Once the blocks had been cut, it took a considerable amount of time to square them off nicely. Sometimes the more readily affordable, less well-shaped chunks and pieces were used to build what were known as "rubble walls" in less pretentious buildings or inside walls. The use of stone in hotels, municipal buildings, and other institutions, not to mention in railroad roundhouses that where subjected to the effects of cinder-spewing steam engines, provided good fire-proofing material at a time when entire towns not uncommonly went up in flames. The faces of the Dakota Hogback continue to show significant light-colored scars where these quarries once operated.

It may be no coincidence that the first stone structure built in Colorado City, two years after its founding, was not only constructed of Bott's building stone, but also was built by Bott himself—the perfect promotional statement for his growing enterprise. Soon the handsome tawny and dun-colored Dakota Sandstone found its way into other architecturally distinguished, historic buildings as well. These included the Midland Railroad roundhouse (later Van Briggle Pottery); a historic Episcopal church (now a bar) next to the downtown post office in Colorado Springs; and the stone sections of the Cog Railroad Depot at the base of Pikes Peak. It's also probable that the Dakota blocks were used in the twin towers, the outdoor pillars, and in the lower half of the exterior walls of the famous Cliff House Inn on Cañon Avenue in nearby Manitou Springs, as well as in the historic house that anchors the Cascade Apartments, and in the Wheeler House Foundation on Cascade Avenue in Colorado Springs. Of even greater historic note is its possible use in some buildings and outside walls on Colorado Springs founder William Jackson Palmer's extensive Glen Eyrie estate. The list of historic buildings in the Pikes Peak region that incorporated quarried Dakota Sandstone from today's open space awaits further study by the experts and will, doubtless, be added to over time.

Although Langmeyer died in 1880, the Dakota Sandstone quarry continued to operate under the Bott-Langmeyer imprimatur. In that same year, Fredericka Langmeyer, Bott's sister and John Langmeyer's widow, joined with her brother in the operation and management of this successful enterprise. She immediately leased the hogback property she owned for the mining and milling of whatever minerals could be found, including gold, silver, copper, and lead. None was found and the lessees soon gave up on the enterprise. Again in the 1950s, the mining tunnels were re-explored in a search for uranium. False hopes were raised when the Geiger counter fluctuated wildly thanks to radon—uranium's equivalent of fool's gold.

General William Jackson Palmer

Born in 1806 and raised as a Hicksite (less orthodox) Quaker in Philadelphia, General William Jackson Palmer, the founder of Colorado Springs, was a fervent believer in civil rights, overcoming his strong pacifist

"The Spirit in which We Act is the Greater Matter."
—**Goethe**

principles to fight with the Union in the Civil War. Guided in life by his favorite Goethe quote, he led the 15th Pennsylvania Volunteer Cavalry while still in his early twenties, and also distinguished himself as a Union spy. Earning the high rank of Brigadier General at an early age, Palmer was awarded the Congressional Medal of Honor for bravery on February 24, 1894.

In founding the city of Colorado Springs in 1871 at the age of thirty-five (now Colorado's second largest city), Palmer helped to transform a high desert plain at the base of Pikes Peak into a city of trees and parks, which grew to a population of 21,085 by 1900. With a backbone of steel, high moral values, intense energy, and a deep sense of order, Palmer soon made his fortune as a developer and industrialist. Owner of the largest coal mine in the region (John D. Rockefeller bought out Palmer's Colorado Fuel and Iron Company by the time labor conditions sparked the 1913 strike that led to the Ludlow Massacre), he helped to develop three railroads: the Kansas Pacific, the National Railroad of Mexico connecting Texas and Mexico City, and his own narrow-gauge Denver and Rio Grande. He built the first road to Denver. In Colorado Springs, he envisioned a "Newport in the Rockies" that would incorporate the best of the East, while leaving behind the worst—with its heavy industry, polluting smokestacks, noise, and congestion.

Yet this highly successful industrial capitalist and civil engineer—who hated smoke as much as he detested litter—was also the area's first environmentalist and open-space advocate, long before the terms had gained currency. A great benefactor, Palmer gifted some 1,278.20 acres of parks to the city (a huge gift in relation to the size of the city at that time). Well ahead of his time in his understanding of the vital importance of parks and open spaces to serve

Colorado Springs founder and Civil War hero General Palmer with daughters and family friends enjoying the perfect idyll of a beautiful day at Glen Eyrie. (Photo circa 1903 from Colorado Springs Pioneers Museum)

the public, Palmer was not only the founder of Colorado Springs, he was also the father of its parks system. On the 100th anniversary of his death (as this is written), and in this book dedicated to the theme of the preservation of a valued and beautiful piece of open space, it is both timely and appropriate to acknowledge the major role William Jackson Palmer played in the preservation of the natural heritage of the Pike's Peak region—both in terms of what he so generously gave and by way of his remarkable example, which served to inspire so many.

Palmer believed strongly in the value of getting outdoors and enjoying the healthful benefits of

> *"He taught me to know the outdoors, and especially to love it."*
> — **Laura Gilpin,** southwestern photographer

fresh air and plenty of exercise. To this end he contributed not only numerous parks, but he laid out one hundred miles of beautiful trails, some with white-painted rocks to mark trails intended for moonlight rides. These include a still extant trail system in Palmer Park as well as the historic Chamberlain Trail.

So deep was Palmer's love of nature that he served as both mentor and inspiration to the young southwestern photographer, Laura Gilpin (1891–1979), born near Colorado Springs, famous for her empathetic photographs of Navajos and dramatic southwestern landscapes, and arguably among the top ten artists produced by the state of Colorado. Palmer took Gilpin riding and taught her to identify and name local flora and fauna. Each year Palmer would present Gilpin with a book at Christmas. One of these gifts was to prove both prescient and far-reaching in its effects. Its title was *Hunting Wild Animals with a Camera*. Gilpin credited Palmer with sparking her own deep love of the natural history and landscapes of the Southwest, which would become the subject of her memorable photographs and enduring artistry.

General Palmer was as egalitarian in his beliefs about who should be able to enjoy the benefits of nature's gifts as he was in his politics. He believed that workers, in particular, as much as the affluent, should enjoy free and equal access to the healthful benefits that accrue to mind and body in the open air. Palmer saw this as a basic human right—with nature's wonders as much our birthright as the air we breathe. Thus, he did not approve of South Cheyenne Cañon being closed off to the public by a private vendor. For him, the idea that such a natural wonder should be run like a popular concession—as it continues to be to this day—went totally against the grain. But the strategically clever general found a way to get around it. He bought property on Mount Cutler from which citizens could view the famous Seven Falls from a convenient vantage point, without having to travel up a dusty road and pay an admission fee, in some cases, one which they could ill-afford.

Moreover, Palmer was nearly unique for his time in another respect. He understood the critical need to preserve and protect the region's communities of indigenous wildlife. He was angered, for instance, when tourists on the Kansas Pacific Railroad mindlessly shot buffalo along the track for blood sport. Palmer foresaw that such wanton killing would eventually lead to the destruction of the great bison herds and would cause problems with the Indians who depended on them for their livelihood and, indeed, for their very survival.

The founder of Colorado Springs also worked with arborists to plant thousands of trees where no trees grew—in the high desert of his new mountain town, which was sometimes called "Little London" because of the number of Englishmen who lived here. Palmer hired a forester to prevent settlers from cutting down trees along the creeks and in Garden of the Gods. Most citizens had every reason to value trees, except when wood was needed for building or fuel. Evidently Palmer's fine example had caught on to some extent—on June 20, 1891, the *Colorado City Iris* reported that, "A Colorado Springs policeman arrested the county commissioners for cutting trees in front of the court house."

Palmer, in keeping with his principled environmental ethos, managed to squelch a plan to extend a streetcar line along Camp Creek to Garden of the Gods, and another to carve presidential busts on North and South Gateway Rocks in Garden of the Gods.

Glen Eyrie: The Grandest Estate in the Pikes Peak Region

In November 1870, Palmer married Mary Lincoln Mellen—nicknamed "Queen" by her maternal grandmother—a nineteen-year-old beauty of cultivated tastes from a prominent East Coast family. It was for Queen that Palmer built the magnificent Glen Eyrie "castle" on his large estate, with its allusions to the Scottish Highlands and grand English manor houses, and its handsome stone tower and twenty-four fireplaces set in hand-sawn oak walls, with antique mantels imported from Europe.

Completed in 1904, Glen Eyrie contained a total of sixty-seven rooms. It was named by the estate's Scottish landscape architect for a large, somewhat disheveled eagle's nest in the red Lyons Sandstone cliffs not far from the castle. A successor nest (possibly made up of portions of the original of a century ago) can still be observed today, clinging to the cranny of a cliff like an aerial condo. Below the larger nest, into which red-tailed hawks have unceremoniously moved, is a smaller version, "perhaps a

General Palmer's beautiful Glen Eyrie castle built next to Garden of the Gods. (Photo courtesy *Castles of Colorado*)

mother-in-law suite," wryly observes Len Froisland, Glen Eyrie's resident historian, who has been employed at the estate for more than three decades. The sandstone cliffs, with their jutting red outcrops, fins, and monoliths, also known as "Little Garden of the Gods," form a stunning backdrop to the castle.

For its time, Glen Eyrie boasted every conceivable modern convenience. There were built-in fire hoses on each floor, a central vacuum, world-class weather monitoring equipment, and one of the first milk pasteurizing plants in the U.S., with cows luxuriating in facilities supervised by a Swiss dairyman. The Glen Eyrie castle, fit indeed for a Queen, was and is one of the most impressive estate homes in the Pikes Peak Region (and perhaps in the Rockies). With its ingenious attention to detail, the estate might best be described as a stylistically different Monticello.

Most historians believe that it was a heart condition that prevented Queen, who died at the age of forty-four, from ever settling permanently in Colorado Springs, with its high altitude and thin air, rather than any underlying antipathy for that "queer, embryo-looking place," as writer Helen Hunt Jackson so unforgettably described the town in 1873. Instead, on doctor's orders, Queen sought out a more temperate climate, and in addition, gained a more culturally enriched one when she settled in England. Palmer, meanwhile, remained at Glen Eyrie where his work was, while enjoying the company of his fine horses and pony-sized Great Danes, including his favorite, Yorick.

(Palmer once praised dogs in a letter to his ten-year-old relation Daisy Mellen because "they rarely die and never resign.")

In the course of his life, Palmer supported a passel of relatives (most of them Mellens), as well as employees, while managing not just the development of a town, but that of a small industrial empire that included the railroad-supporting coal mine and a steel mill in Pueblo, with numerous people on the payroll. And his worries were added to periodically by major cash flow problems and labor strikes. But by the end of his life he had begun to enjoy some of the abundant fruits made possible by his impressive range of skills, his ceaseless work and industry, and his sheer breadth of vision.

While riding near his estate in the autumn of 1906, General Palmer was thrown from his horse, paralyzing him from the waist down. The best care money could afford failed to restore him to his former good health. But, to cheer him in his few remaining years of declining health and mobility, the general's three daughters—Marjorie, Elsie, and Dorothy—were now happily ensconced at Glen Eyrie, having returned to the U.S. after Queen's untimely death.

When the castle's final wing was completed, it served as a venue for Christmas parties, circuses, and festivities organized for the children of workers and local citizens, including Indian youth.

Booker T. Washington: A Guest at Glen Eyrie

Among Glen Eyrie's most distinguished guests was Booker T. Washington, who dined in 1906 with the general. For years Palmer had been among the Civil War veterans who gave generously and quietly to the support of Hampton University, the historically black institution at which Booker T. Washington, one of its earliest students, was educated. At the time of Washington's visit to Colorado, he was lecturing at Colorado College.

It is estimated that, in his lifetime, General Palmer gave away nearly one-half of his entire estate in his many generous gifts to public and to private charities. Palmer's professed concern for the laborer had been formed, in part, by a backpacking trip he made through Europe as a young man, during which he saw first-hand the social ills that resulted from overwork, underpay, and unhealthy working conditions. But Palmer, surprisingly, did little to improve working conditions at his own coal mine—with the important exception that miners' families were provided with better housing, schools, and medical care. Yet when the general sold the Denver and Rio Grande Railroad, he divided half the profits with his employees.

When it comes to the question of where the Dakota building stone for Palmer's splendid castle was mined, not all historians are in agreement, with one writer claiming Red Rock Canyon as a source. However, the weight of historical evidence suggests otherwise. Nonetheless, a probable link is thought to exist between the historic sandstone quarries in Red Rock Canyon and other major structures found on Palmer's estate.

E.C. (Cornelius) van Diest: Engineer for Glen Eyrie

Palmer is reported to have instructed E.C. (Cornelius) van Diest—chief engineer for the Glen Eyrie project from 1903 to 1906 (Glen Eyrie was completed in record time while the general was traveling in Europe)—to use "lichen-veneered" Dakota Sandstone mined from a site on the estate itself.

Born in East India (now Indonesia) in 1865, van Diest was a close friend of Palmer's and served as a pallbearer at his funeral in 1909, when, at age seventy-two, the general tragically succumbed to his riding injuries. A well-respected civic leader with many investments and property holdings of his own, van Diest was known for being a strong advocate of child welfare. Awarded an honorary Ph.D. from the Colorado School of Mines, van Diest is credited with helping to develop lightning protection for buildings. Until his death in 1951, he served as a trustee at Colorado College. And more significantly yet—in terms of open spaces and public parks in the Pikes Peak region—van Diest designed Palmer's superb system of public parks.

According to an article written by van Diest in 1942, at the age of seventy-seven, and titled, "Some Recollections of General William J. Palmer and the Building of Glen Eyrie," the building stone used in Palmer's castle was "quarried or cut from the Dakota Sandstones forming part of the east boundary to the Glen. Each stone, after being cut to the desired thickness [about four-inches thick, since the stones formed a veneer] and selected as to color and mossiness, was brought in straw-bedded wagons to the work. If one views the angles of the hexagonal tower and the numerous right angles in the building, the problem of properly selecting stone to fit these conditions can be appreciated," wrote van Diest in his clear, authoritative prose.

In *Newport in the Rockies*, Marshall Sprague reaffirms that "the lichen crusted [Dakota] stones" used to build Palmer's castle were quarried from outcrops in Blair Athol, the canyon north of Glen Eyrie. While Sprague and van Diest describe the quarry site location somewhat differently, both assert that the sun-warm, beige-gold building stone for the monumental castle was mined on Palmer's extensive estate.

But the convenience of securing building stone from a well-established working quarry in close proximity to Glen Eyrie for those structures that did not require "lichen-veneered, first-cut stone" argues strongly in favor of Red Rock Canyon as a source. In terms of greater ease and convenience, it would have trumped hand-cutting stone on the estate and carting it over uneven terrain. In the absence of documentation or further study by an architectural geologist, much at this stage remains in the realm of conjecture. However, it is a good guess that the quarries did supply some of the tan (Dakota) and red (Lyons) building stone used in other structures on Palmer's Jeffersonian-style estate, including the dairy, the outer walls of the carriage house, the old gatehouse, and the gardener's cottage.

Thanks to the handsomely colored, beautifully dressed stones, the walls of the Dakota Sandstone in Glen Eyrie castle glow warmly like the tawny coat of a lion in late afternoon light. Besides their organically warm, buff-gold color, the stones retained some of their natural appearance as a result of being "first cut," meaning, as per Palmer's precise instructions, that their attractively textured surfaces still claimed original markings, courtesy of Mother Nature. Not only were they stamped with lichens, but they were undiminished in their appeal by any smooth, raw, injurious cuts. This was the aesthetic equivalent of using unpeeled logs—with their natural bark intact—in the construction of a traditional log cabin.

Dressing Building Stone Requires Skill and Patience

Dressing an ashlar, or squared block of building stone, such as the Dakota Sandstone blocks used in Palmer's Glen Eyrie and those quarried extensively from the open space itself and used in buildings in Denver and the Pikes Peak region, required a skilled stonecutter. General Palmer was wealthy enough to employ many stone dressers on site. In the late nineteenth century, such craftsmen were well paid, earning the munificent sum of $6.00 per day. The basic stone-cutting tools included drills, portable toothless saws such as wire saws, and an abrasive slurry made of loose grit, sand, or steel shot. The process of hand-cutting the stone was slow and painstaking.

Among other essentials in the stone dresser's tool kit were "feathers" (a type of shim) and wedges (plugs) of iron, which would be pounded into holes drilled in the rock at carefully spaced intervals to help split it. Masons hewed; bankers cut to specification; settler masons squared and trimmed. Only the sides and front of the building block needed to be finished. High points needed to be eliminated in order to prevent the weight of the layered stone from causing cracks or wobbling and to facilitate the mortaring process.

According to mining geologist Jon Barker, a skilled rock cutter himself, the easiest rock to cut is "green" rock, meaning rock that has not been cured or dried of its sap. (Rock has water in it, poetically called "sap" by stonecutters.) However, before stones can be finished, they need to be cured. The largest building blocks were typically used—as can be seen in the Dakota Sandstone walls of Palmer's Glen Eyrie castle—at the base of a given edifice to lend the impression of solidity.

Gypsum was used in the production of the delicate and graceful plaster-of-Paris Italianate moldings that border the ceilings of several of the castle's grandest rooms. No detail was overlooked by General Palmer in the castle's architecture or that of its beautifully laid-out grounds. For example, multi-faceted, well-formed, pink crystals of gypsum were also used ornamentally to line the bridge on the expansive castle grounds—from which stunning red cliffs form the backdrop for sailing eagles, roaming coyotes, wild turkeys, and big-horn mountain sheep, tame as domesticated herds.

General Palmer wanted his friend, chief engineer van Diest, to construct an edifice that would last for a thousand years and there is every indication that van Diest succeeded in this mandate (while in the process contending with such problems as union labor walkouts). To obtain the roof tiles he admired from a centuries-old church in Europe, General Palmer bought the entire church and shipped the tiles home. When the original tiles recently began to leak, they were removed and replaced with ones that were less attractive, but more functional. Some of the old tiles have been recycled by local artists, who use them as mini canvasses for paintings. But the rest of the castle remains in excellent repair.

Rock Quarrying in Red Rock Canyon

Different dates have been given for the onset of large-scale, heavy industrial quarrying in Red Rock Canyon, which was primarily centered on the mining of the handsome and increasingly fashionable red Lyons Sandstone, formed between 250 and 290 million years ago of Permian Period, wind-blown, red desert dunes. It is generally agreed, however, that it was not until between 1886 and 1888 that the canyon saw what might be regarded as extensive and well-capitalized quarrying operations. John G. Bock in his book, *In Red Rock Canyon Land,* states that the quarries operated from 1884 to 1904. Other historians suggest slightly later dates.

The Lyons Sandstone found in Red Rock Canyon was considered to be some of the best, if not *the* best, found anywhere in the country. According to Bertie Langridge, a mineralogist writing in 1890, there were four other sandstone quarries operating in the country and none had sandstone of comparable quality or functioned on such a large scale. And he further notes in the picturesque lingua franca of geology: "In Kenmuir the formation is such that the waste, riprap, and spalls common in most quarries is minimal. … Almost every particle of stone quarried … is of market value."

The three quarries operating in Red Rock Canyon in the late 1800s were the Snider Stone and Lime Company, the Colorado Stone Company, and the Greenlee family-owned Kenmuir Quarry. The site of the second largest of these operations, the Snider Quarry is located just west of the upper parking lot on the open space at the mouth of Red Rock Canyon. As you head farther south, the Colorado Stone Company, the smallest of the three quarries, was located just beyond the former Bock house and the man-made lakes. Deep slots can be seen in the ridge rocks where this quarry once operated. Farther south still is the site of the Kenmuir Quarry, by far the largest and most successful of the red Lyons Sandstone quarries, which targeted a more upscale, competitive market, producing higher quality and quantity of stone than its smaller competitors who catered more to local demands.

Not all of the rock in the Lyons Formation, despite its uniformly high quality, was worth quarrying. There are places where cutting suddenly stops because the rock is bad. (The conspicuous inky spots seen in the rocks are accretions of ferrous iron oxide, also called "goethite" after the great German poet, writer, and scientist Johann Wolfgang von Goethe.)

The Snider Quarry

The Snider Quarry operation was owned by two brothers, George W. and William Snider, who were based in the nearby town of Manitou Springs. (William discovered the upper level of the well-known Cave of the Winds and turned it into a commercial operation.) A *Weekly Gazette* story, dated August 12, 1888, states that "the Snider Quarry will open in October and will occupy 60 acres of land … extending from the mouth of the canyon half a mile upwards."

The Colorado Stone Company

While the Colorado Stone Company may have been the smallest of the three quarries, it generated big headlines and a certain amount of hyperbole in the *Weekly Gazette* of October 6, 1888. The caption for the story jumps out in large, bold-faced letters. It announces an "Important Industry," and is followed up by four separate subheads announcing the: "Beginning of an Enterprise of Considerable Magnitude; an Association of Wealthy Capitalists Incorporated; To Develop the Red Rock Quarries at Colorado City; The Stone Superior and Shipping Facilities Excellent."

Mr. John L. Stuart, the Vice Present and General Manager of the company, is somewhat quaintly described as being the "representative of a syndicate of wealthy gentlemen from all over the states, whose names are household words ... although it is not desirable to make known the names of many of the men." The article reports that the quarry offices would be in Denver, that the company "was incorporated with a capital of $100,000," and that the machinery being brought in for the operation "will consist of some of the heaviest machinery ever brought to the West." And, indeed, news stories from the time confirm that Ingersoll steam channelers were employed in the operation, and were the first of their kind to be used west of the Mississippi.

The *Weekly Gazette* story noted that brown stone for building had recently gone out of fashion and that the new fashion was to use the bright red and other colored stones. "No more beautiful or durable stone can be found than the red stone near Colorado City. ... The company's quarries at Colorado City are situated in Red Rock canon [sic] and the Midland Railroad [this should be the "Colorado Midland"] is now putting in a line of switches up the canon to them, that the stone may be loaded directly onto the cars for shipping. It is expected the company will be able to begin shipping stone in about twenty days."

The story further quotes Mr. Stuart as rather grandiloquently suggesting that, "The quantity of the rock is unlimited [extending fifty miles into the mountains] ... it could keep thousands of men employed in quarrying the stone for centuries to come without exhausting it." According to references cited by Dr. Jack A. Murphy, Emeritus Curator of Geology at the Denver Museum of Nature and Science, building stones from the Colorado Stone Company quarry were shipped to Fort Worth, Texas, and to Kansas, as well as throughout the West. However, the Colorado Stone operation was not long-lived; and it is thought to have been absorbed, in about 1889, either into the Greenlee Kenmuir Quarry or the Snider Quarry, according to geologist R.E. Lippoth, an expert on quarry history.

The Kenmuir Quarry

Several historic documents exist from the days of the Kenmuir Quarry's peak of operation, which was owned and operated by the Greenlee brothers of Denver: John R., William T., James R., and Robert C. These include a piece of ephemera, dated 1896. It is a handwritten bill in pencil that records on a scrap of paper the sale of one cow to Greenlee Sons for the seemingly exorbitant cost of $30—the equivalent of ten carloads of the coarsest derrick rock available at the Kenmuir-mined quarry. Clearly, cows were a precious commodity, even after the advent in the late 1870s of such great southwestern cattle spreads as the famous JJ Ranch.

A decade earlier, in 1888, historic documents show that the Kenmuir Quarry received permission to use the Knox blasting method in its rock mining operations. The license was renewed again in 1890 and 1892, and probably several times thereafter.

Greenlee & Sons Kenmuir Quarry, which began operations in the late 1880s, was the largest and most successful of the red sandstone quarry operations sited on the future open space. The quality of the stone was reportedly some of the best in the country. Red Lyons mined from the quarries provided building stone for many of Denver's finest civic buildings and grandest mansions. Here workers at the Kenmuir Quarry pause for a photograph, circa 1890. (Photos from Colorado Springs Pioneers Museum)

The historic lower Kenmuir Quarry resembles an Aztec ziggurat except for the large abandoned cranes, circa 1930. (Photo courtesy Don Ellis)

Several bills of lading further record the activities of the Greenlee-owned Kenmuir Quarry in the mid-1890s. Among these is an order sent in April 1895, and a contract signed on the 13th day of May 1895, in which Greenlee & Sons of Denver agreed to load and deliver from their quarries, located in Red Rock Canyon, seventy-five cars of derrick rock (coarse rock or riprap) from three of its steam derricks at the cost of $3.00 per car. Stone loaded from the upper pile with the use of a hand-operated derrick came to $4.75 per car, while bridge stone from the top of the cliff totaled an astronomical $5.75 per car.

The Colorado Midland Railway Company, on the receiving end, required the coarse rock to riprap a new embankment as protection against high water at Colorado City. The Colorado Midland also requested the loan of a "grab hook" to use on a derrick placing the rock as it was unloaded. Another bill of lading, dated August 1896, records charges for several carloads of building stone from Greenlee's quarry to be shipped to the Reduction Works at Colorado City (Penrose and company's gold reduction mill). While most of these archival examples of Kenmuir's early operations are somewhat work-a-day, the red Lyons building stone that was to be harvested at the quarry would soon be destined for much grander things.

It is largely thanks to the archival instincts of the John Bocks, father and son, the subsequent owners of Red Rock Canyon for eighty years, and in particular, John G., the elder, that such records as the ones just cited, and often recorded in black ink in a quaint, spidery hand, were carefully preserved and are today available at the Colorado Springs Pioneers Museum.

Most open space visitors approach the Kenmuir Quarry from the east side, which is its most dramatic view. As it further consolidated its operations in 1888, the Kenmuir quarried deeply and extensively into the massive Lyons Sandstone outcropping on the open space, transforming the rock, with the benefit of radical incisions and "new technology," into an enormous red, pyramidal staircase of stone. The reason for the stair effect is that the channelers used to cut the rocks could not get absolutely flush with the rock wall. Each cut down is called a "lift," thus, a "lift down."

At the historic Kenmuir site, the part of the quarry you arrive at after hiking through Quarry Pass on the west side—with its spiky line of iron pins sprouting from red rock—represents the oldest part of the operation. This is borne out by its use of older technology, seen in its surviving skeletal metal works, rusting like the red rocks themselves. What is sometimes referred to as the "Upper Kenmuir Quarry" is even farther south and higher up.

Both the Snider and Kenmuir quarries were eventually equipped with "modern" heavy machines that were designed to cut rather than cleave stone. These included steam-driven channeling machines mounted on temporary rails. Tracks were laid down for each channel cut, with the top lift having been cut by hand. Then, from that point down, the machines cut individual channels using star bits mounted on long chisels that chattered along at a slow pace, with plenty of attendant dust and noise. According to geologist R.E. Lippoth, the channels were approximately 3 inches wide and 4- to 8-feet deep across the quarry floor. Blocks cut in the Greenlee Quarry, using

6- to 7-foot channels, typically measured 7x6x10-feet and weighed over 25 tons each. The smaller quarries used smaller channeling machines. The Snider Quarry, for example, cut 4-foot channels.

Moving at a rate of about seven linear feet per minute, the channeling machines made several passes to achieve the desired depth. Some channeling machines were capable of cutting two channels at a time. The ancient Egyptians, when building the pyramids, also cut channels, but they did it all by hand, relying on thousands of conscripts to perform the heavy labor. While the nineteenth-century quarry workers in Red Rock Canyon were at least minimally paid labor, they nonetheless operated heavy machinery, toiling for long, hot hours in dusty, noisy work conditions—with silicosis and hearing loss not uncommon occupational hazards.

Once the quarry channeling machines had cut the desired channels in the rock, black powder was poured into a series of three-inch-diameter round holes that were drilled ten feet deep at the base of the rock using gadding drill bits. The process of drilling holes under a block is itself called "gadding." Scoring along the line of the holes helped ensure a clean break in the stone, especially important if one were aiming for an upscale market. Using the patented Knox blasting method (named after its inventor, whose patent on it earned him enormous sums), the holes were plugged to hold the pressure of the blast. When the black powder was detonated, using the "newest" method of electricity to ignite the powder, it blasted the big, square building blocks of red stone free from its parent ledge.

The large, heavy blocks—which had thus been "plugged" down to sizes manageable by the derricks—were now ready to be "lofted," typically with the use of a heavy chain attached to the giant steam-powered derrick, then loaded aboard a waiting railroad car. An early news story—which reads like a puff piece about local boys making good—reported that the homegrown Snider Quarry had the largest derrick in the state, with its seventy-four-foot high mast. But it was surpassed, in this high-vaulting competition, say experts, by the Kenmuir. It was the Kenmuir, with its guy lines that stretched all the way across Red Rock Canyon and its surviving industrial artifacts that ultimately boasted the largest mast-and-boom-style derrick in the state, a hulking structure that in old photographs dominates the landscape like some giant prehistoric craning-necked dinosaur. Sizeable slots can still be observed in the red rocks where heavy timbers once used in the Kenmuir's derrick were solidly planted.

The double-gauge Colorado Midland Railway spur, built in 1888, ran deep into the canyon and served the quarries as a vital transportation link. It is impossible to overestimate the importance of this link to ensuring that the quarry operation was the success it was, both regionally and nationally. One might question, for instance, why so many Denver mansions and institutional buildings made use of stone quarried from Red Rock Canyon instead of the same stone found in its namesake town of Lyons, Colorado. The reason is simple enough. Lyons, although closer to Denver, had no convenient transportation link via rail until the late 1880s.

Today the historic tracks of the Colorado Midland Railway can no longer be seen on the open space, but there are some anchor bolts, not in direct line of sight with the

Kenmuir Quarry, which may have been used to secure a water tower that once serviced the steam-driven train. There was also a small, connecting funicular train at the Kenmuir that ran up with empty cars on the tracks laid beside a newly cut channel, and then ran back down again with loaded ones.

The Colorado Midland spur also boasted a small company town in what is today's open space, consisting of a power plant, rooming houses, cottages, livestock, a post office, and a blacksmith shop. Some of the old offices, after the railway closed, still contained stacks of correspondence and records.

A convenient, hand-built narrow staircase that was cut with a pick, climbs straight up the face of the red Lyons Sandstone where the Kenmuir Quarry once operated, creating the large, temple-like ziggurats. Children love to climb up this ruddy red staircase; acrophobics do not rejoice in it quite so much. By climbing up the quarry face, taking either the trail around to the left or the more direct hand-cut stairs and entering what this writer likes to think of as the "Red Lyons amphitheatre," it is still possible to see gravelly soil blackened by embers. This marks the spot where the large, fired-up boilers, stoked with embers, produced the steam that once powered the rock-cutting channelers.

The Kenmuir's impressive and well-documented inventory included an Ingersoll drill, an Ingersoll bar channeler, a Sergeant drill, three Wardwell machines, forges and bellows (for making tools), various steam pumps, one air compressor, and fourteen derricks (three of which were run by compressed air), just to name a few of the items listed in a report compiled by mineralogical engineer Bertie Langridge in 1890.

By 1890, only Greenlee & Sons (Kenmuir) and the Snider brothers were still operating in Red Rock Canyon, where they continued to extract and ship prodigious amounts of Lyons Sandstone. Greenlee was shipping out ten rail carloads per day of prime building stone (a fully loaded car could carry forty tons), while employing one hundred and twenty men. The Snider Quarry was averaging five carloads a day and employing thirty-five men. Because of the rock's uniform, fine-grained texture, its relative durability (with very little arkose or cobble), and its handsome, hematite-red color, Lyon's Sandstone in the late 1800s enjoyed a national market. It was in such wide demand by the 1890s that shipments of Lyons Sandstone building blocks had topped the charts at over forty-two thousand tons per year. During this period, the Snider Quarry alone recorded a backlog of four hundred carloads.

Of the two Lyons sandstone quarries, the Kenmuir was clearly the better financed and more successful. (Langbridge estimated that the stone from the Kenmuir Quarry should bring in $2.00 per ton and, if the quarry operated double shifts, using "artificial" light, that it could net, in annual profits, the grand sum of $1,750,000.) In its heyday, the site was a buzzing hive of industry and activity, supporting numerous buildings, including ones to house the heavy and expensive machinery the quarry owned. An old safe, perhaps from the quarry superintendent's office, still lies in Greenlee Canyon.

During the depression of 1893–94, the Pikes Peak region was not as severely affected as the rest of the country. Large wealth was beginning to be amassed, thanks to big gold strikes at the Portland and Independence Mines in Victor in the 1890s. The depression's full impact was, however, felt elsewhere, signaling a decline in orders for the widely coveted and expensive red sandstone building blocks. Indeed, since most of the quarried stone was sold outside the region, the impact of the depression on the Red Rock Canyon quarries was the primary cause for their decline and/or ultimate demise. The secondary cause was the onset of new technology. The Snider Quarry, thus, was sold in June of 1894; the Kenmuir Quarry, however, continued its operations at a reduced level throughout the depression, closing its doors sometime before 1915, by which time all quarry activity in the open space had ceased.

A small stone building from the Greenlee operation occupied a place in Greenlee Canyon as recently as the 1950s. And it is still possible to see remains from this enterprise, including large anchor bolts skewered into the rock where heavy cable had once been tied. Suspended across the canyon from the quarry operation itself, the guy line was attached to the east and facing wall of Lyons Sandstone, on the opposite side. The bolts and several deep cuts and scars in the rocks from the Kenmuir Quarry are easy to spot.

Quarried Lyons Building Stone for Colorado's Finest Buildings and Mansions

Red Lyons Sandstone building blocks quarried on what is today's open space grace many fine and historic buildings found in the Pikes Peak region and Denver, as well as in other states. According to reporter and historian Dorothy Aldridge writing in *Historic Colorado City*, stone quarried in Red Rock Canyon was used in the Board of Trade building in Fort Worth, Texas, and in the Union Depot in Des Moines, Iowa. Closer to home its use appears in such charming old structures in nearby Pueblo as the Union Depot, built in 1889, and listed on both state and national historic registers.

In Colorado Springs, the historic Lowell School located on Nevada Avenue dates to 1891, and is listed on the State Historic Register. Blocks of Red Rock Canyon–quarried Lyons Sandstone contribute a handsome border to its foundation wall. Geologist Jon Barker confirms that the lintels and arches of Mackenzie's Chophouse, originally the Alamo Hotel, are also ornamented with stone from Red Rock Canyon. The red Lyons similarly adorns the historic Union Printers Home (1892) and was used at the base of exterior walls in the Denver and Rio Grande train station, built by Palmer (now Giuseppe's Depot Restaurant).

McGregor Hall, one of the women's residences at Colorado College in Colorado Springs, with its stylish gambrel roof and eyebrow dormers, was completed in 1903. Listed on the National Register of Historic Places, its attractive and solidly built walls are constituted entirely of Lyons Sandstone mined from Red Rock Canyon's Greenlee (Kenmuir) Quarry.

In nearby Manitou Springs, two historic buildings that house the sulfa springs are thought to have been built of the material. The town's beautiful and historic "Red Stone Castle," which some knowledgeable researchers believe was built in the 1890s (although earlier dates have been given), and which is listed on both state and national historic registers, incorporated stone from the Red Rock Canyon quarries. One of the oldest and grandest houses in the region, "Red Stone Castle" was built by Isaac Davis on Iron Slope Mountain. Currently a privately owned home and B&B, "Red Stone Castle" is distinguished by its handsome stone turret, its reputation for being haunted, and walls that are between eighteen inches and two-feet thick. With its fairy-tale tower and handsome exterior walls fashioned entirely from the Lyons building stone quarried in Red Rock Canyon, the castle glows with an added intensity in a rose-colored dawn.

The well-known B&B in Manitou Springs called the Red Crags, built in 1889, is also a candidate for the list of historic buildings utilizing Red Rock Canyon–quarried stone in its construction.

There was even more abundant wealth to build even grander edifices in the capital of Denver, thanks to the gold and silver mining booms in the 1860s and '70s in Central City, Black Hawk, and Leadville. Some of the 280-million-year-old Lyons building stone extracted from the present-day open space has been identified in several of Denver's most gracious old mansions and finest historic buildings, giving new meaning to the word "antique."

In his book *Geology Tour of Denver's Capitol Hill Stone Buildings*, geologist Jack Murphy identifies more than a dozen historic Denver homes and public edifices—built between 1887 and 1893—that incorporated building stone quarried from Red Rock Canyon. A few of these architect-designed structures, with their romantic, neo-Gothic details and flourishes and their Victorian charm, were built exclusively from the handsome red Lyons Sandstone from Red Rock Canyon. But because it

top: Described as "a towering sandstone castle," and listed on the National Register of Historic Places, Red Rock Canyon quarried stone was used in the construction of Denver's Croke-Patterson-Campbell Mansion built by Thomas Croke in the 1890s. Croke was a Denver merchant, former state senator, and later ran the *Rocky Mountain News*. (Photo courtesy Don Ellis)

right: Denver's famous Molly Brown House makes use of quarried Lyons building stone from Red Rock Canyon as architectural accents. (Courtesy Molly Brown House Museum)

commanded a high price, the stone was sometimes used only as architectural accents in buildings constructed of the less expensive blond-colored Dakota Sandstone, or used at the base of foundation walls and/or in flagstone steps.

On Murphy's list of memorable, old-world buildings and mansions in Denver that appear both on state and national historic registers and that make use of Lyons building blocks quarried in Red Rock Canyon are: the Central Presbyterian Church, the Molly Brown House (which is a good example of a house using red sandstone for architectural accents), the Boston Block (a commercial building), the Masonic Temple, the Lang House (part of Lang & Pugh Row Houses), the George Schleier Mansion, the Keating Mansion, the Creswell Mansion, and the Croke-Patterson-Campbell Mansion.

Murphy cites six additional historic Denver buildings that are not listed on the national register, but which, more significantly, do incorporate the popular, salmon-colored native stone quarried and shipped from Red Rock Canyon. These include the Whitehead-Peabody House, the Daly House, the Woodward House, and the Lehow-Crebbin House. Two more Denver structures are cited by Murphy as ones that in all probability made use of Red Rock Canyon stone, but the source in these examples is less well established. One is the Sheedy Mansion, an expansive and splendid example of Victoriana in the best sense, complete with diminutive Gothic tower and neo-classic columns; another is the Evans-Strayer-Townsend House.

The North Capitol Hill neighborhood in Denver provides an outstanding showcase for many unforgettably grand and historic buildings and quaint old manses built of the now-famous brick-red Lyons Sandstone quarried in the nineteenth century and at the turn of the twentieth in Red Rock Canyon.

Lyons sandstone had two characteristics in its favor, originally making it much sought after as a building stone—three, if you include its intrinsic beauty. It is easy to cut and, for sandstone, it is a strongly resistant rock. But time shows that it does not, in fact, weather well. When steel and cement began to replace sandstone building blocks, the bottom fell out of the market for Lyons Sandstone. Steel and concrete were not only more durable, they were also more affordable.

As John George Bock wrote quite affectingly in his *In Red Rock Canyon Land*: "Thousands of dollars of stone cutting machinery was left standing idle ... the old canyon heaved a sigh of relief. ... Red Rock Canyon left her mark. She was pawed, robbed, and raped, her beauty destroyed. So for the next few years she went back to the wild. Only the caretaker heard the moan of the night wind as it blew through the silent canyon. The bobcats, bear, mountain lion, deer, and wild horses wandered on the silent trails. Nature would reclaim the canyon and its outlet for her own."

University of Colorado, Colorado Springs geologist Brandon Vogt has made a study of "rock weathering processes" in the open space. These processes are of great interest in a more practical sense in the field of monument and building preservation. As Vogt explains, Red Rock Canyon makes for an interesting comparative study in the relative rate of rock decay. The three types of weathering to which rocks in their various aspects are subjected are physical, chemical, and biological. It is the very process of weathering that, in turn, prepares rock for erosion.

In studying weathering processes, Vogt's students concluded that south-facing rocks in the open space weathered faster than north facing ones, despite the latter formations' lichens and other living rock coverings. The sun, they reasoned, as it controls thermal expansion and contraction, had more apparent impact on weathering the rocks than either moisture or the colonizing lichens and mosses on the rock's surface. In the south-facing rocks there was evidence of pitting and sand flaking, and a hollow sound was produced by the rock when it was tapped.

The study conducted by geologist Vogt and his students provides added scientific evidence of the vulnerability of sandstone when it comes to weathering, as compared to the new, more durable, if also more prosaic, building materials of iron, first; steel later; and concrete. Thanks to such technological advances, the monumental hematite-red Lyons Sandstone outcropping on the open space was spared further dismembering cuts. Instead, it was left undisturbed in its present state, with its rough-hewn, stair-stepping profile, evocative of a crude starter-kit Mayan Temple stained red.

Spencer Penrose

Another hard-driving industrialist to make a name for himself in the Pikes Peak Region and with a historic connection to the present-day open space was the black sheep of a well-heeled, blue-blooded East Coast family. On December 10, 1892, the urbane, deal-making, young Spencer Penrose arrived on the scene and soon would amass a vast fortune as a gold and copper baron, as well as hotelier. While Mogul emperors in India built marble monuments to immortalize themselves, Penrose built the famous luxury resort hotel, the Broadmoor (as well as the Will Rogers Memorial, high on Cheyenne Mountain, where Penrose is buried). The historic five-star hotel, with its Spanish elements of architecture, would soon draw the rich and famous from far and wide—everyone from the heavy-weight boxing champion Jack Dempsey to the child star Shirley Temple, not to mention the popular humorist Will Rogers and several golf-playing American presidents—a role it continues to this day.

The mogul emperors of India built marble monuments to memorialize themselves. Penrose built a resort hotel and the nightly illuminated Will Roger's Shrine high up on the side of Cheyenne Mountain where Penrose is interred.

Like Palmer before him, and John George Bock, the original assembler and owner of today's open space, Spencer Penrose was a Philadelphian. He came West to make good—in more ways than one. As the tall, handsome young bachelor, known as "Spec," he cut a wide swath at all levels of society. He drank hard—and having lost an eye in a sporting accident at Princeton (where his record was abysmal), he later had an extra false eye made-to-order that appeared bloodshot for those occasions when he needed it. He also engaged in brawls and earned a reputation for his exploits with young women whose names would not have been discovered in anyone's blue book or social register.

The Ludlow Massacre

While living in Cripple Creek, where he was in partnership with Charles Leaming Tutt of the C.O.D. Mine, Spencer Penrose proved himself to be both resourceful and determined. In 1894, during the Cripple Creek mining strike, Penrose and his cohorts joined the sheriff's posse of deputies in order to defend big mines. It was a foreshadowing of the terrible violence that would occur in later years between coal miners and owners during the infamous Ludlow Massacre, some of the worst labor-owner violence in U.S. history, an event later memorialized in a pro-union ballad written by folk singer Woodie Guthrie.

At the center of the Ludlow violence was a large and productive coal mine, the Colorado Fuel and Iron Company, originally founded by General Palmer and purchased by John D. Rockefeller in 1902. In response to dangerous working conditions, high prices at the company store, restrictions on free speech and bargaining, and low wages, a strike had been organized by the United Mine Workers of America on April 20, 1914. In the course of the conflict that left twenty-one dead, Colorado National Guardsmen attacked a tent colony where the striking miners and their families had taken shelter after having been evicted from their homes. Tell-tale signs of kerosene on the roofs of the tents offered proof that a fire had been deliberately set there, killing two women and eleven children that were hidden inside who died of asphyxiation and burns. In addition, three union leaders, two strikers, another child, one passerby, and one National Guardsman were killed by gunfire. The Ludlow Massacre represented a major landmark in changing labor relations between the common working man and corporate power.

In 1913, a little before the Ludlow Massacre, Mary Harris Jones, popularly known as "Mother Jones, the grandmother of all agitators," arrived in Colorado (near Trinidad) to support the mine workers engaged in striking to improve their working conditions. She was by then in her eighties, and an organizer of the Industrial Workers of the World (the IWW or "Wobblies"). Both strikers and organizers were jailed. Rallying against Mother Jones' incarceration, a thousand women in Trinidad, Colorado, gathered to march in protest. They were charged by a National Guard cavalry unit armed with sabers. The women were slashed at and cut. One woman had an ear partly severed.

When Spencer Penrose and the members of their so-called "Company K"—who were deputized to defend the mine owners at Cripple Creek—ran out of liquor, Spencer rode a horse all the way (approximately forty miles) down the mountain to Palmer's high and dry Colorado Springs. The drugstores were fresh out of the "medicinal supplies" Penrose sought. But an affluent and friendly mine owner came to the rescue with a barrel of bourbon. Spencer had no way of transporting a barrel, so he purchased a dozen hot-water bottles from Glockner Hospital in which to carry the liquor, saddle bag–style, all the way back to Cripple Creek, demonstrating his considerable mettle and resourcefulness. Penrose went on to become one of the West's most successful mining barons, making untold millions.

Two Historic Gold Refining Mills in Red Rock Canyon

Eventually Tutt and Penrose, joined by mill operator Charles Mather MacNeill, formed a new partnership, betting this time on the gamble that milling gold ore might prove more profitable than mining for gold. In 1896, they opened the Colorado-Philadelphia Reduction and Refining Mill at the foot of the hogbacks on the northeastern edge of today's open space. The site was conveniently located, both for availability of building stone and transport, just south of the Colorado Midland Railroad tracks and within a quarter mile of the Colorado Terminal running up to Cripple Creek.

Early records show that Greenlee & Sons was awarded the contract for building stone for the Colorado-Philadelphia mill. Hundreds of tons of Lyons Sandstone quarried from the Kenmuir Quarry were used in the construction of the mill, with its three foot–thick foundation. Buildings for this operation, including its general office, a stone structure which may have been built of the Lyons as well, and the assay office were located in Red Rock Canyon.

The Colorado-Philadelphia Reduction and Refining Mill was financed with revenues raised from the sale of the C.O.D. mine for $250,000, in addition to backing from East Coast investors and old Philadelphia money supplied by family and friends, who purchased stock in the new venture. At its peak, the Colorado-Philadelphia processed two hundred tons of gold ore per day using a new chlorination method, thanks to expertise brought to the enterprise by Charles MacNeill. It was advertised by its owners as being the largest chlorination mill in the United States and was so successful that, in 1901, the three partners expanded their operation into a "mill trust" under the name United States Reduction and Refining Company (USR&R), capitalized at thirteen million dollars. The merger, in an era before anti-trust laws were enacted, soon incorporated interests in Cripple Creek District gold mines, railroads, and half a dozen gold reduction mills in the region, including ones operating in Goldfield, Florence, and Pueblo.

The three partners built a second mill on the present-day open space. Called "The Standard," the historic mill was also located at the base of the hogbacks—about a quar-

The Colorado-Philadelphia Gold Reduction Mill, owned and operated in the late 1890s by Copper Baron Spencer Penrose, was built on the edge of the open space on a foundation of Lyons building stone quarried from Red Rock Canyon. It was here, and not at Cripple Creek as might be assumed, that the first of Colorado's historic mining strikes took place. (Photo from Colorado Springs Pioneers Museum)

ter mile south of the Colorado-Philadelphia. It, too, would be merged into the ever-expanding "mill trust." Among The Standard's distinguishing features were its elongated flues, designed to channel smoke and fumes from huge furnaces through tall smokestacks, built of fire-resistant red brick. However, pains were taken not to show photographs of industrial sites such as the coal-burning, black smoke–belching reduction mills because Colorado Springs, with its many sanitariums, was noted for having clean air. The mills were providentially equipped with fire extinguishing systems, in event of the ever-present danger of fire, and sufficient electricity to provide for night lighting.

Tutt, Penrose, and MacNeill, still in their thirties, soon claimed an absolute monopoly on the transport and refining of gold from Cripple Creek. They held controlling interest in the Midland Terminal and Florence & Cripple Creek Line. By 1905, they had also gained control of the popularly known "Short Line" (Colorado Springs Cripple Creek District Railroad), originally promoted by Irving Howbert and James F. Burns of the Portland Mine and financed by gold king Winfield Scott Stratton. The Short Line was built to provide lower-cost competition for the "mill trust" monopoly on rail shipping. When the three partners gained control of it, too, they were able to charge the highest possible prices the market would bear, sparking outrage on the part of their competition. However, within a short period, the three partners had all become multimillionaires.

Stranger than Fiction:
John G. Bock's Sketches of Prominent Figures

John G. Bock's brief history booklet, *In Red Rock Canyon Land,* is nothing if not a pastiche of historical detail. Some is dry as dirt, but other passages, written in the omniscient, third person, brim with lurid flourishes of purple prose, imitative of popular dime-store fiction of the day. The opening pages reproduce numerous, detailed patents, spelled out in legal language, that were held by early owners of parcels of land in Red Rock Canyon Open Space. These might have been better served, with their useful dates, in an appendix.

The chronicle begins to pick up when Bock switches to his preferred literary voice. In this mode, he profiles several famous local characters and personages, whom he coyly refuses to name, but whose familiar historic identities are hard to miss. These include the dream-chasing, hard-drinking, n'er-do-well cowboy Bob Womack, who struck it rich (only to lose it all again) when he discovered the first gold in Cripple Creek. Another "mysterious" character, who looms larger than life as the scene described by Bock unfolds, may have been his old friend Spencer Penrose.

First—as Bock sets the scene—the unnamed personage, a mill owner, holds a meeting with a presumed business contact. The meeting concludes with a handshake and the words: "I sure could take a drink or a pretty girl. I think I'll take both before the night is over." The mysterious character then hires a hack and drives to the big gold refining mill on the northeastern section of what is today's open space. Here he spends some quiet time admiring the "thousand glistening lights" of the Colorado-Philadelphia

Reduction and Refining Mill as he listens to its sounds of "steam blowing off, the rumble of the machinery, and the screech of the switch engine as it backed the ore into the hoppers." (A nice descriptive touch was achieved by Bock in this historic reminiscence.)

The next day an important meeting is held with several mining engineers. At the meeting the unnamed mill owner, in Bock's boilerplate account, argues forcefully for the immediate closure of the Colorado-Philadelphia Reduction and Refining Mill—even as, across town, miners were "discussing a strike for higher wages."

Labor Strike in Mill on Today's Open Space
Marks the Beginning of Colorado's Labor History

In *A Colorado History*, Ubbelohde et al. state that, "It was in the reduction works at Colorado City, where Cripple Creek ore was processed, rather than in the goldfields themselves, that the battle [over working conditions for labor] originated." *Colorado: Federal Writers' Project* (first published in 1941) states that the labor conflict between miners and owners began with a strike in the reduction mills at Colorado City in February 1903. The first to strike were employees of The Standard mill "in protest against the discharge of union men."

Writing in the February 2008 issue of *West Word* of the Old Colorado City Historical Society, Paul Shepard reports that beginning in 1903 "the Mill and Smelter Workers Union No. 125 of the Western Federation of Miners (WFM) had gone on strike at three gold processing mills," including The Standard. The workers were demanding $3.00 for an eight-hour day, an increase from $1.80 for twelve hours, and the right to bargain collectively—rights to which Penrose and other mine owners, it should be noted, were strenuously opposed.

In short, the 1903 labor strike at The Standard mill, located on today's open space and owned by Penrose, Tutt, and MacNeill, represented an important turning point in Colorado's labor history. It was the spark that ignited the conflict between workers and owners. Black and Norman in *A Pikes Peak Partnership: the Penroses and the Tutts* affirm that The Standard mill, which was the first to strike, proved to be the catalyst for "the 1903–1904 Cripple Creek Labor Wars," that followed, and that the strikes began first, not in the mines, but in the mills.

At this juncture Bock's account departs from that of Sprague in *Newport of the Rockies*. Sprague reports that the Colorado-Philadelphia mill "opened in September of '96 and prospered." Bock, in contrast, states that the mill closed two million dollars in the red. Perhaps both are correct and merely chart the rise and the fall of the Colorado-Philadelphia and The Standard, in particular, and of chlorination mills, in general. "Not until 1906," state Noel and Norman, "would the partners [Penrose, Tutt, and MacNeill] sell the USR&R to the Guggenheims, operators of the Pueblo-based American Smelting and Refining Company."

In any case, the chlorination mills, an innovation originating in the Transvaal of South Africa, were soon to be supplanted by the far more efficient cyanide mills. The triumvirate of Penrose et al., having seen stocks in their trust plunge, had wisely decided to invest in Utah copper, which turned out to be the greatest, long-term source of Penrose's vast fortune. Astute in reading the handwriting on the wall, the three partners in the "mill trust" had done well to sell their holdings to the Guggenheims. The Colorado-Philadelphia mill would soon be replaced by the most modern cyanide mill in the world—the commercially successful Golden Cycle, with its seventeen buildings and huge dumps. The mill was first built in 1906; then after a huge fire demolished it, a more modern version was completed by its owner, John Milliken, in 1908. Within four or five years, all other mills had shut down—including the Colorado-Philadelphia and The Standard. Buried along the northeastern edge of Red Rock Canyon Open Space, the foundations of the early Colorado-Philadelphia and The Standard gold refining mills are still observable today.

The Golden Cycle continued in its operations until 1948, at its peak milling eight hundred tons of gold ore a day from Cripple Creek. Established on a site south of Highway 24 (of Ute Pass fame), the mill was conveniently located a short distance from the Midland Terminal's roundhouse on 21st Street in Colorado Springs.

The current site of a large new development in the city named "Gold Hill Mesa," also located on 21st Street, is in reality no "hill" in any ordinary sense. Rather than a naturally occurring geological rise in the landscape, it is a product of the Golden Cycle's tons and tons of irreducible gold tailings, laced with lead, cyanide, and arsenic. New homeowners are promised protection from exposure by a cover of four feet of dirt, combined with plastic lining. Two new ponds at the development have been designed specifically to capture and hold toxic runoff from drainage and downpours.

Other relics from Red Rock Canyon Open Space's recent industrial past appear in what archeologists describe as its "historic engravings." The most prominent and historically interesting of these is chiseled into one of the red rock faces of the quarried Lyons Sandstone. It boldly proclaims "Workers of the World Unite" and harks back to the early 1900s, a reminder of tumultuous times of labor unrest marked by protest over low wages and poor working conditions. This example of crudely carved graffiti from the past is a clear expression of sympathy for the IWW labor movement on the part of Red Rock Canyon's quarrymen.

Ironically, Colorado's geological riches have usually generated the most wealth for the fewest, not infrequently outside investors (such as today's cyanide heap-leach gold mine in Cripple Creek owned by a South African consortium), while non-renewable resources are sucked dry and landscapes that formerly were alive with natural and human history—endowing it with a uniquely defined sense of place and helping to attract tourist dollars—are destroyed. Parts of that larger story can be seen dramatically illustrated in Red Rock Canyon land after the white man arrived.

Unlike the more modern archeology of the landfill on the Bock property, a more poignant and far more meaningful footnote to, and reminder of, the fragility of human history on the open space was documented in a 1920s news story reporting the existence of an early cemetery that had first been in use there in 1859, located on a bluff between Red Rock Canyon and the old reduction mill. Parts of coffins could still be observed in the 1920s, protruding like the prows of marooned ships, along the edges of what was later to become the John S. Bock gravel quarry. The cemetery was eventually abandoned because it was too hard to dig there in winter. The dead, who seemed to have had no final rest, were later removed to the nearby Mesa Cemetery, by which time it, too, was beginning to be abandoned.

"Morning Glory"—Landscape painting in Red Rock Canyon. (by Laura Reilly)

Wind-blown tidal pool ripples in the Dakota Sandstone. (Photo courtesy Don Ellis)

Cross-bedding in Lyons dunes. (Photo courtesy Bill Koerner)

top, left to right: Blue penstemon, Indian paintbrush
above, left to right: Prickly pear cactus, Locoweed (Photos courtesy Bill Koerner)

A Fountain fin aflame in the sun. (Photo courtesy Bill Koerner)

Ancient leaning towers. (Photo courtesy Bill Koerner)

A historic Dakota Sandstone quarry on the open space. Quarried Dakota Sandstone from the open space was used in several of the buildings and walls in Colorado Springs and may also have figured into the construction of walls and outbuildings on General Palmer's grand estate, Glen Eyrie. (Photo courtesy Bill Koerner)

Processing Fountain fins, view from Garden of the Gods to Red Rock Canyon. (Photo courtesy Bill Koerner)

In a constituency building effort, Joe Fabeck leads a Red Rock Canyon hike, framed by sandstone outcrops in the background. (Photo courtesy *Westside Pioneer*)

View from a hill of the dedication in June 2009 of the award-winning, native stone open-air pavilion. (Photo courtesy *Westside Pioneer*)

First Red Rock Canyon trail building day, August 2004.
(Photo courtesy *Westside Pioneer*)

Gnarled juniper, seasoned survivor of mountain storms, with piñon pine in background, known as "sister trees" by the Utes. (Photo courtesy Bill Koerner)

CHAPTER 6

The Bocks

*"The people who came West were either
dreamers or they were driven."*
—**Chuck Murphy,** Local Builder and City Leader

John George Bock was born in New Jersey in 1889, and, like General William Jackson Palmer and Spencer Penrose before him, grew up in Philadelphia. Following the advice of Horace Greeley, he decided to go West as a young man. Looking to reinvent himself and make good on the western frontier, Bock arrived in Colorado in 1907. By the mid-1920s, he had begun to assemble the parcels making up today's beautiful Red Rock Canyon Open Space.

John George Bock's parting memory upon leaving Philadelphia was of a quarrel with his mother, who called him a "worthless, fighting, lazy spendthrift." In his forty-one-page history, *In Red Rock Canyon Land*, the first of the two autobiographical accounts he wrote, Bock describes in a few brief lines his arrival in Colorado Springs at the town's Santa Fe Station in 1907, and his first glimpse of the snow-capped Pikes Peak. Upon his arrival, Bock had hoped to locate some distant kin, but never succeeded in realizing this goal. The journey by rail that delivered him at the Santa Fe Station was not without event. A few miles west of Limon, Colorado, Bock witnessed the explosion of a train's steam engine that cost the lives of both the engineer and fireman as it hurtled the boiler one hundred feet off the tracks.

Bock decided not to remain in the small, front-range town of Colorado Springs. Instead, at age eighteen, he managed to secure a job for a brief period weighing sugar beets in Rocky Ford, in southeastern Colorado, with the help of fellow Philadelphian Charles Evans. Evans was, at the time, assistant manager of the Holly Sugar Company in the town of Swink. When Bock and Evans were still living in the East, Bock had saved Evans' two sons from drowning and Evans was now repaying the favor.

In the early 1900s, southeastern Colorado was largely devoted to free-range cattle operations. Many a youth like Bock, without benefit of higher education or family wealth, would be hired by powerful cattle kings as ranch hands and wranglers—their Sunday-best western attire and handsomely tooled leather boots attesting to new-found identities. In time, some of these "greenhorns" even mastered the art of lassoing a balky or runaway steer. Bock was proud to be hired as a ranch hand at one of the largest, most famous of the free-range spreads in the entire Southwest, the JJ Ranch, where "by 1879 cowboys were riding herd on hundreds of thousands of cattle" according to the history *Colorado*, produced by the Federal Writers' Project. At the JJ ranch, Bock helped on the chuck wagon, did odd jobs, and worked as a horse wrangler.

The JJ Ranch in the Lower Arkansas Valley was a sprawling, 225-million-acre operation with half a million head of cattle and an estimated twenty thousand watering holes, which extended across the states of Colorado, Oklahoma, and Texas. Headquartered thirty-four miles south of La Junta, it comprised several ranches (many of the larger ones were controlled by English and Scottish interests), with the original ranch having been owned by James J. Jones, hence the "JJ" brand name.

In his second book, *In Canyon Land*, a cloth-bound eighty-page memoir published in 1964 by Vantage, Bock describes his life at the JJ Ranch in lively, often colorful detail, as well as his time later as a homesteader in southeastern Colorado; a World War I veteran; and, finally, a family man and real estate developer with interests in the tourist trade.

John G. Bock as a newly minted cowboy with hat, horse, and sidearm. (*Colorado Springs Gazette Telegraph*, August 10, 1952, courtesy Don Ellis)

Bock was thrilled when, after his arrival in 1907 at the JJ Ranch as a mere "tender-foot," he was issued his first pair of chaps, some spurs, and, most exciting of all, a Colt six-gun with holster and cartridge belt. The other cowboys working on the ranch also gave him a new name, calling him "Philadelphia." For a short time, Bock continued to work for the JJ free-range spread, learning the ropes of being a cowboy and rancher. Bock's story, as it unfolds, is in microcosm the story of the history of the American West in the twentieth century.

In his memoir, Bock's description of what brought about dust bowl conditions and the conflict between cowboys and "nesters," as captured in the western dialect of a "seasoned old fighter [who had] trailed cattle through blinding snowstorms," represents an insightful piece of historical reporting.

In the meantime, Bock's relationship with the JJ Ranch (as was to be the case in so much of his life and with so many of his relationships) is both conflicted and ambivalent. He fell deeply in love with the lifestyle (and the perceived romance) of a cowboy, but he also documents its undoubted hardships, privations, and loneliness—a constant underlying theme throughout Bock's narratives.

While employed at the JJ Ranch, Bock developed several youthful crushes. The first of these unrequited passions was directed at a young woman he refers to in his memoir as "Belle." "Belle," Bock writes, was "dressed so daintily with her calfskin boots, neat silver spurs, well-fitted riding skirt and plaid shirt, she looked to him [Philadelphia] like the loveliest, most desirable human being he had ever seen." But Belle wasted no time in letting the smitten young Philadelphian know that as the daughter of "one of the richest cattlemen in the region" she would not deign to give him the time of day. Equally taboo and off limits for relationships in the prevailing western caste system, the wealthy young woman informed him, were both the "nesters" and the roughneck "cowboys." At that moment, Bock made up his mind to make something of himself. He dreamed of striking it rich in the gold fields in order to support a lifestyle that was like that of "a rich and powerful cattle king."

In addition to thwarted romance, Bock's adventures during the two-year period he was employed at the JJ Ranch included herding cows through quicksand, attending cowboy dances at La Junta, and being caught up in a wild stampede of hundreds of spooked cattle. One night at camp, Bock had a knock-down, drag-out fight with another ranch hand named Tex. This occurred after a "blow-out" at La Junta, following a day spent at the La Junta stockyards loading bawling cows onto railroad stockcars. As a result Tex quit his job at the ranch. Bock, too, departed, leaving behind the people and country he'd come to love and appreciate. The brawl between Tex and Bock was probably triggered by jealousy over the girl Bock so mysteriously continued to refer to as "the belle," and whom he speculates had also driven the smitten Tex "loco," too. But before Tex and Philadelphia went their separate ways, the two did make up.

Bock decided to head off for New York City, whose narrow deep canyons he found to be every bit as, if not more, lonesome than the red canyon lands of the Southwest. From New York he boarded a steamer for Florida and New Orleans. Then he worked his way back across the country towards the West. Eventually he earned enough money from odd jobs, Bock writes in his memoir, to buy a string of pack mules for prospecting in the desert and hills of Arizona. One night camping in the forests of Arizona, he and the mules were frightened "in deep virgin forest" by an enormous bear. Bock took careful aim and shot it between the eyes, whereupon "the monster lunged and fell." Then, "for some time Philadelphia watched the dying brute."

It was after his return to southeastern Colorado from Arizona in 1910 that Bock changed course and joined the ranks of the hated "nesters," buying and fencing off a small homestead of his own, while closing off a canyon with brush as a corral for his cattle. Since cattle require many acres when grazing on native grass, his actions were deeply resented by local ranchers. Bock's early days homesteading were difficult in other respects as well. Reduced to his last tin of beans, Bock nearly starved to death until help came, when he least expected it, in a letter with money from his family in Philadelphia.

At the onset of World War I, Bock became a draft-dodger. He did not support U.S. policy in entering the war. As a result, he was forcibly "trapped and handcuffed" by the law. Then he was shipped off to training and sent overseas where he experienced action on the front lines. By this time, Bock had learned not just to fight and to shoot straight, but to survive.

During World War I, Bock served as a member of an infantry regiment that distinguished itself by capturing a German machine-gun nest, helping to save the lives of many allied soldiers. As a result of war injuries sustained in the autumn of 1918 at the Battle of St. Mihiel (one of the most significant battles of WWI), and a combination of other illnesses, Bock was hospitalized for six months. He suffered from an injury to his ear that caused dizziness and, in later years, "fits and convulsions" (indicating there may have been other head injuries). He was also gassed and afflicted with tuberculosis. Twenty-nine years later, Bock was awarded a Purple Heart, but as he writes in his memoir, "'Philadelphia' felt he should have been awarded the Medal of Honor."

Discharged in May 1919, after a year in the military, Bock returned to find his homestead—with its three hundred head of cattle—in good shape and just the way he left it, thanks to the excellent care of a local rancher named Tom Tate, who had generously looked after it in his absence. Shortly thereafter, John Bock met his future wife, Sylvia Seay, born August 11, 1902, the daughter of a "nester" family originally from Kentucky. The two met at a Fourth of July dance held in a local schoolhouse. This proved to be a harmonious, if short-lived, period in their relationship, marked by a certain awkward innocence and amiability, and even tinged with romance. "What a sweet name for a sweet girl," Bock writes. ... "It was late that evening before he [Philadelphia] rode back to his ranch, a happy, singing cowboy." John and Sylvia were married on September 12, 1919.

It was on the Bock's isolated, rock-ribbed, arid, canyon-land homestead, with its blistering summers, near Higbee, Colorado, that Bock's two sons would later be born. John S. (Seay, after his mother), the late owner of the Red Rock Canyon property, was born on April 19, 1921, followed two years later by Richard on July 21, 1923.

Due to the nature of his war injuries and subsequent tuberculosis, however, Bock was soon forced to give up ranching altogether. Bock complained not only of dizziness and a "burning" head, but of reduced function and severe pain in his arm. Some of Bock's physical complaints and his more erratic behavior patterns also suggest that he may have been suffering from what is known today as post-traumatic stress syndrome—the result of being shell-shocked, gassed, and wounded by German mortars that killed many soldiers.

Bock thus decided to divest himself of his homestead in the spring of 1923, which he sold to Jim Hagen, the former wagon boss for the JJ Ranch. He then bought a Ford automobile with the idea of returning in it with his family to Colorado Springs, where he hoped to devote himself to the promising new enterprises of real estate and tourism and to indulge in his hobbies of penning verses and collecting historic pioneer relics.

The Famous JJ Ranch Redux: Bootleggers and Gun-Slingers

During the time that Bock was still homesteading in southeastern Colorado, he had a run-in with his former employer, the JJ Ranch. The ranch managers had decided they wanted access for grazing to the land Bock now owned and which he had fenced off for his own cattle. When Bock denied them access, the JJ ranch owners and management allegedly used their considerable influence to secure a right-of-way for a road through Bock's holding to open it up for grazing. Bock was furious. Well over a decade later, in 1938, after the famous JJ Ranch fell on hard times, Bock decided to buy what was left of the much diminished, seven hundred and twenty–acre spread and to keep its famous brand name. Bock was motivated, as he describes it, by a deep mixture of nostalgia for the ranch and searing hatred for its managers.

In order to finance the purchase, Bock sought the assistance of his old friend Spencer Penrose, who had contacts with major bankers. Then he systematically bought up the few parcels remaining of the JJ Ranch, which had become deeply mired in debt and decay. Grand old trees had been chopped down, buildings were in shambles, and no one was left but a few tenants.

In 1938, after his purchase of the down-at-heel remnant of the JJ Ranch, with its old corrals and bunkhouse, Bock decided to reopen the former dance hall and hold Saturday night dances. But he never knew "when a big fight would start and someone would get killed. The bootleggers were trying to take over," writes Bock, "and they finally did." Bock's long-term vision, never realized, was to turn the JJ Ranch into a tourist destination spot, complete with rodeos, sightseeing, and a hotel. In 1946, after "a world of trouble," including the perennial problem of water rights, Bock sold what was left of the famous spread back to the Texans from whom he'd originally purchased it.

Bock tells a pair of notorious gun-slingers, known as "Shag" and "Blackie," that he really didn't want the JJ Ranch itself, or what little remained of it, he just wanted a couple of dead ranch managers. The narrator and star protagonist then reveals to his reader that "Philadelphia began to pack a gun." And he even went so far as to threaten to kill a ditch rider if he didn't stay off his land. While stylistically Bock's narrative tends to read, at times, a bit like dime-store western fiction, this episode has the ring of unvarnished truth to it. According to one family friend, toward the end of his life John Bock made a habit of sleeping with a pistol and a shotgun. Indeed, such episodes were to be become an oft-repeated theme in the Bock family saga, somewhat in the best traditions of what we've come to think of today as the, perhaps, not-so-mythic "Wild West."

Bock's wife Sylvia was not happy about Bock's investment in the JJ Ranch. She had no desire to return to the hard life she had once known as a "nester" in southeastern Colorado. She appreciated living in Colorado Springs and the fact that her sons were being better educated in the city than they might have been in rural schools. Thus, she never set foot on the much-reduced JJ ranch owned by her husband.

One historic trophy that Bock proudly retained from his JJ Ranch venture was the right to own the "JJ" brand, reputedly the most famous cattle brand in the West. According to an interview with Bock in the *Gazette Telegraph* of August 10, 1952, Bock intended to continue paying the renewal fee for the famous

John G. Bock, developer and owner of Red Roc Canyon, featured with the famous JJ Ranch branding irons. (Colorado Springs *Gazette Telegraph*, August 10, 1952, courtesy Don Ellis)

brand and, eventually, to will it to his sons. By the early 1950s, Bock was actively and productively using the "JJ" brand on twelve saddle horses he owned that were "ridden mostly by children to Red Rock Canyon" in today's open space.

Bock's Early Investments

Bock was quick to grasp the new economic realities ushered in at the turn of the century when Colorado's land and its spectacular scenery had begun to replace gold as the best possible investment. Indeed, land was the new gold. Having very little formal education, Bock decided, first, to earn a diploma in real estate through a correspondence school. Then, he started to invest in property in and near today's Old Colorado City, the quaint, historic Victorian neighborhood that once, for a brief four-day period, served as the state's Territorial Capital. Bock even bought the former "house" of the famous Laura Bell, the successful and beautiful madam of the back streets, which was located near the entrance to Red Rock Canyon at 31st Street and Colorado Avenue. This house was to remain the family home until 1965. Bock had by this time joined with D.V. Pruitt in his burgeoning real estate business, and before long, the two partners had bought up most of the property that had been the former "Red Light" district in the then Colorado City.

Roundup Saddle Stables

Another of Bock's early investments was in property close by the Red Rock Canyon entrance, where he "started the Roundup Saddle Stables with his spotted horses." There were western pintos, saddle ponies, and burros. Among the stable's features that were popular with tourists and locals alike were long guided rides, sometimes in the moonlight. Bock's two sons, John S. and Richard, led some of the horse rides.

John S. Bock related a story about his father's horse riding operation to Chelley Gardner-Smith, whose family would later rent one of the Bock-owned houses in Red Rock Canyon. Sometimes Bock Sr. allowed children to go out on rides on their own, unaccompanied. But he would always issue a stern warning to them in the form of a story, telling the young riders about a great old wild stallion who lived in the canyon, and who would lure their horses away unless the children returned on time.

William Eddy, now in his eighties, was a former horse wrangler employed at the Roundup Saddle Stables in the 1940s. After the city purchased Red Rock Canyon as open space in 2003 and built a trail link, Eddy visited the property, renewing some of his fondest memories. Eddy recalled with pleasure his work at the stable when he was a mere teenager. He remembered seeing John G. Bock—who, at the time, seemed to be a "pretty old" man of fifty—wearing a battered cowboy hat and sitting in the sun on a bench all day, playing with his dog.

Eddy's reminiscences included rides up to the old cave, found high up on the present-day open space. The rides were followed by cookouts of baked beans, hot dogs and hamburgers prepared over a campfire, with someone playing a guitar. The horses were so familiar with the trail that they never had a problem finding their way back to the stable after dark in the starry night (*Westside Pioneer*: 18 August 2005).

Assembling Red Rock Canyon Holdings

By the mid-1920s, Bock had already begun systematically to purchase and lease parcels of land in Red Rock Canyon in today's open space. These parcels ranged in size from 32 to 200 acres. Slowly, patiently, over the next two decades, he continued to build up his holdings. He kept a detailed record of the parcels he purchased and the amounts he paid for them. For example, he purchased the 32-acre Gypsum Canyon parcel for $3.00 an acre; he procured 129 acres from the Greenlee Stone Company for $1,300; 45 acres from the Earth Products Company for $500; 40 acres from the Colorado Stone Company for $500; 200 acres from the Union Land and Cattle Company for $4,000; and the 87-acre Swope property for back taxes. Before long, Bock had pieced together 650 acres, for which he had paid $7,100, averaging out to a little over $10.00 per acre—a steal by today's standards. The Bock family held ownership of these properties for approximately eighty years.

As Bock, writing about himself in third-person, observes in his memoir, *In Canyon Land*: "Soon six hundred and fifty acres were owned by this man from Philadelphia and his wife, Sylvia. It was dished out to him on a silver platter, although it took years to acquire all the property." In his personal history, *In Red Rock Canyon Land*, Bock laments his earlier inability, for the lack of $300, to buy the Colorado-Philadelphia and Standard gold reduction mills sold in 1911 "for twenty-five hundred dollars, with land consisting of two hundred acres, more or less. Its only worth was the private trails for his horseback riders. It was like a big dump with the ruins of the old Standard mill evident everywhere. The faithful old Midland Terminal Railroad" Bock continues, "still hauled the low grade ore to the Golden Cycle," in Colorado Springs.

At least one of the parcels Bock held in Red Rock Canyon also contained water rights, although not very significant ones. Water rights in the West have traditionally been hotly contested, and the laws governing them are complex. Such rights, historically, had been handed down with parcels of land from seller to buyer. Different laws govern water originating on the land of a property owner and water flowing through the land from drainages higher up. Water originating higher up is owned by the city. However, the Bocks, both father and son, operated on the principle that they had clear and legitimate claim to whatever water flowed down the several drainages from above them and thence through their property.

The first time he set eyes on it, Bock was struck by the "rack and ruin" of Red Rock Canyon. "Steel rails, railroad ties rotting away here and there, the big derrick was still standing; thousands of dollars in iron lay scattered about; the old boiler room; piles of debris and rock from the big quarry," he wrote. The property was, in short, a disaster area, an industrial wasteland in one of the world's most beautiful settings.

After the Kenmuir Quarry closed sometime around 1915, the tracks from the Colorado Midland Railroad—which had been granted a right-of-way into Red Rock Canyon in 1888 and which had provided such a vital transportation link for the Lyons stone being quarried at the time—remained in place. At the height of the gold rush, the "faithful, old Midland Terminal" to which Bock refers had been built to connect Cripple Creek to Divide and was used by Penrose, Tutt, and MacNeill for their gold mining monopoly. Meanwhile, the first Midland Railroad underwent foreclosure and sale, but managed to steam along under new ownership until it went bankrupt in 1917. As a result, several of the Midland's unused or disabled cars had simply been left standing on their tracks in the company's Red Rock Canyon spur. This posed another problem for John G. Bock. In addition to the scrap iron that littered the area—most of which Bock cleaned up, but some is still in evidence—small boys took a delight in releasing the parked cars. A story in the Colorado Springs Independent (unrelated to today's newspaper by the same name), dated April 24, 1947, reported that, "The Midland spur was used ... for crippled cars until boys turned [them] ... loose" to run down and pile up at the main line. Although car brakes would be set and rocks and logs put before the wheels, the youngsters would remove them and "watch the smash."

Over the next decades, John G. Bock engaged in what appeared to be well-intentioned, if sometimes ill-advised, conservation measures in today's Red Rock Canyon Open Space. Concerned about erosion and washouts caused by torrential rains, he built earthen dams to divert water. He planted trees, shrubs, and grasses, not knowing that some would later prove to be invasive. Among the varieties of trees Bock planted and replanted is the invasive weed tree, the Siberian elm. However, Bock undoubtedly deserves credit for having cleaned up and restored much of the pocked and pummeled landscape brought about by decades of human use and abuse. Indeed, Bock attempted to introduce conservation measures based on the best knowledge of the day.

Bock was equally quick to exploit the land's resources in order to make money. He dredged a canal and diverted water flowing down from the Pikes Peak massif through the several drainages on his property. The diverted water, at one time, supplied the Bott-Langmeyer quarries, the gold mills, and Colorado City neighborhoods. It was later used to fill up the numerous small lakes that dotted the Bock property. Whether Bock was entitled to the use of this water is a moot point, but there is little doubt that he profited from it.

Local historians are indebted to Bock for his sense of Red Rock Canyon land's history and for recording it in his own inimitable style. In addition, Bock deserves to be acknowledged for the initial generosity with which he shared the gift of the magnificent landscape that, as he himself said, had been virtually handed to him "on a silver platter." For example, in a happier time, visitors and groups, such as the Colorado Mountain Club, had been welcomed. They were free to hike and explore Red Rock Canyon land and to enjoy picnics there. But soon enough all of that was to change dramatically.

Bock became embittered when the city refused his request to build an access road to his property (and better yet, one that would link up with the Broadmoor and help promote his riding stable). But he wanted the road, first and foremost, because the entrance to his property had been blocked by the owners of a trailer camp, a fact he blamed, in part, on his wife's "religion" and "good-neighborliness." The suit Bock subsequently filed against the Norris and Newby families, who owned the trailer camps, went all the way to the Colorado Supreme Court. Bock lost the suit, however. He was eventually forced to buy more property and spend his own money to build an access road. Later, when he had income at his disposal to do so, Bock derived great satisfaction from his ability to buy the offending trailer park for the "extraordinary price" of $73,000.

The late Jim Phillips, a close friend of John S. Bock and former executive director of Colorado Springs Utilities, stated that the senior Bock harbored a deep antipathy for the city of Colorado Springs and its employees, convinced that they were out to cause trouble. For one thing, Bock wanted all the water that flowed through his property for free. "That was one reason why he was never happy with the city of Colorado Springs."

Bock was equally unhappy with and deeply angered by the state of Colorado when it built U.S. Highway 24 that divided his property and Garden of the Gods—in the process, blasting through a large red bluff about which he felt strongly proprietary. Bock was thus thwarted both in his effort to prevent the highway from going in and, earlier, to preserve the right-of-way of the Midland Terminal Railroad winding its way up Ute Pass to Cripple Creek, which he valorized in verse. Another defeat was his failure to save "Old 160," one of the last steam locomotives to run on the Midland tracks. It is easy to sympathize with Bock. Besides the handsome red sandstone bluffs that were dynamited, the area lost its once-stretching riparian plain—with the crystalline waters of Fountain Creek meandering through it and grand old cottonwoods casting their shadows—and the uninterrupted connection between Garden of the Gods and Red Rock Canyon.

Bock's succession of frustrations and defeats, among other causes, resulted in the Red Rock Canyon property being declared off limits to the public "by an act of law." It was during this period that Bock also declared his intent of willing the property to his sons. Instead, the sons themselves purchased the property in 1962. From the 1950s on, visitors to Red Rock Canyon might well have found themselves confronted by armed guards, warned off the property, and possibly even shot at.

While the beauty of Red Rock Canyon stirred strong sentiment in Bock, prompting visitations of his muse and the penning of sentimental verse, he made no bones about the fact he wanted to see the area developed. And his sons, John and Richard, would have big plans to do just that in the 1960s and '70s. But former wrangler and local citizen William Eddy counts himself among those who were more than happy to see the property preserved. "I was afraid it would go to a contractor who would tear the place up. It's too beautiful a place to build houses."

John G. Bock's Later Years

After developing his real estate business and tourist interests, Bock found time to establish a museum in the old city hall, which later became a fire station. Here he housed his collection of pioneer relics—a catalog that, according to a 1964 newspaper interview, included: "beaver and bear traps, horns, the Old Colorado City Volunteer Fire Department hose nozzle, a canteen Bock found while prospecting on the Arizona desert in 1909, and disintegrating cowboy hats." "The varmints cleaned off the felt," Bock noted. The collection also included antique guns, knives, and other weaponry. Among Bock's most prized possessions was a Colt revolver said to have belonged to Kit Carson.

The war injuries sustained by Bock, however, had made him irritable and, ultimately, it would seem, unstable. In describing his ungovernable outbursts of anger, Bock was open and forthright. Bock was not only dispatched to the Fort Logan Mental Hospital in Denver, but the Veterans Administration in Colorado "ordered that a guardian be appointed over him." The guardian in this case, somewhat unexpectedly, was the First National Bank of Colorado Springs.

Bock describes his reaction to this development. He "flew into a rage. When a man [possibly an unnamed Veteran's hospital or bank official] violates his profession, Philadelphia felt, he is the same as a rattlesnake." Later, Bock was awarded total disability pay by the U.S. government for injuries sustained under fire.

The episode with the Veterans hospital precipitated Bock's departure from Colorado Springs. A story in the *Gazette Telegraph* of August 10, 1952, stated that Bock was leaving for Arizona "to seek a lower altitude." The combination of being gassed and suffering from T.B. may have reduced his lung capacity. After he fled the mental hospital and due to his failing health, Bock sold the old family home and riding stables on 31st Street and Colorado and developed the Red Rock Shopping Center, featuring one of the region's largest Safeway grocery stores. John George Bock then returned to Arizona where, as a young man, he had once attempted unsuccessfully to do some gold prospecting. It was, however, his son John S. who shepherded the shopping center project through and who appears in a relatively youthful, 1950s-era photograph occasioned by the center's official opening—at which a dozen or so VIPS, in suits, are shown gathered for a ribbon cutting ceremony.

In Scottsdale, Arizona, Bock began to recover some of his health, and, as he documents in his short autobiography, "Philadelphia purchased forty-acres of farm land at 68th Street and East McDowell Road." (Apparently his wife Sylvia was unaware of this holding or the small stash of cash Bock had squirreled away that made the Scottsdale land purchase possible.)

For some time, the aging Bock lived alone in an old trailer in Scottsdale until the city, with its burgeoning population, decided to build a road through his semi-rural property. By this time, property values had shot sky high. When the city declared eminent domain, Bock hit the jackpot, realizing a small fortune on the deal. Suddenly his long-held dreams of striking it rich had been fulfilled. With the merest shake of the dice, Lady Fortune had favored him, this time with more than just a smile—as Bock himself might have written.

Bock immediately hired a chauffeur (he had recently become unable to drive) and a "secretary" to help him write the books he had always dreamed of writing. The elder Bock then returned to Colorado Springs (where he spent his summers) in a big Cadillac and with a lady friend in tow, according to one of his son's closest associates. Thus does the saga of the elder Bock's life, as he himself narrates it, draws to a close with the fitting literary device of a dream sequence, nailed down to the realistic and concrete detail of considerable wealth suddenly being realized. As he approached his last days and final roundup, "Philadelphia" would now enjoy all the personal wealth any man could possibly hope for, desire, or need.

Regardless of his wealth and comfortable life in Scottsdale, the elder Bock continued, until the end, to hold fast to his determination to see the Red Rock Canyon property fully developed. And he also stubbornly persisted in his on-going campaign against taxes.

John George Bock died December 4, 1966, at the age of seventy-seven in the Veterans Hospital in Phoenix, Arizona, after a short illness. His son, Richard, wrote somewhat grandiloquently in the obituary notice appearing in the *Gazette Telegraph* of December 15, 1966: "Mr. Bock belonged to that breed of man who helped shape the West. With a determined mind, rough courage and steadfast stamina needed to match the perils of the wilderness, he carved his mark high and for all those that followed to see. Believing firmly in America, he put his country above personal belief and yielded to no one in his belief in the rights and freedom of the individual."

The Bock Brothers

Born on the old homestead near La Junta in southeastern Colorado in the 1920s, John and his younger brother Richard spent a somewhat idyllic youth riding, hiking, fishing, and exploring in Red Rock Canyon after the family moved to Colorado Springs. Here

> *"John S. Bock once said he had 'earned a Ph.D. in shoveling manure."'*
>
> **—Erwin Cook,**
> personal physician and friend

the late owner of the property, John S. Bock, would remain, except for a brief interval in South America and trips to Hawaii, until his death in Kailua-Kona, on March 9, 2002.

The elder Bock was a notably tough taskmaster and disciplinarian and expected the boys to work hard. Both John and his brother Richard helped out with the Roundup Saddle Stables that their father had established with an eye to the tourist industry. Their chores included mucking out stalls and, doubtless, the far more enjoyable assignment of leading trail rides for locals and tourists. John once said, according to close family friend and personal physician Erwin Cook, that he had "earned a Ph.D. in shoveling manure."

John and Richard both attended Colorado College (CC). They enjoyed the benefits of the education their father never had.

John began his studies at Colorado College in the early 1940s, but was interrupted by WWII, when he was drafted into the Army Air Corps. Sometime in the early '60s he completed his studies at CC as a "mature" student, earning a degree in geological engineering. One of his geology instructors was Professor John Lewis. Lewis recalls student field trips that included John Bock and ended with everyone having a beer together afterwards. Later Bock would call on Lewis when he wanted a geology consultation regarding one of his many enterprises or if he needed him to testify in a lawsuit. Bock spent a period of time, probably as a petroleum engineer, in South America.

Bock married more than once. A son, born April 29, 1961, was the probable offspring of a first marriage which there seems to be no record of. He, unfortunately, died in his youth in a vehicular accident. A second, and apparently, brief marriage occurred in the 1960s, according to a notice in the *Gazette-Telegraph* of October 3, 1963, stating that John S. Bock was issued a marriage license to Eunice M. Pisciotta, age twenty-six, of Pueblo. He met and married his last wife, Joan, in Hawaii in the 1970s, when he was managing the various condominiums in which he had invested and where she was engaged in high fashion and retail, an interest reflected in her up-to-the-minute stylishness even when rusticated in Red Rock Canyon.

Richard Bock was of a different cut of cloth than either of the other Bock males. Gentler and more inclined toward the arts, he studied architecture and never married. He is listed in the Colorado College Yearbook, the *Nugget,* as having been in both the class of 1946 and 1948, indicating he may have had a break in his studies at the college, where he was a member of Kappa Sigma social fraternity.

While both Bock sons served in the military in World War II, it was John, as a bombardier in the Army Air Corp, who, like the elder Bock, was awarded a Purple Heart. John S., indeed, bore some of the same genetic markers as the elder Bock. One informant described John S. Bock as "somewhat irascible—and that's an understatement." Both father and son seemed to take their cues from the local landscape, with dispositions as prickly as cacti and as rough and sharp-edged as the rocks. And if there is a gene for such a thing, they both had a low tolerance for being crossed—whether by bureaucrats, bankers, or local businessmen, all of whom were regarded with a degree of suspicion and mistrust.

When John S. died in 2002 in Hawaii at the age of eighty, he was with his wife Joan. An obituary notice of John's death was never published in Colorado Springs, reportedly because Joan wanted to keep the death secret, possibly due to sensitive and on-going negotiations still in progress over the prospective sale of the Bock property. John's younger brother, Richard, who was clearly overshadowed by his older sibling, and about whom somewhat less is known, is currently a resident of Scottsdale, Arizona.

The Hitch Rack Stables

Dick and Joan Lambert are the former owners of Hitch Rack Stables, built by them in the late 1960s, near 31st Street, not far from Old Colorado City. It was a "dude" riding operation with rental horses aimed primarily at tourists. The Hitch Rack Stables was located on property that was then owned by John S. Bock. Dick and Joan Lambert became friends of John and his wife, Joan. However, because John was *In those days it was perfectly safe to ride a horse from the Hitch Rack Stables across the highway to the Garden of the Gods.* known to be difficult, Joan Lambert tended to keep her distance, not wanting to offend him. Bock had granted the Lambert's permission to establish their stables on his property and to allow their riders to ride through it. The Lambert's "bread and butter" depended on Bock's good will. Fortunately, Dick Lambert and John Bock "spoke the same language." Early on, Lambert and Bock had a little disagreement. Lambert wasted no time in expressing his views in a direct, down-to-earth manner. "After that we got along good," says Lambert. As a result of the friendship, the Lamberts sometimes stayed in the townhomes Bock owned in Hawaii.

Joan Lambert recalls how different the area was then. It was not uncommon to see men in cowboy hats and boots on the west side of town, in Old Colorado City. In those days, there was so little traffic that it was perfectly safe to ride stable horses across the highway between Red Rock Canyon and Garden of the Gods, where the Lamberts and other riders put on nightly shows for the tourists. Later on, the stables were closed and the Lamberts established an excavation business. They subsequently had an arrangement whereby they used a lot on the Bock property to store their heavy equipment and in return Lambert maintained the roads on the Bock property, some still in use today.

Dick Lambert reports that many people were mad at Bock—whether in Colorado Springs, the town of Manitou Springs, or the state highway department. "If you wanted a fight, he was, by God, ready." He was a strong property rights man. It was no one else's "god damn business what he did with his property," and especially the blankety-blank "tree huggers."

A Liability of Unknown Proportions

Among the many money-making enterprises developed by the late John S. Bock in Red Rock Canyon was "the world's most beautiful dump," described in earlier chapters, which opened on June 22, 1970. The fifty-one-acre dump (with another eight to ten acres spilling over into Manitou Springs Section 16) resembled an enormous bathtub of trash, more than a hundred feet deep in places. As noted earlier, the Certificate of Designation/Solid Waste Disposal Site was issued by El Paso County to John S. Bock for a fee paid of $25.00, signed by the chairman of the board of county commissioners, on a form provided by the Colorado Department of Health. As noted in Chapter 1, the dump filled up all of Gypsum Canyon, the deepest on the Bock property, with most of the garbage generated by the citizens of western Colorado Springs over a period of nearly two decades in an era that predated regulations.

Bock did not manage the dump himself. He leased it to local entrepreneur Nick Pinello, who ran the dump in the 1980s and oversaw its first reclamation. The job done was said to have been something of a textbook model for its time. Pinello enjoyed a reputation for setting high standards in any enterprise he undertook. Even so, the dump represented an environmental liability of unknown proportions and nearly derailed attempts to save today's open space.

In addition to the potential toxicity of the dump, which raised a number of troubling questions about what hazardous wastes it might contain, there were also related concerns about the possibility for ground water contamination. The fact that its contents had not been compacted also meant that, according to one engineering report, "Any structures placed on the filled area would eventually sustain structural distress of an intolerable magnitude."

There was yet another unanticipated problem with the dump of no small dimensions. The dump was located below several drainages flowing into the property and acted as a natural dam, turning the area above it into a virtual lake during periods of excessive rainfall. In the spring of 1999, the water that accumulated behind the landfill rose to a level of nearly thirty feet, creating a lake that covered close to two acres.

Today, numerous methane vents sprout like periscopes from the clay with which the dump is capped. For the next two decades the dump will continue—like a living, breathing organism—to decay, with some related subsidence, and with the need periodically to recap with clay to smooth out depressions and fissures, and then, to revegetate it.

Other Bock Enterprises

Cash flowing from the dump reportedly helped John S. Bock raise some of the money he later invested in his Hawaiian condos. In addition to the dump, one of Bock's most successful money-making enterprises on his property was a sizeable gravel quarry (also described in earlier chapters), which supplied, among other construction projects, paving gravel for Pikes Peak Highway. Bock capitalized on the convenient and abundant dumps of Verdos alluvial mesa gravels (mostly disintegrated Pikes Peak granite) located at the toe of Gypsum Canyon in the north of the open space. These gravels had been washed down during the Pleistocene Epoch, between one and two million years ago. Here the land was flat and shallow, slowing the water's flow and thus bringing to a halt the downward transport of the gravels, which top the nearby mesas.

In a Sisyphean task, the ready-made gravel, once it had been sold to the city, was carted back up Pikes Peak again to the highway in an attempt to help stem erosion caused by vehicular traffic. Instead, and somewhat ironically, the paving gravel washed off the highway again into fragile tundra below it, causing even greater damage over the long run. (The constantly eroding mesa gravels, however, do afford a more stable base on which to build than the sticky, more expansive clays and shale found in the region.)

At the front of the Bock property, until after its purchase by the city on November 25, 2003, stood a view-shed polluting stand of three large elevated billboards facing Highway 24. These rentals also added to the revenues Bock earned off the land.

John Bock, in another of his enterprises, leased space to approximately thirty-eight trailers scattered about on his property. The largest trailer encampment, with about seventeen households represented, was located at the mouth of the beautiful Red Rock Canyon itself, with another dozen in Sand Canyon, and up to nine more on the east side—each with its own trailer-shaped lot. The tenants paid their rentals on a month-by-month basis. (The combined revenue from the Bock dump, gravel quarry, billboards, and trailer camps was thought to be an estimated $100,000 a year.)

One of the tenants with a mobile home in Sand Canyon, who prefers not to be named, remembers the time when she and her husband arrived on the Bock property to inquire about renting a lot for their mobile home. Bock did not exactly threaten them, she says, but "he was a different sort of person" and "very territorial. He came out with his gun, which he always carried." On another occasion when a car drove in and parked opposite their mobile home, someone reported it to Bock. By the time the hiker returned from his scramble over the rocks, he found his tires had been blown out.

When John Sr. was still a presence on the land, the mobile home owner recalls that he used to ride around in his ten-gallon hat and with a gun strapped to his side, inquiring who people were and what they were doing there, although he knew (or should have known) that most were tenants in the trailer parks.

The two brothers, the tenant remembers, did not get on at all, and "darned near killed each other." Their mother, Sylvia, once said: "I have two sons: one is Cain; the other Abel." It was clear who was Cain and who Abel in this Bockian parable. The mobile home tenant regarded Richard as being "a very nice person." John, however, was another matter. He even forbade the police to come on his property. A law unto himself, "Bock wanted his own little kingdom and had the money to do it."

Although it is not quite clear who was responsible (he had lots of enemies), John was once locked in the garage without food and water, and it was several days before anyone found him—which is why he built stairs to the roof when he added the bomb shelter in the 1960s.

For nearly two decades, Lou Colson, another former trailer camp tenant, lived happily in Red Rock Canyon land. She relished this western-style peaceable kingdom (that is, when it came to the four-leggeds) with its great natural beauty. One day when Lou opened her front door she discovered a young mountain lion asleep on her steps. She let him continue his snooze, undisturbed, since he clearly needed the rest.

One day Lou Colson opened the front door to find a young mountain lion asleep on her steps. He was clearly all worn out from his ranging, so she left him undisturbed.

Lou also recalls the day she watched a sow bear take a tumble off the rocks. The acrobatic black bear was good at this and made a soft landing, face up, just in the right position for her two hungry young cubs to jump aboard and take advantage of the nutrition on tap. Lou describes Red Rock Canyon land as a place "that was full of beauty. It was full of wildflowers, including Colorado's state flower, the mountain columbine. There was plentiful wildlife. And you could hike all over and find fish fossils in the rocks. It was also fun to watch the deer. It had everything you could want in your backyard," she says.

Joan Lambert's father, John Hussman, was hired as a guard and keeper of the trailer encampments, which most observers agree were substandard in just about every respect except the setting itself. The water lines were in horrible shape and some tenants had no water at all. In addition, not all of the trailer camp occupants were necessarily upstanding citizens. John Bock's instructions to John Hussman were, if you see anything strange, "Don't ask questions, just shoot." Unfortunately, John Hussman had a little problem with alcohol and he almost shot John Bock himself. Bock was not amused. In the spring of 2002, security was further tightened on the Bock property when two homeless men, who had been camping in the quarry, were arrested and later convicted in connection with the murder of a local taxi driver. They had established a camp and were cutting down old trees to use as firewood.

"Don't ask questions. Just shoot!"

John Lewis, professor emeritus of geology at Colorado College, is not afraid to call a spade a spade. He states that John Bock was basically a "slum landlord." Another close associate, however, insists that Bock was generous to his tenants, keeping the rents low. One cold, wintery day, Bock called Lewis in about a problem that had developed with his trailer park located on 26th Street, at the mouth of the canyon. "Look at this," Bock said. What Lewis saw appeared to be "a miniature glacier growing out of the gravel, pushing at a trailer." Its source was a broken water line. At the time, Jack McCullough (after whom the water treatment plant in the area is named) was head of the city water department. Lewis was well acquainted with McCullough because both belonged to the same poker group (also attended by former Colorado College professor and well-known cartographer and climber, Robert Ormes). McCullough was none too pleased with Lewis for calling him to deal with the problem at hand, and also with

Bock himself, who was already in contention with the city over water, pressing one of his many lawsuits. The city was forced to jackhammer the frozen soil in order to get to the broken line and repair it.

The House in the Hole

The Bock brothers, John and Richard, owned five houses and four commercial structures on what is today's open space, including three pole barns used for storing tack and feed. At least three of these homes the brothers themselves designed, built, and lived in, with one being occupied by their mother, Sylvia. John's house was a 1960s-era ranch style, flat-roofed structure with wrap-around plate glass windows nearly covering the length of the sixty-foot-long living room, with its white wall-to-wall carpeting and its exterior walls composed of the sun-glowing, red Lyons building stone.

According to Dr. Erwin Cook, John's long-time friend and personal physician, John held many parties at this house. The parties were typically barbeques and primarily held for his business contacts—of which he had many, given his extensive holdings of real estate in Old Colorado City and elsewhere.

The three-bedroom Bock house, built in 1909, in which John's mother Sylvia originally lived, was most unfortunately located near a leveling project that involved the removal of several large mounds of dirt after the state highway department built an extension of Highway 24. Sylvia Bock, however, refused to let the house be moved. A Bock associate explains this refusal saying, "Sylvia was just as stubborn as the rest of them." So John instructed the construction crew to plow the dirt right up to and around Sylvia's house. Soon people began referring to Sylvia's house as "the house in the hole," since it now sat eight to twelve feet below its surroundings. All that could be seen was the roof with its TV antennae peaking out. A steep driveway to the house acted as a natural conduit during a hard rain. The house, not surprisingly, flooded out a couple of times. "In a frog-strangling downpour, it got pretty damp," says Dick Lambert, with picturesque understatement. (A long-time tenant of the trailer park, who prefers not to be named, tells a similar story. One winter after a big snow, in an attempt to bury it, John plowed snow up high over "the underground house" that his mother rented.) After Sylvia moved to Arizona, Bock rented the house to "some hippie," Lambert recalls.

In the early 1980s the "house in the hole" was rented out by John S. Bock to Chelley Gring (now Gardner-Smith), a then stay-at-home-mom and now a Middle School performing arts teacher, her husband, Scot Gring, and their two children, Shawn (age four) and Olivia (age three). Chelley remembers John S. as always being respectful to her, and as always carrying a shotgun. His wife Joan was kind, and neighborly enough to bake cookies for the Gring children.

Chelley was struck by the fact that the Bocks were frequently dressed in white, and she began to think of Joan as "the woman in white," reminiscent perhaps of the Wilkie Collin's novel. But there may be a simple explanation for the Bocks' somewhat odd partiality for their ghostly apparel, not the best choice it would seem, for a place like

Red Rock Canyon with its abundant red dust. The Bocks spent a great deal of their time in the tropical climes of Hawaii, where white is a popular choice in view of the climate.

Chelley remembers "the house in the hole" as being attractive, with its hardwood floors, cedar closets, and blond paneling. The exterior walls were a combination of logs and red Lyons building stone and a large front window framed a beautiful view. It was well equipped with modern appliances. Someone, probably Sylvia herself, had gone to considerable pains to make it so. The house, facing due east, caught the morning light.

Chelley devoted hours to weeding and restoring the front garden, with its partially buried wishing well. She took the time and trouble to plant trees and cultivate beds of flowers. Bock was visibly touched by her efforts and even choked up: "This is how my mother used to keep it," he said, revealing a side to his nature few were privileged to see.

Apparently, Sylvia had been heartbroken when Highway 24 went in. At one time, her house had been in a pristine setting. Visitors crossed a bridge over Fountain Creek to approach it. Now it was nearly flat up against the highway and the creek was no longer there. This may help explain Sylvia's stubborn refusal to allow "the house in the hole" to be moved. It may also have been Sylvia Bock's way of protesting—even though she understood that the march of "progress" is unstoppable.

Before the Gring family moved into "the house in the hole" they had been warned by Bock that they would be drinking well water. Unfortunately, the well was downstream from the dump and the many septic tanks at the three trailer camp sites. Chelley reported having been ill several times in the course of her family's eighteen-month stay. Once they moved she had no problems, however, and believes the well water may have been the cause.

Because Bock was always armed, Chelley was fearful of hiking out on the property or of taking her two small children beyond the long driveway. As a result, she feels she missed some of the great beauty of the place. Similarly, the Gring family never went up to the Bock house without first informing him, having been met once with a shotgun when they stopped to drop off the monthly rent. Chelley considered Bock "a very private person."

Chelley recalls, with enthusiasm and unqualified pleasure, the wildlife she enjoyed in her own front yard in Red Rock Canyon. She once identified a tiger salamander, which she didn't know existed in Colorado. She also rejoiced in the visit on one occasion of a magnificent buck deer, numerous does, the presence of Colorado bluebirds, hummingbirds, a family of skunks, and a tree in their yard with an active beehive.

A very small Bock house of 306 square feet, built in 1924, and located west and a bit north of "the house in the hole," was occupied by a caretaker.

From Hawaiian Condos to Former Bachelor Pad

As Erwin Cook, who had known Bock for twenty-five years put it, "John could be rough-and-tumble when it came to business dealings. He was purely a businessman. But when it came to his personal friends, he could be outgoing and generous."

John held extensive properties not only in Colorado Springs, but also in Maui, Hawaii, including several condos on the tropical island. He also owned the presidential suite on the top floor of the high-rise resort condominium "The Whaler," with its glorious ocean views, large lanais, and its prime location on Kaanapali Beach in Maui. The suite was luxuriously appointed, with gold-plated faucets in the bathroom. Bock made this suite available to Dr. Cook and his wife during a vacation trip the couple made to Hawaii, sending them a basket of fruit with a personal note wishing them a nice stay. And he offered them the use of his personal car kept in the basement parking, a Cadillac convertible. As luck would have it, the battery was dead.

Joan Lambert remembers Bock as having been a playboy before meeting his wife Joan in Hawaii. He was tall, well built and very smart, she recalls. His house in Red Rock Canyon, with its swimming pool and its spectacular setting, was "quite the bachelor pad."

Richard's frame house, with its bank of windows, was nicely perched on the red Lyons ridge, above and north of the site John's house occupied. Richard thus enjoyed the superior view, but John's was the more attractive structure of the two. As mentioned, the walls of John's house were built of the native stone quarried from the site. The centerpiece of John's living room was its handsome stone fireplace and chimney. Somewhat incongruously, the side view from John's picture window looked out to the six-car-garage-cum-bomb-shelter.

The Bomb Shelter

In the 1950s at the height of the Cold War when alarms in schools rang, children were trained to duck under desks for protection while their parents horded supplies of water and stocks of tinned goods in their basements for emergency use in the event of a direct nuclear strike. For the next decade or so, families with the means to do so even built their own bomb shelters. Among these were the Bock brothers. At least that is what observers believe the earth-implanted, three-room structure the Bocks built on their property was intended for—with its attached "earth-sheltered" office with double steel doors, a fireplace, and a workshop.

Those who visited the bomb shelter, built into the side of a hill (before its agreed-upon demolition after a public process), recall its dark, dusty, cobweb-festooned, dank interior, its steel doors, its tattered, musty furniture. But most of all, visitors remember the gigantic, lighted topographical model of the Utopian, new-age city that the Bock brothers, in their 1975 Red Rock Canyon Development Plan, envisioned building on what is today's open space.

While the Bocks' bomb shelter did boast earth-filled masonry walls that were approximately three to four feet thick, it was neither sealed nor ventilated. There was plenty of shelf space to store supplies, but it lacked a filtration system. If the Cold War had heated up and Colorado Springs had been attached by nuclear-tipped missiles, the Bocks' shelter (in use in the '60s), was probably not well enough designed to survive a blast—although the dirt ridge above it might have worked as something of a shield, offering enough protection to increase the chance of survival. Dr. Erwin Cook, among others who saw the bomb shelter, agrees that the structure appeared poorly designed.

Bock's Lake

On a more aesthetically pleasing note, the one-acre lake in front of John Bock's house was inspired in the 1960s by a commercial artist named Dick Williams. Williams did a landscape painting that featured the red rock outcroppings in John Bock's front view to which he added a lake in the foreground to give Bock an idea of how it would look. Bock was so taken with the idea that, in a case of life imitating art, he created the artificial lake. The manmade lake mirrored the spectacular view from the front window of jutting red sandstone cliffs, and possibly the added flourish of a great blue heron poised on a tree branch above the glistening water.

The water for the lake was supplied by a small stream that the city owned, but Colorado Springs Utilities never challenged Bock's use of it because diverting the stream for city use, according to a city utilities' employee, would have been both difficult and costly. A notice in the *Gazette Telegraph* on July 22, 1976, however, captioned a news story with the headline, "City Sells Water to Bolster Private Lake's 'Aesthetics.'" Evidently Bock's lake (one of several on his property) needed to be refilled and the Colorado Springs Utilities agreed to sell him water for that purpose that would be pumped directly from nearby Fountain Creek, a special favor not granted to everyone.

A World Trade Center Planned for Red Rock Canyon

For twelve years, from the early 1960s through the mid-1970s, John and his brother Richard worked on their vision to turn the Bock property into a large, resort-style, space-age city within a city of "international scope" for an estimated eight thousand residents and an additional sixty-eight thousand visitors and employees. In recognition of the sheer scope and magnitude of the Bock brothers' 850-acre Red Rock Canyon Development Project for Colorado Springs, Manitou Springs, and El Paso County, the Master Plan notes, in Volume V, almost as an afterthought: "It may be possible with a land exchange program to work out certain mutual and desirable trades." A platoon of engineers, surveyors, and aerial photographers had been hired to help in the fabrication of blueprints and designs for the Red Rock Canyon Project.

> *"He wanted his own little kingdom and he had the money to do it."*
> —trailer camp tenant

The plan, published in 1975, filled nine volumes and was translated into six languages. Volume V, the "Land Use Master Plan," runs to 108 pages alone. Given the publishing cost of the prospectus, work of the planning consultants, aerial photographers, and other experts, and the sizeable project model, the big ideas, in the end, no doubt came with a price tag attached.

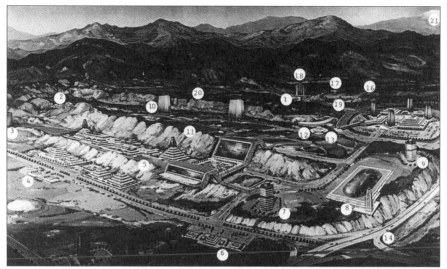

The Bock brothers' 1975 Red Rock Canyon development plan was more ambitious and grandiose than anything dreamed up before or since. Shown in architectural plans are a proposed World Trade Center with aerial tram (8), and an office tower (17). (Photo from Colorado Springs Pioneers Museum)

Water for the new-age Utopian city on the eastern slope, a location noted for its aridity and high desert climate, was to be supplied first and foremost by the construction of a new dam, sited in Wild Bear Canyon north of Colorado Springs and west of Castle Rock. In the drawings, the dam appears sizeable. Another source of water the plans spell out, in a classic case of counting chickens before hatching, would be nearby Manitou Springs. Energy was to be provided by Colorado Springs Utilities.

Among its numerous futuristic and imposing structures, the Master Plan features a spectacular, multi-story World Trade Center connected to an aerial tram that loops like a roller coaster throughout the extensive development. A design for a Regional Plaza and Restaurant Unit, with multiple restaurants, is shown topped with a tall, slender, antennae-thin spire. The tallest of the many high-rise towers rose to three times the height of the tallest building in the city of Colorado Springs—potentially competing for air space with rodent-hunting red-tailed hawks. Some of the tallest buildings, with their antennae-like spires, not only had a distinctly space-age appearance, but also featured building-top landing pads for helicopters.

The Red Rock Canyon Development Project allocates additional space for an impressive array of on-site facilities and services that include: parks, sculptures, fountains, waterways, canals, biking and hiking and saddle trails, water pumps, roads, bus and truck transportation systems, underground horizontal elevators—described as a somewhat "star-gazing concept" of "flying belts for individual people." It provides for such critical services—essential to any burgeoning new metropolis—as fire and police stations to be located on site.

Other buildings and complexes included three employee towers and a world-class resort and convention center. The center would be equipped with a worldwide communication tower—known as a "teleport" to telecommunication experts. Individual rooms in the center were given exotic names, such as "Fjord North, Macau, Kowloon, Mai Tai, Bikini Bay, and Bora Bora." Visitors and convention-goers could check into an executive hotel, or opt for the so-called Sand Canyon Motel, with its 804 rooms. Residents would live in one of the 3,600 residential units found in a three-winged condominium high-rise, consisting of 25 towers of varying heights.

For the convenience of consumers and office goers, there was to be a Regional Shopping Center, with a roof garden of over one million square feet, and as a part of the unit, an office tower. In the meantime, sports enthusiasts could choose between two championship-style eighteen-hole golf courses with driving ranges, then bask in the conveniences and luxuries offered at the Executive Center and Canyon Land Country Club Complex. Additional recreational areas were designated for a ski lift and a rifle range. For the culturally attuned, there was a World Cultural Center and a fine arts theatre. And for the more socially inclined, the project showcased a schematic for the eight-storied, multi-towered Allegro Nightclub Center.

Four large domes were designed to cover the sports center (to include a movie and bowling facility, and indoor tennis courts), and the cultural complexes. The largest of these domes covered the Gourmet Dining Club located in the Allegro Nightclub Center. This complex alone consisted of twenty-two towers of varying heights—with the three largest towers each rising to thirty-six stories—and boasted a banquet building, nightclub sphere, spa dome, and underground parking.

Additional space was available (at least on the huge model and in the Land Use Master Plan) for a Medical and Research Center, Museum and Science Building, and a four-building Technological Center and Industrial Park.

A sizeable computer and finance center is included in the schemata of the Bocks' 1975 Red Rock Canyon project. (Photo from Colorado Springs Pioneers Museum)

Of particular interest is the fact that the red Lyons Sandstone quarry in Red Rock Canyon was to be turned into a historical monument and further "enhanced" by waterfalls, night lighting, and music—a concept possibly inspired by the nightly illumination of the cascading Seven Falls in South Cheyenne Canyon, southwest of Colorado Springs.

Theoretically, the buildings in the proposed new development would have occupied only 25 percent of the land in the erstwhile "kingdom" in the canyon, with the rest of the property being partially devoted to the thirteen lakes that were designed to accommodate sailboats and to permit all varieties of water sports, including scuba diving. In addition, the plan provided for the infrastructure needs of service and supply centers and water treatment and sewage plants, necessary to a population center of the size anticipated by the developers.

In the Land Use Master Plan, one architectural notation of interest specifies that whenever a conflict should arise between principles of design and dictates of function, design will take precedent. Roofs were to be considered "with the same respect and consideration" as walls. "There are no back doors, no back yards in this type of project; everything is right out in front."

Teleports Are the Wave of the Future

Reportedly, John Bock had second thoughts about the advisability of building a World Trade Center when friends pointed out the drawback of not having ready access to major transportation hubs and ports in landlocked Colorado. "The other burr in Bock's saddle," notes former El Paso County official P.J. Anderson, was that the state had promised Bock to build an interchange at the entrance of his property on Highway 24. The letter containing the promise was couched in "weasel language," says Anderson, and Bock never got it locked in contractually. But, Anderson also acknowledges that building such an interchange, promised or not, would have been an expensive proposition.

Information Technology expert and local historian David Hughes worked with Bock on addressing the problem of lack of "access" when it came to the proposed World Trade Center in the isolated canyons of the Bock property. Hughes encouraged Bock to include a worldwide communications tower or teleport for the proposed city within a city. Consisting of a huge disk and big antennae connected to a satellite, a teleport would facilitate global wireless communication and, as Hughes explains it, would serve to open up business and service activities around the world. It would also, states Hughes, enable people to live and work on the same premises, while providing global access in a landlocked setting.

While the concept of a "teleport" may sound futuristic, it is, in fact, a very real part of today's IT global communications world, insists Hughes. Bock was so taken with Hughes' ideas that he paid for an information-gathering trip made by Hughes to the World Trade Center in New York. A teleport or world communications tower is prominently featured in both the model and the 1975 Land Use Master Plan of the Bocks' Red Rock Canyon Project.

Bock, who traveled widely in connection with his World Trade interest, was a dues-paying member of the World Trade Center Association, which is best described as "a global chamber of commerce." Among its mandates is to promote trade, business, and development on a global scale. At some point, Bock secured licensing approval from the association to build a World Trade Center on his intended site under the name "The Rocky Mountain World Trade Center," with affiliates in New York and around the world.

Promoting the Red Rock Canyon Development Project

Bock also reportedly traveled to Washington, D.C., and to Texas, seeking financial backing for the Red Rock Canyon Development Project. And he never missed an opportunity to get publicity and to promote his interests. For example, John and his brother Richard arranged for a high-level meeting with then-Colorado Governor John Love, who served from 1963–1973. One photograph of the event shows Love and the brothers bent over a schematic of the Bock's visionary development plan—although it had yet to be published in its current voluminous form.

Dave Hughes, who was a friend of John Bock's, indicates that at one time, big Japanese interests may have taken a look at the Bock brothers' project, with a view to backing the ambitious plan, but nothing more came of it.

The Red Rock Canyon Project boasted an intricately designed seal that was intended perhaps to be cast in bronze and engraved with the grand and noble-sounding motto, "Serving the World." Yet this resounding sentiment was countered, if not actually contradicted, by the following declaration: "The project is *not designed for the welfare worker* or for *these people in the lower income bracket....* This project is a luxurious type of thing: it is designed to be that way. *We are only interested in a certain portion of the people ...*" [Italics added].

> *"We are only interested in a certain portion of the people."*
> —from the **Bock Red Rock Canyon Master Plan** (1975)

John A. Love, Colorado governor from 1963 to 1973, is shown here (from left to right) with John and Richard Bock. (Photo from Colorado Springs Pioneers Museum)

The Bock brothers never realized their dream of building a futuristic city on the Red Rock Canyon property. There were problems right from the start, with utilities such as water and electricity, although the Bocks had secured an agreement to buy water from the Twin Lakes Reservoir, south of Leadville. Richard Bock thought that the Broadmoor Hotel played a part in blocking the Bocks' visionary plans. The Broadmoor, he believed, could never have competed with a resort city of the size and scale the Bocks envisioned, even with the hotel's renowned golf course that for decades had drawn the rich and famous from all over the world, including several past U.S. presidents.

Richard Bock credited the Colorado voters' defeat of the proposal to host the 1976 winter Olympics as contributing to the plan's failure, since the Olympics would theoretically have brought in interested investors and buyers.

Between 1974 and 1979, P.J. Anderson was planning director and then county administrator for El Paso County. He dealt with Bock regularly. Despite his professed dislike for the federal government, Bock wanted Anderson to write a letter to the Department of Housing and Urban Development (HUD) to get federal funding for his Red Rock Canyon Development Project. In order to secure federal grants, however, an official letter was required. Anderson refused to write such a letter on the grounds that there was "an illegal landfill on the property that didn't meet specifications, multiple septic systems that were deficient and backed up; and, then, there were the mobile homes, which were always in violation of something." Bock next went to a well-known Denver lawyer, Joe Montana, to get him to apply pressure on Anderson to write the letter. When that failed, Bock wrote a letter to President Ford questioning Anderson's competence and asking that he be fired, with a copy of the letter sent to then-Colorado State Representative Bill Armstrong.

Even after all of that, at some later date Bock and Anderson became friendly. However, Anderson believes that Bock was more of a dreamer than an implementer when it came to his Red Rock Canyon project. Bock never submitted a "sketch plan" for approval, a requirement before a development project can go forward, says Anderson. Everything was

> *The Bocks' Red Rock Canyon Development Project "was totally meaningless in the real world."* —P.J. Anderson

on paper, but nothing was ever officially approved. At some later date, in the mid-1970s, the county did have a copy of Bock's Land Use Master Plan in its records, where it continues to gather dust. A further check of El Paso County Development Office files confirmed that Bock, subsequent to Anderson's departure, never bothered to submit the necessary "sketch plan." Records do, however, indicate numerous land-use violations, in addition to special use requests in the 1970s for the sanitary landfill and for open pit gravel mining.

Moreover, Bock needed big financial backing for his ambitious project. He couldn't have financed it himself. But the project, says Anderson, with its space-age teleport, was just too futuristic. "It was totally meaningless in the real world."

Richard, after twelve years of work devoted to the effort, deeply regretted that the Bock vision of a futuristic city on the Red Rock Canyon property was never realized. He, like his brother, did not appear, however, to entertain any deep abiding sentiments about the site itself—a man for whom, in any case, such memories were rapidly beginning to fade. Nor was there any thought of preserving the land for its own sake. The family already had had its fun there—horseback riding, picnicking, hunting, and fishing in an area of unparalleled natural beauty, populated with abundant wildlife. Moreover, there were no direct descendants to consider. It was time to move on. Still, if the plan had to fail, then, as Richard conceded to *Gazette* reporter Bill Vogrin in a 2004 interview, the alternative of a park was "a nice one."

Architect Morey Bean, who met with him on several occasions, confirms that Richard Bock was the "prime architect and ambassador" of the Bocks' Red Rock Canyon project. Bean described Richard as someone who "was outspoken and outgoing," and, at the same time, endowed with a pleasant disposition and personality, making him easy to deal with.

Nonetheless, most would agree that nothing about the Utopian vision of the Bock brothers for Red Rock Canyon land's development was on a small, or even a realistic, scale—not even the three-dimensional, highly detailed, topographical model itself. (Today the cumbersome model, the size of a ping-pong table, resides at the Colorado Springs Pioneers Museum.) Indeed, the Red Rock Canyon Development Project was, in almost every respect, more ambitious and far-reaching, more grandiose even than that of the schemes of a subsequent developer who later rode into town with a proposal for developing the spectacular red rock country, the money to back it up, and the eponymous name of "Zydeco," a subject to be fully explored in the next chapter.

At some point the Bock brothers, not unexpectedly, came to a parting of ways. Richard, who remained a life-long bachelor and who reportedly was "quite artsy," and of a very different temperament from his brother, moved to Scottsdale, Arizona, as did their mother Sylvia, after John bought them both out. For a time, while he was in Scottsdale, Richard pressed on with his efforts to sell the Red Rock Canyon project. From 1963 through the mid-1970s, he continued to write promotional letters touting the ambitious plan—one of which was addressed, somewhat surprisingly (given the Bocks' concern for having a bomb shelter), to the USSR Chamber of Commerce. Another was addressed to the World Trade Center of Japan.

By 1978, it had become clear to most, including the brothers themselves, that the grand vision embodied by the Red Rock Canyon Development Project had failed—partially due to a lack of financial backing; and also because of the widely reported family schism. Dick Lambert echoed the observations of many in saying that John and Richard did not get along and were in frequent conflict. The late Jim Phillips suggested that fuel was added to the fire when John came back from South America and found that Richard, unbeknownst to him, had sold off a sizeable chunk of real estate on the eastern side of the extensive Bock properties. Lambert added that he remembers Richard as being "one of those professional college students, which probably did not sit very well with his older brother, John."

Unlike his brother John, however, Richard Bock appears to have enjoyed a close relationship with his mother. In Vogrin's *Gazette* story, Richard is quoted as saying that "John always ran the roost. We had a falling out in the family. My mom finally moved to Arizona. My brother stayed in the canyon. ... I never came back." Richard and John's mother died at the age of ninety-nine in Scottsdale, Arizona, on September 26, 2001.

Back in the Canyon—a Pre-existent Wild West

In the meantime, John S. Bock appeared to become more and more reclusive over the years. Like many people who enjoy considerable wealth, however, he was a wise investor. He was also, as has been reported by his close associates, notably tight; and, as the record over the years so clearly demonstrates, he tended to be litigious. Dick Lambert reports that John took his mother and brother to court, possibly when he was engaged in actively buying them out.

John kept up the practice started by the elder Bock of warning off trespassers not only with signs, but with a shotgun. This is perhaps in the best tradition of a pre-existent and possibly mythic West in which problems were often settled by violence. At any rate, the Bocks worked hard to keep people off their property. Bock was "extremely proprietary about his property," states John Lewis. His attitude was: "'No one walks on my land.' I think he got that from his father."

Notable Trespassers and the Sting of Buckshot

When he was about fifteen or sixteen years old, Chuck Miller, a former city executive, recalls a fateful day when he and some friends dared to trespass on the Bock property. It was a time in their lives when they considered themselves to be invincible. It was also a time when kids could be off all day long—disappearing early in the morning and not returning until supper—and parents would not worry.

Part of the allure in sneaking up to the Bock house, Miller remembers, was putting yourself in harm's way—it was that element of risk that made it so much fun. Another attraction was seeing whether or not you could provoke Bock into chasing you and what form that chase might take, whether hot pursuit might be conducted by foot or in a jeep.

As the chase began on this particular day, Bock fired a shotgun at the trespassing gang of teenage boys. The boys took off running, with Miller, quite literally, bringing up the rear. Fortunately, the gun was fired from long range. But Miller felt the sudden, sharp sting of buckshot in his derrière—like the pins in a cushion or porcupine quills in a dog's nose. When he got home his mother was able to extract the bead-sized pieces of lead, performing the delicate surgical removal with a needle and tweezers.

Robert Ormes was a professor of English at Colorado College. Ormes is well known for his excellent early maps of trails in the Pikes Peak Region. His *Guide to the Colorado Mountains* was for many years considered the most authoritative book on Colorado's 13,000- and 14,000-foot peaks. John Lewis and Robert Ormes, as mentioned previously, were poker buddies and friends. Lewis says that Ormes "walked around, just in the natural order of things. He walked any place he wanted. He always took the most difficult route, so if you were with him, you might end up bushwhacking." One day, when in the natural order of things, Robert Ormes was hiking on the Bock property, Bock took a pot shot at him.

John S. Bock used his gun in other ways as well. He once eliminated a raccoon that had taken up residence in the Bock home fireplace chimney—first, by lighting a fire under it. Then, when the raccoon dropped down the chimney dazed, but unharmed, Bock shot the creature on the spot—spattering the living room with raccoon remains.

John S. Bock has variously been lauded as a "conservationist" and decried as an "environmental pig." Or does the truth lie somewhere between? One of Bock's close friends and business associates (who asked not to be named) remarked that "Bock loved the land, but not so much he wouldn't let it work for him." Or to put it another way, "He loved the land, but he loved money more. The dump, for example, tided him over, albeit he didn't need the revenue. He wasn't poor."

Bock may have loved the land, but as the same former associate emphasizes, "He wasn't going to give it away." And yet there were several well-established precedents for such gifts—both in the generous example of city founder General William Jackson Palmer and in the Perkins family's magnificent gift to the public of the Garden of the Gods in 1909.

Later, when New Mexico developer Richard Yates and his company Zydeco came into the picture, John Bock was pleased, says his former representative, real estate broker Tom Kay. Bock saw the Yates' plan as "a sort of extension of his own plans for development, with some not-unappealing changes," says Kay. These included development of the frontage of the Red Rock Canyon property, which Bock thought held promise—but that is yet another chapter in the long and colorful history of Red Rock Canyon.

CHAPTER 7

The Secret Garden of the Gods—
The Community Saves Red Rock Canyon

*"Just a little more than a century ago there was a bill before Congress
that set aside all the land from the Garden of the Gods to the top
of Pikes Peak* [an area that presumably would have included
Red Rock Canyon] *as the second national park in the United States.
That should be publicized!"*

—Dr. Richard Beidleman,
Chairman Emeritus, Dept. of Biology, Colorado College

*"Red Rock Canyon is at the very heart
of that wonderful eruption of geology."*
—An open space proponent

John S. Bock may have loved the 789-acre Red Rock Canyon property owned by his family for eighty years—with its stunning red rocks that are a natural geological continuation of Garden of the Gods, its colorful canyons, and its richly historic hogbacks—but it appeared that what Bock most wanted was to get $15 million for it. Still, those who had dealings with Bock over the years tend to think he was somewhat ambivalent about giving up his land and that what he really wanted was to remain a player in the game.

The Perkins Family's Magnificent Gift of Garden of the Gods
There was little doubt, however, that the Red Rock Canyon property was not destined to become a gift to the city in the historic manner of it sister park, Garden of the Gods. Few, indeed, will forget the magnificent gift the Perkins family so generously made to the city of Colorado Springs, on Christmas Day in 1909, when they bequeathed the Garden of the Gods. A wealthy railroad baron, Charles Elliott Perkins was a good

friend of General William Jackson Palmer, whose beneficent example of many generous gifts of land for city parks was an inspiration to him. Perkins never built on the 480-acre site he owned in Garden of the Gods, which is at the very heart of the spectacular red sandstone outcroppings, with their spires and fantastically shaped rocks, and which he once so aptly described as "a marvel of nature."

Unlike most successful entrepreneurs and developers, Perkins did not believe in turning nature's beauty into profit. To him the idea of Garden of the Gods as a beer garden (one of the earliest development proposals for its use, made only partly in jest) or, for that matter a world-class golf course, would have been anathema. The Perkins' family gift, presented to the city by his eldest daughter Alice Perkins and other family members, fulfilled their father's dying wish that the land at the heart of today's Garden of the God's Park remain undeveloped in perpetuity—free and open to all. Seldom has a city awakened on a Christmas morning to so splendid and enduring a gift under its collective Christmas tree. (Out-of-state visitors are often surprised when they discover that Garden of the Gods—given its unique character and unsurpassed grandeur—is not a national monument, but instead a city park.)

Bock's Non-negotiable $15 Million

For several years, the hard-headed and famously testy John S. Bock had been trying to sell the Red Rock Canyon property and the price he set, as already stated, was a non-negotiable, take-it-as-it-is $15 million. Complicating the equation was the nearly sixty-acre landfill—a part of which was in nearby Manitou Springs Section 16—a hazard of unknown proportion and a risk that few wanted to take on. Moreover, the price set by Bock exceeded anything the city of Colorado Springs could realistically afford.

But Bock was mad at the city for, among other things, not granting him what he considered his due in water rights. Bock, as previously noted, only owned a small water right on his property. But it was insufficient for the grandiose scheme first dreamed up by the Bock brothers in their "Red Rock Canyon Project," and more recently by a newly arrived, out-of-state developer whose plan held strong appeal for Bock. Nonetheless, and despite this major obstacle, Bock remained, as geologist and friend John Lewis put it, "messianic" in his desire to develop the land.

The One Bureaucrat Bock Trusted

Furthermore, as even the most sympathetic observers have confirmed, Bock not only mistrusted, but actively hated bureaucrats of every stripe. He denigrated them, states one informant, as "pettifogging, grubbing pipsqueaks," to put it politely—with expletives deleted. But there was one important exception. The one bureaucrat Bock had learned to trust was the well-respected former director of City Utilities, Jim Phillips.

Jim Phillips had once helped Bock straighten out some bills for his trailer tenants. In addition, the city had needed to exercise domain over a small portion of the Bock property in order to build a power substation on 31st Street. John had gone to court over the issue. One day Phillips came to Bock and said, "I can settle this is no time. We can cut you a check in compensation right now." Phillips and Bock walked together downstairs to the city clerk's office and Bock got his check in a matter of minutes. That was the end of the court case and the beginning of a friendship. Bock subsequently told Phillips he was the only honest bureaucrat he'd ever met. Later, Jim Phillips would serve Bock as a trusted consultant when he was attempting to sell the Red Rock Canyon property.

> *"If we're going to keep anything open or keep the big mansions out of the foothills, we have to do something now."*
>
> **—Mark Cunningham,** member of the Red Rock Canyon Committee

The Bock brothers with their Red Rock Canyon Project were not the first or the last of the well-financed investors eager to develop the area that formed a natural geologic continuation of Garden of the Gods. At one time nearly every major developer in the area, and some well beyond it, had looked at the property or been approached.

Arizona Developer Draws Up Plans for Development, then Admits Defeat

Bob Fairburn, now in his eighties, and currently of Phoenix, Arizona, is an architect and major developer who has designed, among other projects, military bases and installations, a giant mall outside Phoenix, and more than two-hundred resort hotels located both in the U.S. and countries abroad. Learning of his reputation, John S. Bock contacted Fairburn and they began to work together in the late 1960s, a relationship that continued off and on throughout the '70s. At Bock's behest, Fairburn drew up various plans and designs for development projects in Red Rock Canyon—one of which included a golf course. On at least one occasion, Fairburn also brought in potential investors—several of whom flew in from the East Coast and the Chicago area. But every time Fairburn and Bock got to the point of finalizing a deal, often in terms of multi-million dollar projects, "Bock would kill it," says Fairburn. (In the case of the investors who flew in from other parts of the country, this was more than a little awkward, Fairburn recalled.)

Fairburn describes Bock as being both "enigmatic" and "erratic," someone who liked to travel a lot and "play the big shot." At the same time, he was capable of turning on the charm when the occasion required. As Fairburn sees it, Bock's sense of identity was tied to the Red Rock Canyon property. He relied on it not just for cash (at that time in the form of the lucrative gravel pit), but also for cachet—helping to explain, perhaps, some of his chronic indecision when it came to selling off the property.

Fairburn says he "gave a lot of services" to Bock, but was never compensated. Indeed, in a pattern that would become increasingly familiar, Fairburn was spun off. He had flown Martin B26 Marauders in WW II and led fifty-one missions over Germany. He had known success on a global scale—but, concedes Fairburn, "I could never conquer John."

Local Developers, Nike, and Donald Trump— All Consider Property

Well-known Colorado Springs developer Steve Schuck of the Schuck Corporation reports that he likewise explored the Red Rock Canyon property, sometime in the late 1960s or early '70s, and found it "fraught with challenges, not least of which was dealing with the Bock family." Schuck decided to give it a pass.

According to Bock's representative, real estate broker Tom Kay, the people from Nike had at one time also toured the property and sent in helicopters to survey it, looking for a possible location for their headquarters. In the end, it was too big an area for them. There were also rumors that a California developer had raised the possibility of building a hotel and golf course on the site.

Real estate agent Jeany Rush devoted six years to showing the Bock property to prospective buyers. She had a letter of commission from Bock and worked with him under a system whereby the property owner pays when the realtor brings in the client. Rush never scored, but she did enjoy what few others did—a "friendly relationship" with John Bock, with whom she liked to "shoot the bull." Rush describes Brock as smart, happiest when he was on the land, and in his younger years could have been described as "charismatic."

Rush sent large, carefully prepared binders of promotional and due diligence material to such well-known personalities as John Denver, Robert Redford, Donald Trump, and Ted Turner, among other prospects. Trump's people were sufficiently interested to fly over the property. Then came a brief letter from New York, typed on elegant letterhead paper, emblazoned with a gold "T," in essence saying thanks, but no thanks.

Big Fish Not Biting—Dump a Liability and Insufficient Water

The big fish were not biting for at least four important reasons. First and foremost, the dump was a potential "vicarious liability," especially under federal superfund site laws. Others variously note that water rights were a huge issue, the price was too high for the property, and the seller was widely known to be nearly impossible to deal with.

Colorado Springs real estate broker Zoltan Malocsay showed the Bock property to a client who wanted to build a large house there and enjoy it for two generations, including with his grandchildren, and then make a gift of the property to the city. While Bock liked to declare himself "the king of water," says Malocsay, in fact all he had was a two-inch water main and no permit for his dams. Since all water belongs to the public, it is illegal to hold water in a dam that is more than ten feet high (whereas the upper dam, when the water was up, held fifteen feet), but the city had humored Bock by providing extra water. Bock would never believe that he didn't own the water that ran over his property, says Malocay. He wanted to turn his property into "the land of lakes." But any serious developer or buyer needed to look at the water issue first. Ultimately, Malocsay's client decided the property was not developable. More recently, Malocsay and his wife Dolores have enjoyed picnics in today's Red Rock Canyon Open Space, which they fondly refer to today as "the twin sister of Garden of the Gods."

Broadmoor Hotel Holds Option, Vice President Considers Zoo Site

According to Tom Schmidt, vice president of development for the Broadmoor Hotel, who built the Broadmoor West Residences condominiums and the Broadmoor Brownstones townhouses, the Broadmoor Hotel held a six-month option on the Bock property in the late 1990s. One idea Schmidt briefly entertained was that of moving the Cheyenne Mountain Zoo to Red Rock Canyon. Schmidt says this was solely his idea, based on the fact that the zoo had limited parking, was not easy to find, and was located on a steep hill, which made it "tough to expand." The Bock property by contrast had "no steep hill, lots of parking, and the backdrop of the red rocks," which would have been a great setting for the animals, Schmidt observed.

Schmidt also considered using only the front acres on the property for development, while leaving the rest as open space. Ultimately, Schmidt decided that the property "would not work out financially for development." He couldn't afford Bock's asking price, he said, especially when you factored in the cost of cleanup. There was also the water issue and the fact that there was "a lot of rock to bore into." In addition, Schmidt had the impression that Bock was using him to jack up the price when the next customer came along, a strategy he did not want to be a part of.

Schmidt says he's glad the deal didn't work out. He didn't want to be in conflict with the community, which was eager to acquire the property. "Purchasing that property," affirms Schmidt, "is the best thing TOPS ever did."

Despite the obstacles, any number of potential buyers continued to discuss the idea of purchasing the property once Bock made it clear his plans were to sell. Indeed, people were agitating for it—whether they were realtors, open space proponents, or developers. Among these was niche developer Mark Cunningham, because he lived on the west side of Colorado Springs and the Bock property was in the near vicinity, and real estate broker Tom Kay.

From the beginning, and for all the reasons just outlined, no open space prize loomed larger or appeared more impossible to achieve than the saving of the 789-acre, breathtakingly beautiful and unique, legacy-quality, undeveloped property of Red Rock Canyon. And because of such environmental pitfalls as the landfill, no public open space purchase would prove more complex to negotiate. (Another potential liability was the torn-down 1950s-era motel that was buried somewhere on the property, along with its forgotten memories, while raising once again the specter of toxicity, this time in the form of asbestos.)

Tom Kay first met Bock in 1972 when Kay, a student at Colorado College, rode a bicycle over to Bock's property. T.K., as he's known to business associates and friends, remembers that first meeting well. "It was at the wrong end of the double barrel of a shotgun, and I got to know him. Later Bock hired me to represent him," Kay recalls.

Red Rock Canyon Rated "A/Unique" for its "Significant Natural Features"

In support of their grand and seemingly unrealizable objective of preserving Red Rock

Canyon, open space advocates pointed to the fact that, in 1990, the landscape and urban design firm of Thomas and Thomas was commissioned by the city to conduct an "Urban Growth Area Inventory of Significant Natural Features of Colorado Springs." The study began by tipping its hat to the City's Comprehensive Plan that "emphasized that the preservation, promotion and enhancement of [its] significant natural features have historically contributed to the desirable environment and image of the region." In an evaluation of twelve geographic sub-areas in the Pikes Peak region, Red Rock Canyon received top marks. In terms of both its "natural features" and "visual variety," two-thirds of the Bock property—including Red Rock and Greenlee Canyons and the hogbacks—was given the highest rating of "A/Unique." The remainder of the land, largely in the eastern-most Sand Canyon, was given a second level "B/Distinctive" rating.

In the City of Colorado Springs' 1997 Open Space Plan, Red Rock Canyon was identified as a "candidate area" for possible acquisition under the generic title "the hogbacks," in a loosely drawn circle on the map, which also included the parcel later known as "White Acres," as well as lower portions of adjacent Manitou Springs Section 16. A subsequent technical evaluation under the city's new Trails, Open Space and Parks (TOPS) program likewise gave the property one of its highest ratings. Ann Oatman-Gardner, a leader of the campaign to pass the original TOPS sales tax and former chairperson of the TOPS Working Committee said, "That property has got to be literally some of the last, best undeveloped land in the area."

Passage of TOPS Critical to Open Space Acquisition

With the successful passage of the TOPS tax in April of 1997, citizens had, for the first time, a mechanism for actually realizing the dream of saving special pieces of land as open space. The 1/10th of a percent sales tax (1 cent on every $10.00 spent on sales-taxable goods purchased) was projected to generate six million dollars per year in a good economy. The cost to an average household was about $16 a year. Sixty percent of funds raised must be spent on open space acquisition and stewardship.

On March 30, 1999, a citizens group, the Red Rock Canyon Committee (RRCC), was formed to promote the preservation of Red Rock Canyon as open space. Scott Flora, the Deputy Director of Trails and Open Space Coalition (TOSC), played a key role in bringing the committee together. He set up a public meeting, identified volunteers, and reviewed strategies to be adopted by the committee in working toward the acquisition of the Bock property as public open space. The RRCC was initially headed by Denise DeLeo of Manitou Springs, followed by former Holly Sugar executive Joe Fabeck. Later the committee was co-chaired by Don Ellis and Shanti Toll. Every month, several individuals contributed to the operating expenses of the RRCC. They were, in turn, acknowledged in the *Red Rock Rag*, a monthly journal newly established by Don Ellis. Initially, Ellis even financed the small, but effective *Red Rock Rag* out of his own pocket, with its timely announcements and reports on the status of the effort to save the property and its short topical columns on the property's stunning geology and rich natural and human history. As Terry Putman, planning chief for the city parks and recreation department, observed, the RRCC was the only open space advocacy group in town to be able to claim its own news publication. With its carefully targeted audience of political leaders and activists, the *Red Rock Rag* was truly the mouse that roared.

One of the first problems the RRCC faced was educating the public. For years the Bock property had been posted and off limits (and a live-fire zone). Most were unaware of the property's stunning beauty, although local residents and neighbors who did know it referred to it as "the secret Garden of the Gods." In order to educate people as to what was really out there—back behind the trailer park and the stand of giant billboards, the RRCC, with the help of broker Tom Kay, secured permission from owner John Bock to conduct hikes on the property.

Don Ellis of the RRCC conducted a follow-up survey of the hike participants. The response to the Red Rock Canyon property was highly enthusiastic. More than half the respondents ranked it "slightly higher" than Garden of the Gods, "somewhat higher than the beautiful regional park of North Cheyenne Cañon," and "significantly higher" than Palmer Park, with its distinctive southwestern topography, for all of the qualities rated.

Zydeco Arrives Backed by Money and Powerful Interests

The walks continued until a big-time developer named Richard Yates, with pockets full of money and powerful connections, and his development company Zydeco out of New Mexico, arrived on the scene with a proposal that John Bock thought held promise. Zydeco quickly secured a multi-year renewable option on the property. The development specter had become real. After that the hikes were forbidden, and Tom Kay shifted the focus of his attention to working with Yates.

> "We aren't against anything. We're for something."
> —**Joe Fabeck,** Chair,
> Red Rock Canyon Committee

Undeterred, the RRCC persevered in its efforts. Slide shows were created and articles written and placed in local journals in an ongoing effort to educate the public on the desirability of saving Red Rock Canyon. A picturesque flier emblazoned with the words "Save Red Rock Canyon" was distributed and informational meetings were held to which the public was invited. Activist, former teacher, and local business owner Shanti Toll not only developed a slide show, but also gave talks.

Once again it was a case of a determined, quick-witted David matching his otherwise limited resources against an incredible Goliath, with everything going for him. In this case Goliath was lent reinforcement (at no cost) by the *The Gazette's* editorial page, which for weeks ran often personal attacks against the RRCC and its project. *The Gazette* boasts the largest circulation in the greater city of Colorado Springs. Its editorial page-writer had a well-honed penchant for flinging outrageous slurs and insults. He suggested in one editorial (7 January 2004), for example, that the process to save the open space was "driven by politicians and activists trying to burnish their do-gooder credentials and assure their place in posterity, no matter what the near and mid-term costs."

In Volume I, No.1 of the newly launched *Red Rock Rag* (May 2000), Chair of the Red Rock Canyon Committee Joe Fabeck wrote eloquently and even poetically: "During almost every meeting I'm told how pleased everyone is with our stand against development of the Canyon. I'm quick to correct them. We aren't against anything. We're for something. It's the other guy who is against. We're for preservation of Red Rock Canyon as accessible open space. We're for defending the Canyon's wildlife habitat, flower-filled meadows and historic sites from the bulldozer's blade. We're for preserving the geologic treasures and scenic beauty of unique red rock formations—natural extensions of the Garden of the Gods. We're for open space with hiking trails and picnic sites for everyone's pleasure."

Over the next two years, the most difficult and controversial choice to be put before the preservationists was: Do you try to cut a deal with the developer to save part of the land or do you go all out trying to defeat the developer and his plan. Negotiations took place at countless meetings and planning sessions in both Manitou Springs and Colorado Springs, in repeated presentations before both city councils, and at numerous sessions of the TOPS Working Committee—the citizen advocacy group which advises the Colorado Springs Parks, Recreation and Cultural Services on open space purchases. Participants matched wits, stratagems, and a don't-blink-first brand of toughness and optimism that reminded some observers of an old-fashioned poker game.

The out-of-state developer from New Mexico, Richard Yates, came to the table with millions of dollars to play with. The New Mexico-based Yates family is one of the wealthiest in that state. It owns a multi-million-dollar oil and gas drilling empire, with nearly three times more oil and gas leases on public western land than any other entity, and international ventures as far afield as Morocco and Spain. (In the Bush administration, a Yates lobbyist was second in command at the Department of Interior.)

Many notable elements of Yates' development plan—with its exclusive clubs, palatial residences and world-class golf course—bore similarities to the Red Rock Canyon Project previously conceived by the Bock brothers. But the state-of-the-art, 346-acre golf course Yates had in mind would have outstripped in sheer ambition and scale even what the Bocks had visualized for their futuristic city of thousands.

Indeed, the eighteen-hole course in Yates' plan would have covered all of the valleys on the Bock property, including Sand Canyon, Greenlee Canyon, Red Rock Canyon, and what is now known as Hogback Canyon (once known as No-Name Canyon), as well as the dump in the former Gypsum Canyon. The stunning hematite red sandstone towers, spires, and monoliths that bracket the valleys, contrasted with the lush, emerald-green expanses of the resort-style golf courses, planed by Yates, would have afforded a prize-winning and unique world-class backdrop. By occupying the site of the crown jewels of the former Red Rock Canyon land, Yates' proposal would also have rendered the most desirable part of today's open space the most inaccessible to the public.

"We Like Manitou!"

And for the next two years it looked as if Zydeco, as it engaged with citizens and local officials in an effort to realize its ambitious schemes, might succeed. Yates and company tried every strategy in the book, including lawsuits, and they hired the best consultants and attorneys money could buy. But history was disregarded in the grand proposal, and insufficient consideration was given to the site's location in a high, arid desert ecosystem, where water is such a precious commodity that in the past it had sparked water wars, as it continues to do to this day (albeit with a bit less gun-toting violence). As the old saying goes: "Whisky is for drinking; water is for fighting over."

Because the former Bock property is located in El Paso County, Zydeco's first decision was where to pitch its development vision and annexation application—whether Colorado Springs or Manitou Springs—so that water and electricity would be provided at the expense of local entities, while citizens' taxes covered the cost of critical infrastructure, ranging from fire and police protection to roads and local schools that the development would require.

Zydeco opted for the small town of Manitou Springs, an art mecca full of old Victorians, boutique stores, and independent-minded citizens. But why Manitou Springs? Critics suggest that Zydeco probably saw the smaller town as "an easier roll" than Colorado Springs in terms of approval of development plans for a challenging piece of real estate. Then-Mayor Marcy Morrison observed that the small town had only one city planner and its review process for such proposals was less stringent than elsewhere.

Zydeco's own explanation, voiced by one of its local representatives, for why the out-of-state developer chose the small town of slightly more than five thousand souls to pitch their development to was simply that, "We like Manitou."

Manitou Springs Fights Back

In making their initial presentations to the Manitou Springs City Council, Zydeco argued that the development would broaden the town's tax base from $41 million to $75 million, and increase annual sales tax revenues from $1.9 to $3.1 million. Less was said about what supplying the needed infrastructure would cost Manitou Springs— particularly after Zydeco said it wanted Manitou Springs to provide Tax Incentive Financing (TIF) because of the "blighted" nature of the property. This would have involved setting up a special tax district called an Urban Renewal

Zydeco billboard: A game of bluff? (Photo courtesy *Westside Pioneer*)

Authority—a practice generally reserved for slum renewal in urban areas. The TIF provided obvious benefits to Zydeco; what Manitou Springs got out of it was less clear. Manitou Springs City Council member Kathy Verlo confessed to having real problems "getting my head around the idea that this lovely piece of land is blighted."

To back up their projected tax revenue numbers, Zydeco presented a "concept plan" for "The Quarry" (a brand name intended to suggest the idea of "blight," but not a name one imagines the developer using at the luxury home/resort hotel stage of development) to a working session of the Manitou Springs City Council. Included would be two hotel resort complexes with 600 rooms, an 18-hole/346-acre golf course, driving range and club, 512,000 square feet of retail space, 700 apartments, 800 single-family units and 60 luxury estates. Nothing was said about open space.

Zydeco's professed fondness for Manitou Springs, however, was not reciprocated by the town's citizens. First Zydeco promised to hold a series of public meetings in the city hall in Manitou Springs. In the *Red Rock Rag,* Editor Don Ellis announced that Parry Thomas, representing Zydeco, was working on plans for "The Quarry" development. In order to get public input, a meeting was scheduled for May 17, 2000, at the Manitou Springs City Hall. A precursor meeting held in Manitou Springs Council Chambers on April 25, 2000, "was packed to overflowing and reporters were present from Channel 11 and several newspapers. Despite the overflow crowd, Mayor Hankin declined to move the meeting to the larger Memorial Hall because recording equipment for the meeting had been set up in Council Chambers. The recording equipment malfunctioned and was inoperative during the meeting."

"The Best Public Uprising of 2000"

At the subsequent public meeting held in mid-May at the Manitou Springs City Hall, the anger among the standing room–only crowd was so palpable you could cut it with a knife. In a classic demonstration of grass-roots democracy in action, citizen after citizen, eloquently and with great conviction, backed up by reasoned, fact-based argument, testified against Zydeco. One white-haired woman (in tennis shoes) did not mince words. "We don't want you here. Go home," she admonished the Zydeco representative.

Citizens were left even more frustrated when Zydeco representatives Kyle Blakely of the Muir Agency and Parry Thomas of Thomas & Thomas refused to go beyond outlining their "concept plan" rather than to spell out specifics or answer questions. Citizens were aware that a more detailed plan had already been presented to city council. They wanted to know the specific numbers for such things as housing units, apartments, luxury homes, resort hotels, and the square footage of retail space. The representatives, with cool suavity, stood their ground and stonewalled. The *Colorado Springs Independent* had this to say about the Blakely-Thomas performance: "Anybody who can stand in front of an entire town and do a fairy dance around the truth deserves recognition." Finally, one exasperated woman demanded, "Is John Bock here? Is Richard Yates here? Tell them to get their butts in here."

> *"They want to construct a couple of square blocks of Manhattan up there."*
> —Rick Laurenzi,
> Manitou Springs activist

No further meetings were held and the Red Rock Canyon Committee received notice a week later that the public meeting scheduled by Zydeco for June 7 had been cancelled. Beyond that, it was difficult to know what the developer's next move might be or what his intentions were.

In the meantime, a September 21–27 story in the *Colorado Springs Independent* by Bob Campbell quoted Rick Laurenzi, one of the Manitou Springs activists who initiated a petition drive against the project, as saying: "Even if all Zydeco did was to build the office and retail space that it outlined that night at Council, that development would be the size of the Citadel Mall. Visualize that with all the parking acreage it would require. They want to construct a couple of square blocks of Manhattan up there."

Laurenzi's sentiments reflected the general fear of Manitou Springs' citizens that the proposed development would double their population of slightly over five thousand. City councilwoman Kathy Verlo reported that she had received lots of calls from "people who are upset," according to a *Denver Post* story (15 April 2000). They want to see Red Rock Canyon preserved as open space. "They are concerned that its [development] would totally destroy the small-town image we [in Manitou Springs] have." Tobe Easton, another resident and open-space activist echoed the sentiment. "When you walk downtown," she said, "you always run into somebody you know. Manitou Springs as we know it would disappear."

The mayor of Manitou Springs Nancy Hankin further outraged many by suggesting that the project "is probably our best opportunity" to grow. Running counter to opinion in Manitou Springs, Hankin appeared to support the idea of setting up an "urban renewal authority (or "TIF")."

The TIF plan was not only ironic, it was logically flawed. The dump was the worst blight on the Bock property. But it was centered amidst the glorious red spires, and was widely acclaimed as being one of the most beautiful sites in the Pikes Peak region. This is precisely where Zydeco, indeed, intended to locate its upscale, lush, green, water-guzzling, world-class golf course complete with exclusive luxury resort club and hotels.

In a letter addressed to Joe Fabeck in April of 2001, in response to Fabeck's earlier letter questioning Zydeco's information about its project, which was published in the *Gazette* and *Independent,* Richard Yates asserted that his proposal aimed to create "a greenbelt equal to almost 500 acres. ..."

"No Annexation without Voter Approval"
Almost immediately several petition drives were started by volunteers such as Verlo and Laurenzi to put "no annexation without voter approval" measures on the November ballot. Volunteers stood in grocery store parking lots and knocked on doors to collect signatures. Before long, hundreds of signatures had been collected. Reading the handwriting on the wall, the Manitou Springs Council preemptively passed its own ordinance requiring voter approval for all annexations of over three acres. Described by the *Colorado Springs Independent* as the "Best Public Uprising" of 2000, this effectively ended the Zydeco/Manitou Springs romance. Hankin was not re-elected.

In the meantime, citizens had been lobbying in support of Amendment 24 to the state constitution, which would have required voter approval for any developer-initiated, council- or commissioner-approved plan to annex properties. In September of 2000, on the last possible date before a deadline that would have been imposed had

Amendment 24 passed, Zydeco turned to Colorado Springs and filed an application for annexation there.

Zydeco Offers Colorado Springs "a Bit of the Rest without the Best"

Zydeco's approach to Colorado Springs was markedly different from that made to Manitou Springs. The TIF became history. No grandiose revenue generating development plans or concepts were floated. Instead, and probably correctly anticipating that the battle would be over open space, Zydeco chose to lead with their "open space" plan first, in a series of private briefings to select city leaders and opinion molders, and then, in a public presentation to the TOPS Working Committee in December.

The question for the city and open space proponents now became whether to negotiate a deal in which the property was divided between use for development and open space where citizens could recreate. However, Zydeco's plan was described by one open space proponent as "a bit of the rest without the best." Its proposal was divided between two separate parcels, totaling 245 acres. One parcel, of a little less than 100 acres, would have been part of the broad valley, on the Red Rock Canyon property, between the Niobrara and Dakota hogbacks. While visually significant from downtown Colorado Springs, this parcel would have been surrounded by development and, in all likelihood, would not have constituted a piece of open space that would have drawn many visitors. The larger parcel would have been in Sand Canyon on the far western side of the property beneath Crystal Hills.

Yates, in his letter to Fabeck, refers to these parcels as "two gorgeous canyons including hiking trails to Section 16…." Although this land does connect to the adjacent Manitou Springs Section 16 (a plus), much of it is very steep and thus less usable by the average hiker. One observer noted: "You'd have to hack your way through it with a machete." For the same reason, much of the land would not be buildable—a point surely not missed by the developer. Almost all this western parcel falls in the second-desirability, "B" category in the 1990 Thomas and Thomas evaluation. The crown jewels—Red Rock Canyon, Greenlee Canyon, plus almost all of the other dramatic red rock outcroppings on the property—would have fallen within the Zydeco development, much of it being devoted to the large private golf course and resort.

> *"Whenever something has been saved, it's because people have stood up for it."*
> —Dr. Richard Beidleman,
> Chairman Emeritus,
> Dept. of Biology, Colorado College

Joe Fabeck remembers these developments well. He believes that the biggest obstacle the committee and its supporters faced was that Zydeco "had money and spent a lot of it." The elements that helped save the land for open space were manifold. First, says Fabeck, was the no-compromise stance. The developers, he says, weren't offering much of anything anyone wanted in the way of open space or good hiking. Even so, several people wanted to compromise, says Fabeck. It was a question of patience and out-waiting the developers. It was also a question of working with and educating people who were influential. The first effort along these lines was directed at city council members whose position on the issue was unclear at the time.

A Cheyenne Mountain Heritage *Kiva* article written by this author was featured in the award-winning quarterly in the winter of 2001. Its founder-editor, Colorado historian and author Richard Marold was quick to appreciate the importance of such a piece. The story was subsequently picked up and carried as a front-cover feature by the widely circulated *Colorado Springs Independent* (21 June 2001). Copies of *Kiva* were purchased in large numbers by the Red Rock Canyon Committee to be presented to city council members and circulated among other decisionmakers. Councilwoman Sally Clark credited the article with giving her the first real understanding she had had of Red Rock Canyon, and she became a supporter of the citizen-driven preservation effort. It was a proud moment for the journal's editor and this author when Zydeco owner Richard Yates held the *Kiva* up at a meeting and said, "This is the sort of thing we're up against!"

Volunteer Work Continues to Save One of the State's Premier Endangered Places

In the winter of 2001, Red Rock Canyon was nominated by Colorado Preservation, Inc. for its list of "Most Endangered Places" in Colorado "because of the significance of its historic quarries, archeological sites, and imminent threat of development" (*Red Rock Rag*, November 2001).

Don Ellis followed up various citizen initiatives by inviting all candidates for city council positions running for election in 2001 to state their position on the goal of preserving Red Rock Canyon in the *Red Rock Rag*. A majority responded and their statements were published in the April issue. Discussions were also held with people at Colorado Springs Utilities. Fabeck agrees that one of the biggest nails in the coffin of Zydeco's development plans was the water issue and the legal questions that surrounded it. Fabeck added that he was surprised at what an effective tool e-mail proved to be in helping to reach out to and build a constituency.

Clearly the countless hours of volunteerism contributed by Fabeck and other civic-minded and committed individuals helped level the playing field in an otherwise unequal battle, where the hired guns on the opposite side were presumably well compensated for their time and for the skills they brought to the table.

As stated by Fabeck, public reaction to the Zydeco open space offering was almost entirely negative. The Trails and Open Space Coalition, the region's leading trail and open space advocacy group, directed by former Air Force Vice Director for Operations for Space Command, Dan Cleveland, called the Zydeco open space offering "insufficient [and] incompatible" with the TOPS committee's "original vision to preserve approximately 500 acres of the Red Rock Canyon as quality open space." Similar sentiments were expressed by Cheyenne Commons, the citizens group that led the campaign to save the Stratton Open Space and the Skyway Homeowners Association.

The Manitou Springs City Council, the Manitou Springs Open Space Committee, and the El Paso County Parks Advisory Board passed resolutions endorsing the RRCC effort to save the maximum amount of quality open space on the Red Rock property. All of these groups argued strongly against annexation based on the limited Zydeco open space offering.

Over the months of negotiations and back-room meetings, the fate of the Zydeco open space proposal and, ultimately, how much and what kind of open space would be saved in Red Rock Canyon was in the hands of a rising chain of Colorado Springs advisory groups and decisionmakers, including the TOPS Working Committee, the Parks and Recreation Advisory Board, the Planning Commission and, finally, the city council. When Zydeco turned away from Manitou Springs and to the Colorado Springs City Council in its annexation efforts, it made a strategic error, one among several. Zydeco and Bock threatened a lawsuit against the city in order to secure water for their development based on water rights dating back to laws set forth in the late 1800s, when limited water rights existed to the Bott-Langmeyer quarry on the eastern portion of today's open space. This did not please the city council, at that time led by Mayor Mary Lou Makepeace, and with a few—but not necessarily a majority—of open space advocates among its members, such as former City Council Vice Mayor Richard Skorman, City Councilwoman and local bookstore owner Judy Noyes, and Councilwoman and journalist Margaret Radford. Moreover, many local residents had not forgotten that some of the worst drought conditions in recent history had necessitated adherence to strict water rationing schedules. Dirty cars they could abide, but not watering gardens proved a hardship.

Locally there was an almost daily flow of news stories about the city's growing infrastructure backlog—miles of new streets to maintain and repair; greater demands on schools, police, and fire-fighting services; a dwindling ratio of snowplows to miles of road to cover. The list went on and on (as it does to this day). Many also questioned the logic of annexing such a special place for development when 60 percent of the city's existing annexed area had not been developed.

A "Giving," not a "Taking"

University of Colorado (Colorado Springs) economist Daphne Greenwood argued that annexation involves a "giving"—a bestowing of value that was not there before annexation. Refusal to annex is not a "taking" in the traditional property rights sense, but rather simply not a "giving" of a large financial benefit to the developer or owner. Moreover, Colorado Springs' annexation policy says a proposed annexation must be "beneficial to the city." Even on purely economic terms, open space is arguably a more beneficial alternative than development for the city. More than two-dozen studies support the premise that park and open space contribute to an increase in "proximate property values," with a positive impact of up to 20 percent on property values. Because the costs of park maintenance is very small (and even smaller with open space) compared with the costs of infrastructure needs for new development, when the proximate value is added over a period of years, parks and open space can end up being a benefit, not a cost. According to one study, "The incremental increase in revenues that governments receive from the higher property taxes is frequently sufficient to pay the acquisition and development costs of the amenities." This could be doubly true if the "amenity" is one of world-class quality and would draw tourists and their dollars as well.

The City Refuses to Annex—Zydeco Tries a New Ploy

Ultimately the city refused to annex. In early March, the Colorado Springs Parks, Recreation and Cultural Services received notice that Zydeco had withdrawn its offer to sell 245 acres of the Red Rock Canyon property to Colorado Springs as open space. The March 9 *Gazette* quoted Zydeco attorney Bruce Warren as saying that "Zydeco withdrew because there seemed to be no consensus about it and no positive response [but that] Zydeco will remain open to proposals from TOPS and the city and certainly consider them."

At this juncture Zydeco approached El Paso County, which like the rest of the state of Colorado, has a minimum of thirty-five acres on lot sizes for development in unincorporated areas. The objective of this requirement is to prevent an eruption of dense, helter-skelter, handkerchief-sized developments on open lands. With this in mind, Zydeco swiftly reconfigured its plans to include palatial mansions on thirty-five-acre lots—re-dividing the entire property into long, thin strips. Under the newly formulated plan, estate homeowners would retain direct ownership of an acre or so of the thirty-five, while granting an easement on the rest for the proposed golf course.

On Tuesday, May 8, Zydeco held a series of meetings, at one of which Zydeco's attorney Bruce Warren announced the developer's intention to sell Red Rock Canyon property as thirty-five-acre lots. In a convincing, poker-faced game of bluff and bluster, Zydeco then put up an enormous billboard in a prominent part of town advertising thirty-five-acre luxury homes in Red Rock Canyon and providing a dot.com contact.

Less than a week after the Zydeco ploy (although at the time no one could be certain that that was indeed what it was), the Red Rock Canyon Committee met to determine whether or not to pursue a compromise agreement. The decision not to compromise at that time was approved, among others, by Jan Doran, President of the Council of Neighbors and Organizations (CONO), representing one hundred and forty neighborhoods.

On June 8, 2001, the Colorado Department of Public Health and Environment received a request from Stewart Environmental Consultants, Inc., of Fort Collins, on behalf of Zydeco, requesting approval of a "voluntary" cleanup plan drawn up by the consultants for the Bock landfill. Everyone, it seemed—from the developer to the city—was concerned about exercising due diligence when it came to the Bock landfill.

On August 30, 2001, Zydeco played host, with Tom Kay moderating and Richard Yates present, to a small homeowners meeting whose members had no vested interest in preserving the Red Rock Canyon property as open space, but who owned property adjacent to Red Rock Canyon. The neighbors had previously received a letter of intent from Zydeco spelling out the developer's desire to discuss the building of a links-style golf course in Red Rock Canyon as a form of environmental mitigation that would cost the city and its citizens nothing. The attendees were told they were among the chosen because they were the "most effective" neighbors of the Bock property. But it was clear that the meeting represented a last ditch effort by Zydeco to get the proverbial camel's nose under the tent.

The meeting began with a presentation by environmental engineer Dave Stewart of Stewart Environmental Consultants, Inc., of Fort Collins, who reviewed the multiple problems of solid waste disposal associated with the Bock property. These were twofold, with both the potential for ground water contamination from the dump and air pollution from methane—which is ten times more toxic than carbon dioxide (some studies indicate that the figure is closer to twenty-six times). Recapturing the methane with pumps and then reusing it as fuel is something the EPA would approve, Steward said. But, the first capping of methane at the dump had occurred in the 1980s. The ability of a landfill to produce methane has an estimated half-life of thirty-five years. The Bock dump was already well into its remediation period. Thus, at this stage in its history, there was insufficient methane being emitted from the landfill to make recapturing of bio-fuels, and the consequent prevention of the release of greenhouse gases into the atmosphere, a viable proposition. (Bock himself—presumably for the money and not any environmental concerns—had at one time investigated the possibility of recapturing methane from the landfill as bio-fuel.)

A hard downpour of rain, with the accumulation of six inches in thirty-six hours, had at least on one occasion, Stewart reminded his audience, created yet another concern. It opened a fissure in the dump, emitting both methane and a strong smell that prompted one visitor to call the health department. Steward described this as being an "explosive" situation. Moreover, a deep fissure in the oxygen-less dump would spell doom for any small creatures that stumbled in.

Yet another problem related to the fact that the dump sits on top of the Morrison aquifer and that Bock had dug a deep well nearby, raising some very real concerns about water contamination, Stewart said. After the city purchased the Bock property, Colorado Springs Utilities inspected the well and found that, indeed, the water in it was contaminated. The use of contaminated water is illegal. This means that the man-made lakes on the open space must now depend on hard, concentrated rains and run-off for water. In dry years the lakes tend to run low, creating less than desirable conditions for riparian plants and such iconic water birds as the Great Blue Heron.

In addition to the solid waste dump on the Bock property, Stewart further noted the presence of a second dump filled with construction materials.

Stewart's briefing left little doubt that an environmental cleanup was bound to be difficult, complex, and above all, costly. But, the message was clear, it could all be accomplished at no extra expense to the city or its taxpayers by Zydeco, and in the process, citizens would gain a beautiful, state-of-the-art golf course.

"The Broadmoor and More"

In the letter of intent sent by Zydeco to neighbors to set the stage for the meeting, several details of their latest plan were highlighted. In addition to the eighteen-hole PGA standard golf course, the plan spelled out the need for a new irrigation system and reservoirs to provide water for the course, a parking lot near the Bock house (at the threshold of Red Rock Canyon), as well as additional maintenance and driving range buildings. The plan would also rely on such already *existing* (my italics) facilities as city gas and electricity to the Bock residence, septic tanks from the Bock residence and *maintenance buildings*, as well as potable water from the city "to the Bock residence, *maintenance buildings, and driving range.*" The Bock residence was to be converted into a club house (although given its deteriorating state, it's a reasonable bet the developer would have torn it down instead). Disingenuously, nothing was said of the potential Zydeco plan to develop the frontage of the Bock property or to build luxury estate homes on thirty-five-acre lots.

As Stewart concluded his remarks, more than one of the developer's team chimed in with the refrain that "the state really wants us to move ahead with this project." Clearly, some unnamed state official had agreed that a golf course was one of the approved methods for remediation of a landfill. In short, the golf course was being sold as an easy way to do a massive cleanup operation, while meeting exacting federal and state requirements and regulations (ones that had not existed when the dump was originally put in place). It was beginning to sound as if the developer considered he'd be doing the community and the taxpayers a great big favor.

The merits of the proposed golf course were next addressed by high-end, golf course architect Kevin Atkinson, representing Phelps/Atkinson Golf Course Design of Evergreen, Colorado. Unstinting in his praise of the beauty of the Red Rock Canyon site, Atkinson proclaimed it one of the ten best golf course sites he had seen anywhere in the country. It would not only gain national and worldwide attention, he observed with a flourish, but it would be "the Broadmoor and more." With those seventy-foot-tall rock walls, the spires of red rocks, the monolithic Lyons Sandstone, it would make the cover of any slick, glossy, architectural or sporting magazine in the U.S, he concluded.

Citizens Question Water Use, Future Development Plans, Impact on Wildlife

When questioned by some of the more thoughtful citizens in attendance, the developer and his representatives were unable to say how much water would be required to keep the links green. Audubon International estimates that the average American golf course uses 312,000 gallons per day. A links-style course, with a well-designed watering system, does help to reduce the volume of water consumed. But the reduction is not sufficient, many would argue, to make it acceptable in the context of diminishing water resources and accelerating demand in a high desert climate with periodic droughts and rapidly falling water tables. Furthermore, the city, like so many across the nation according to recent studies, is already overstocked with golf courses, built by developers to anchor high-end housing developments.

Questioned about whether Zydeco had additional plans for development on the property once the golf course was completed, the presenters were at best vague. They were also unable or unwilling to specify to what extent traffic flow would be impeded at the property's busy access point on Highway 24, if and when further development should take place. The implication was that such a prospect was so distant and remote it had no business even being introduced into the discussion. The only thing the developers were currently asking for, they insisted, was to build a golf course. The presenters then moved nimbly on to the next question.

One neighbor, clearly impressed, opined that Zydeco's plan to build a golf course was certainly a whole lot better than what Bock had done with his property. Another neighbor wanted to make certain the red rock formations themselves would not be in any way altered. Not only was he given reassurance on this point, but he and others were informed that they would be incredibly proud to be neighbors of so splendid a golf course.

Another savvy neighbor wondered if the thirty-five-acre luxury homes (called "homesteads" by the developer) that had previously been presented for approval to El Paso County, if built, would be in a gated community. The question basically went unanswered. One woman voiced her fears that the developer might have designs, in the future, on adjacent Manitou Springs Section 16, should the Red Rock Canyon development go through. Yet another expressed concern about what impact a golf course would have on wildlife corridors. The developers acknowledged they had not done a wildlife study, though a rare plant study had been conducted, they said. Questions about run-off from chemical pesticides and fertilizers that might have a negative impact on indigenous and/or rare plant communities never came up.

One brave soul, a woman, quietly but pointedly observed that there was currently a new trend in urban planning that allowed for community spaces. "How does the development of a golf course fit in?" she asked. She also wondered why the city had not purchased the property. Tom Kay answered by saying that the developer had stood aside for the city to give it a chance to make the purchase and it had shown no interest.

In the course of the exchange that took place between developers and their targeted audience in August of 2001, the golf course plan was presented as a fait accompli— not a question of "if," but merely a question of "when." The presentation was skillfully couched in the "green" language most often associated with environmentalists. But the implication was clear and unmistakable. It was just a matter of time before the bulldozers started to roll.

Zydeco Withdraws

Richard Yates continued to negotiate until the end of the year at which time, it is believed, his elder brother who had given him some money to play with pulled the plug.

It is estimated that Yates spent roughly a million dollars on Zydeco's option to purchase the Bock property, on which he took a hit, not to mention thousands of additional dollars needed to hire lawyers, planners, surveyors, architects, and other experts in order to exercise due diligence, produce a site plan, and address the requirements of the health department. There were those, both among supporters and detractors, who questioned whether the thirty-five-acre luxury estate homes, one of Yate's last proposals, were economically viable in the first place given the glut of luxury estate homes standing empty on the market. And the world-class golf course came with its own set of problems, not least of which was water.

On January 7, 2002, Zydeco withdrew its Special Use Permit application filed with El Paso County Planning for the 346-acre Red Rock Reserve golf course. On February 25, 2002, Bock's real estate broker, Tom Kay, announced that he had been authorized by Bock to approach other interested buyers of the Red Rock Canyon property.

The ups and down of the political process and strategic moves and negotiations between preservationists and Zydeco reminded some of the rough terrain and intemperate weather that characterizes the Front Range.

Yates Underestimated the Opposition
However, open space supporters were aided by the fact that, as one astute political observer pointed out, "Yates was not of this community, and he made some key mistakes." For example, he did not take the Red Rock Canyon committee or anyone connected with it seriously enough to ever attempt to hold a meeting with them or connect in any other way. In short, Yates seriously underestimated the opposition. And, he also managed to antagonize a fair number of people. As columnist John Hazlehurst wrote in the *Colorado Springs Independent* in the winter of 2002, if you want to be a successful developer "you emphatically do not do what Yates had done: infuriate the preservationists, treat the folks in government like know-nothing hicks, submit incomplete plans full of apparent misstatements, and sue the entities whose assent you need to annex/develop."

A final and definitive nail was driven into the coffin of Yates' development plan when he received the second resounding "no" to water, this time from the city of Colorado Springs. The groundwork was laid at a utilities board meeting on which City Council members also serve. These included Mayor Mary Lou Makepeace and council members Judy Noyes, Ted Eastburn, Jim Null, Richard Skorman, and Sally Clark, all of whom voted not to give Yates water.

In the end, aided by several maladroit political choices by the developer and the unwillingness on the part of most of the preservationists—including the TOPS Working Committee—to buy into any of the limited open space scenarios offered by him, the Zydeco development plan was stymied. Joe Fabeck and Don Ellis were two of the key players in this triumph, personalities that complimented each other—Ellis, the detail man and local historian, and Fabeck, the former corporate executive and make-no-compromise hard-liner, because as he put it, "Once you make a compromise, you'll never get more than what you ask for."

In a *Westside Pioneer* interview (5 February 2004), Ellis, in turn, credited Kent Obee, Chair of the TOPS Working Committee, with helping to smooth over differences "when Joe and I got too abrasive." Obee, a retired senior career diplomat said, "I was always willing to talk to people, to find the best way to present the case. ... We had to decide when to push, where to push." Obee admitted he was not overly confident about stopping Zydeco. "The single biggest political decision was whether to hold out or make a deal," he said. "It helped that Yates never came up with a compromise that was good enough to tempt people."

When the Zydeco option lapsed in late 2002, preservationists and the city quickly stepped forward, even while Yates was still engaged in talks with Bock for renewing it—although some sources say that Bock had already decided not to renew. Shortly thereafter, John Bock died. Fabeck matter of factly states that if John Bock hadn't died when he did, none of what followed would have been possible.

In the meantime, the TOPS Working Committee recommended that the Trust for Public Land (TPL), a national non-profit land conservation organization, be brought in as a negotiator. TPL had been involved in the city's first big open space success story, the purchase of the Myron Stratton land in the southwestern portion of the city in 1998.

> "I met Bock just once through a screen door. He was wearing pajamas, his Hugh Hefner robe, and he had a gun in his hand."
> —**Woody Beardsley,** TPL Program Manager

Months of negotiations followed with myriad ups and downs. The TPL project manager and negotiator for the deal was Woody Beardsley—an astute, young, six-foot four-inch Coloradan from Denver with a ready smile and a partiality for cowboy boots and tweed coats, who comes from a Colorado cattle ranching family. It was Beardsley who managed to surmount the many obstacles, and survive the cliff-hangers, to successfully negotiate a deal.

The Critical Need to Pass a TOPS Extension

Among the remaining variables in bringing the Red Rock Canyon purchase to closure was the question of "would the voters support a proposal to extend TOPS beyond its original twelve-year limit?" While there was enough money in the TOPS funds to purchase the Red Rock Canyon property, in order to make it acceptable to people in other quadrants of the city, it was important to have funds available for purchases in addition to the Red Rock Canyon property.

The TOPS extension campaign drew for its support on a wide spectrum of Red Rock Canyon open space advocates and civic groups—at the forefront of which were the Trails and Open Space Coalition (TOSC), the Sierra Club, the Friends of Red Rock Canyon, and numerous neighborhood associations.

It was the hope of this broad coalition and the TOPS extension campaign leaders to build on the success TOPS had realized in purchasing the Stratton Open Space in the city's southwest, and Big Johnson Reservoir (now called "Blue Stem Prairie") on the east side, as its first major open space purchases, not to mention the J.L. Ranch purchase, which became Cheyenne Mountain Park. The latter purchase, made for sixteen million dollars, represented a site that had received top ratings for its conservation values and may have taken priority over Red Rock Canyon. Its purchase removed it from the docket at a strategically important time.

TOPS' Signature Success—the Purchase of Red Rock Canyon

By this time, Red Rock Canyon had become such a popular cause that it could effectively serve as "the flagship property" for the ultimately successful TOPS extension campaign. Results exceeded all expectations. The extension not only passed, but with an overwhelming two-to-one margin of voter approval in the spring of 2003. It was, indisputably, the passage of the TOPS extension—after the carefully crafted campaign waged to convince voters of the critical importance of continuing with the ordinance—that made the purchase of the Red Rock Canyon property possible. As long-time open space activist Lee Milner states, "It wouldn't have happened without TOPS [and its subsequent extension]. Our ability or lack of ability to purchase the Red Rock Canyon property would be the signature piece of TOPS' success."

In retrospect, negotiating the Red Rock Canyon Open Space deal was fairly straightforward in terms of the way having been paved with TOPS and a GOCO grant, says Beardsley, but it was complex in terms of the owner, land titles, and, of course, the liability issues, including the dump and trailer park. Beardsley credits the late-Jim Phillips from city utilities and real estate broker Tom Kay with helping to keep all the pieces together and on track. "Kay anticipated problems," says Beardsley. "He kept the deal together through the variety of morphs or forms it took." Beardsley also got on well with the widow, Joan Bock, and thinks that that helped in cinching the deal.

Possibly the Largest TPL Acquisition in Colorado

In November of 2002, Beardsley brought negotiations to a head when he managed to nail down the option on the land, opening the way for the city to finalize the deal. Red Rock Canyon Open Space, Beardsley says, represented one of the Trust for Public Land's largest (and maybe the largest) of its acquisitions in Colorado at the time. It was most unusual in being an opportunity to buy such a major and beautiful property "that close to an urban center."

Former Colorado Springs City Councilman and Vice Mayor Richard Skorman credits Beardsley as being "one of the unsung heroes" of the Red Rock Canyon Open Space success story. Tom Kay echoes the sentiment saying, "This was a complicated transaction with a

In a constituency building effort, Joe Fabeck leads a Red Rock Canyon hike, framed by sandstone outcrops in the background. (Photo courtesy *Westside Pioneer*)

landowner who had little faith in government entities. It is safe to say the deal would never have come together without the involvement of the Trust for Public Land."

Another major unknown in the purchase of the Red Rock Canyon property was an almost complete turnover of the city council in April of 2003. Would the new council support the vision of saving Red Rock Canyon as its previous members had done? The answer to the question was a resounding "yes," thanks, in large part, to a well orchestrated and highly focused effort by both citizens and the city parks and recreation department to educate the council's newly elected members on the desirability of the purchase. After TPL bought the Bock property, the city—under the old council—had agreed, in turn, to buy it from TPL. But nothing is ironclad until the money is appropriated. The massive change in the council's membership made it necessary at a critical turning point in negotiations to virtually start over again. Colorado Springs Parks, Recreation and Cultural Services Director Paul Butcher and his deputy, Terry Putman, played a key role in bringing new council members aboard on the plan. Without Butcher and Putman's timely expertise and support, the plan to purchase the Bock property might well have failed.

New City Council Approves Red Rock Canyon Purchase

In May 2003, the new city council voted unanimously to approve the Red Rock Canyon acquisition at $12.5 million dollars, a price TPL negotiated with John Bock's widow. Jerry Heimlicher, former city councilman from District 3 and now of Tennessee, later commented that he regarded his vote in favor of the purchase of the Bock property as "a tombstone vote"—something worthy of an epithet on his own final marker.

Then, in October 2003, came the long-awaited and exciting moment when the Trust for Public Land closed on its purchase of the Red Rock Canyon property.

Tom Kay says that much is owed to Joan Bock, the widow, who was "the gracious one" in these negotiations, and who, in his opinion, gave up three million dollars. He concurs with most observers that it's a figure John Bock never would have agreed to. "He was proud." says Kay. "He hadn't changed that price in thirty years."

In November of 2003, the city, in turn, closed on its purchase of the Red Rock Canyon property from the Trust for Public Land, after authorizing Certificates of Participation, (COPs), similar to bonds, of up to $15.5 million for the purchase. In a second vote required to approve the funding of the purchase, the vote was 6 to 2 in favor, with Mayor Lionel Rivera and Councilman Darryl Glenn voting against (Richard Skorman, who had worked for TPL, recused himself). Both Rivera and Glenn were lukewarm, at best, on open space and justified their switch on the grounds of the extra costs beyond the $12.5 million for which they had originally voted—giving them a chance to further burnish their fiscally conservative credentials.

The council's approval of the purchase was a moment not only of great jubilation, but also of vast relief for many, not least of whom were the TPL negotiators, who having initially paid for the purchase might have been left awkwardly holding the bag.

In the end, the cost of the Bock property added up to $15.5 million because of the extra expenditures, among others, necessitated by having to extend the option to purchase the property. This amounted to $250,000—thanks to Doug Bruce, a Colorado Springs libertarian and anti-tax crusader, who sued the city for what he said was misleading in the TOPS renewal ballot language—arguing that "extending" meant "increasing" an existing tax. Bruce was ultimately overruled by the Colorado Supreme Court, but the delay in the city's ability to purchase the open space ultimately cost the taxpayer.

In addition, there were costs associated with relocating the mobile home dwellers (an estimated $675,800), of cleaning up the gravel pit, and ameliorating leaks in the dump (hikers could smell the methane), not to mention demolition costs (an estimated $57,200), and insurance, as well as debt service reserve to pay the cost of issuing the COPs. On the other hand, the assessed value of the property was $17 million dollars. Most citizens felt that this was a gift they could not afford *not* to give themselves.

In December 2003, just in time for Christmas, Great Outdoor Colorado (GOCO), whose funds come from the lottery, gave Colorado Springs a grant of $1 million to help pay for the purchase of Red Rock Canyon—GOCO's largest grant ever to Colorado Springs.

In March of 2004, the Manitou Springs City Council declared the Red Rock Canyon Committee "Environmentalist of the Year," and approved a gift of $50,000 to Red Rock Canyon to be dispersed over a number of years.

In short, after five long years of what has been described as one of the most intensive periods of citizen lobbying in local history, the community had scored a major victory. And now even the spirits of the Utes, the first historic occupants of the area, may have rested a bit easier.

While water had proved to be a big stumbling block for developers, equally important, citizens had begun to ask themselves: What is going to be most beneficial to our community in the future—a hotel, golf resort, and housing complex in Red Rock Canyon or having the land available as open space for a growing population? And grow we will. The Colorado Springs Utilities, one of the most careful monitors of where we are headed, predicts a population of 800,000 in less than forty years. Another question people were beginning to ask themselves was that will the resources of our current foothill parks and open space—and particularly Garden of the Gods, which is already being "loved to death" by some 1.7 million visitors annually—be adequate? In considering the best possible use of Red Rock Canyon, the public did not overlook those deeper and more human needs we all share, as population densities grow, for space where we can both recreate and get away from it all. As Wallace Stegner observed, "It is a good question whether we may not need that silence, space, and solitude for the healing of our raw spirits more than we need ..." a mega-resort and housing/business complex.

> "As the country at large grows more stressful as a dwelling place ... quiet, remoteness, and solitude ... become more and more precious to more and more people." —**Wallace Stegner**

The Perennial Problem of What to Do about the Dump

When it came at last to questions of finalizing the purchase of the Bock property as open space, the dump was something everyone wanted to pretend simply did not exist. Today, the Palmer Land Trust holds an easement on Red Rock Canyon Open Space (which protects it and its conservation values in perpetuity), but the PLT could not, for obvious reasons, place an easement on the dump itself. The large grant from GOCO was raised to cover the purchase of the open space, but the grant money could not be spent on the area occupied by the dump. The Trust for Public Land, which negotiated the purchase of the open space, came up with an imaginative arrangement whereby the city itself bought the dump for the grand sum of $1.00. No one on the city council wanted to be held accountable for spending big dollars on a landfill.

One of the supreme ironies of the Bock dump was that, on the one hand, it posed environmental risks of an unknown magnitude as well as significant cleanup costs. This caused developers to mostly back away from its purchase. In a sense the dump protected Red Rock Canyon from mega developments—while at the same time nearly derailing the effort to save it as public open space. One way or another, there was now a great deal of work to be done, and it was time to shift focus from celebrating the hard-won victory to beginning the cleanup.

A Time to Steward

Thus, many of the same open space proponents and citizens who worked toward the preservation of Red Rock Canyon and voted for TOPS, would now model how to practice good stewardship by contributing to trail building, noxious tree removal, tree plantings, the development of multiple-use trails, climbing walls, bicycle freerides, and other recreational facilities.

A Time to Reflect

In the year 2000, former *Independent* columnist and city council member John Hazlehurst, whose family has been in the Pikes Peak region since 1859, received a request for a letter for a new time capsule at Colorado College. In the letter he wrote to future generations of Colorado Springs citizens, he asked: "Do you still believe, as we did, that you live in a special place, one worth fighting for, one worth preserving? I hope so. … We may have been selfish screwups, but if we managed to save Manitou Springs Section 16 and Red Rocks, at least we did one or two things right."

The Utes once again take us most directly to the heart of the matter. As one Ute elder commented about the Garden of the Gods, in an observation that applies equally to Red Rock Canyon: "It's a cathedral. And you don't live in a cathedral."

At dawn on Friday, October 29, 2004, Red Rock Canyon Open Space officially opened to the public. And there was much to celebrate. The preservation of the Red Rock Canyon property as open space was the biggest and best story related to the city's open space and parks' legacy to occur in the past hundred years. Nothing quite so big and important or historic had happened locally—in the realm of preserving such a stunning piece of public open space, with its remarkable red sandstone geology and richly diverse, millennia-old history—since the day the Perkins family so generously presented Colorado Springs with the immemorial gift of Garden of the Gods.

Colorado Springs Mayor Lionel Rivera addresses celebrants at July 2005 Red Rock Canyon dedication. (Photo courtesy *Westside Pioneer*)

A Time to Celebrate

To celebrate the historic event, a Red Rock Canyon dedication was held on July 16, 2005. It featured picnics, bicycle freeriding, rock climbing demonstrations, guided hikes, a blues band, and a ribbon-cutting ceremony with speeches by local leaders. Today Red Rock Canyon Open Space, second only to its nationally known sister park, Garden of the Gods, and possibly Cheyenne Canyon, is one of the most frequented and beloved parks in the Pikes Peak region—with an estimated fifty thousand annual visitors.

Epilogue: A Greater Red Rock Canyon

"Each generation has its own rendezvous with the land,
for despite our fee titles and claims of ownership,
we are all brief tenants on this planet. By choice, or by default,
we will carve out a land legacy for our heirs."
—Stewart Udall from *The Quiet Crisis and the Next Generation*

The joy and jubilation generated by the successful citizen-driven effort to save the beautiful Red Rock Canyon as public open space created its own momentum for more good works and creative projects. This included the preservation of two additional, high-priority parcels, critical to the completion of the open space map itself—the adjacent White Acres and the 640-acre Manitou Springs Section 16, to be described later. The purchase of these properties took on an added urgency after Red Rock Canyon had been saved.

In the meantime, one of the first orders of business for the Colorado Springs Parks, Recreation and Cultural Services department and engaged citizens was to hold a public process to facilitate discussion of ideas and concerns related both to recreation in and the stewarding of the spectacular new open space. A series of five public meetings was scheduled to help formulate an Open Space Master Plan, for which public input was sought on a multitude of wide-ranging issues: from layout and design of trails and trailhead locations to the ultimate use of the Bock compound, and the thorny question of how most equitably to manage the parts of the property still occupied by several small mobile home parks, and the best use of the less desirable, smaller parcels fronting Highway 24 and 31st Street.

Other questions, such as areas to be designated for rock climbing, access to the quarry sites, and overall security for the large property, would also have to be addressed. High on the list of concerns was the question of how to achieve a reasonable balance between public access and related educational signage and exhibits, along with the protection of the area's rich fossil resources.

Adding to the complexity of the issues to be dealt with was the fact that TOPS-funded purchases allow for only minimal development of infrastructure on open space—essentially only trails, trailhead parking, and restrooms. Six hundred and fifty-three acres of Red Rock Canyon Open Space fell under this provision. The remaining less desirable acreage fronting Highway 24 and along 31st Street was bought with state lottery funds (GOCO). As such, it was not designated as open space, nor would its intrinsic conservation values justify its being included in the Master Plan as open space since it was neither as pristine nor as spectacular as the interior of the property.

Ultimately, it was decided, thanks to a thinking-out-of-the box proposal put forward by Terry Putman, then-parks department's Manager of Design and Development and the TOPS program, that the best possible use for these two frontage areas might be as a nicely landscaped public park with a picnic area, and most of the parking for the open space conveniently located at the same sites. The concept proved to be both an imaginative and effective hybridization, one that answered to a variety of public interests and needs. Today these less pristine parcels also include an off-leash dog walking area and a "freeride" bicycle park.

Grass Roots Democracy in Action

The first of the series of Master Plan meetings inviting public input began in the winter of 2004 and was facilitated by the team of Tweed Kezziah and Susan Watkins, an experienced, city-contracted, Colorado Springs consulting firm, working in conjunction with Design Concepts of Boulder, a planning company who would help draw up the Master Plan. The Master Plan meetings yielded an abundance of new ideas and proposals and proved an impressive example of thoughtful citizen input, decisionmaking, and grass roots participation in local governance.

In any process of deciding how best to use a newly acquired open space, there is bound to be some disagreement and dissension, even among its most committed advocates. Individual interests, values, and preferred modes of recreation vary greatly among any group of outdoor enthusiasts and pro-active citizens. In order to reach agreement and arrive at an optimum plan, striking a balance is essential.

Chris Lieber at the parks and recreation department, who for more than a decade played a key role in the negotiation for and purchase of many of the city's last remaining open spaces at a time when the window of opportunity was rapidly closing, regards these moments of disagreement, conflict, and dialogue as being signs and symbols that define the "verb" in community. Dialogue, plus different ideas and difficult moments, says Lieber, lead to a point where we all come together. The results crystallize into what Lieber describes as "action moments"—hence the "verb" in community.

As a part of the public process and in order to make the public aware of the educational potential of the open space, a series of lectures was presented covering topics such as geology, paleontology, early and modern human history, the quarries and mills sited on the open space, and its diverse ecology. The well-attended lecture series was sponsored by the Friends of Red Rock Canyon in conjunction with the city parks and recreation department. (The Friends group had morphed out of the original Red Rock Canyon Open Space Committee and played, as it continues to do, a critical role in fundraising and spurring volunteer action on behalf of the open space.) In follow-up questionnaires at the conclusion of the lectures, participants expressed great enthusiasm for, interest in, and a desire to learn more about the long and varied history of the open space.

Subsequent planning sessions fostered lively discussions concerning what trails to build and where to locate them, the appropriate use of non-intrusive signage, ways and means to further educate the public on the rich history of the open space, and how best to protect precious fossils and ecologically sensitive areas.

A Tempest on Mt. Olympus

In formulating the Master Plan, one of the earliest and most important decisions to be made was on an appropriate name for the newly acquired open space. An activist group of women, known as "the Garden of the Goddesses Club" (GGC), generated national publicity when it proposed that Red Rock Canyon Open Space be named "Garden of the Goddesses." They argued a need to help redress an imbalance in masculine energy apparent in everything from local statuary to city place names, and, most specifically, in the name of the famous Garden of the Gods Park. Others participants were quick to point out, in the course of the impassioned debate that followed, that according to their own understanding, the word "Gods," in its plural usage, embraced not only male, but equally powerful female deities.

The problem of naming the open space was rendered more complex by the fact that, in the past, the "Garden of the Gods" signs had been defaced by Christian fundamentalists who objected to the plural usage in "Gods." Vandalized park signs were sometimes found with the "s" in "Gods" systematically blotted out. This presented just one more maintenance problem for the already cash- and personnel-strapped city parks and recreation department.

For this and other reasons, the vote at the conclusion of the public debate came out overwhelmingly in favor of retaining the property's original and geologically inspired, historic name. The Garden of the Goddesses Club, among whose leaders is open space activist Coreen Toll, put forth a strong lobbying effort, and then graciously conceded to majority opinion despite their considerable disappointment.

In the meantime, the naming brouhaha raised in the public process prompted the libertarian editorial writer of the Colorado Springs *Gazette* to have a field day as he dipped his quill into battery acid in an editorial titled "Garden of the Gags" (7 January 2004). The writer suggested as alternative names for the open space: "Legacy-Chaser Acres," "The Gas Fields," and "Arsenic Acres." Some of his other comments were even more derogatory. His underlying complaint was simply a sour grapes lament that the Red Rock Canyon Open Space advocates had been successful in their effort to save the area through the TOPS program.

Ultimately, the publicly vetted Master Plan would feature seventeen miles of multiple-use trails and a variety of recreational resources, including trails which are handicap accessible, three areas for technical rock climbing, an off-leash dog area, a freeride mountain bike area, equestrian parking, and picnic areas. In 2004, the team of Kezziah and Watkins received an award from the Partnership for Community Design in Colorado Springs for the Red Rock Canyon Open Space project and public process.

"A Neighborhood, Small and Humble ..."

Once the Bock property had been purchased for public use, the trailer camp tenants had to be relocated in a manner that was as fair as possible to all concerned. In mid-June of 2003, mobile home tenants on the Red Rock Canyon property received a notification from Joan Bock, the wife of the late property owner, which advised residents "to find other places to live and terminate ... tenancy on the premises no later than September 1, 2003." Local historian and committed open space supporter Don Ellis was a strong advocate for the trailer camp tenants, insisting that they be treated fairly when it came time for them to be relocated. As Ellis wrote in the *Red Rock Rag* (October 2002): "Now there's ... a neighborhood, small and humble, only about two dozen households. Some of the householders are elderly and disabled. All have very modest incomes. Most have lived in the neighborhood a long time and own their homes. Now, this neighborhood is threatened. ... And, we have become the threat."

The city, to its lasting credit, responded to the appeal of Ellis and other concerned citizens in a remarkably successful relocation process that was led by Terry Putman and his deputy Chris Lieber, working together with a hired consultant.

Addressing the problem of what to do about the trailer camp "community" continued to pose some very real challenges for city park officials, who nonetheless pressed ahead, working long and hard on imaginative solutions. Open space advocate Lee Milner noted that the soft-spoken, low key, Terry Putman, with more than two decades of working experience under his belt and a faint Texas drawl "did a lot of the grit work. He did a yeoman's job" when it came to dealing with the enormity of such complex problems as the mobile home parks and, of course, the dump, that had scared off so many of the big-time developers, said Milner.

The Good, Bad, and the Ugly

Terry Putman, who is now retired, says that one of his proudest achievements while serving as a city parks' official was the preservation of the Red Rock Canyon property as open space under his watch.

When Putman presented the case for purchasing the property before the city council, he covered all the liabilities, omitting no detail. The title of his presentation was "The Good, Bad, and the Ugly." Fortunately, the city council by this time knew enough to be persuaded of the fact that "the good" far outweighed "the bad and the ugly." Once council approved the purchase, the city parks and recreation department began to deal with the problems one by one. The first issue they had to address, says Putman, was what to do about the four "junk houses," excluding the Bock house, which had been moldering on the property. Next came the need to tackle the relocation of mobile home tenants. When they looked into the matter, Putman and his deputy, Chris Lieber, soon discovered that only one mobile home was up to code. This meant the city had to purchase new mobile homes, in addition to paying rent differentials as mobile home owners were relocated. Total cost for the relocation of mobile home residents came to $650,000, while demolition costs totaled $57,000—less than the originally estimated cost and an amount that struck most as being remarkably cost effective.

The citizens of what Ellis referred to as this "little neighborhood" were understandably more than a little reluctant to leave. If Red Rock Canyon Open Space was the site of "the world's most beautiful dump," it was also the location of the world's most beautiful trailer park.

In the course of the relocation, the city worked months and went to great lengths to identify good affordable housing in convenient locations for the soon-to-be-displaced trailer park residents. Decisions on re-locations were made on a case-by-case basis, keeping in mind expressed preferences and individual needs. Tenants were queried at length

"... And right action is freedom From past and future also."
—**T.S. Eliot,** "The Dry Salvages"

and their stated wishes given the highest consideration and priority. The move included generous compensation packages, which ranged between $25,000 and $35,000, plus moving expenses and payments for at least a period of four months to cover differences between the tenants' Red Rock Canyon rent of $245 per month and their new accommodations. Most occupants were aware that they could not have expected such generosity from a developer.

In order for the relocation process to work, it was essential for the city officials engaged in the process to possess both genuine empathy and strong negotiating skills. What they were working to overcome, in most cases, was a combination of inertia, a reluctance to leave, and in some cases outright hostility. It was a painful process for all concerned. One tenant was angry and another, although a short-timer there, expressed heartbreak over having to leave the wild beauty of the canyon. Another said he wouldn't miss the wind roaring down the canyon—no doubt, a bit like the freight trains out of Wyoming with their mile-long cargoes of coal. One tenant, a woman, proved almost impossible to track down, though eventually city officials did locate her. Still another couple, Audrey and Michael Quigley, both of whom were disabled and in their late sixties, had lived in the canyon with their four basset hounds for twenty-seven years. They professed delight at being able to make a fresh start in their own modest new home in Stratton Meadows in Colorado Springs.

Because Bock never issued leases to the occupants of his trailer camps, several trailers were being sub-let. While most tenants were decent, law-abiding citizens, there were one or two bad apples in the lot. One of these, for example, was serving a jail sentence for possession of methamphetamine. This raised a number of complicated questions about the legality of compensation when it came time to relocate the trailer camp occupants. City officials ended up having to visit the meth dealer in jail to work out the details of his future relocation.

One former tenant, who informally served as Bock's "security officer" and used to ride around the property in his truck with a gun on the seat, said he never would have dreamed it, but, after his relocation from the trailer camp, he found himself living in zip code "80906," considered one of the most desirable addresses in town.

Some tenants of the trailer park chose to relocate to working-class neighborhoods in Colorado Springs; others moved to small, nearby mountain towns such as Florissant. Most, whether individuals, families, the disabled, or the elderly were persuaded of the advantages to be enjoyed by moving either into permanent, low-cost housing of their own, or new mobile homes with reliable hookups to sewage and utilities. Civic leader, businessman, and former vice mayor of Colorado Springs Richard Skorman describes Terry Putman's handling of the mobile homes' relocation as one of the "shining moments" in the otherwise difficult and complex restoration process. Woody Beardsley, TPL's negotiator, notes that the city "went beyond what was legally required and did what was right."

A Model of "Adaptive Reuse"

Another problem that needed to be tackled by the city parks and recreation department and engaged citizens was what to do with the houses and garage/bomb shelter built by the Bocks in the late 1950s and early '60s. John Bock's L-shaped, flat-roofed home built up against the Lyons Sandstone Formation was a typical 1960s structure, with its red walls of native stone, expanse of large picture windows, and fireplaces providing its most distinctive features.

Proponents for saving the Bock-owned house and six-car-garage-cum-bomb-shelter on the estate, which included five ranch-style houses and four commercial structures, argued that the former were a part of the history of the land. They pointed to the architectural significance of the John Bock house, which appeared to have drawn inspiration from Frank Lloyd Wright with some of its features, such as its stone fireplaces.

Those against saving the structures believed that they lacked architectural merit and that the costs of both restoration and maintenance would be prohibitive. Colorado Springs architect Elizabeth Wright Ingraham, the granddaughter of Frank Lloyd Wright, lent weight to this latter position, saying of the John Bock house: "The building has no architectural value. It wouldn't have won any awards." There was never any clamor in support of preserving Richard's house or Sylvia Bock's "house in the hole."

Arizona Architect and developer, Bob Fairburn, who knew Richard Bock personally, reports he got on well with him because of their shared interest in architecture. While Richard had some "inventive" ideas, says Fairburn, the Bock houses were not, in his opinion, exceptional. Richard, however, had played a part in their design and then billed the estate for work done, which infuriated John, who subsequently pressed a lawsuit. This was one reason for the bitter hostility that arose between the brothers, says Fairburn.

A final argument against saving the John Bock house was its location at the mouth of Red Rock Canyon, at the heart of one of the most beautiful landscapes of the entire open space. As one open space advocate put it, it's one of the sites that immediately provokes the "Oh, Wow!" response. The Bock house and garage/bomb shelter left standing in this location represented an unwanted distraction.

Ideas were floated and supported by the preservationist community about using the Bock house for a visitors' center or letting a non-profit with relevant interests adopt it, but the city didn't have the money for the former and none wanted to take it on for the latter. Another concern was that because of the relative isolation of both the houses and the bomb shelter, these structures were vulnerable to acts of vandalism.

In addition, city park planners worried that the Bock house location, if it were turned into a visitors' center or office space, would have resulted in too many cars driving too far into the open space at one of its most scenic vantage points. As city parks and recreation department's landscape architect Sarah Bryarly noted: "The open space has the same rock formations as the Garden of the Gods, without all the traffic. It's the local's Garden of the Gods."

And the fact remained that both Bock houses were in a bad state of repair. The roof of John's house leaked like a sieve, with costs of restoration calculated at more than the value of the structure. Because of ongoing concerns about acts of vandalism, the Bock house was for a time occupied by a custodian. Then, from 2004 to the time of its demolition and the subsequent start of construction on a newly planned open-air pavilion in 2008, it was boarded up. It was at this point that the garage and bomb-shelter were broken into and stripped of all their copper wiring.

As for the garage/bomb-shelter, which at 2,063 square feet was half again as large as the Bock house, the preservationists fought equally long and hard to save it, arguing eloquently at times, in the words of Don Ellis, that "the Bock bomb shelter may well be the only privately constructed Cold War era shelter in the Pikes Peak region which would ever be publicly owned. As such, it may offer our only opportunity to preserve such a shelter for the education of future generations, our only opportunity to offer future generations concrete evidence of the degree of anxiety and the extent of preparation which engaged citizens during the Cold War era." Ellis further stated that, "friends of the late John S. Bock have affirmed that Mr. Bock was greatly concerned with the possibility of a Soviet attack and that he had, indeed, constructed this as a bomb shelter."

After examining all of the arguments presented in the course of the public process and elsewhere, and although public opinion was divided, the city ultimately decided that the Bock houses should be demolished. In the meantime, several citizens had proposed that a good use of the building materials from the demolished Bock houses and garage/ bomb-shelter might be in the construction of an outdoor pavilion to be used for educational exhibits and to provide a welcoming, visually pleasing, but not too intrusive landmark, strategically located where the Bock house had once stood at the entrance to the open space.

The Lyons building stone quarried in Red Rock Canyon that formed the walls of John Bock's house and that faced the exterior walls of the garage were subsequently salvaged and incorporated into the pavilion's backdrop and stone pillars, manifesting

View from a hill of the dedication in June 2009 of the award-winning, native stone open-air pavilion. (Photo courtesy *Westside Pioneer*)

the visionary work of architect Timothy Stroh and that of the innovative Charlie Paterson of Charlie Paterson Construction.

Several massive wood beams from the Bock garage/bomb-shelter were also salvaged and effectively reused in the new structure. These beams, while undamaged, showed dark burn marks that were possibly from a shower of sparks emitted from an old steam engine. The beams are of the right dimension and heft to suggest, based on research that has recently come to light, that they may have been trestles for the Midland Terminal Railroad. The Midland was torn down in the late 1940s in plenty of time for Bock to consider recycling the beams later in his garage/bomb-shelter.

The handsome new pavilion, with its fine stonework, cantilevered roof, "flying beams," and geometric angles is suggestive of the natural geologic configurations of rock outcroppings in the open space itself and is a successful example of adaptive reuse. "The challenge was in keeping the unique history of the home and making it [the pavilion] the entrance to the open space," said Stroh, whose Colorado Springs firm specializes in historic preservation. "There's an echo of the memories of the house [in the pavilion], an honoring of what was there."

The new pavilion, which most agree represents a good compromise between the preservationists and the purists, was built at a cost of $359,000 by Paterson Construction, a sizeable investment, but far less than the full restoration and continuing maintenance of the properties would have cost. Funding for the pavilion and interpretive signage on the open space was made possible by a gift of $100,000 from the Friends of Red Rock Canyon group, including a generous contribution of $50,000 from members Bob and Ellen Hostetler. The remaining $259,000 came out of TOPS money.

Its striking design earned the pavilion an AIA merit award and a center-spread story in *Architect Colorado* magazine in the fall of 2009. Dedicated on June 13, 2009, the 1,500-square-foot pavilion, with its 600 square feet of covered area, houses educational exhibits and signage and provides a convenient shelter during sudden summer downpours.

Trails Have their Own Stories to Tell

Among the major concerns, both of the Master Plan and its effective implementation, was the building of seventeen miles of sustainable and environmentally friendly trails in the open space. The goal was, wherever possible, to make full and appropriate use of Bock's already vast network of pre-existing roads and social trails. However, many of the original Bock roads were not well engineered. Although they were unsustainable, requiring constant maintenance with the use of heavy equipment, they could be redesigned and restored.

According to Chris Lieber, more than 13.8 of the 17 miles of sustainable trails targeted for construction under the Open Space Master Plan have been developed. Of these, 5.8 miles follow Bock's original and rather primitive roads. The restored trails represent 42 percent of total construction, while newly built trails make up the rest.

Notable Trail Blazers— from the Early Clovis People to Fred Barr

Historic trails, whether unsustainable and poorly designed or beautifully built like those of city founder General Palmer, have their own stories to tell, not unlike the ancient rocks themselves. Some of the earliest trails through the open space followed the natural contours of the land. These routes were tramped down by mule deer, bears, and other creatures. It is likely that the earliest humans to pass through the open space were the Clovis people. As Pettit observes in her *Ute Pass* history, Clovis points discovered in the area suggest that these early peoples wandered up Ute Pass some ten thousand years ago. One possible "archeological anomaly" identified in Red Rock Canyon Open Space may trace its origins back to early hunter-gatherers. Later on, the Utes followed some of these same early trails or blazed new ones of their own through the open space and up toward Ute Pass. In more recent human history, guided horse rides and old railroad beds left their tracks. Then came the mountain loving, solitude-seeking Fred Barr, who almost single-handedly built the Barr Trail up Pikes Peak in the 1920s. Barr also built many of the more modern, original trails on the present-day open space.

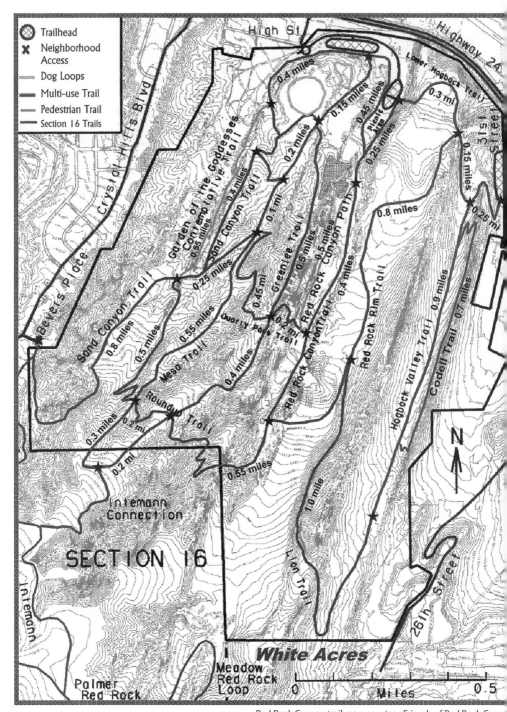

Red Rock Canyon trail map, courtesy Friends of Red Rock Canyon

Ultimately, trails are about getting back in touch with Mother Nature, says professional trail builder Dave Dessel. A well-designed, sustainable trail, despite heavy use, should last for years because it avoids serious erosion problems. It rises and falls against the contour of the land at a grade of no greater than between 8 to 10 percent. By virtue of its carefully engineered design, a well-built trail provides out-slopes to shed water—avoiding the need for water bars—while including dips and curves pleasing to cyclists.

Adhering to such guidelines as these, Red Rock Canyon's trails have been designed for multiple use by cyclists, horses, and hikers; while dogs have their own small off-leash park. Many volunteers—from Boy Scouts and members of the Sierra Club to the Colorado Youth Corps (modeled on the Civilian Conservation Corps (CCC) of the Depression era)—have helped build, improve, maintain, repair, beautify, and/or extend trails. Trail building on the open space also provides seasonal employment and training programs for youth.

"Solvitur Ambulando."
(It can be solved while walking.)
—**Saint Augustine**

Trails not only lead to destinations, ideally they can also serve to strengthen bonds between friends and family members, connecting one generation to the next. Children who experience the wonders of a trail hike are also more apt to experience a reconnection with the earth's wild places and a desire to help protect wildlife habitat, native plants, and historic landscapes.

In August of 2004, nearly one hundred Volunteers for Outdoor Colorado (VOC), under the supervision of Lieber, added another mile of trail to the open space, at which stage, Lieber was quoted as saying, "Three miles down and fourteen to go." In the summer of 2006, the trailhead on 31st Street, just south of Highway 24, was opened. The trailhead parking lot features an open gravel area designed for horse trailers. The Lower Hogback Trail, connecting the new trailheads to the Red Rock Canyon Trail, was also constructed. This trail connects to the hogback area via already existing tracks now known respectively as the Hogback Valley Trail and the Red Rock Rim Trail.

In the autumn of 2006, REI and Friends of Red Rock Canyon cleared

First Red Rock Canyon trail building day, August 2004. (Photo courtesy *Westside Pioneer*)

Second Red Rock Canyon trail building day, September 2004. (Photo courtesy *Westside Pioneer*)

the trail corridor for the Roundup Trail. The trail construction was funded in part by a grant from the Colorado State Parks Trails Program awarded to Friends of Red Rock Canyon (FoRRC). By the winter of 2006, FoRRC had formulated new plans and raised more funds, courtesy of a grant from GOCO, to support the development of a mile of trail linking the southern portion of Red Rock Canyon to the Intemann Trail connection. Volunteers for Outdoor Colorado assumed most of the responsibility for organizing the project, with sweat equity worth an estimated $50,000 provided by local volunteers.

> *"Spaces to reflect on the journey of our lives are essential to our well-being."*
> —**Coreen Toll**

Karlee Thomson, who served as president of the Friends of Red Rock Canyon, says that the wonderful thing about being involved with the organization is that, "You get to witness people doing things they never thought they could do." She says she will never forget the family who volunteered to work on the Section 16 trail connection linking the Intemann Trail with the Red Rock Canyon trail system. It was the first time the family, with two boys of about ages nine and eleven, had participated in such a project. The day started out foggy, but when the mist cleared and the sun came out, the family was stunned by the beauty they saw around them of the red rock canyons. Thomson says she will always remember the look of surprise and wonder on their faces when they looked back at the results of their day's work along the flagged-out route, and realized that through their efforts they had completed a good hundred feet of new trail.

Members of the Garden of the Goddesses Club (GGC) deserve special attention in the project to complete seventeen miles of new or restored trails on the open space. The club generously contributed over a thousand hours of volunteer labor at an estimated cost savings to the city of $16,300. In addition, they contributed building materials to the new trail, three-quarters of a mile long, that they personally adopted. They worked tirelessly, together with other volunteers, in the development of one of the open space's most beautiful trails. Called the "Contemplative Trail," the name was arrived at through compromise between the club and the city parks and recreation department. Although the members of the GGC were disappointed in their initial inability to persuade the city and the public to adopt the name "Garden of the Goddesses" for the open space, and then in a later attempt to adopt the same name for a new trail, they remained graceful compromisers. They swallowed their disappointment, rolled up their sleeves and set to work, dedicating their skills, energy, and imagination to the job of creating a trail of great and enduring beauty as one of their unique legacies. In doing so, they were guided by the ideal described by Coreen Toll that "spaces to reflect on the journey of our lives are essential to our well-being."

In addition, the GGC's installation of stone and timbered stairs along the Contemplative Trail has rendered erosion-prone sections more user-friendly and attractive. The club also contributed five exceptionally beautiful, honey-colored pine-log benches, designed by Bears of Manitou, and strategically sited at scenic viewpoints along the trail. One of the view-centered turnouts with bench enjoys the shade of a venerable old ponderosa pine.

The Contemplative Trail is located on the west side of the open space, starting near the main Highway 24 trailhead and skirting the east side of Sand Canyon, which is the western-most canyon. It passes dramatically leaping red fins and sky-opening arches, wends its way through high, narrow, vertical sandstone walls and around knobbed boulders the size of houses, composed of composite rock and 323-million-year-old Fountain Formation Sandstone. On the Contemplative Trail you can both reach your destination and experience the journey.

"Meet Me in Montana"—
Rock Climbers Install Bolted Climbing Routes

In the fall of 2005, a group of climbers known as the Colorado Springs Climbers Alliance (CSCA) helped develop a climbing plan for the new open space. Among those involved were Ric Geiman, Stewart Green, Bob Hostetler, and Brian Shelton. Since the red Lyons Sandstone in Red Rock Canyon, where the climbing wall is located, is smooth-faced and with few cracks, a majority of its climbing routes needed to be bolted. The CSCA volunteers worked to camouflage bolts and to limit damage to sensitive environments. "Standards included no dangerous runout, placing route termination/rap anchors under the top of the [Lyons Sandstone] faces to reduce rock fall risk and discourage 'tourist' scrambling," says Bob Hostetler. In a two-month period, eighty-five new routes—from fourth class (top rope) to challenging 5.12 class climbs—were established, Hostetler reported in the *Red Rock Rag* (Fall 2005).

"The Best and Largest [Climbing] Cliffs in the Pikes Peak Region"

Rock climber Stewart M. Green has published a useful climbing guide on the open space titled *Red Rock Canyon Open Space: A Rock Climber's Guide, Colorado Springs, Colorado*. In his guide, featuring illustrations by Martha Morris, Green exults over the abundant rock slabs and steep faces available for climbing in Red Rock Canyon Open Space. Describing the richness of it all, Green writes: "The cliffs that wall Red Rock Canyon's flanks form a marvelous climbing area, the best and largest in the Pikes Peak region." Both in terms of the quality of the sandstone rock and the numbers and varieties of routes available—ranging from moderately difficult to highly technical—Red Rock Canyon Open Space, Green asserts, is better than Garden of the Gods. "The quiet, serenity, and isolation that climbers experience here is an added bonus compared to the usually busy, automobile-dominated atmosphere at the Garden," Green states.

Perhaps because of their up-close and personal tactile intimacy with the rocks, climbers are quick to recognize their intrinsic poetry. This can be seen in the catalog of evocative names the Climbers Alliance members have bestowed on the climbing routes, such as Solar Slab, Ripple Wall, Storm Surge, The Whale, Aphrodite, Among the Stars, Venus, Autumn Leaves and Burning Feet, Fit to be Tied, and Meet Me in Montana.

In his guide, Green reminds readers that rock climbing is a dangerous sport and that it is important to exercise care and be responsible. For those interested, a permit is required before undertaking a climb in Red Rock Canyon Open Space. Permits are easy to get, good for a year, and can be secured, free of charge, from the Garden of the Gods Visitor and Nature Center.

On any good-weather weekend, one can see rock climbers of every size, age, level of competence, and description spidering up the sandstone walls. During a summer visit to Colorado, this author's grandchildren, at ages five and eight, even attempted a short climb up a bolted beginner's route under the close supervision and watchful eyes of parents and grandparents.

The Friends of Red Rock Canyon, the city parks and recreation department, and CityRock (formerly the ROCK Climbing Center)—an indoor climbing and adventure center with locations in downtown Colorado Springs and in Manitou Springs—jointly sponsored a first-time rock-climbing competition open to all ages and abilities. To enter, participants needed first to demonstrate "their ability to climb safely outdoors." The competition used the "Redpoint" format, which requires that roped climbers reach the summit of the climb without falling or weighting the rope. Competitors, who provided their own equipment and belayers, had five hours to complete as many climbs as they desired, but were scored only on their top ten climbs. Prizes of climbing equipment and clothing donated by local sporting businesses were awarded at the competition, which is slated to become an annual event. Part of the money raised from the competition was donated by CityRock to the Friends of Red Rock Canyon.

Freeriding over Teeter-Totters, Drops and "Skinny's"

In the winter of 2004–2005, the volunteer mountain bike advocacy group, Medicine Wheel, began to assist the city parks and recreation department with plans for a freeriding area in the front park section of Red Rock Canyon. The group adopted the portion of the park that had previously been set aside as a freeride area and helped with fundraising and technical expertise. One day while meeting on site, the group devoted a morning to picking up "a dumpster's worth of trash," wrote Josh Osterhoudt in the *Red Rock Rag* (Winter 2004–5). By January of 2007, Phase 1 of this plan, "the beginner area" was scheduled to open. Dr. Cory Sutela wrote in the *Red Rock Rag* (Winter 2007) that one focus of this phase was "to provide an area for skills development in a safe environment. We tried to include several levels of 'beginner' stunts that will allow users to progress to more difficult stunts as their skills improve. You can see this progression in the various sizes of teeter-totters, drops, and bridges (or 'skinny's'). It would be impossible to completely eliminate all hazards in a park of this nature, but we have done our best to reduce the risk of needless injury through the location, type, and landscaping around our stunts."

A Celebration of Red Rock Canyon Open Space

On September 30, 2006, REI co-sponsored the National Public Lands Day project on Red Rock Canyon Open Space, which was an opportunity to thank and remember all of the volunteers who participated in and supported open space projects and activities. The list of contributions made is epic and includes trail building, clearing and clean-up, weed and noxious tree eradication, and tree planting. The list also includes citizens who, early on, were active in petition drives, attended countless public meetings, contributed to fund raisers, lobbied elected officials, made possible the publication of timely and educational newsletters and articles, and otherwise supported the Red Rock Canyon Committee in the successful drive to save the Bock property from development.

From Moonlight Hikes to Yoga Programs and Poetry Readings for Youth

Research shows that people living near parks and open spaces exercise more and enjoy better health. This is important for all age groups and particularly the young. The numbers of ways in which Red Rock Canyon Open Space can be used in this regard are proving to be as limitless as the protean shapes of the rocks themselves. For example, the open space has been the venue for the annual Catamount Institute-sponsored "under the hunter's moon hike; a poetry hike for Woodland Park Middle School students who read a poem they've written in a special spot of their choosing; a yoga for youths program held in the summer; performances by drumming groups; an academic study by students at Pikes Peak Community College that resulted in a Master Use Plan—and the list goes on of the myriad ways in which the public has found to enjoy this unique and health-promoting, recreational and educational resource in our own backyard.

In addition, Red Rock Canyon Open Space, with its light-filled landscapes, wild flora and fauna, and its incomparable red sandstone outcroppings, is an ongoing inspiration to such artists as landscape photographer Bill Koerner and impressionist painter Laura Reilly, whose works are featured in this book.

A Secret No More and a Legacy for Future Generations

Among the superlatives that accurately describe Red Rock Canyon Open Space today is that it's one of the "most often visited parks" in the city. And its splendid red rocks continue to develop their own narratives and lore. A secret no more, it is a great credit to the city and to its city park's and recreation department, and most of all to its many citizen volunteers, whose stories have already been documented, that this much-loved and beautiful property was saved for the pleasure and benefit of the many, instead of the few.

In the meantime, the Friends of Red Rock Canyon (FoRRC) are continuing to work on such projects as major noxious weed removal, trail building, and repairs. One of the more historic work days sponsored by FoRRC took place in the spring of 2010 and featured the highly symbolic removal of some old barbed-wire fence that for years separated Red Rock Canyon Open Space from the newly acquired White Acres. In September 2010, FoRRC assisted in the building of the new Codell Trail, headed up by volunteer Chris Lieber. It runs along the crest of the Niobrara ridge and provides a link in the History and Geology Interpretive Trail loops, while affording great views east to the city and west to the Dakota ridge. To this day, the Friends of Red Rock Canyon see their continued strong advocacy for and committed stewarding of the land as the legacy they will leave future generations.

Completing the Puzzle:
White Acres and Manitou Springs Section 16

The forty-five-acre White Acres parcel and the 640-acre Manitou Springs Section 16 are two contiguous and scenic properties that make up the larger puzzle of the Red Rock Canyon Open Space map. Both have long been considered high priorities for preservation. White Acres hugs the southeast corner of the expanded open space. Manitou Springs Section 16, which is used by thousands of visitors per year, occupies a sizeable wedge on the southwest side of the open space, and is almost as large as Red Rock Canyon Open Space itself. The Niobrara and Dakota Sandstone Formations described earlier continue into White Acres, while the red Lyons and Fountain outcroppings are found in Section 16.

Many old and historic roads and trails—some made by wagons, others well-used social trails—in addition to wildlife corridors, crisscross back and forth between Red Rock Canyon Open Space, Section 16, and White Acres—with Section 16, in turn, connecting with Bear Creek Park and the Pikes National Forest.

Ute fortifications and/or drift fences along the ridge of the Dakota Hogback. (Photo courtesy Merrilyn Caduff)

White Acres and Section 16 also share overlapping human history with Red Rock Canyon Open Space. The stone walls that line the spiny ridge of the Dakota Hogback in the open space continue along that same ridge into White Acres. Archeologists say the walls are either drift fences or Ute fortifications and overlooks. There are, moreover, possible signs of two historic Indian (probably Ute) camps in the same area. The Dakota Hogback in White Acres is likewise rich in fossil-bearing rocks, offering historic proof of the long-ago presence of ancient seas—just as does the same formation in Red Rock Canyon Open Space. For this reason, White Acres is a popular site with Colorado College students conducting field studies in geology.

The thread of the story of the historic arrival of Europeans on the open space is similarly taken up and continued in White Acres. As noted in the chapter on modern human history, one of Old Colorado City's founders, Anthony Bott, mined limestone on the site beginning in the late 1860s. White Acres was also where the more successful Bott-Langmeyer Dakota Sandstone quarries commenced operations in the 1870s and '80s. According to experts, the handsome, leonine gold blocks cut from these quarries provided building stone used in the major outbuildings and possibly in the stone fences on William Jackson Palmer's monumental Glen Eyrie estate.

After her husband's death, Fredericka Langmeyer continued to operate the quarry business with her brother, Anthony Bott, leasing out a strip of land in today's White Acres, where hopeful miners conducted what turned out to be fruitless explorations in the hogback for gold, silver, copper, and lead. During the Cold War, in the 1950s, the search was on once again, this time for uranium, but with equally disappointing results.

Indeed, both in terms of their fascinating millennia-old geology and their diverse human and rich natural history, White Acres and Manitou Springs Section 16 are so closely related to the open space that many visitors believed that the two parcels had already been acquired.

A White Acres Christmas

From the mid-1930s until the mid-1960s, the White Acres parcel was owned by W.C. and Pearl E. White, who deeded the property to Bethany Baptist Church in Old Colorado City. The church gave the property the name "White Acres" to honor the gen-

erous donors, whose original intent was that the property be used as a retreat. However, in the summer of 2008, church officials decided— much to the dismay of the family's descendants—to put the property up for sale to raise money to replace a leaky roof and to cover costs of other repairs needed on the church.

Open space advocate Don Ellis, seizing the opportunity, wasted no time in submitting a TOPS application to purchase the property through the TOPS funding program. For several years preservationists had eyed White Acres as a possible site to purchase, but believed that the larger, more widely used Manitou Springs Section 16 should have priority.

Pearl and Cloe White, who generously made a gift of White Acres. (Photo courtesy Merrilyn Caduff)

At least twice in the recent past the church had indicated the property might be up for sale. But this time it was for real.

In order to facilitate the property's sale, the church decided to form a (some would say "ill-advised") partnership with Infinity Land Corporation owned by Colorado Springs developer Paul Howard, and transferred title to the property to a new joint entity called Proverbs 3.5. The partners then proceeded to set the price for the property at $1.375 million and offered it to the city for purchase through the TOPS program. After extended staff and TOPS Working Committee deliberation, the city council vetoed the proposed purchase as being too costly and more than the land was actually worth. The decision the church made to partner with Howard had effectively doubled the asking price for the land. Had it been half that amount, the city would have snapped it right up. As it now stood, Howard would profit to the tune of approximately $700,000.

When the Colorado Springs City Council turned down the White Acres proposal, it appeared likely that the hillside subdivision Howard and company had in mind as their back-up plan for the site was destined to go in, despite growing public opposition.

The developer signaled the seriousness of his intent to develop the area by taking initial steps toward getting the city to annex the property to gain access to city utitlities.

Many neighbors and engaged citizens were becoming increasingly concerned about a plan that would contribute urban density, visual blight, and increased traffic to a historic area distinguished by its wooded slopes, rocky outcrops, and wildlife—and one that was ideally suited for recreation.

At one public meeting where citizens had gathered to express opposition to Infinity's plans, Merrilyn Caduff, a retired high school English teacher and the niece of the original owners of the White Acres property, drew strong applause when she said: "This was my aunt and uncle's pastureland. I played there as a girl. It is exceedingly beautiful … I know if they knew about this plan, they would be devastated."

Merrilyn Caduff's feelings for the White Acres property can only be described as deeply personal, full of "beautiful memories," and infused with an abiding a sense of place. She remembers as a child discovering fossilized sea shells and Indian arrowheads in White Acres, rejoicing in spring's first anemone, and the later splashes of red of the Indian paintbrush, and being serenaded of a summer day by the western meadowlark, with its flute-like song. The hills were covered with gooseberry and chokecherry bushes, and the rocky landscape was pocked with a splattering of small holes and concretions that one geologist had indentified as having resulted from a meteorite hit.

Merrilyn's Uncle Cloe and Aunt Pearl, she recalls fondly, were life-long nature enthusiasts and animal lovers. They pastured their horses, King, a big black stallion, a pinto named Patches, as well as a decommissioned army mule called Mickey, and a rescued white stallion known as Toby, on the hillside property. When Merrilyn's uncle watered the horses, he would

top: Merrilyn gathers White Acre memories in the company of Patches, the pinto, and decommissioned army mule, Mickey.
above: Uncle Cloe with Mickey. (Photos courtesy Merrilyn Caduff)

carefully place a heavy wood plank or log in the water trough, resting it on the bottom so that it leaned diagonally against the tank's rim—thus providing an escape bridge for small creatures such as squirrels and rabbits who tumbled in.

During World War II, the White property provided a welcome and peaceful refuge for family and friends to spend time with loved ones during a period of turmoil. The Whites wanted to give others an opportunity to experience this special place in the same way they had. Their vision included making it available as a retreat, particularly for young people. They thought by deeding their land to the church they could count on its remaining in its pristine state to be enjoyed by future generations. The decision to sell it for development, Merrilyn Caduff says, was "just not right," and the church as a result of the actions of a few got "a black eye."

It is worth noting that the White family's generous gift of their land to Bethany Baptist Church occurred in the mid-1960s, prior to the time when land easements, such as those made available through the Colorado Springs Palmer Land Trust, came into widespread use as an essential tool for protecting hundred-year-old heritage ranches and rapidly vanishing open spaces from being bulldozed and paved over into giant malls and sprawling subdivisions. Had the Whites been able to place such an easement on their property, with its built-in legal safeguards, it would have remained a church-owned and operated open space to be enjoyed as a retreat according to the White family's express wishes and clear expectations.

It was only after the national recession hit and the housing market went flat that developer Paul Howard was forced to reduce his asking price for White Acres by 28 percent. When that happened in the spring of 2009, the property once again moved to the forefront as a candidate for purchase. Paul Howard once more professed to want to see White Acres saved as open space and again approached TOPS. He would now receive only 30 percent of the profits from the potential $1 million sale, but said it was a sacrifice he was willing to make as a Christian whose first concern was for the church.

Ironically, a bad situation (the market) had resulted in a good outcome. As preservationists and city planners are quick to note, a market downturn is an ideal time to maximize on TOPS funding by making open space purchases—when land is being sold at not just reasonable, but sometimes even at discount rates. As a result of the reduction in price for White Acres, the city now became willing and able to strike a deal.

Arguments cited in favor of the White Acres acquisition were its location adjacent to Red Rock Canyon, its vital trail linkages, and its inherent conservation values. And most significantly, White Acres forms a prominent and highly visible backdrop to Colorado Springs. It was this salient feature—perhaps more than any other—that afforded a "tipping point" in the effort to preserve the property as open space.

Once citizens and city leaders understood how much they stood to lose of their scenic view if White Acres were to be developed—thanks to imaginative advocacy and informational efforts on the part of volunteers—they quickly rallied in support of purchasing the parcel. Don Ellis helped to bring home the reality with photographs he took of White Acres from various vantage points on the property and around the city. Then, he produced a computer-generated image of what a subdivision in that conspicuous hillside backdrop would have looked like. Forty-eight luxury estate homes and townhouses lumbering up the side of the Dakota Hogback like elephants in Hadrian's legions, in full view of much of the city and beyond, no longer struck most as an appealing option.

Furthermore, had this rural, craggy hill country been converted into an urban development, it is quite possible that an access road into Manitou Springs Section 16 may have opened up—in turn complicating Section 16's future as open space and impinging on the peace and natural beauty of Red Rock Canyon Open Space itself.

Because TOPS funds were limited, the Friends of Red Rock Canyon, under the leadership of President Karlee Thompson, and with volunteer Don Ellis at the forefront, swung into action, working with the Colorado Springs Palmer Land Trust to raise $75,000 toward the White Acres purchase. The effort also gained support from the Bear Creek neighborhood, the Trails and Open Space Coalition (TOSC) and more than three hundred citizens, along with businesses and foundations.

On one of the coldest days of the year, in December 2008, a neighborhood gathering was held to publicize White Acres. "The Tree of Hope" event featured the singing of the adapted Christmas carol, *"I'm Dreaming of a White Acres Christmas,"* conducted by former music instructor and State Representative Michael Merrifield. An evergreen growing in the yard of the White's former house was decorated. One of the most popular features of the event, in addition to the steaming mugs of hot chocolate, was a fire in an old oil drum that helped keep the chilly revelers warm.

In the spring of 2009, the Colorado Springs City Council voted unanimously to approve the million-dollar purchase of the property from real estate company Proverbs 3.5. Many were overjoyed, and none more so than Merrilyn Caduff, when on December 1, 2009, the city's TOPS program closed on the deal, with the city scheduled to purchase the land in phased allotments over a four-year period. Today Merrilyn Caduff's gratitude for the preservation of this public open space, with its "beautiful memories," is as daily as the mountain sunrise.

And the successful, community-supported effort to save White Acres as a part of the expanded Red Rock Canyon Open Space, with its upbeat and positive ending, has yet one more finale. Clint Tafoya, a young pastor who ministers to youth, has lived on White Acres for a decade, where he rented the modest ranch-style house once owned by the White family. The Whites and the Tafoyas were and continue to be good family friends.

For years young people had enjoyed the outdoor retreats in White Acres presided over by Tafoya, a third-generation Coloradan and a rock climber, who works in his family-owned surplus store in Old Colorado City. From the beginning Tafoya had requested Bethany Baptist Church to sell him the house he rented. The church, however, was reluctant to do so—not wanting to divide its property. But not long ago Tafoya got married and the church serendipitously decided to sell. Today Tafoya is a married man, who retains a 2.5-acre portion of the property and owns his own home.

Another small strip of land, donated by Proverbs 3.5, has been set aside with a city easement in the event the Public Works department decides to re-route the adjoining 31st Street. But, as Don Ellis says, everyone affected "fervently hopes the road will never be built."

What Is a Section 16?

Like twenty-two other states that manage trust lands (except for Alaska and Utah, which obtained four sections), the State of Colorado is dotted with Section 16s and 32s. These sections owe their existence to the Land Ordinance Act passed by the Continental Congress in 1785. The act's objective was to make funds available for schools and to provide land on which centrally located schoolhouses could be built. However, the lands held in trust for the public are not, strictly speaking, entirely "public" and have, in the past, been used in a variety of ways—from agriculture to mining. Thus, while public schools and education may be the ultimate beneficiaries of revenues raised, there are also and inevitably vested interests looking for ways to cash in as well.

The Colorado State Land Board (SLB), which exercises control over the state's Section 16s and 32s, is made up of five citizen land commissioners appointed by the governor. It was established in 1876 to manage the three-million acres of land; plus an additional four-million acres of mineral rights that comprise the state's many sections. The SLB, explains Scott Campbell, executive director of the Palmer Land Trust, "can do whatever it wants with either 16s or 32s—including lease, sell, mine, log, etc. Our own Manitou Springs Section 16 is no different. If the city purchases it, the State Land Board will still retain the mineral rights. Then the city will either have to lease the rights so that they are not used or a geologist will have to issue a qualified opinion that the chances of mineral development is so remote as to be negligible." "The State of Colorado," adds PLT Programs Director and environmental attorney Josh Tenneson, "has taken the position that it must retain mineral rights even if the surface rights are sold to another party." While the prospect of drilling or excavating for minerals in Manitou Springs Section 16 is remote, this interesting facet of Colorado's current mining laws cannot be totally overlooked or casually dismissed, even as it reflects back to much earlier laws and a mind-set rooted in Colorado's nineteenth-century mining history.

Manitou Springs—A Vocal Constituency for Section 16

In 1972, El Paso County first leased the Manitou Springs Section 16 property for recreational purposes and began to minimally maintain it. Red flags were raised in the mid-1990s when a proposal was broached by El Paso County to sell the developable quarter of Section 16 to developers. The Morley Brothers' development firm in Colorado Springs had indicated an interest, making a proposal that included a complex (and in some cases far-flung) series of land swaps.

The result was an immediate public outcry—particularly in Manitou Springs. A public hearing was held and concerned citizens, including former Manitou Springs Mayors Bill Koerner and Marcy Morrison, spoke out strongly against the plan. Longtime activist Tobe Easton, a leader of "Section 16 Intact," an advocacy group formed to fight the proposed sale, and its spokesperson Zoltan Malocsay, among others, registered equally strong protests, both at public meetings and in the media. The plan to sell to the developers was soon scuttled.

Had the sale of Manitou Springs Section 16 gone forward, however, there is little doubt that the future of today's Red Rock Canyon Open Space would have been seriously jeopardized. In all likelihood, John Bock would have conceded the right to build a permanent road through his property that would logically have run through Greenlee Canyon, while an enclave of luxury estate homes would have been built higher up on the plateau, just south of today's open space.

Amendment 16 Establishes the Benefits of Land beyond "Maximum Economic Value"

The prospect of development in Section 16, and Manitou Springs' well-organized opposition, helped spur the passage of Colorado's Amendment 16 in 1996. The amendment states that land has natural resources and social and wildlife habitat benefits beyond those that are purely monetary and exclusively tagged to the idea of realizing "maximum economic value." Amendment 16 required the State Land Board to set aside 10 percent of its land for conservation, which would make it difficult—if not impossible—for the SLB to sell off a certain percentage of designated sections for development.

Over the years, El Paso County officials had hoped to buy Manitou Springs Section 16, but were never able to set aside sufficient funds to do so. Meanwhile, in 2004 the SLB sharply increased the annual rent on the property to the point where continuing the lease became an impossibility for the county.

The city with its greater resources, thanks to the TOPS program, agreed to take the lead in the effort to preserve Section 16. In 2004, it secured a Great Outdoors Colorado (GOCO) grant of $200,000 to extend the lease on Section 16 for a five-year period, from 2005 through 2010, in preparation for purchasing the land. The GOCO-negotiated agreement with the SLB included an option for the city to apply whatever remained of that amount toward a final purchase on the land.

Starting in 2004, the city park and recreation department's Chris Lieber began working in an all-out effort to reach some kind of agreement with the State Land Board. However, these discussions ended when anti-tax activist Douglas Bruce filed a lawsuit against the extension of the TOPS program, which tied things up in the courts for three years until the Colorado Supreme Court ruled in the city's favor. Negotiations resumed again in 2008. By this time the city had secured an additional $1 million grant from GOCO toward the purchase of the land and a pledge for funds to be raised by PLT. But the city and the SLB could not bridge differences of opinion over the value of the land itself.

In addition, the State Land Board was angered by the city's purchase of White Acres, which had effectively denied Manitou Springs Section 16 its last easy access point unless a hugely expensive road was cut through the hillside from Gold Camp Road, greatly complicating any future development option for the parcel. The State Land Board, in response, darkly threatened to fence off Section 16, if a plan for purchase of the property or payment of an even higher rent were not hammered out in a timely fashion.

The dispute over the value of the land boiled down to wildly differing appraisals of what constitutes "value." Appraisals are both an art and a science, involving complex variables and methodologies. In recent years, several had been done on Manitou Springs Section 16. The price of land value can vary tremendously depending on which methodology for a given appraisal is applied. Usually, the "highest and best use" of land in our society is for residential or commercial development. However, in the case of Section 16, being valued for its development potential and appraised accordingly would lower the land's value, since only a small part of it was developable and it had no access road. Based on the development methodology, the lowest figure suggested in any past appraisal was arrived at in 2009 when the land was valued at $2.8 million, a figure unacceptable to the SLB. The highest proposed figure, based on an open-space methodology, was $8.9 million, an amount arrived at by comparing the price paid for adjacent Red Rock Canyon Open Space. Yet by any measure, the two properties were far from comparable. In addition to its stunning aesthetics and park-like features, Red Rock Canyon Open Space held far more developable acreage than Section 16, with potential for commercial development on the property adjoining Highway 24. The high-end appraisal was as unacceptable to Colorado Springs' conservative city council as the low appraisal had been to the State Land Board.

Finally, in 2010, two positive developments broke the impasse. First, State Representative Michael Merrifield introduced House Bill 1165, which would allow for the direct negotiation for purchase of selected SLB parcels by local government before a sealed bid process opened it up to developers and other vested interests. The bill allows for just two such transactions per year. Manitou Springs Section 16 was one of the poster children for the introduction of the bill, which was approved by the Colorado State Legislature and signed into law by Governor Ritter in the spring of 2010. Colorado Springs immediately requested that Section 16 be the first sale to be considered under the new guidelines. To underscore the hope generated by the new bill, GOCO had once again extended the deadline for its $1 million grant to the end of 2010.

The State Land Board agreed to have yet one more appraisal done—one that the city urged to more accurately reflect the land's true value in terms of actual economic development potential. In the summer of 2010, this appraisal was done and happily the results proved to be acceptable to both the SLB and the city. A convergence between timing and price was, at long last, about to be achieved.

After Nearly Four Decades of Negotiations, Manitou Springs Section 16 Purchase Wins Unanimous Approval

Once the price was approved by all parties, additional terms were negotiated. These included the state's agreement not to develop mineral rights for ninety-nine years, at which time the agreement could be re-negotiated. In return, the state would be paid $321,000 out of the grand total to cover an estimated thirty-five acres of potentially extractable gravel.

Capital to purchase the six hundred and forty acres for the agreed-upon price of $4.12 million would mostly be provided out of TOPS funds. Additional funds included

GOCO's $1 million and a contribution of $200,000 from El Paso County. Smaller contributions also came from Manitou Springs, the Trails and Open Space Coalition, the Intemann Trail Committee, and the Palmer Land Trust, which agreed to raise funds to cover its own costs of providing the GOCO-required easement.

In the end, the net cost to the city for Manitou Springs Section 16 was only $2.927 million—little more than the lowest earlier appraisal of $2.8. It was clearly too good a deal to pass up. The TOPS Working Committee and the Parks Advisory Board (made up of volunteers appointed by the city council who advise the parks and recreation department on all matters related to parks, trails, and open space) gave the purchase unanimous votes of approval. In late September of 2010, the city council surprised and delighted many observers by also voting unanimously in favor of the proposed purchase. This included unexpected positive votes by some of the council's most reluctant open-space enthusiasts.

A number of factors beyond the attractive price resonated with council members. They liked the fact that all trail building and upkeep of the open space parcel has in the past and will continue to be done by volunteers, reducing cost of maintenance and upkeep to a minimum. And since the county and then the city had been renting the popular foothills property for nearly forty years, the savings realized on rent would also help defray costs. The view-shed of the city was another important consideration. As Mayor Lionel Rivera commented at the conclusion of the council's landmark vote to purchase the parcel, Section 16 is visible from anywhere in the city. "If it were ever excavated," he said, "it would look terrible."

Section 16 had been decades in the making and ultimately proved one of the longest open space land deals ever to be negotiated by the city. The vote by the city council represented a triumph not only for citizens, but also for visionary city park officials. Following the city council's approval, the State Land Board in early October of 2010 added its own formal stamp of approval to the purchase of the six hundred and forty acre hillside parcel by Colorado Springs. Aimee Cox, formerly of the parks and recreation department, who helped negotiate the final agreement, and senior manager Kurt Schroeder, along with representatives from the Palmer Land Trust, signed papers on the closing of the historic Manitou Springs Section 16 sale, making it official on December 7, 2010. Thus was the forty-year-long process brought to a successful close on a note of festivity and celebration—thanks to the efforts of so many over the decades, not least of whom were those farsighted area conservationists who never gave up and never gave in.

A Second Garden of the Gods

By early December of 2010, with the addition of the adjacent Manitou Springs Section 16, and prior to that, of White Acres, Red Rock Canyon had nearly doubled its open space from a total of 789 acres to 1,474, making it larger than its sister park to the north. It had become nothing less than a "second Garden of the Gods" for not only the citizens of Colorado Springs, but also for future generations. Its preservation, further ensured by PLT land easements, continues to represent an enduring victory for all who care about one of the most beautiful sites in the Pikes Peak region and, indeed, of the entire Southwest.

Today the greater Red Rock Canyon Open Space serves as a critical refuge and wildlife corridor for literally dozens of species of plants and animals, some of them rare and/or endangered. It boasts scenic views of the Garden of the Gods and figures prominently as a mountain backdrop to the city. Its varied recreational opportunities abound for citizens of all ages. As a city-owned open space and with some ADA-accessible trails, it assures access to all visitors from across the region, state, and from abroad.

Last, but not least, the open space represents an economic good—as even developers, the Chamber of Commerce, and the Economic Development Corporation admit to when pushed. Studies show that populations living near parks are healthier, requiring fewer human and social services, and that properties located in the vicinity of parks and open spaces increase in value, often offsetting city purchasing and maintenance costs over the long term. In addition, a well-developed and beautiful city park system is among the magnets that draw outside investors and new enterprises, as well as tourists, bringing in needed tax dollars.

In retrospect, there is no easy path to saving a parcel of public open space for future generations to enjoy. Success depends on unwavering commitment and relentless hard work by a multitude of volunteers, citizen groups, and private and public organizations over the long haul. It requires tenacity, patience, steely optimism, and vision, backed up by creative partnering within the community itself. It also relies on vast reservoirs of diverse skills and know-how brought to bear by neighbors and volunteer groups to address a wide, and frequently daunting, range of complex issues and challenges. Finally, it depends on a fair measure of luck and good timing, while drawing on that indefinable quality known as "generosity of spirit."

The story of Red Rock Canyon Open Space is as multi-layered and many angled, as historic and timeless, as the red rocks themselves. Its broader narrative takes in the history and geology of the American West and includes one of the best environmental success stories in the region—a story that deserves to be made a matter of public record and celebrated. It is proof positive that engaged citizens working together can make a significant difference to the quality of life we all enjoy while protecting Colorado's great outdoors. Indeed, the very process of working together towards a greater public good helps build community and contributes to an abiding sense of place.

Red Rock Canyon Open Space thus stands as an enduring reminder of a larger truth: that it takes a community not only to save, but to restore, protect, and steward an open space. This variant on a wise and ancient proverb, tracing its origins back to the deep African past, has now been written in stone in Red Rock Canyon's long and continuing, 1.75 billion year history.

In Praise of Red Rock Canyon

"... when we first see [this country] *we know it's beautiful.* [But] *we cannot take everything. We have to leave some for the next generation."*
—"Red Ute" Eddie Box, Sr.

We sing the praises of these sculpted red rocks
that have stood the test of time for three-hundred-million-years—
vertical as the plummeting, vole-hunting drop of
a red-tailed hawk—sharp as an arrowhead,
flint-lapped and chisel-edged.

We sing the praises of these ancient frozen dunes—
the hematite-red Lyons Sandstone, stretched like sleeping basilisks
rounded like a whale's humped back;
We praise the tilted Fountain fins—leaning towers of stone,
Mother Earth's curved ribs, shaped like a bow,
tapered center poles,
the color of madder root and sun-lit rose,
propping up the sky's blue tent, blue as a robin's egg.

We sing the praises of these up-thrusting, salmon-red leaping
pinnacles; the blunt, snub-nosed, time-worn mesas,
the chalky, shell-white, Dakota Hogback ridges,
spiny and bent, wizened as ancient grandmothers—
hunched like wickiups.
We celebrate the copper-red cañons—glowing
with the first uncontained fires of a western dawn.

We lift up our voices in infinite praise of the sacred homes of
Eagle, Coyote, Skunk, Owl, Rabbit and Crow, home of Puma
in his secretive, bleached-bone-littered lair. Home of the silver-fluting
notes of the cañon wren, home of zigzagging shuttles and serpent-
twisting bolts of light, home of the scrub oak and piñon,
the needle-shimmering, hushed chants
of wind rivers in the sky-touching pines.
We praise the high rocky ledges,
the protective shaded hollows,
the cave-dark home of Black Bear.
We sing the praises of those early first inhabitants
whose eagle-winged and soaring spirits still hunt and gather here.

— **Ruth Obee**

Select Bibliography
and Recommended Reading

Flora, Fauna, and Natural History

Cameron, George. *Vascular Plants of North Cheyenne Canyon and the Stratton Open Space, Colorado Springs, Colorado.* Colorado Springs, CO: Manuscript, Penrose Public Library, Special Collections, 2001.

Craighead, John J.; Craighead, Frank C. and Davis, Ray J. *Peterson Series: A Field Guide to Rocky Mountain Wildflowers.* Boston, MA: Houghton Mifflin Co., 1963.

Dunn, Jon L. and Blom, Eirik A.T. (Chief Consultants). *Birds of North America.* Washington, D.C.: National Geographic Society, 1992.

Fisher, Chris; Pattie, Don and Hartson, Tamara. *Lone Pine Field Guide: Mammals of the Rocky Mountains.* Renton, WA: Lone Pine Publishing, 2000.

Fitzberald, James P.; Meaney, Carron A. and Armstrong, David M. *Mammals of Colorado.* Denver, CO: Denver Museum of Natural History and University Press of Colorado, 1994.

Guennel, G.K. *Guide to Colorado Wildflowers: Plains and Foothills (Vol. 1).* Englewood, CO: Westcliffe Publishers, 1995.

Guennel, G.K. *Guide to Colorado Wildflowers: Mountains (Vol. 2).* Englewood, CO: Westcliffe Publishers, 1995.

Hammerson, Geoffrey A. *Amphibians and Reptiles in Colorado: A Colorado Field Guide.* Niwot, CO: University Press of Colorado and Colorado Division of Wildlife, 1994.

Hoyt, Erich and Schultz, Ted. *Insect Lives: Stories of Mystery and Romance from a Hidden World.* Cambridge, MA: Harvard University Press, 1999.

Kelso, Tass. *Botany of the Pikes Peak Region.* Colorado Springs, CO: Colorado College, 2004.

Kelso, Tass; Halteman, Phillip and Reis, Scott. *Plant Communities of the Red Rock Canyon Open Space, Colorado Springs.* Colorado Springs, CO: Colorado College, 2003.

Little, Elbert L. *National Audubon Society: Field Guide to Trees, Western Region.* New York, NY: Alfred A. Knopf, 2001.

Milne, Lorus and Margery. *National Audubon Society: Field Guide to Insects & Spiders*. New York, NY: Alfred A. Knopf, 2003.

Peterson, Roger Tory. *Peterson Field Guides: Western Birds*. New York, NY: Houghton Mifflin Co., 1990.

Petrides, George A. and Petrides, Olivia. *Peterson Field Guides: Western Trees*. New York, NY: Houghton Mifflin Co., 1998.

Powell, John and Travis, Tina. *Noxious Weed Field Guide: El Paso County, Colorado*. El Paso County Environmental Services Department, (N.D.).

Stokes, Donald. *Guide to Bird Behavior (Vol. 1)*. Boston, MA: Little, Brown and Co., 1979.

Stokes, Donald & Lillian. *A Guide to Bird Behavior (Vol. II)*. Boston and Toronto: Little, Brown and Co., 1983.

Stokes, Donald & Lillian. *Guide to Bird Behavior (Vol. III)*. Boston, MA: Little, Brown and Co., 1989.

Troublesome Weeds of the Rocky Mountain West. Colorado Weed Management Association, Eighth Edition, 2004.

Walker, Melissa. *Pikes Peak Region Traveler*. Englewood, CO: Westcliffe Publishers, 1998.

Weber, William A. and Wittmann, Ronald C. *Colorado Flora: Eastern Slope (3rd Ed.)*. Boulder, CO: University Press of Colorado, 2001.

Young, Mary Taylor et al. *On the Trail of Colorado Critters: Wildlife Watching for Kids*. Denver, CO: Denver Museum of Natural History and Boulder, CO: Westcliffe Publishers, 2001.

Geology

Finlay, George Irving. *Colorado Springs: A Guide Book Describing the Rock Formations in the Vicinity of Colorado Springs*. Colorado Springs, CO: The Out West Company, 1906.

Foutz, Dell. R. *Geology of Colorado Illustrated*. Grand Junction, CO: Dell. R. Foutz, 1994.

Halka, Chronic. *Roadside Geology of Colorado*. Missoula, MT: Mountain Press Publishing Co., 1980.

Johnson, Kirk R. and Raynolds, Robert G. *Ancient Denvers: Scenes from the Past 300 Million Years of the Colorado Front Range*. Denver, CO: Denver Museum of Nature and Science, 2006.

Mathews, Vincent; Kellerlyn, Katie and Fox, Betty (edited by). *Messages in Stone: Colorado's Colorful Geology*. Denver, CO: Colorado Geological Survey, 2003.

Noblett, Jeffrey B. *A Guide to the Geological History of the Pikes Peak Region*. Colorado Springs, CO: Colorado College, 1994.

Weissenburger, Ken; Milito, Sharon and Ellis, Don. *Geologic Folio: Red Rock Canyon Open Space, Colorado Springs, Colorado*. Colorado Springs, CO: Old Colorado City Historical Society, 2010.

Euro-American History of the West

Aldridge, Dorothy. *Historic Colorado City: The Town with a Future.* Colorado Springs, CO: Little London Press, 1996.

Bock, John G. *In Red Rock Canyon Land.* Colorado Springs, CO: Old Colorado City Historical Society, 1999.

Bock, John G. *In Canyon Land.* New York, NY: Vantage Press, Inc., 1964.

Colorado: Federal Writers' Project American Guide Series. New York: Hasting House, 1951.

Gehling, Richard and Mary Ann. *Man in the Garden of the Gods.* Woodland Park, CO: Mountain Automation Corp., 1991.

Howbert, Irving. *Indians of the Pike's Peak Region.* Glorieta, NM: The Rio Grande Press, Inc., 1914.

Howbert, Irving. *Memories of a Lifetime in the Pikes Peak Region.* New York and London: G.P. Putnam's Sons, Knickerbocker Press, 1925.

MacKell, Jan. *Brothels, Bordellos & Bad Girls—Prostitutes in Colorado, 1860–1930.* Albuquerque, NM: University of Mexico Press, 2004.

Murphy, Jack A. *Geology Tour of Denver's Buildings and Monuments.* Denver, CO: Denver Museum of Nature and Science, 1995.

Noel, Thomas J. and Norman, Cathleen M. *A Pikes Peak Partnership: The Penroses and the Tutts.* Boulder, CO: University Press of Colorado, 2000.

Sprague, Marshall. *Newport in the Rockies.* Anthens, OH: Sage/Swallow Press Books; Ohio University Press, 1980.

Ubbelohde, Carl; Benson, Maxine and Smith, Duane A. *A Colorado History.* Boulder, CO: Pruett Publishing Co., 1995.

West, Elliott. *Contested Plains: Indians, Goldseekers, and the Rush to Colorado.* Lawrence, KS: University Press of Kansas, 1998.

Wilcox, Rhoda Davis. *The Man on the Iron Horse.* Manitou Springs, CO: Martin, 1996.

Paleo and Historic Indian History of the West

Cassells, E. Steve. *The Archaeology of Colorado.* Boulder, CO: Johnson Books, 1983.

Crum, Sally. *People of the Red Earth.* Santa Fe, NM: Ancient City Press, 1996.

Becker, Cynthia S. and Smith, P. David: *Chipeta, Queen of the Utes: A Biography.* Montrose, CO: Western Reflections Publishing Co., 2003.

Gunnerson, Dolores A. *Apache History and Jicarilla Origins, 1525–1801.* Lincoln, NE: Augstums Printing Service, Inc., 2006.

Howbert, Irving. *Indians of the Pike's Peak Region.* Glorieta, NM: Rio Grande Press, Inc., 1970 (written in 1914).

Kroeber, Alfred L. *The Arapaho*. Lincoln, NE: University of Nebraska Press,1983.

Marsh, Charles S. *People of the Shining Mountains: The Utes of Colorado*. Boulder, CO: Pruett Publishing Co., 1982.

Patterson, Alex. *A Field Guide to Rock Art Symbols of the Greater Southwest*. Boulder, CO: Johnson Books, 1991.

Pettit, Jan. *Utes: The Mountain People*. Boulder, CO: Johnson Books, 1990.

Schaafsma, Poly. *The Rock Art of Utah*. Salt Lake City, UT: University of Utah Press, 1994.

Smith, P. David. *Ouray: Chief of the Utes*. Ridgeway, CO: Wayfinder Press, 1990.

Snyder, Stephen; Flowers, Michael and Morad, Raymond L. *Red Rock Canyon: An Archeological Investigation*. Survey prepared for Colorado Springs Parks, Recreation and Cultural Services of City of Colorado Springs, CO, 2004.

Williams, Jack R. *Ute Culture Trees: Living History*. Florissant, CO: Pikes Peak Research Station, 2001.

Williams, Jack R. *Jicarilla Apaches: The Forgotten People of Pikes Peak and Southern Colorado*. Florissant, CO: Pikes Peak Research Station, 2004.

Wroth, William (Ed.). *Ute Indian Arts and Culture: From Prehistory to the New Millennium*. Colorado Springs, CO: Taylor Museum of the Fine Arts Center, 2000.

Paleontology

Clark, Neil and Lindsay, William. *Pockets Dinosaurs*. New York, NY: DK Publishing, 2003.

Johnson, Kirk and Troll, Ray. *Cruisin' the Fossil Freeway*. Golden, CO: Fulcrum Publishing, 2007.

Lockley, Martin and Hunt, Adrian P. *Dinosaur Tracks*. New York, NY: Columbia University Press, 1995.

Milito, Sharon A. *Fossils and Geologic Points of Interest in Red Rock Canyon Open Space, Colorado Springs, Colorado*. Colorado Springs, CO: Abstract of 2007 study, Colorado Springs Parks, Recreation and Cultural Services.

Urban Studies

Fodor, Eben. *Better Not Bigger: How to Take Control of Urban Growth and Improve Your Community*. Stony Creek, CT: New Society Publishers, 1999.

Greenwood, Daphne T. and Holt, Richard P.F. *Local Economic Development in the 21st Century: Quality of Life and Sustainability*. Armonk, NY: M.E. Sharpe, 2010.

Rogers, Richard. *Cities for a Small Planet*. Boulder, CO: Westview Press, 1998.

Index

(Italic page numbers refer to illustrations)

About the Author

Since her return to her western American roots, writer Ruth Obee has been advocating for open space through her writings. Over the years, she has called many places home, and has been engaged in a life-long exploration of what Wallace Stegner called being "placed."

Ruth Obee has been an English teacher (U.S. and India), an editor (Washington, D.C.), and a writer and poet who accompanied her husband, a career diplomat, to posts in India, Nepal, Pakistan, Tanzania, and South Africa—countries where they lived for more than two decades. She is the author of two collections of poetry, *Looking out from the Hindu Kush* and *A Sense of Place*; and of a literary biography, *Es'kia Mphahlele: Themes of Alienation and African Humanism* (Ohio University Press, 1999) and is a regular contributor to the Cheyenne Mountain Heritage Center *Kiva* magazine. Her poems and feature stories have appeared in a variety of national and local journals and anthologies, including: *Pulse of the River* (Johnson Books, 2007), *The Journal of Commonwealth Literature, The Christian Science Monitor, The University of Denver Quarterly, Short Story International, World magazine* (Peace Corps), *Ranger Rick* wildlife magazine, *Cricket, Spider,* and *Cicada* magazines for children, the *Colorado Springs Independent, Peak and Prairie* (Rocky Mountain Chapter, Sierra Club) and *The Silver Lode* (anthology of the Colorado State Poetry Society). She is a Gill Foundation grant recipient, as well as of a recent state-wide poetry award. In keeping with her commitment to the preservation and stewardship of Colorado's historic ranches and legacy open spaces, she has served locally on such boards as Cheyenne Commons and the Palmer Land Trust.

Ruth and her husband, Kent, make their home in Colorado Springs in Cheyenne Cañon, where they count among their numerous summer visitors: black bear, red fox, bandit-masked raccoons, mule deer, and possibly a secretive mountain lion or two, as well as those heroic, long-distance migrants, hummingbirds.